A TEXT BOOK OF

DATA STRUCTURES

For

Semester - II

SECOND YEAR DEGREE COURSE IN
COMPUTER ENGINEERING/INFORMATION TECHNOLOGY

As Per New Revised Syllabus of
North Maharashtra University, Jalgaon,
June 2013-2014

G. R. PATIL
M.E. (Electronics),
Associate Professor in E & TC Department,
Army Institute of Technology,
Dighi, PUNE.

NIRALI PRAKASHAN
Advancement of knowledge

N3096

DATA STRUCTURES (NMU) (SE COMP./I.T. - Semester - II) ISBN 978-93-83971-13-8

First Edition : January 2014

© : Author

The text of this publication, or any part thereof, should not be reproduced or transmitted in any form or stored in any computer storage system or device for distribution including photocopy, recording, taping or information retrieval system or reproduced on any disc, tape, perforated media or other information storage device etc., without the written permission of Author with whom the rights are reserved. Breach of this condition is liable for legal action.

Every effort has been made to avoid errors or omissions in this publication. In spite of this, errors may have crept in. Any mistake, error or discrepancy so noted and shall be brought to our notice shall be taken care of in the next edition. It is notified that neither the publisher nor the author or seller shall be responsible for any damage or loss of action to any one, of any kind, in any manner, therefrom.

Published By :
NIRALI PRAKASHAN
Abhyudaya Pragati, 1312, Shivaji Nagar,
Off J.M. Road, PUNE – 411005
Tel - (020) 25512336/37/39, Fax - (020) 25511379
Email : niralipune@pragationline.com

Printed at
Repro Knowledgecast Limited
India

DISTRIBUTION CENTRES
PUNE

Nirali Prakashan
119, Budhwar Peth, Jogeshwari Mandir Lane
Pune 411002, Maharashtra
Tel : (020) 2445 2044, 66022708, Fax : (020) 2445 1538
Email : bookorder@pragationline.com

Nirali Prakashan
S. No. 28/25, Dhyari,
Near Pari Company, Pune 411041
Tel : (022) 24690204 Fax : (020) 24690316
Email : dhyari@pragationline.com
bookorder@pragationline.com

MUMBAI
Nirali Prakashan
385, S.V.P. Road, Rasdhara Co-op. Hsg. Society Ltd.,
Girgaum, Mumbai 400004, Maharashtra
Tel : (022) 2385 6339 / 2386 9976, Fax : (022) 2386 9976
Email : niralimumbai@pragationline.com

DISTRIBUTION BRANCHES

NAGPUR
Pratibha Book Distributors
Above Maratha Mandir, Shop No. 3, First Floor,
Rani Jhanshi Square, Sitabuldi, Nagpur 440012,
Maharashtra, Tel : (0712) 254 7129

BENGALURU
Pragati Book House
House No. 1, Sanjeevappa Lane, Avenue Road Cross,
Opp. Rice Church, Bengaluru – 560002.
Tel : (080) 64513344, 64513355,
Mob : 9880582331, 9845021552
Email:bharatsavla@yahoo.com

JALGAON
Nirali Prakashan
34, V. V. Golani Market, Navi Peth, Jalgaon 425001,
Maharashtra, Tel : (0257) 222 0395
Mob : 94234 91860

KOLHAPUR
Nirali Prakashan
New Mahadvar Road,
Kedar Plaza, 1st Floor Opp. IDBI Bank
Kolhapur 416 012, Maharashtra. Mob : 9855046155

CHENNAI
Pragati Books
9/1, Montieth Road, Behind Taas Mahal, Egmore,
Chennai 600008 Tamil Nadu, Tel : (044) 6518 3535,
Mob : 94440 01782 / 98450 21552 / 98805 82331, Email : bharatsavla@yahoo.com

RETAIL OUTLETS
PUNE

Pragati Book Centre
157, Budhwar Peth, Opp. Ratan Talkies,
Pune 411002, Maharashtra
Tel : (020) 2445 8887 / 6602 2707, Fax : (020) 2445 8887

Pragati Book Centre
Amber Chamber, 28/A, Budhwar Peth,
Appa Balwant Chowk, Pune : 411002, Maharashtra,
Tel : (020) 20240335 / 66281669
Email : pbcpune@pragationline.com

Pragati Book Centre
676/B, Budhwar Peth, Opp. Jogeshwari Mandir,
Pune 411002, Maharashtra
Tel : (020) 6601 7784 / 6602 0855

PBC Book Sellers & Stationers
152, Budhwar Peth, Pune 411002, Maharashtra
Tel : (020) 2445 2254 / 6609 2463

MUMBAI
Pragati Book Corner
Indira Niwas, 111 - A, Bhavani Shankar Road, Dadar (W), Mumbai 400028, Maharashtra
Tel : (022) 2422 3526 / 6662 5254, Email : pbcmumbai@pragationline.com

Preface ...

It gives me immense pleasure to present this book on "**Data Structures**".

The book is written mainly for the second year students of Computer Engineering and Information Technology courses of North Maharashtra University for the subject **"Data Structures"**.

The book includes information about basic concepts of Data Structures. Various Concepts of the Data Structures are explained in detail. Mathematical treatment of various concepts are given wherever necessary. Number of Solved Problems and Exercises are included in each unit.

Unit I provides the Introduction to Data Structures.

Unit II provides the Concepts of Stack and Queue.

Unit III provides the Concepts of Linked Lists.

Unit IV provides the Concepts of Trees.

Unit V provides the Concepts of Searching and Sorting.

I sincerely thank to Shri. Dineshbhai Furia, Shri, Jignesh Furia and Shri. M. P. Munde. The books could be completed in time, due to sincere and hard work of Nirali Prakashan's staff namely Mr. Malik Shaikh, Mrs. Anjali Muley and Miss Pallavi Kumari. I thank them all.

Valuable suggestions from our esteemed readers to improve the text will be most welcome and highly appreciated.

January 2014   **Author**
Pune.

Syllabus ...

1. Introduction to Data Structures (08 Hours, 16 Marks)
   (a) Introduction of Data and Data Object.
   (b) Data Structure and Abstract Data Type (ADT).
   (c) Implementation of Different Data Structures.
   (d) Basic Terminologies with Data Structures, Types of Data Structures.
   (e) Data Structure Operations.
   (f) Concept of Arrays, Pointer and Structures.

2. Stack and Queue (08 Hours, 16 Marks)
   (a) Detailed knowledge of Data Structure like Stack, Queue and Circular Queue.
   (b) Polish Notations and Interconversions by using Stack.
   (c) Use of Stack in Function Call, Recursion, Tower of Hanoi.

3. Linked Lists (08 Hours, 16 Marks)
   (a) Understand the Concept of Linked List Data Structure.
   (b) Pros and Cons of Array compared with Linked List.
   (c) Creation, Traversing, Searching, Insertion, Deletion Operations w.r.t. Single Linked List.
   (d) Pros and Cons of single linked list, double linked list
   (e) Ice Polynomial addition using single linked list as well as storing multivariable polynomials using generalised list.

4. Trees (08 Hours, 16 Marks)
   (a) Creation, Traversing, Searching, Insertion, Deletion Operations w.r.t. Binary Search Tree.
   (b) Concept of Threaded Binary Tree, Tree Traversals (Recursive and Non-recursive).
   (c) Concept of Huffman Algorithm.
   (d) Height Balanced Tree(AVL Search free).

5. Searching and Sorting (08 Hours, 16 Marks)
   (a) Basics of Searching Techniques.
   (b) Basics of Sorting Techniques.
   (c) Different Sorting Algorithms including Bubble, Insertion, Selection, Quick, Merge, Heap, Radix.
   (d) Time and Space complexity of an algorithm with big 'O', 'θ', 'Ω' notations.
   (e) Best, Worst, and Average case time complexity of each of these algorithms.

***

Contents ...

1. **Introduction to Data Structures** — 1.1 - 1.64

2. **Stack and Queue** — 2.1 - 2.72

3. **Linked Lists** — 3.1 - 3.66

4. **Trees** — 4.1 - 4.72

5. **Searching and Sorting** — 5.1 - 5.54

***

UNIT I

INTRODUCTION TO DATA STRUCTURE

1.1 INTRODUCTION

In this chapter, basic concepts of data structures and algorithms will be introduced. We will see how data can be organised and how various operations can be performed. Algorithms and their time complexity will also be discussed alongwith space complexity.

1.1.1 Basic Terminology: Elementary Data Organisation

First let us look at the various terminologies that will be used throughout this text.

(i) **Data:** It is a collection of values or information.
For example, A set of integers.

(ii) **Data item:** It is a single value in the set of data.
For example, A number 10 in set of integers.

(iii) **Group items:** It is a data item that can be divided into subitems.
For example, A record of student containing his Roll No, name, date of birth, marks etc.

(iv) **Entity:** It is something that has certain properties (attributes) which may be assigned values.
For example, In students list, each student is an entity.

(v) **Entity set:** Entities with similar attributes is called entity set.
For example, All students in a list of entity set.

(vi) **Range of values:** A set of all possible values that could be assigned to a particular attribute.
For example, Roll Nos of students may range from 1 to 70.

(vii) **Information:** It is meaningful or processed data.
For example, Sorted list of students.

(viii) **Field:** It is a single elementary unit of information representing an attribute of an entity.
For example, rollno, name, date of birth are fields because they represent attribute of student.

(ix) **Record:** It is a collection of field values of a given entity.
For example, Record of a student.
101 Amit 05 April 1994.

(x) **File:** Collection of records of the entities in a given entity set.

(xi) **Primary key:** The field which uniquely identifies the record.
For example, Roll no of student is primary key.

(x) **Fixed-length record:** All records in the file having same amount of space requirement i.e. they have same number of fields.
(xi) **Variable length record:** Records in the file may have different lengths.

The way in which data is organised is called data structures. Collection of records as discussed above is also a data structure. But data may be organised in a more complex types of structures as well. So that we can maintain and process the data more effectively.

1.1.2 Data Structures

The logical or mathematical model of a particular organisation of data is called data structure. There are two criteria on which the choice of data model depends:
   (i) It should reflect the relationship of data in real world.
   (ii) It should be simple so that the processing of data can be done effectively.
Thus, a data structure can be defined as a set of domain D, designated domain d∈D, a set of functions F and set of Axioms A. Thus, the triple (D, F, A) denotes data structure d, where,
   D is domain means range of values.
   F is functions means operations.
   A is Axioms means semantics of operations i.e. rules of operations.
Data object is a set of values. In a data structure, we describe a set of data objects and how they are related.

Data structure may be divided into two types:
(i) **Primitive:** The data structures related to atomic data types i.e. they cannot be further divided are called primitive data structures or simple data structures or primary data structures. For example, int, float, char.
(ii) **Non-primitive:** The data structures which are composite in nature or derived from basic data types are called non-primitive data structures. For example, array, structures, file, lists etc. They are also called as secondary data structures.

Non-primitive data structures can be further classified as:
(i) **Linear data structures:** In this the elements form a sequence or arranged in hierarchical manner. For example, arrays, linked list, queues, stacks.
(ii) **Non-linear data structure:** In this data is not arranged in sequence, i.e. each element may have multiple successors or predecessors For example, trees, graphs.

Now, let us briefly discuss the various data structures.

Arrays:
A linear or one-dimensional array is a list of finite number of similar data elements referenced by a set of consecutive numbers called indices.

For example, $a_0, a_1, a_2, \ldots, a_n$ are elements of an array. In C language they are denoted using brackets as a[0], a[1], a[2], …, a[n].

We can have array of integers, array of real numbers, array of names, array of records etc.

Linked lists:

It is a list elements in which each data element is stored alongwith address of its successor as shown below in Fig. 1.1.

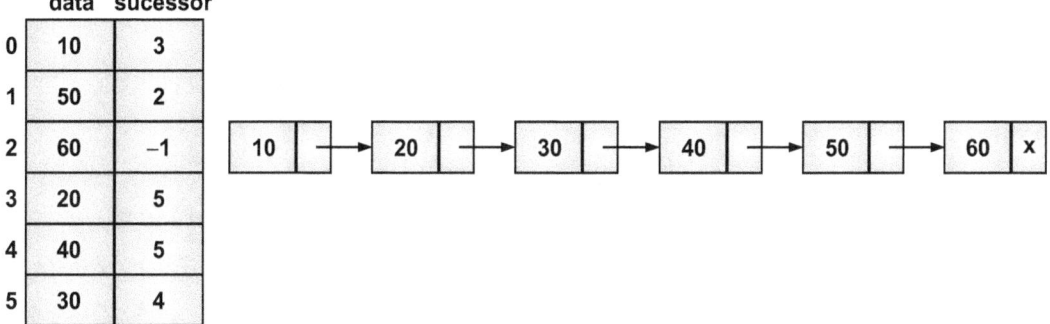

Fig. 1.1: Linked organisation of data

Stacks:

It is a Last In First Out (LIFO) type of data structure in which insertion or deletion can be made only at one place called top as shown in Fig. 1.2.

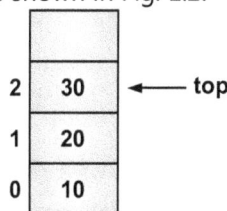

Fig. 1.2: Stack

Queue:

It is a First In First Out (FIFO) type of data structure in which deletion can take place at one called front and insertion can take place at the other end called rear as shown below.

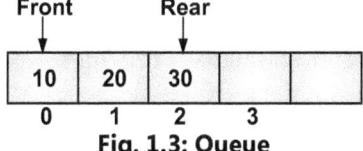

Fig. 1.3: Queue

Trees:

Data may contain hierarchical relationship between elements. This data can be stored using a tree type structure whose starting element will be at the root of the tree as shown below in Fig. 1.4.

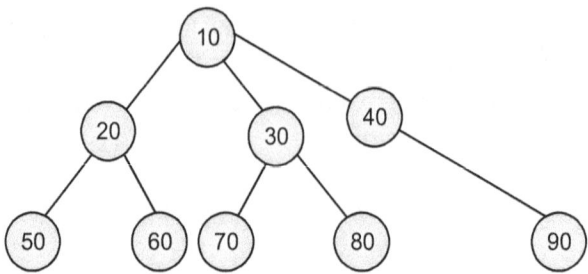

Fig. 1.4: Tree

Graph:

Information to be stored some times contain a complex relationship which may be represented in the form of graph. For example, In a computer network the packets are transmitted from one node to another. The cost of transmission of these packets can be represented as below in Fig. 1.5.

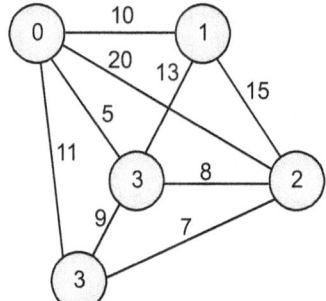

Fig. 1.5: Graph

1.1.3 Data Structure Operations

The various operations that need to be performed on the data stored in the data structure are:

(i) **Searching:** It is finding between location of a record or records based on a particular key. For example, in a student database we may need to find student or students with more than 50% marks.

(ii) **Sorting:** Arranging the records in some logical order. For example, we may need to arrange the student records in descending order of percentage.

(iii) **Traversing:** Accessing each record exactly once so that we can process the records one by one.

(iv) **Inserting:** Adding a new record in the data structure.

(v) **Deleting:** Removing a record from the data structure.

(vi) **Merging:** Combining records from two different structures. For example, we may want to combine two linked lists.

(vii) **Copy:** Making one or more copies of the record or records in the data structure.

(viii) **Reverse:** Reversing the order of the data stored in the data structure. For example, We may want to reverse the list of numbers stored in an array.

1.1.4 Abstract Data Type (ADT)

Abstract Data Type (ADT) is a tool for specifying the logical properties of a data type. Data type as you know is set of values and the operations on these values.

ADT is a mathematical concept that defines data type. In ADT, we do not specify how the set of operations is implemented. So when we define an ADT, we are not concerned with implementation details.

The ADT is a useful guideline for the implementers and a useful tool for programmers so that they can use data type correctly.

If we have an ADT, there will be some operations specified in it as functions. If a program wants to perform these operations it can do so by calling the appropriate function. Now, suppose the implementation of these functions in ADT is changed, that will not affect the program in which these functions are used. Then if you have some addition to ADT, that will also not affect the program.

With an ADT, we are not concerned with how the task is done. We know that it can be done. ADT consists of set of definitions that allow programmers to use the functions while hiding the implementation. This generalisation of operations with unspecified implementation is known as abstraction.

ADT is defined as data declaration packaged together with the operations that are meaningful for the data type.

There are many ways in which ADT is specified. An ADT consists of two parts:
1. Value definition
2. Operation definition.

1. **Value definition:** It has collection of values for the ADT. It consists of two parts:
   (i) **Definition clause:** It consists of actual data.
   (ii) **Condition clause:** It consists of restriction on data.
2. **Operation definition:** It defines operations in ADT in 3 parts:
   (i) **Header:** Similar to function header.
   (ii) **Precondition (Optional):** It specifies restrictions that must be met before operation is done.
   (iii) **Post condition:** Specifies what operation does.

Example: Array as ADT
    value
    /* Definition
    Array_type a [size];

/* Operation Definition

/* To store n elements in array */
    void store (Array_type a, int n);

/* To display n elements of array */
    void disp (Array_type a, int n);

/* To find length of array */
    int length (Array_type a);

/* To append an element in array */
    void append (Array_type a, int x);

/* To modify an element in array */
    void modify (Array_type a, int p, int x);

/* To remove an element */
    void remove (Array_type a, int p);

/* To search an element */
    int search (Array_type a, int x);

/* To sort the array */
    void sort (Array_type a);

/* To insert an element */
    void insert (Array_type a, int p, int x);

1.2 ARRAYS (ONE DIMENSIONAL AND TWO DIMENSIONAL)

When we declare variables as:
    int a, b, c;
Compiler reserves 3 memory locations to store 3 integer numbers.

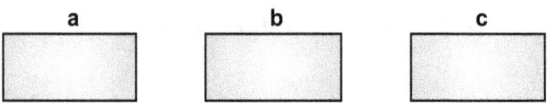

Fig. 1.6: Memory allocation for variables

In case, we want to store more numbers, say 1000 we have to have those many variables declared. But this is going to be inconvenient for the programmer.

C provides a convenient way to declare as many variables as you want using arrays. Arrays are defined in number of ways:
1. An array is a group of related data items that share a common name.
2. An array is a collection of elements of same type which are stored in continuous locations in memory. For example, suppose we want to store marks of 50 students or salaries of 25 employees, we can use arrays. In short, a list of data items of same type can be stored in an array. Arrays can be single or multidimensional. Let us first look into single dimensional arrays.

1.2.1 Defining an Array

We can declare any array variable to store them. Array is declared as
    data_type array_name [size];
    For example, int a[100];

It means we declared 100 variables of integer type. These variables have the same name a. The size can be any integer constant. The above declaration reserves 100 locations in the memory to store integer numbers.

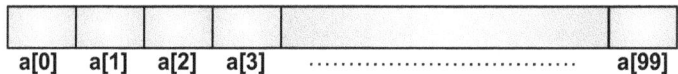

a[0] a[1] a[2] a[3] .... a[99]

Fig. 1.7: Memory allocation for single dimensional array

These locations are a[0], a[1], ..., a[99] are called elements of array. They are just like any other variable names.

1.2.2 Reading into an Array

To read elements into an array we can use for loop as,
    for(i=0;i<n;i++)
        scanf("%d", &a[i]);

where n is the number of elements in the array, n can be any number less than size of the array. When i=0, first element entered from keyboard gets stored in the location a[0], when i=1 second number entered is stored in location a[1] and so on.

Similarly, if array elements are real (say float x[100]) then we can write,

```
for(i=0;i<n;i++)
    scanf("%f", &x[i]);
```

1.2.3 Printing an Array

The elements in the array can be displayed using for loop as

```
for (i=0;i<n;i++)
printf("%d \n", a[i]);
```

Thus, when i = 0 the element stored in the location a[0] gets displayed. When i = 1, the second element in the array gets displayed and so on.

1.2.4 Processing an Array

Array elements can be processed the same way we process other variables i.e. just like we write c = a + b; we can write,

```
a[2] = a[0] + a[1];
```

Numbers stored at location a[0] and a[1] in the array are added and the sum is stored in the location a[2]. Similarly we can have,

	sum = a[0] + a[1];
or	avg = (a[0] + a[1]) / 2;
or	a[10] = 20;
or	a[5] = 4;
or	a[9] = a[8]; etc.

It means we can take any element in an array randomly and process it.

1.2.5 Examples on Array

Now let us write some programs to understand how single dimensional arrays are used.

Program 1.0: To store and display the elements in an array.

```
void main( )
{
    int a[10], i;
    clrscr( );
```

```
        for(i=0;i<10;i++)
            a[i]=i*10;
        for(i=0;i<10;i++)
            printf("%d \n", a[i]);
        getch( );
}
```

Explanation:

1. The declaration int a[10]; will reserve 10 integer locations a[0], a[1], a[2], ... a[9].
2. The first for loop puts values 0, 10, 20, ..., 90 in the locations a[0], a[1], a[2], ...a[9].
3. The second for loop displays the values 0, 10, 20, ..., 90.

Program 1.1: To display first 10 Fibonacci numbers.

```
void main ( )
{
    int a[10], i;
    clrscr( );
    a[0]=0;
    a[1]=1;
    for(i=2;i<10;i++)
        a[i]=a[i-1]+a[i-2];
    for(i=0;i<10;i++)
        printf("%d \n", a[i]);
    getch( )
}
```

Explanation:

1. The declaration int a[10]; will reserve 10 integer locations a[0], a[1], a[2], ... a[9].
2. Since first two Fibonacci numbers are 0 and 1 they are stored in a[0] and a[1].
3. The first for loop starts with i=2 and calculates the ith Fibonacci number.
4. The second for loop displays all the Fibonacci numbers.
5. The output will be 0 1 1 2 3 5 8 13 21 34.

Program 1.2: To accept numbers from users and display them in reverse order.

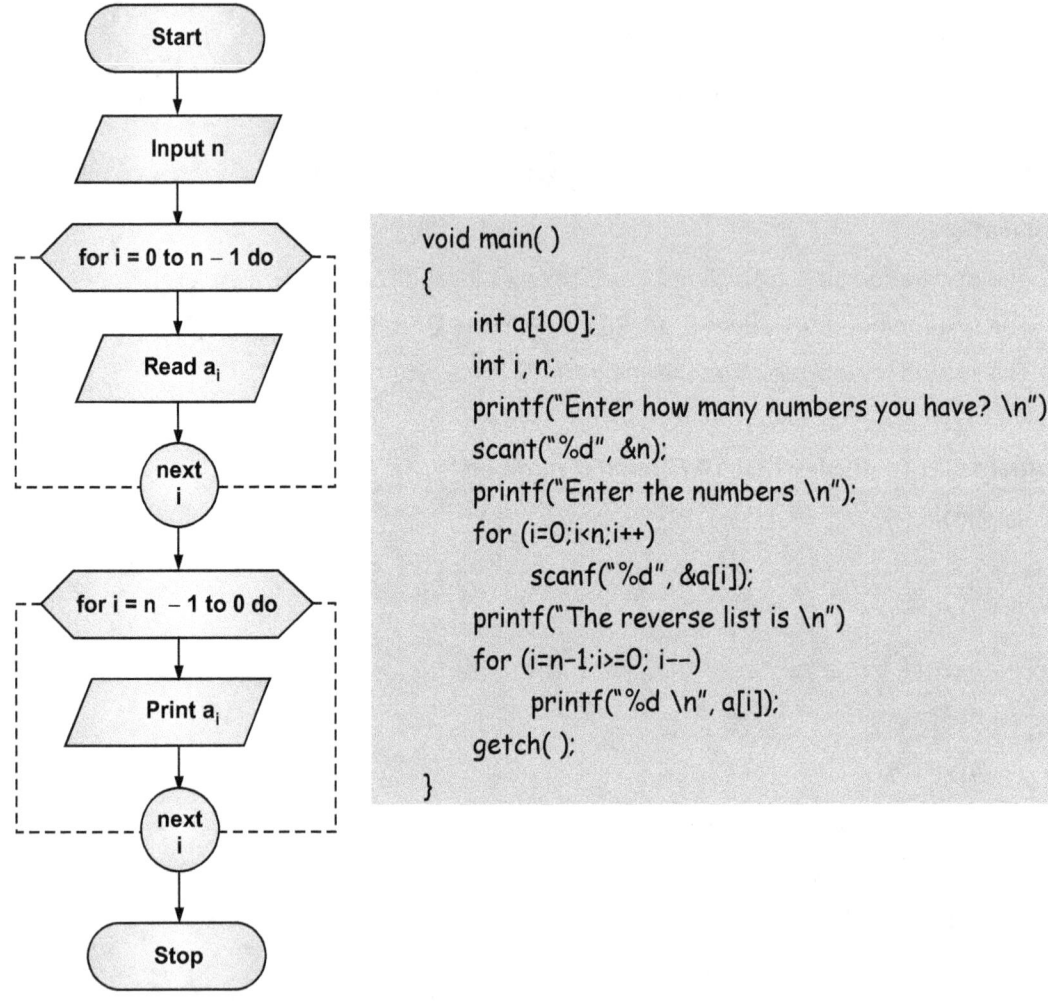

```
void main( )
{
    int a[100];
    int i, n;
    printf("Enter how many numbers you have? \n")
    scant("%d", &n);
    printf("Enter the numbers \n");
    for (i=0;i<n;i++)
        scanf("%d", &a[i]);
    printf("The reverse list is \n")
    for (i=n-1;i>=0; i--)
        printf("%d \n", a[i]);
    getch( );
}
```

Fig. 1.8: Flow chart for program 1.2

Explanation:
1. First, for loop accepts numbers from users and stores them into an array.
2. Since, the last numbers will be in an $(n - 1)^{th}$ location, the second for loop which displays the elements starts with i = n – 1 and goes upto 0.

Note: Most of the array related programs will have 3 parts, viz. reading the elements in an array, processing the array and printing results.

Program 1.3: To count number of odd and even numbers in a list.

```
void main( )
{
    int a[100];
    int i, n, oc = 0, ec = 0;
    printf("Enter how many numbers? \n");
    scanf("%d", &n);
    printf("Enter the numbers \n");
    for (i=0;i<n;i++)
        scanf("%d", &a[i]);
    for (i=0;i<n;i++)
    {
        if (a[i]%2==0)
            ec ++;
        else
            oc ++;
    }
    printf("Even numbers are %d \n", ec);
    printf("Odd numbers are %d \n", oc);
    getch( );
}
```

Program 1.4: To count number of positive numbers, negative numbers and zeros in a list.

```
void main( )
{
    int a[ 100];
    int i, n;pc=0;nc=0;zc=0;
    printf("Enter how many numbers? \n");
    scanf("%d", &n);
    printf("Enter the numbers \n");
    for (i=0;i<n;i++)
        scanf("%d", &a[i]);
    for (i=0;i<n;i ++)
    {
        if(a[i]>0)
```

```
        pc++;
    if(a[i]<0)
        nc++;
    if(a[i]==0)
        zc++;
}
printf("Number of positive numbers=%d \n", pc)
printf("Number of negative numbers=%d \n", nc)
printf("Number of zeros=%d \n", zc)
getch( );
}
```

Program 1.5: To find sum, average, standard deviation of n numbers.

Explanation: We can write a program to find sum and average of numbers without using array. But to find standard deviation, we have to have an array because the numbers accepted from the user will be required second time to find standard deviation. It is given as

$$sd = \sqrt{\frac{\sum_i (a_i - \bar{a})^2}{n}}$$

where, $\bar{a}$ is Average of the umbers.

Hence to find standard deviation, we have to first find average and then find the $\sum_i (a_i - \bar{a})^2$ where, i = 0 to n – 1.

```
#include <math.h>
void main( )
{
    float a[100];
    float s, avg, sd
    float i, n;
    printf("Enter how many numbers? \n");
    scanf("%d", &n);
    printf("Enter the numbers \n");
    for (i=0;i<n;i++)
        scanf("%f", &a[i];
    s=0;
    for (i=0;i<n;i++)
```

```
        s=s + a[i];
    avg = s/n;
    printf("Sum is %f \n", s);
    printf("Avg is %f \n", avg);
    s=0;
    for (i=0;i<n;i++)
        s=s + pow(a[i] - avg, 2);
    sd=sqrt (s/n);
    printf("Standard deviation is %f sd);
    getch( );
}
```

Program 1.6: To find maximum of given n numbers.

```
void main( )
{
    int a[ 100];
    int i, n, max;
    printf("Enter how many numbers? \n");
    scanf("%d", &n);
    printf("Enter the numbers \n");
    for (i=0;i<n;i++)
        scanf("%d", &a[i]);
    max = a[0];
    for (i=1;i<n;i++)
    {
        if (a[i]>max)
            max = a[i];
    }
    printf("Maximum is %d \n", max);
    getch( )
}
```

Program 1.7: To search a number from a given list of numbers.

```
void main( )
{
    int a[100];
```

```c
    int i, n, s, flag;
    printf("Enter how many numbers? \n");
    scanf("% d ", &n);
    printf("Enter the numbers \n");
    for (i=0;i<n;i++)
        scanf("%d", &a[i]);
    printf("Enter number to be searched \n");
        scanf("%d", &s);
    flag = 1;
    for(i=0;i<n;i++)
    {
        if(a[i]==s)
        {
            flag = 0;
            break;
        }
    }
    if(flag==1)
        printf("Found");
    else
        printf("Not found");
    getch( );
}
```

Program 1.8: To convert decimal number into binary.

```c
void main( )
{
    int a[50];
    int i, x, q;
    printf("Enter the number \n");
        scanf("%d", &x);
    i=0; q=x;
    while (q>0)
    {
        a[i] = q%2;
        q = q/2;
```

```
        i++;
    }
    n=i;
    printf("The Binary number is .... \n");
    for(i=n-1;i>=0;i--)
        printf("%d", a[i]);
    getch( );
}
```

1.2.6 Initializing an Array

Just like we initialize memory variables at the time of declaration e.g., int x = 10; array elements can also be initialized as

    int a[ ] = {10, 20, 30, 40};

It will initialize the elements of the array a as

    a[0] = 10, a[1] = 20, a[2] = 30, a[3] = 40;

Here note that there is no need to declare size, since we are specifying the data to be stored in array. Let us consider following example.

```
    void main
    {
        int a[ ] = {10, 20, 30, 40};
        for (i=0;i<4;i++)
        {
            a[i] = a[i] + 10;
        }
        for (i=0;i<4;i++)
            printf("%d \n", a[i]);
    }
```

Output of the above program will be

    20
    30
    40
    50

1.2.7 Two Dimensional Array

Sometimes, we have a group of numbers represented in terms of rows and columns. e.g., table of values.

Table 1.1

	Item 1	Item 2	Item 3
s1	10	40	10
s2	20	30	20
s3	30	50	50
s4	10	20	60

In mathematics, this table of values is represented in terms of matrix. It consists of rows and columns. The table given above can be represented in C using two dimensional array as

    int table[4][3];

Thus, two dimensional array can be declared as

    var_type   name [row_size] [col_size];

e.g. int a[10][10];

It will reserve 100 locations in the memory to store 100 integer numbers. The names of the locations will be

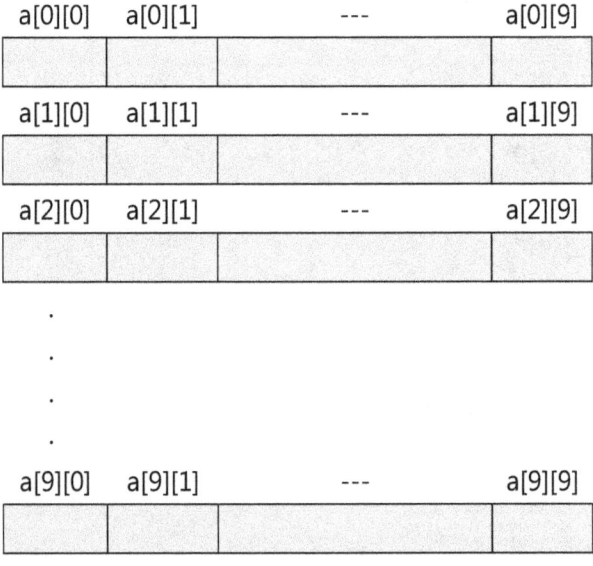

Fig. 1.9: Memory allocation for 2-D array

1.2.8 Reading into two Dimension Array

To read data in single dimensional array, we use single for loop. Here, we have to use nested for loop. Foe example if an array consists of m rows and n columns. We can write

```
for(i=0;i<m;i++)
    for(j=0;j<n;i++)
        scanf("%d", &a[i][j]);
```

The outer for loop runs for m times and the inner n times. The elements will be accepted row wise. This is called as row major representation of the two dimensional array.

1.2.9 Displaying the Two Dimensional Array

To print the elements stored in two dimensional arrays, nested or loop will be required as follows:

```
for(i=0;i<m;i++)
{
    for(j=0;j<n;j++)
        printf("%d", a[i][j]);
    printf("\n");
}
```

Note: printf ("\n"); statement is used to transfer the cursor to next line after a row is over.

1.2.10 Processing Two Dimensional Arrays

Just like we access any element in a single dimensional array randomly, we can access any element in two dimensional array for storage of value or calculation purpose.

e.g. a[0][0] = 10;
    sum = a[0][0] + a[1][1] + a[2][2];
    a[0][0] = a[0][0] + b[0][0];
    a[2][2] = a[0][0] + a[1][1];

1.2.11 Examples on Two Dimensional Arrays

Now let us write some programs based on two dimensional arrays.

Program 1.9: To find sum of two matrices.

There will be three matrices involved here. Three two dimensional arrays will be required to store the three matrices. The addition is carried out element by element.

    i.e., c[i][j] = a[i][j] + b[i][j];

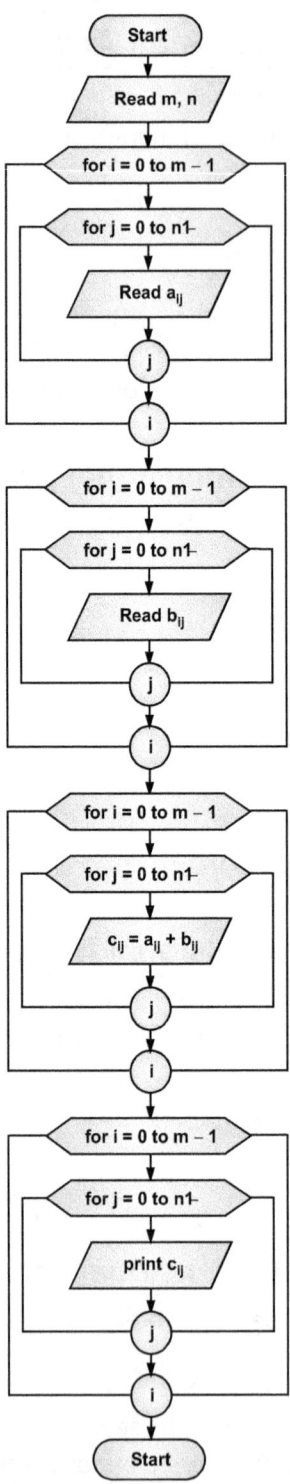

Fig. 1.10: Flow chart for matrix addition

```
void main( )
{
    int a[10][10], b[10][10], c[10][10];
    int i, j, m, n;
    clrscr( );
    printf("Enter order or matrices \n");
    scanf("%d%d", &m, &n);

    printf("Enter first matrix \n");
    for(i=0;i<m;i++)
        for(j=0;j<n;j++)
            scanf("%d", &a[i][j]);
    printf("Enter second matrix \n");
    for(i=0;i<m;i++)
        for(j=0;j<n;j++)
            scanf("%d", &b[i][j]);
    for(i=0;i<m;i++)
        for(j=0;j<n;j++)
            c[i][j] = a[i][j] + b[i][j];
    printf("Resultant matrix is \n");
    for (i=0;i<m;i++)
    {
        for(j=0;j<n;j++)
            printf("%d", c[i][j]);
        printf("\n");
    }
    getch( );
}
```

Explanation:
1. Order means number of rows and columns of the two matrices to be added. It is same for both matrices hence same variables m and n are used.
2. The two matrices are accepted from user and stored in 2-D arrays a and b.
3. The third nested for loop adds the elements of a and b and stores the result in c.
4. The matrix c is displayed by the 4"h Nested for.

Program 1.10: To find sum of all major and minor diagonal elements in a given matrix.
```
void main( )
{
    int a[10][10];
    int m, n, i, j, s, s1;
    printf("Enter order or matrix \n");
    scanf("%d%d", &m, &n);
```

```
        printf("Enter the matrix \n");
        for(i=0;i<m;i++)
            for(j=0;j<n;j++)
                scanf("%d", &a[i][j]);
        s = 0; s1 = 0;
        for(i=0;i<m;i++)
        {
            for(j=0;j<n;j++)
            {
                if (i==j)
                    s = s + a[i][j];
                if(i +j==m - 1)
                    s1=s1 + a[i][j];
            }
        }
        printf("Sum of major diagonal %d, minor diagonal %d", s, s1);
}
```

Explanation:
1. Diagonal elements will have row and column number same hence the condition i == j is tested for adding the elements.

Program 1.11: Write a program to find transpose of a matrix.
```
    void main
    {
        int a[10][10], b[10][10];
        int i, j, m, n;
        printf("Enter order of matrix \n");
        scanf("%d%d", &m, &n);
        printf("Enter the matrix \n");
        for(i=0;i<m;i++)
            for(j=0;j<n;j++)
                scanf("%d", &a[i][j]);
        for(i=0;i<m;i++)
        {
            for(j=0;j<n;j++)
                b[j][i] = a[i][j];
        }
        printf("The transpose is \n");
```

```
for(i=0;i<n;i++)
{
    for(j=0;j<m;j++)
        printf("%d", b[i] [j]);
    printf("\n");
}
}
```

Explanation:
1. Array a stores the matrix of the order m x n whose transpose is to be stored in matrix b.
2. After reading the elements in a, the elements of a are copied to b one by one. The element in the ith row and j^{th} column of a is copied to j^{th} row and i^{th} column of b.
3. Note that third loop which prints the elements of b has n first and m next because the transpose will have order n × m. i.e., it will haven rows and m columns. e.g. Transpose of 3 × 2 will be 2 × 3 matrix.
4. We cannot write the statement b[i][j] = a[j][i] instead of b[j][i] = a[i][j]. Find out the reason.

Program 1.12: To print product of two matrices.
```
void main
{
    int m, n, k, p, 1, i, l;
    int a[10][10], b[10][10], c[10][10];
    clrscr( );
    printf("Enter order of 1st matrix \n");
    scanf("%d%d", &m, &n);
    printf("Enter order of 2nd matrix \n");
    scanf("%d%d", &p, & l);
    if (n!=p)
    {
        printf("Invalid order");
        exit (0);
    }
    printf("Enter 1st matrix \n");
    for(i=0;i<m;i++)
        for(j=0;j<n;j++)
            scanf("%d"; &a[i][j]);
    printf("Enter 2nd matrix \n");
```

```
            for(i=0;i<p;i++)
                for(i=0;j<l;j++)
                    scanf("%d", &b[i][j]);
            for(i=0;i<m;i++)
            {
                for(j=0;j<l;j++)
                {
                    c[i][j] = 0;
                    for(k=0;k<n;k++)
                        c[i][j] = c[i][j] + a[i][k] * b[k][j];
                }
            }
            printf ("Product is \n");
            for(i=0;i<m;i++)
            {
                for(j=0;j<l;j++)
                    printf("%d", c[i][j]);
                print("\n");
            }
            getch( );
}
```

Explanation:
1. First matrix is stored in array a and has order m × n. second matrix is stored in array b and has order p × l.
2. Number of columns of first matrix should be equal to number of rows of second matrix. Hence, if n!=p the error message "Invalid matrices" is displayed and exit(0) statement terminates the program.
3. The process of multiplication will require Nested for loops. The outer for loop with variable 1st will keep on changing the row number of 2nd matrix. The second for loop with variable j will keep on changing column of 2nd matrix. The third for loop will do the sum of multiplication of ith row elements of first matrix and j^{th} column element of second matrix and the result will be stored in 3rd matrix's i^{th} row and j^{th} column.
   e.g., when i = 0, j = 0, k runs from 0 to n − 1. The value
   a[0][0] * b[0][0] + a[0][1] * b[1][0] + ... + a[0][n − 1] * b[n − 1][0] will be stored in the location c[0][0] and so on.

4. The resultant matrix c is of the order m × l. Hence, the last nested for loops run for m × l times.

1.2.12 Initializing Two Dimensional Array

Just like we initialize one dimensional array, we can initialize two dimensional arrays as follows:

    int a [ ][3] = {10, 20, 30,40, 50, 60, 70, 80, 90};

It means we are storing the numbers in the array as follows:
    a[0][0] =10   a[1][0] =40
    a[0][1] = 20   a[2][1] =50
    a[0][2] =30   a[1][2] =60 etc.

Note that it is necessary to have column size mentioned as a[][3] otherwise it will become difficult for the compiler to allocate memory.

If number of columns is not specified, the array can be initialized as

    int a[ ] [ ] = {(10, 20, 30}, {40, 50, 60}, {70, 80, 90};

Program 1.13: To find sum of elements in a matrix

```
void main( )
{
    int i, j, s = 0;
    int a[ ][3] = {10, 20, 30, 40, 50, 60, 70, 80, 90};
    for(i=0;i<3;i++)
        for(j=0;j<3;j++)
            s = s + a[i][j];
        printf("Sum is % d", s);
        getch( );
}
```

Multidimensional Array:
We can have more than two dimensional arrays as well. For example, a three dimensional array can be declared as

    int a[2][2][3];

There will be total 12 elements in this array. These elements will be a[0][0][0], a[0][0][1], a[0][0][2], a[0][1][1], a[0][1][2], a[1][0][0], a[1][0][1], a[1][0][2], a[1][1][0], a[1][1][1], a[1][1][2].

While initialising the multidimensional array the leftmost dimensional can be omitted.
e.g. int a[ ][2][3] = {0, 1, 2, 3, 4, 5, 6, 7, 8, 9, 10, 11}

1.3 POINTERS

Pointer is a very powerful tool which allows programmer lot of flexibility and help in improving efficiency of the program. This concept is important because almost all data structures are based on pointers.

1.3.1 Basic Concepts of Pointer

First thing that should be clear to you is, we are writing a program which is going to be executed by a machine which has memory and each location in memory has an address. When we declare a variable say int a; a location in the memory is reserved to store an integer number.

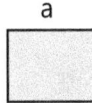

Fig. 1.11: Memory allocation for a

We have the location name as 'a'. The computer which is a digital device. gives number to the location which is called as address of that location. It is just like we give some nice name to our home and Municipal Corporation identifies it with House Number or Survey No. etc. Thus, the memory variable will have associated with it an unique address as shown in Fig. 1.12.

Fig. 1.12: Address of a

What if I want to know the address of that variable? It is possible to access the address of a variable using & operator. The operator & (ampersand) gives address of the corresponding variable. Thus, in above case, &a will be 10000. The address will be solely decided by the computer and not by the programmer. Let us write a program to understand this concept.

Program 1.14: Program to illustrate address of (&) operator.

```
void main( )
{
    int i = 4, j = 8;
    printf("value of i = %d\n", i);
    printf("Address of i = %u\n", &i);
    printf("Value of j = % d\n", j);
    printf("Address of j = %u\n", & j);
}
```

Explanation:

1. In program 1.14, we have two variables declared as i and j. The situation in the memory will be as shown in figure 1.13.

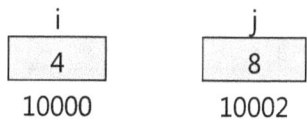

Fig. 1.13: Memory allocation and address of i and j

Here we are assuming that the address of i and j are 10000 and 10002 respectively. The output of the program will be as follows.

Value of i=4
Address of i = 10000
Value of j=8
Address of j = 10002

2. Note that while displaying address %u is used because the address will never be negative number. It is displayed as unsigned integer.

When C program is executed the RAM consists of operating system, the program and the data involved in the program in separate areas. The data area is nothing but the space reserved for the variables in the program. The space in RAM is measured in bytes. Each cell in RAM is of 1 byte. The address is given to each byte in RAM.

Generally, following is space allocation for each variable type
1   byte for char
2   bytes for int
4   bytes for float and long time
8   bytes for double

Hence, when we declare variables as below the memory allocation will be as shown in Fig. 1.14 (Refer Appendix A for further details).

int a, b;
float x, y;
char ch;

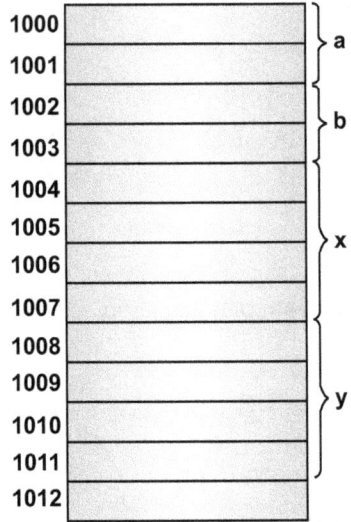

Fig. 1.14: Memory allocation for variables

Just like we have & operator giving address of a variable, there is another operator called operator which gives value stored at a particular address. It is called indirection operator. e.g. *(&a) will give value stored at address of a, which is nothing but value stored at a only. Let us consider one more program to illustrate the concept.

Program 1.15: Use of & and * operator.

```
void main( )
    {
        int i = 3;
        printf ("Value of i = %d \n", i);
        printf ("Address of i = %u \n", &i);
        printf ("Value of i = %d \n", *(&i));
    }
```

1.3.2 Pointer Declaration and Initialisation

There are three basic types of variables in C viz. int, float, char. If a variable is of type int, it will store only integer type data. It is possible to store address of a variable in memory. C provides a pointer type variable which is capable of storing address of another variable but of same type.

A pointer variable is declared as,

$$int\ *p;$$

Thus, a pointer variable is declared like any other variable with * preceding the variable name. It means we are declaring a variable p which is a pointer type variable and it is capable of storing address of any integer variable. We can use this variable to access the value stored in another location. Suppose we have 2 variables declared as follows:
    int a = 10;
    int *p;

Two locations will be reserved in the memory as shown in Fig. 1.15.

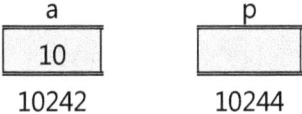

Fig. 1.15: Memory allocation for a and p

Now, if I write a statement as
    p = &a;
address of a (i.e., &a) will be assigned to p as shown in Fig. 1.16.

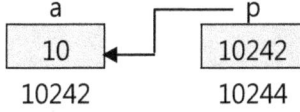

Fig. 1.16: Pointer p pointing to location a

It means p has the address of a i.e., p is pointing to a as shown and *p will give value stored at a. Thus, if we store address of a variable in a pointer type variable we can access the value stored in that variable through the pointer type variable.

Let us consider a program:

Program 1.16: To illustrate pointer variable & operator.
```
void main( )
{
    int *p;
    int a = 10;
    p = &a;
    printf ("Value of a = %d \n", a);
```

```
    printf ("Address of a = %u \n", &a);
    printf ("Value of p = %u \n", p);
    printf ("Value of a = %d \n", *p);
}
```

Output of the program will be
    Value of a = 10
    Address of a = 10242
    Value of p = 10242
    Value of a = 10

Note: We can have float and char type pointers also. The float type pointer can store only address of float type variable. It cannot store address of int or char variable. Similarly, char type pointer can store only address of char type variable. Following program has all the three pointers.

Program 1.17: To illustrate pointer variable & operator.
```
void main( )
{
    int *pi, a=10;
    float *pf, x=1.2345;
    char *pc, c = '*';
    pi= &a;
    pf= &x;
    PC= &c;
    printf ("%d \n", *pi);
    printf ("%f \n", *pf);
    printf ("%c \n", *pc);
}
```
Output: 10
               1.2345
               *

Now, consider some more programs.

Program 1.18: To illustrate operations with pointer variable.
```
void main( )
{
    int a = 10, b = 20, *p, *q, c;
    p = &a;
    q = &b;
    c = *p + *q;
    printf ("Sum is %d \n", c);
}
```

Output: 30

Explanation:
1. Address of a is stored in p (a is pointed by p) and address of b is stored in q (b is pointed by q).
2. *p will be 10 and *q will be 20.
3. Variable c will store sum of value stored at a location pointed by p (i.e., a) and value stored in a location pointed by q (i.e., b).

Note: The indirection operator * has higher precedence than the arithmetic operators +, –, *, /.

Program 1.19: To illustrate operations with pointer variable.
```
void main( )
{
    int a = 10, *p;
    p = &a;
    *p = *p + 100;
    printf ("Sum is %d \n", a);
}
```

Output: 110.

Explanation:
1. p = &a will store address of a in p (a is pointed by p).
2. *p will be 10.
3. The statement *p = *p + 100 means the sum of value stored in a location pointed by p and 100 will be assigned to a location pointed by p.
4. Hence, *p = *p + 100 is equivalent to a = a + 100.

Program 1.20: To illustrate operations with pointer variable.
```
void main( )
{
    int a = 10, b = 20,.c, *p;
    p = &c;
    *p = a + b;
    printf("Sum is %d \n", c);
}
```
Output: 30

Explanation:
1. p = &c will store address of c in p (c is pointed by p).
2. *p will be garbage initially.
3. The statement *p = a + b means the sum of a and b will be assigned to a location pointed by p which is nothing but c. Hence, *p = a +.b is equivalent to c = a + b.

Program 1.21: To illustrate operations with pointer variable.
```
void main( )
{
    int *p;
    *p = 100;
    *p = *p *10;
    printf ("%d\n", *p);
}
```
Output: 1000

Explanation:
1. *p = 100 will store the constant number 100 in a temporary location and p will point to this location as shown in Fig. 1.17.

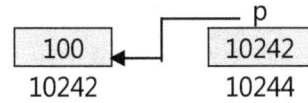

Fig. 1.17: Pointer to a constant

2. The statement *p = *p *10 will store product of location pointed by p and 10 into a location pointed by p itself.

1.3.3 Pointer to a Pointer

Let us consider a program to illustrate this concept.

Program 1.22: To illustrate double pointer.
```
void main( )
{
    int a = 4,*b, **c;
    b = &a;
    c = &b;
    printf("%u \n", &a);
    printf("%u \n", b);
    printf("%u \n", c);
    printf("%u \n", &b);
    printf("%d \n", a);
    printf("%d \n", *b);
    printf("%d \n", **c);
}
```

Note that there are two pointers b and c. b is a single pointer and c is a double pointer. b stores address of integer variable. c can store address of another integer variable.

1. Let us assume following situation in memory when a, b and c as declared.

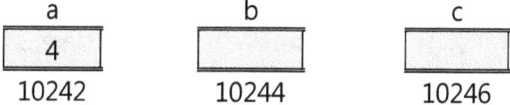

Fig. 1.18: Memory allocation for a, b and c

2. When the statements
    b = &a;
    c = &b; are executed, the memory contents will be as shown in Fig. 1.19.

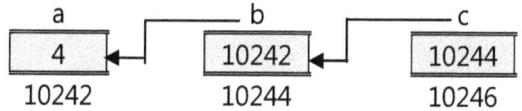

Fig. 1.19: Pointer to a pointer (double pointer)

*b will be value stored at 10242 i.e., a
**c = value stored at (value stored at 10244)
    = value stored at 10242
    = 4

3. Hence, output of program will be,
    10242
    10242
    10244
    10244
    4
    4
    4

1.4 INTRODUCTION OF STRUCTURE

Storage of complex data item is an important task a programmer has to perform. Complex data items involve set of records having variety of information. This calls for a data type that can manage this variety at ease. C provides a constructed data type known as structures. We can combine different data types of our choice using structures. These structures help to organize complex data in a more meaningful way. Thus, structure is constructed or user defined data type which can group together different data types.

1.4.1 Structure in C

It is a user defined data type. We have seen basic data types like int, float and char. We can store only one type of value in these variables. But in case we want to store a record containing name, age and income of person, we need to store it in three different variables viz. char, int and float. Also, if we have to store a list of persons having name, age and income then we need three arrays of same types. It is going to be very difficult to manage the different arrays. As an example, Let us see a program which can store a list of persons have name, age and income and sorts it age-wise. We need to declare 3 arrays char name[50][20], int age[50], float income[50] (the size is assumed to be 50).

Program 1.23: List of employees using arrays

```
void main( )
{
    char name[50] [20], temp1 [20];
    int age[50], temp2;
    float income [50], temp3;
    int i, j, n;
    printf("Enter how many persons\n");
    scanf("%d", &n);
    for(i=0;i<n;i++)
    {
        printf("Enter name \n");
        fflush(stdin);
        gets(name [i]);
```

```
            printf("Enter age\n");
            scanf("%d", &age [i]);
            printf("Enter income \n");
            scanf("%f', &income[i]);
    }
    for(i=0;i<n-1;i++)
    {
            for(j=i+1;j<n;j++)
            {   if(age[i] > age[j])
                {
                    strcpy(temp1, name[i]);
                    strcpy(name[i], name[j]);
                    strcpy(name[j], temp1);
                    temp2 = age[i];
                    age[i] = age[j];
                    age[j] = temp2;
                    temp3 = income[i];
                    income[i] = income[j];
                    income[j] = temp3;
                }
            }
    }
    printf("The list is \n");
    for(i=0;i<n;i++)
            printf("%s \t %d \t %f \n"; names[i], age[i], income[i]);
}
```

Note that in above program while sorting the records, in the list, we had to handle each array separately as these records are stored using 3 different arrays. The program also becomes lengthy. Therefore we are structure type variables to store the record, which allows us to store different data types in one variable making manipulation of records easier.

1.4.2 Defining Structure

There is a difference between structure declaration and definition. The declaration tells the compiler about prototype of structure, whereas definition creates the structure variable. The definition allocates space in memory for structure variable.

Structure is declared as,

    struct <name>
    {
        data_type member1;
        data_type member2;
          :
        data_type membern;
    };

where member1, member2, ..., membern etc. can be int, char, float, array, struct itself. Also note that the declaration ends with semicolon. The structure declared is called structure template.

For example,

    struct person
    {
        char name[20];
        int age;
        float income;
    };

The fields name, age and income are called structure members.

Thus, we have declared a variable type or template called as struct person which is capable of storing name, age and income of one person. To store data items, variables of type struct person are to be defined.

    For example, struct person p, q, r;

This will reserve space for storing 3 records in p, q, r as follows:

	name	age	income
p			
q			
r			

The structure declaration and variable definition can be done together as follows:

    struct person
    {
        char name[20];
        int age;
        float income;
    }   p, q, r;

Storing data in structure variables

Once we have declared the structure type variable, we can store the values in these variables. We have to store the values in the individual fields. This is done using dot(·) operator.

For example,

    strcpy(p.name, "abc");

    p.age = 30;

    p.income = 30000.00

Consider following program which stores a record in a structure type variable and copies into another variable of same type.

Program 1.24: To store and display data in structure variable.

```
void main( )
{
    struct person
    {
        char name[20];,
        int age;
        float income;
    };
    struct person p, q;
    strcpy(p.name, "abc");
    p.age = 25;
    p.income = 5000.00;
    q = p;
    printf("%s \t %d \t %f \n", q.name, q.age, q.income);
}
```

Output of above program will be

    abc   25   5000.00

Thus, we see that the different types of data can be handled by structure type variables and it becomes very easy to manage this data.

1.4.3 Array of Structures

An array of records is used to store number of records, for example, a list of persons having name, age and income. In the previous Section, we had defined a structure for the same. Now, we can have a variable declaration as.struct person p[100]. It will reserve 100 locations as shown below to store list of 100 persons.

	name	age	income
p[0]			
p[1]			
p[2]			
:			
:			
p[99]			

To access or store data into these locations, we can use dot operator.

For example, p[0].name is the name field of first record, p[0].age is the age field of first record, etc.

To read data into this array, we can use for loop. Similarly, to process data sequentially and display, a for loop can be used. Any record or field can also be randomly accessed.

Program 1.25: To store a list of persons and display the names of persons whose age is above 40.

```
void main( )
{
    struct person                          // Structure declaration
    {
        char name[20];
        int age;
    };
    int i, n;
    struct person p[100];                  // Array of structure
    printf("Enter number of persons \n");
    scanf("%d", &n);
    for(i=0;i<n;i++)                       // Read n records
    {
        printf("Enter name \n");
```

```
            gets(p[i].name);
            printf("Enter age \n");
            scanf("%d", &p[i].age);
        }
        print("Persons above 40 years are \n");
        for (i=0;i<n;i++)                          // Display records
        {
            if(p[i].age>40)                         // if age > 40
            printf("%s \t %d \n", p[i].name, p[i].age);
        }
}
```

Program 1.26: To prepare a list of persons having name, age and salary and sort the list age wise.

```
    void main( )
    {
        struct person                              // Structure definition
        {
            char name[20];
            int age;
            float sal;
        };
        int i, j, n;
        struct person p[100], temp;,               // temp and array of structure
        printf("Enter how many persons \n");
        scanf("%d", &n);
        for(i=0;i<n;i++)                           // Read n records
        {
            printf("Enter name \n");
            gets(p[i].name);
            printf("Enter age \n");
            scanf("%d", &p[i].age);
            printf("Enter salary \n");
            scanf("%f", &p[i]sal);
        }
        for(i=0;i<n-1;i++)                         // sort the records age wise
        {
            for(j=i+1;j<n;j++)
```

```
            {
                if(p[i]..age>p[j].age)
                {
                    temp = p[i];
                    p[i] = p[j];
                    p[j] = temp;
                }
            }
        }
    printf("Sorted listed is \n");          // Display records
    for(i=0;i<n;i++)
        printf("%s \t %d \t %f \n", p[i].name, p[i].age, p[i].sal);
}
```

Program 1.27: To read a list of students having roll number, name and marks in 3 subjects. Find total and percentage. Sort the list in descending order of percentage.

```
void main( )
{
    struct student                          // Define structure
    {
        int rollno;
        char name[20];
        int m1, m2, m3, total;
        float per;
    };
    struct student s[100], temp;            // temp and array of structure
    int i, j, n;
    printf("Enter number of students \n");
    scanf("%d", &n);
    for(i=0;i<n;i++)                        // Read roll no, name and marks in 3 subjects
    {
        printf("Enter rollno \n");
        scanf("%d", &s[i].rollno);
        printf("Enter name \n");
        flushall( );
        gets(s[i].name);
        printf("Enter marks in subjects \n");
```

```
            scanf("%d %d %d", &s[i].m1, &s[i].m2, &s[i].m3);
            s[i].total = s[i].m1 + s[i].m2 + s[i].m3    // Calculate total
            s[i].per = s[i].total/3.0;                  // Calculate percentage
      }
      for(i=0;i<n-1;i++)
      {
            for(j=i+1;j<n;j++)                          // Sort records in descending order
            {
                  if(s[i].per<s[j].per)
                  {
                        temp = s[i];
                        s[i] = s[j];
                        s[j] = temp;
                  }
            }
      }
      printf("Sorted list is \n");
      for(i=0;i<n;i++)
      printf("%d \t %s \t %d \t %d \t %d \t %f \n", s[i].rollno, s[i].name, s[i].m1,
      s[i].m2, s[i].m3, s[i].total, s[i].per);
}
```

Initializing structure variables

Just like initialization of other variables can be done at the time of declaration [For example, int a = 10], structure variables can also be initialized.

For example,   struct person p = {"abc", 20, 2000};
or   struct person p[ ] = {"abc", 20,1000, "pqr", 30, 3000, "xyz", 40, 4000};

Rules for initializing structure variables:

1. Structure members cannot be initialized inside structure declaration or template.
2. The structure can be partially initialized like struct person p = {"abc", 20};
3. The order of the values inside braces should be same as order of definition.
4. Default initial values will be 0 for int and float members and '\0' for char type member.

Program 1.28: To store a list of items having items number, item name, rate. Search an item in the list if item number is entered.

```c
void main( )
{
    struct item
    {
        int item_no;
        char name[20];
        float rate;
    };
    struct item lst[ ] = {10,"Rin", 15.50, 11,"Lux", 10.50, 12,"Surf", 50.60};
    int s, i, flag = 1;
    printf("Enter item number \n");
    scanf("%d", &s);
    for(i=0;i<n;i++)
    {
        if(lst[i].item_no==s)
        {
            flag = 0;
            printf("%s \t %f \n", lst[i].name, lst[i].rate);
            break;
        }
    }
    if (flag==1)
        printf("Not available");
}
```

1.4.4 Structure and Pointers

Just like we can have pointer variable of int, float or character type, we can also have pointer variable of structure type. For example, if we have structure declared as,

```c
struct person
{
    char name[20];
    int age;
    float sal;
}
```

Now, let us have two variables as:
   struct person p = {"abc", 25, 6000};
   struct person *ptr;
   two locations in the memory will be reserved as:

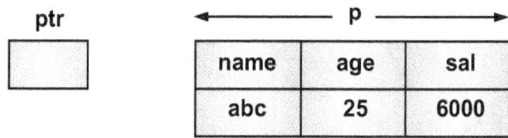

p is simple structure variable and ptr is structure type pointer variable.

Let us store address of p in ptr.
$$ptr = \&p;$$
This will store address of.p say 1000 in ptr.

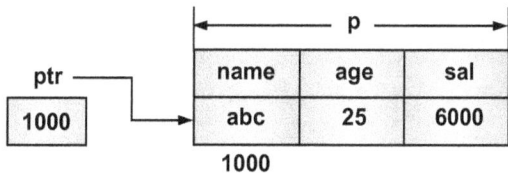

To access data stored in p, dot operator can be used.
   p.name will give "abc".
   p.age will give 25.
   p.sal will give 6000.

Since ptr is a pointer to p, we can access the data through ptr also. An arrow operator (->) is used to access the fields through the pointer type structure variable.
   ptr ->name will be same as p.name i.e., "abc".
   ptr ->age will be same as p.age i.e., 25.
   ptr -> sal will be same as p.sal i.e., 6000.

To access entire structure variable through ptr we can use * operator, i.e., *ptr is same as p. We can also access the fields through ptr using . operator as
   (*ptr). name will be same as p.name i.e., "abc".
   (*ptr). age will be same as page i.e., 25.
   (*ptr). sal will be same as p.sal i.e., 6000.

Now let us write a simple program to illustrate this.

Program 1.29: Use of structure type pointer.
```
void main( )
{
    struct person
    {
        char name[20];
        int age;
        float sal;
    }
    struct person p = {"abc", 25, 6000}
    struct person *ptr, temp;
    ptr = &p;
    printf("%s \t %d \t %f \n", ptr->name, ptr->age, ptr->sal);
    temp = *ptr;
    printf("%s \t %d \t %f \n", temp.name, temp.age, temp.sal);
}
```

Explanation:
1. ptr is pointer to p. hence, output of first printf will be,
   abc   25   6000
2. temp = *ptr will store a value (entire record in p) pointed by ptr in temp. Hence, the output of second printf will also be same.

1.4.5 Array of Structure and Pointer

A pointer variable can be used to store address of an array of records. We can extend this idea for array of structure also. If we have single pointer variable
   struct person *p;

This declaration will reserve only two byte of memory for p at the time of compilation. This variable can be allocated memory block, to store an array of records using malloc as:
   p = (struct person *)malloc(n*sizeof (struct person));

The function malloc will allocate memory block for storing n records of the size of struct person, i.e., 26*n bytes and the address of first record will be stored in p. p+1 will be address of 2nd record, p+2 will be address of 3rd record and so on. In general, p+i will be address of i+1th record. We can use -> operator to access the locations pointed by p, p+1, p+2 etc.

i.e., (p+i) -> name will access name in i+1th record.

(p+i) -> age will access age in i+1th record.

(p+i) -> sal will access sal in i+1th record.

Let us write a program to illustrate these concepts.

Program 1.30: To store a list of n persons and sort it on the basis of age.

```
void main( )
{
    struct person
    {
        char name[20];
        int age;
        float sal;
    };
    struct person *p, temp;
    int i, j, n;
    clrscr( );
    printf("Enter number of persons \n");
    scanf("%d", &n);
    p=(struct person *)malloc(n*sizeof(struct person));
    for(i=0;i<n;i++)
    {
        printf("Enter name \n");
        gets ((p+i)->name);
        printf("Enter age \n");
        scanf("%d", &(p+i)->age);
        printf("Enter salary \n");
        scanf("%f ", &(p+i)->sal);
    }
    for(i=0;i<n-1;i++)
    {
        for(j=i+1;j<n;j++)
        {
            if((p+i)->age>(p+j)->age)
```

```
                {
                        temp = *(p+i);
                        *(p+i) = *(p+j);
                        *(p+j) = temp;
                }
            }
        }
        printf("Sorted list is \n");
        for(i=0;i<n;i++)
                printf("%s \t %d \t.%t \n", (p+i)->name, (p+i)->age, (p+i)->sal);
}
```

Explanation:
1. p=(struct person *)malloc(n*sizeof(struct person)); will allocate memory for storing n records, where n will be known at run time. Thus, depending on value of n, memory is allocated to the pointer variable ptr. If we have 10 records to store, memory for 10 records (260 bytes) will be allocated.
2. The first for loop runs for n times accepting every time name, age and salary and it is stored in the locations whose addresses are p, p+1, p+2, ..., .
3. The second nested for will sort the records age wise using selection sort. Here, *(p+i) refers to the record pointed by p+i which is equivalent to p[i]. *(p+j) refers to the record pointed by p+j which is equivalent to p[j].
4. The third for loop displays all the sorted records.

1.4.6 Nested Structure

We can have another structure variable as a part of a structure. Consider that we want to store name and date of birth of a person. Date of birth can contain 3 fields day, month and year. Hence, we declare it as another structure as shown below:

```
    struct dob
    {
        int dd, mm, yy;
    }
    struct person
    {
        char name[20];
        struct dob d;
    };
```

Thus, we have name and d as two fields in struct person where d is a structure type variable nested inside struct person. If we define
    struct person p;
p will be allocated memory as:

Name	\multicolumn{3}{c}{d}
	dd	mm	yy

If we want to access name we write p.name. If date of birth is to be accessed, we can use p.d.dd, p.d.mm and p.d.yy.

Let us write a simple program which stores name and date of birth of n persons and displays list of person whose date of birth is in the month of June.

Program 1.31: To store name and date of birth and display list of persons whose birthday is in June.

```
void main( )
{
    struct dob
    {
        int dd, mm, yy;
    };
    struct person
    {
        char name [20];
        struct dob d;
    };
    struct person p[100];
    int i, j, n;
    printf("Enter number of persons \n");
    scanf("%d", &n);
    for(i=0;i<n;i++)
    {
        printf("Enter name \n");
        gets(p[i].name);
```

```
            printf("Enter data of birth in dd:mm:yy format");
            scanf("%d : %d : %d", &p[i].d.dd, &p[i].d.mm, &p[i].d.yy);
                                    //Note that there is : in between two %ds
                                    // You should use : while giving input
        }
        printf("List of persons whose date of birth in June is \n");
        for(i=0;i<n; i++)
        {
            if(p[i].d.mm == 6)
                printf("%s \t %d:%d:%d \n", p[i].name, p[i].d.dd, p[i].d.mm, p[i].d.yy);
        }
        getch( );
}
```

1.4.7 Passing Structures to Functions

A function can be passed parameter of type int, float, char etc. We can also pass structure type data to a function and a function can return a structure. We can pass
1. Structure members individually,
2. Structure variables by value,
3. Structure variables by address,
4. An array of structure.

Let us see how we can do these:
1. **Passing structure members individually: Consider following program.**

Program 1.32: Passing structure member to function
```
    void cal_bonus(float);
    void main( )
    {
        struct person
        {
            char name[20];
            int age;
            float sal;
        };
        struct person p = {"aaa", 20, 2000}
        cal_bonus (p.sal);
    }
```

```
void cal_bonus(float salary)
{
    float bonus;
    bonus = salary * 0.5;
    printf("Bonus is %f", bonus);
}
```

In program 1.32, we have passed salary of the person and calculated bonus in the function. The parameter is a float, hence the function argument is also float.

2. Passing structure by value:
Consider following program.

Program 1.33: Passing structure variable by value.
```
void disp(struct person);
void main( )
{
    struct person p = {"abc" 20, 2000};
    disp (p);
}
void disp(struct person p)
{
    printf("%s \t %d \t %f \n", p.name, page, p.sal);
}
```

Output: abc 20   20000

Here, we are passing. the variable p to the function and all the fields will be available to the function which can be displayed.

Typedef:

Whenever one writes function that requires passing of structure, we have to repeatedly write the word struct and name of structure. In order to avoid this, we can create a short cut or alias for this using keyword typedef as:

```
typedef struct person
{
    char name [20];
    int age;
    float sal;
}PER;
```

This means PER is an alias (another name) for struct person.

3. Passing structure by address:

Read the given program and find what will be its output.

Program 1.34: Passing structure by value.

```
typedef struct person
{
    char name s[20];
    int age;
    float sal;
} PER;
void disp(PER);
void modify(PER);
void main( )
{
    PER p={ "abc", 20,20000};
    disp(p);
    modify(p);
    disp(p);
}
void disp(PER p)
{
    printf("%s \t %d \t %f \n", p.name, page, p.sal);
}
void modify(PER p)
{
    p.age=p.age+1;
    p.sal=1.1 *p.sal;
}
```

Output: abc 20 20000
abc 20 20000

Explanation:
1. There are two functions disp and modify to which structure variable is passed by value.
2. When disp is called for the first time, main will pass the contents of p in main to p in disp and the records get displayed.

3. When modify is called, main will pass the contents of p in main to p in modify. The function modify will change age field of p to 21 and sal field to 22000; but these changes will be made in local variable p of modify and not of main. Hence, when control is back in main, its p is unchanged.
4. When disp is called second time, main will pass the contents of p in main to p in disp and they get displayed.

Now, what if I want the function to modify the contents of structure variable passed to it? The answer is, we have to pass it by address as shown in program 1.35.

Program 1.35: Passing structure by address.
```
typedef struct person
{
    char name 2[0];
    int age;
    float sal;
}PER;
void disp(PER);
void modify(PER *);
void main( )
{
    PER p={"abc",20, 20000};
    disp(p);
    modify(&p);
    disp(p);
}
void disp(PER p)
{
    printf("%s \t %d \t %f \n", p.name, page, p.sal);
}
void modify(PER *ptr)
{
    ptr->age-ptr->age+1;
    ptr->sal=1.1 *ptr->sal;
}
```
Output: abc 20   20000
          abc 21   22000

Explanation:
1. There are two functions disp and modify to which structure variable is passed by value and by address respectively.
2. When disp is called for the first time, main will pass the contents of p in main to p in disp and they get displayed.
3. When modify is called, main will pass the address of p in main to pointer ptr in modify. Hence, ptr is a pointer to location p. The function modify will change age field of p to 21 and sal field to 22000. Note that we have used operator -> to access the members of p. Hence, when control is back in main, its p has changed values.
4. When disp is called second time, main will pass the modified contents of p in main to p in disp and they get displayed.

4. Passing structure type array to function:

As we know if we have to pass an array to a function, we have to pass address of first element in the array to the function. Function argument should be pointer type variable. In this case, it should be pointer to structure. Let us consider a program to read a list of persons and sort it on the basis of age. We will write separate function for reading, sorting and displaying the records.

Program 1.36: Program to sort list of persons using separate functions for read, sort and display.

```
typedef struct person
{
    char name [20];
    int age;
    float sal;
}PER;
void read_recs(PER *);
void disp_recs(PER *);
void sort_recs(PER *);
int n;
void main( )
{
    PERSON p[100];
    int i;
    printf("How many persons? \n");
    scanf("%d", &n);
```

```c
        read_recs(p);              // Call read records function
        sort_recs(p);              // Call sort records function
        disp_recs(p);              // Call display records function
    }
    void read_recs(PER *ptr)
    {
        int i;
        for(i=0;i<n;i++)
        {
            printf("Enter name \n");
            gets((ptr+i) -> name);
            printf("Enter age \n");
            scanf("%d", &(ptr+i) -> age);
            printf("Enter salary \n");
            scanf("%f", &(ptr+i) -> sal);
        }
    }
    void sort_recs(PER *ptr)
    {
        int i, j;
        PER temp;
        for(i=0;i<n;i++)
        {
            for(j=i+1; j<n; j++)
                if((ptr+i)->age>(ptr+j)->age)
                {
                    temp *(ptr + i);
                    *(ptr+i) = *(ptr+i);
                    (ptr+j) = temp;
                }
        }
    }
    void disp_recs (PER *ptr)
    {
        int i, j
        for(i=0;i<n;i++)
            printf("%s \t %d \t %f \n", (ptr+i)->name, (ptr+i)->age, (ptr+i)->sal);
    }
```

Explanation:
1. The main function has array p[100]. Its address p is passed to each function.
2. The function accepts the address in pointer variable ptr. Thus, ptr has address of first record, ptr+1 is address of second record. In general, i+1th record can be accessed through ptr+i.

1.4.8 Returning a Structure from Function

Individual structure members or entire structure can be returned back via a return statement at the access point in the calling function. If individual structure member is returned, return type of the function will be the same as type of structure member. If structure is returned, the return type of the function is same as that of structure type.

Consider following example of addition of two rational numbers represented as struct type.
Program 1.37: Addition of two rational numbers.
```
typedef struct rational
{
    int num, den;
} RAT;
RAT add(RAT, RAT)
void main( )
{
    RAT r1 = {2,3}, r2 {4,5}, r3;
    r3 = add(r1, r2);
    printf("%d /%d", r3.num, r3.den);
}
RAT add(RAT rl, RAT r2)
{
    RAT r3;
    r3.num = r1.num r2.den + r1.den r2.num;
    r3.den = r1.den r2.den;
    return(r3);
}
```

Explanation:
1. The num and den are numerator and denominator of rational numbers.
2. The function add accepts two struct type(RAT) variables r1, r2; calculates numerator and denominator of resultant rational number r3 and returns it.

1.4.9 Arrays as an ADT Insertion, Deletion and Traversals of Array

An ordered or Linear List is most simple and common data object. A Linear List consists of set of elements. It is represented as,

$$L = \{e_1, e_2, e_3, ..., e_n\}$$

where $e_1, e_2, e_3, ...,$ etc. are elements in the List. Here, $e_1, e_2, e_3,$ etc. can be integers, real numbers, characters, strings or records. They can be even enumerated data items also. An example of list is shown below:

(i) List of integers:
   L_1 = {10, 20, 30, 40, 50}
(ii) List of real numbers:
   L_2 = {2.5, 7.5, −8.3, 3.8, 11.57}
(iii) List of characters:
   L_3 = {'a', 'b', 'c', 'd', 'e'}
(iv) List of names:
   L_4 = ("Sunil", "Anil", "Nitin", "Seema", "Rima"}
(v) List of records:
   L_5 = {{"abc", 20}, {"xyz", 25}, {"pqr", 30}}
(vi) List of days:
   L_6 = {Monday, Tuesday, Wednesday, Thursday}

The data structure that we can use for storing these lists is array. For example, the list L_1 can be stored in an array of integers, L_2 can be stored in an array of float, etc. There are number of operations that can be done on these lists. These operations are:
1. Display the list.
2. Search an element.
3. Find length of the list.
4. Modifying an element.
5. Insert an element in the list.
6. Delete an element in the list.
7. Sort the list.
8. Reverse the list.

We might require to perform all these operations or part of these operations on the list. The efficiency of these operations will depend on the way in which the data is stored i.e., data structure. Since, the only data structure we know now is an array. Let us implement a list of records using array.

Program 1.38: Write a program to implement list of employees having empno, name and age and perform following operations:

(i) Display,
(ii) Search,
(iii) Insert,
(iv) Delete,
(v) Sort,
(vi) Append.

Let we write a menu driven program. For each of the operation specified eve need to write separate functions.

```c
#include<conio.h>
#include<stdio.h>
typedef struct employee
{
    int empno;
    char name[20];
    int age;
}   emp;
#define max 100
void disp( );
void search( );
void insert( );
void delete( );
void sort( );
void append( );
EMP e[MAX];
int n;
void main( )
{
    int i, ch;
    printf("Enter number of number of records\n");
    scanf("%d", &n);
    for(i=0;i<n;i++)
    {
        printf("Enter empno \n");
```

```c
            scanf("%d", & e[i].&empno);
            printf("Enter name \n");
            gets(e[i].name);
            printf("Enter age \n");
            scanf("%d", &e[i].age);
    }
    do
    {
        clrscr( );
        printf("1. Disp \n 2. Search \n 3. Insert \n 4. Delete \n 5. Sort \n 6. Append \n 7. Exit\n");
        printf("Enter your choice \n");
        scanf("%d", & ch);
        switch (ch)
        {
            case 1:  disp( );
                    break;
            case 2:  search( );
                    break;
            case 3 : insert( );
                    break;
            case 4:  delete( );
                    break;
            case 5:  sort( );
                    break;
            case 6:  append( );
            getch( );
    } while (ch!=7);
}
void disp( )
{
    int i;
    for(i=0;i<n;i++)
        printf("%d \t %s \t %d \n", e[i].empno, e[i].name, e[i].age);
}
```

```c
void search( )
{
    int i, s;
    printf("Enter employee number \n");
    scanf("%d", &s);
    flag = 1;
    for(i=0;i<n;i++)
    {
        if (e[i].empno==s)
        {
            printf("%s \t %d \n", e[i].name, e[i].age);
            flag=0;
            break;
        }
    }
    if (flag==1)
        printf("Not found");
}
void insert( )
{
    int i, loc;
    printf("Enter location for new record (location starts from 0) \n");
    scanf("%d", &loc);
    for (i=n-1;i>=loc;i--)
        e[i+1] = e[i];
    printf("Enter empno \n");
    scanf("%d", &e[loc].empno);
    printf("Enter name \n");
    gets(e[loc].name);
    printf("Enter age \n");
    scanf("%d", &e[loc].age);
    n++;
}
void del( )
{
    int i, loc;
```

```
        printf("Enter record number to be deleted (location starts from 0) \n");
        scanf("%d", &loc);
        for(i=loc;i<n;i++)
            e[i-1] = e[i];
        n--;
}
void sort( )                    // namewise sorting
{
    int i, j;
    Emp temp;
    for(i=0;i<n;i++)
    {
        for(j=0;j<n-1-i;j++)
        {
            if (strcmp(e[j].name, e[j+1].name)>0)
            {
                temp = e[j]
                e[j] = e[j+1]
                e[j+1] = temp;
            }
        }
    }
}
void append( )
{
    printf("Enter empno \n");
    scanf("%d", &e[n].empno);
    printf("Enter name \n");
    gets(e[n].name);
    printf("Enter age \n");
    scanf("%d", &e[n].age);
    n++;
}
```

Note:
1. We have declared array e[ ] globally, so that it will be available to all functions and we need not pass it to them.
2. The variable n which stores number of records is also global. Since it gets changed in insert and delete, it should be made available to these functions.

3. In insert function, we have shifted all the records down from the location onwards, so that there is a space created to insert new record and since one record is added n is incremented by 1.
4. In delete function, the records are shifted up from the location onwards. Since one record is deleted, n is decremented by 1.
5. The sort function sorts the records namewise. Bubble sort is used.
6. Append function adds one records at the nth position because, last record is at $(n-1)^{th}$ position.
7. If the array e[ ] and n declared local as variables in main function, we need to pass these to the function. We may require to pass n by address wherever it gets changed otherwise it can be passed by value.

SUMMARY

- A pointer can be used to store address of a location in the memory and it can access all the successive locations also.
- A malloc function is used to allocate a block memory to a pointer variable which can access data stored in the block. In other words, a single pointer variable can be used to-replace one dimensional array variable.
- An array of pointers can be used to represent a two dimensional array. Each element in the array of pointers will store the address of each row.
- String is an array of characters, used to store group of characters such as words, names, sentences etc.
- In built string functions are used to manipulate characters in a string.
- A char type pointer can be used to access characters stored in a string.
- An array of strings is used to store number of separate strings.
- An array can be passed to a function by passing address of first element in the array or name of array.
- Structure is a user defined or constructed data type which can combine different data types. So that the collection of data can be represented using single name.
- A structure definition consists of structure name and structure members called fields.
- A dot (·) operator is used to access structure members.
- An array of structure is used to store records which are nothing but collection of related fields.
- We can have a structure type pointer variable which can store address of structure variable.
- An arrow (→) operator is used to access members of structure through structure type pointer variable.

- We can declare structure variable inside another structure definition which is called nested structure.
- A structure variable can be passed to a function by address or by value.
- Unions are similar to structures except that the members of union share the same memory location, whereas each member of structure is allocated separate memory.
- Bit wise operator &, |, ^, ~, <<, >> are used to manipulate individual bits stored in memory.
- The sequential representation of data elements is called ordered list. We can do various operations on the list such as display, insert, delete, modify etc.
- A polynomial in single variable can be represented using two techniques:
  (i) Simple array,
  (ii) Array of structures.

SOLVED PROBLEMS

1. Write a program to add two complex numbers.

Solution:

```
void main( )
{
    struct complex
    {
        float real, image;
    };
    struct complex c1, c2, c3;
    printf("Enter first complex number's real and imag part \n");
    scanf("%f%f", &c1.real, &c1.imag);
    printf("Enter second complex number's real and imag part \n");
    scanf("%f%f", &c2.real, &c2.imag);
    c3.real = c1.real + c2.real;
    c3.imag = c1.imag + c2.imag;
    printf("The addition is %.2f + %.2f \n", c1.real, c3.imag);
}
```

2. Define a structure called cricket that will describe following information:
   (i) Player name,
   (ii) Team name,
   (iii) Batting average.

Using this, declare an array player with 50 elements. Write a function in 'C' to print the player name, team name and batting average for that player having highest batting average.

Solution:

```c
struct cricket
{
    char pname[20];
    char tname[20];
    float avg;
};
struct cricket player[50];
void display (struct cricket player[ ], int n)
{
    int i, pos=0; float max;
    max = player[0].avg;
    for(i=1;i<n;i++)
    {
        if(player[i].avg>max)
            pos = i;
    }
    printf("%s \t %s \t %f \n", player[pos].pname, player[pos].tname, player[pos].avg);
}
```

3. What will be output of following program?

Solution:

```c
void main( )
{
    int a = 10, b = 20, c, d, e;
```

```c
        c = a & b;
        d = a | b;
        e = ~a;
        printf("%d %d %d", c, d, e );
    }
```

a = 10 ⇒ 0000000000001010
b = 20 ⇒ 0000000000010100
Hence,
c = a & b ⇒ 0000000000000000 ⇒ 0
c = a | b ⇒ 0000000000011110 ⇒ 30
e = ~a ⇒ 1111111111110101 ⇒ −11
Hence output will be,
0 30 −11

4. Database of 100 students is required to be stored. Each student record contains fields such as roll no, name, total marks. Write a program in 'c' to input the database with above fields mentioned above. Using:
   (i) arrays,
   (ii) Array of structure. Display record of students who scored maximum marks.

Solution:

(i) Program using arrays:

```c
void main( )
{
    int m[100];
    char name[100][20];
    int marks [100];
    int i, max, index;
    for(i=0;i<100;i++)
    {
        printf("Enter roll no \n");
        scanf("%d", &rn[i]);
        printf("Enter name \n");
        gets(name[i]);
```

```c
        printf("Enter marks \n");
        scanf("%d", &marks[i]);
    }
    index = 0;
    max = marks[0];
    for(i=1;i<100;i++)
    {
        if (marks[i])>max)
        {
            max = marks[i];
            index = i;
        }
    }
    printf("%d %s %d", rn[index], name[index], marks[index]);
}
```

(ii) Program using structure:

```c
void main( )
{
    struct student
    {
        int m;
        char name[20];
        int marks;
    }s[100];
    int i, max, index;
    for(i=0;i<100;i++)
    {
        printf("Enter roll no \n");
        scanf("%d", &s[i].rn);
        printf("Enter name \n");
        gets(s[i].name);
        printf("Enter age \n");
```

```
        scanf("%d", &s[i].marks);
    }
    max = s[0].marks;
    index = 0;
    for (i=1;i<100;i++)
    {
        if(s[i].marks>max)
        {
            max = s[i].marks;
            index=i;
        }
    }
    printf("%d %s %d \n", s[index].rn, s[index].name, s[index].marks);
}
```

EXERCISE

1. Define the following terms.
   (i) Data structure
   (ii) ADT.
2. What is pointer and how it is initialized?
3. Illustrate the following parameter passing techniques with suitable example.
   (i) Call by value.
   (ii) Call by reference.
4. Explain how a pointer can be used to replace an array.
5. Explain with example how pointer variable can be used to access elements in contiguous locations.
6. Explain how array of pointers can be used to replace 2-D array.
7. What do you mean by array of pointers? Differentiate between array of pointers and pointer to array with the help of suitable example.
8. Explain different methods of storage representation in 2-D array.
9. What are structures? Explain its use. Define structure having name, age and salary.

10. Explain structure and union in 'C' in detail with suitable example.
11. What is union? Explain with some suitable examples. How union is declared and used in C?
12. Compare structure and union in 'C'.
13. Differentiate between structure and union
14. Explain structure and union in 'C' in detail with suitable example.
15. Write difference between union and structure with example.
16. Write a program to print whether the bit 2nd, 4th and 6th are set or not in a given number.
17. With example explain any one bit wise operators.
18. What is meant by an ordered list?

STACK AND QUEUE

2.1 INTRODUCTION

Stack is a linear data structure where the element which is inserted last can only be taken out first. Thus, it is called LIFO (Last In First Out) type of data structure.

Stack is also defined as a data structure where all addition and deletion are made only at one end called top. It is similar to a real life situation of stack of things. If we keep things stacked one on to the another, we can take out the thing at the top. Similarly, we can keep a new thing on the top.

Stack can be implemented using:
1. Arrays,
2. Linked lists.

Following four operations can be done on a stack.
1. **Push operation:** In this, an element is stored at a location indicated by top.
2. **Pop operation:** In this operation, the element at the top is removed.
3. **Stack Full:** When all the locations reserved for stack are occupied, we can't insert any more elements. This condition is stack full condition.
4. **Stack empty:** When there is no element left on a stack, we can't pop any element. This condition is called as stack empty condition.

2.2 STACK AS AN ABSTRACT DATA TYPE (ADT)

The ADT for stack can be given as follows:

Definition: A stack is a restricted list in which entries are added and removed from the same end, called the top. This strategy is known as last-in-first-out (LIFO) strategy.

Operations (methods) on stacks:

push(item)	Inserts item on the top of the stack
pop( )	Removes the top item
size( )	Returns the number of items in the stack
empty( )	Returns true if the stack is empty
full( )	Returns true if the stack is full
ontop( )	Returns the top element without removing it from the stack

Multiple stacks using single array:

We have seen that multiple stacks can be implemented using multiple arrays. We can use single array also to implement multiple stack. For this we can divide the array into number of parts. Each part will be used as one stack. The top of each stack will be initialized to the starting index of each part in the array. For implementing stack full or stack empty condition, we can use a counter for each stack. The counter will be incremented when push operation is done and decremented when pop operation is done. Stack full condition occurs when the counter reaches maximum value (size of each stack). Stack empty condition occurs when counter becomes starting index of each stack.

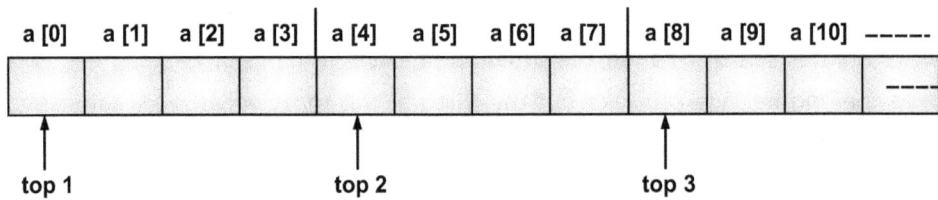

Fig. 2.1: Multiple stacks using single array

Two stacks can be efficiently implemented using single array by using the upper part of the, array for first stack and lower part for second array, The top of first stack will be initialized to -1, it will be incremented when push operation is done and decremented in pop operation. The top of the second stack is initialized to MAX (size of the array). It is decremented in push operation and incremented in pop operation.

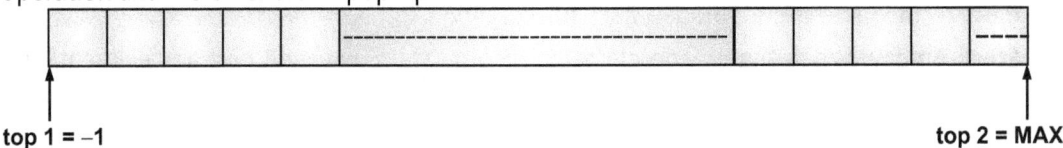

Fig. 2.2: Two stacks using single array

2.3 STACK USING ARRAY

To represent a stack using array, we require an array of some size to be declared say int a[4]. This will create a space for storing elements on stack. The size of the stack is 4. We will require one more variable say top which will be an index to the top element of the stack. Initially, the stack is empty. The variable top will be initialized to -1.

Push operation:

Now, if we want to store a number 10 on the stack, we can increment top and the element 10 will be stored at location a[0].

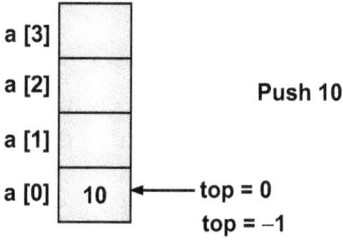

Fig. 2.3(a): Push (10)

Next, we store a number 20 on the stack, top will be incremented to 1 and element 20 will be stored at location a[1].

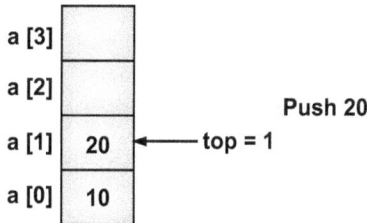

Fig. 2.3(b): Push (20)

Next, we store a number 30 on the stack, top will be incremented to 2 and element 30 will be stored at location a[2].

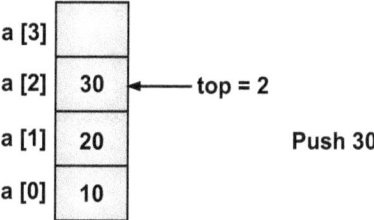

Fig. 2.3(c): Push (30)

Next, we store a number 40 on the stack, top will be incremented to 3 and element 40 will be stored at location a[3].

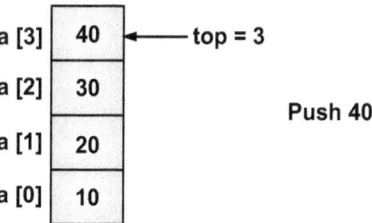

Fig. 2.3(d): Push (40)

Now there is no space left on the stack, hence, the stack is full. The condition for stack full is top becomes equal to maximum size of array −1.

Pop Operation:

Now, suppose we want to remove an element from the stack, we can access element at the top which is given by the index value in top. Consider the stack where we have already pushed four elements. If we carry out pop operation, the element at the top i.e., 40 will be accessed and top is decremented to 2.

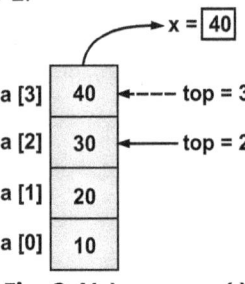

Fig. 2.4(a): x = pop( )

The next pop operation will remove 30 from the stack and top will be decremented to 1.

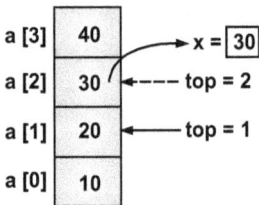

Fig. 2.4(b): x = pop( )

Another pop operation will remove 20 from the stack and top will be decremented to 0.

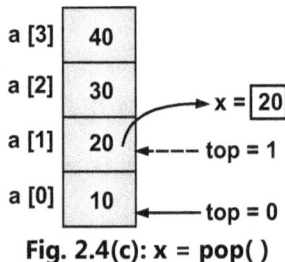

Fig. 2.4(c): x = pop( )

If the operation is carried out again, element 10 will be removed and top becomes −1.

Fig. 2.4(d): x = pop( )

Then we can't remove any more elements because stack is empty. The condition for stack empty is top == −1. The program for implementation of stack will require two functions push and pop whose algorithms areas follows:

1. **Push (x):**
   (i) If top == MAX −1
       print "stack full";
   (ii) else
       top ++;
       a [top] = x;
   (iii) Return.

Every time we do a push operation, we need to increment top and store the data at the location given by top in the array. But before we do this operation, we have to check whether the stack is full or not. Hence, the condition top ==MAX −1.

2. **x = pop( )**
   (i) If top=-1
       print "stack empty";
       return −9999;
   (ii) else
       x = a [top]
       top --;
       return x;

Every time we do a pop operation, we remove an element and then decrement top. But before we do this, we have to check whether the stack is empty or not. Hence, the condition top == −1. Note that we are returning −9999 when stack is empty. This is an indication for the calling function, so that it takes appropriate action when the stack is empty. The complete program for stack implementation is as follows:

Program 2.1: To implement stack using array. (Version 1)
```
#define MAX 5
int a [MAX];
int top = -1;
void push (int x)
{
    if (top == MAX - 1)
```

```
            printf("Stack is full");
    else
    {
        top ++;
        a[top]=x;
    }
}
int pop( )
{
    int x;
    if (top == -1)
    {
        print("Stack is empty \n");
        return (-9999);
    }
    else
    {
        x = a[top];
        top --;
        return (x);
    }
}
main( )
{
    int ch, x;
    do
    {
        clrscr( );
        printf(" 1. Push \n. 2. Pop \n. 3. Exit \n");
        printf("Enter your choice \n");
        scanf("%d", &ch);
        switch (ch)
        {
            case 1: printf("Enter a number \n");
                    scanf("% d", &x);
                    push (x);
```

```
                    break;
              case 2: x = pop( );
                    if (x!= -9999)
                          printf("% d", x);
        }
        getch( );
    } while (ch!=3);
}
```

We can implement separate functions for stack full and stack empty conditions as follows:

```
int stk_full( )
{
    if (top == MAX -1)
    {
        printf("Stack full");
        return (1);
    }
    else
        return (0);
}
```

The function returns 1 when stack is full otherwise 0.

```
int stk_empty( )
{
    if (top == -1)
    {
        print ("Stack is empty");
        return (1);
    }
    else
        return (0);
}
```

The function returns 1 when stack is empty otherwise 0.
These functions can be used in functions 'push' and 'pop' as follows:

```
void push (int x)
{
    if (!stk_full( ))
    {
        top ++;
        a[top] = x;
    }
}
int pop( )
{
    if (!stk_empty( ))
    {
        int x;
        x = a[top];
        top --;
        return x;
    }
    else
        return (-9999);
}
```

The stack consists of an array and top. If multiple stacks are to be implemented in single program, we need to define separate arrays and tops for each stack. Instead, we can define a stack variable for a stack which combines array and top together.

```
typedef struct stack
{
    int a[4];
    int top;
} STK;
```

Now if we declare a variable STK s1; it consists of an array and top as shown in Fig. 2.5.

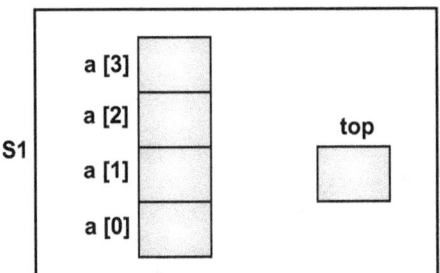

Fig. 2.5: Stack using structure

The elements in the stack can be accessed using dot operate, e.g., if top of the stack is to be initialized, we can write s1.top = −1 or if 10 is to be stored at the top of the stack; we can write s1.a [s1.top] = 10. But the major advantage of this struct type stack will be when more than one stack is to be implemented. The push and pop functions require the stack variable to be passed to them. Since these functions are going to modify the contents of the stack variable, we have to pass it by address. Hence, the function parameter will be pointer to a structure.

The push function will have prototype as,

void push (STK*, int)

The first argument is the pointer to the stack in which we are going to store the element and second argument is the integer number to be stored on the stack.

The pop function will have prototype as,

int pop (STK *)

The argument is the pointer to the stack from which number returns will be popped. A complete program using this is given as follows:

Program 2.2: Implementation of stack

```
#define MAX 5
typedef struct stack
{
    int a[MAX];
    int top;
} STK;
void push (STK*, int);
int pop (STK *);
main( )
{
    STK s1, s2;
    s1.top = -1;
    s2.top = -1;
    push (&s1, 10);
    push (&s1, 20);
    push (&s2, 100);
    push (&s2, 200);
    x = pop (&s1);
    printf("%d", x);
    x = pop (&s1);
    printf("%d", x);
```

```
        x = pop (&s2);
        printf("%d", x);
        x = pop (&s2);
        printf("%d", x);
}
void push (STK *s, int x)
{
    if (s->top == MAX -1)
        printf("Stack is full");
    else
    {
        (s->top) ++;
        s->a [s->top] = x;
    }
}
int pop (STK *s)
{
    int x;
    if (s->top == -1)
    {
        printf("Stack is empty");
        return (-9999);
    }
    else
    {
        x=s->a [s->top];
        (s->top) --;
        return (x);
    }
}
```

Explanation:
1. The main function has two variables s1 and s2 which are stacks.
2. The functions push and pop are passed addresses of stack. It is because the functions are going to change the contents of stack. Since we are passing the structure variable by address, the structure members are accessed using -> operator, e.g., top of stack is accessed through s as s -> top.

3. Note that though we are using two stacks, we have only one structure declaration and same functions push and pop for both the stacks.
4. We can modify the menu driven program we had written earlier for implementation of stack.

Program 2.3: To implement stack using array (version 2).

```c
void push (STK *, int);
int pop (STK*);
void main( )
{
    STK s1;
    int ch, x;
    s1.top = -1;
    do
    {
        clrscr( );
        printf(" Push \n 2, Pop \n 3. Exit \n");
        printf("Enter your choice");
        scanf("%d", &ch);
        switch (ch)
        {
            case 1:  printf("Enter data \n");
                     scanf("%d", &x);
                     push (&s1, x);
                     break;
            case 2:  x = pop (&s1);
                     if (x! = -9999)
                         printf ("%d \n", x);
                     break;
        }
        getch( );
    } while (ch!=3);
}
```

2.3.1 Stack Using Linked List

The array implementation of stack is not efficient from the point of view of memory utilization. The fixed size of array is required and it remains allocated for the entire duration of the program. Linked list implementation will have advantage over the array implementation because we can allocate memory as and when it is required.

The stack using linked list consist of nodes having data and address of next node. The node definition will be,

    typedef struct node
    {
        int data;
        struct node *next;
    } NODE;

A pointer called top can be declared (NODE *top) which will always point to the top of the stack. The operations push and pop will be implemented as follows:

Push Operation:

Step 1: Create a node.
Step 2: Store the data in the node.
Step 3: Link the next field of the node to the node where top is pointing.
Step 4: Point top to the recently created node.
Following figures show this operation.

Push (10):

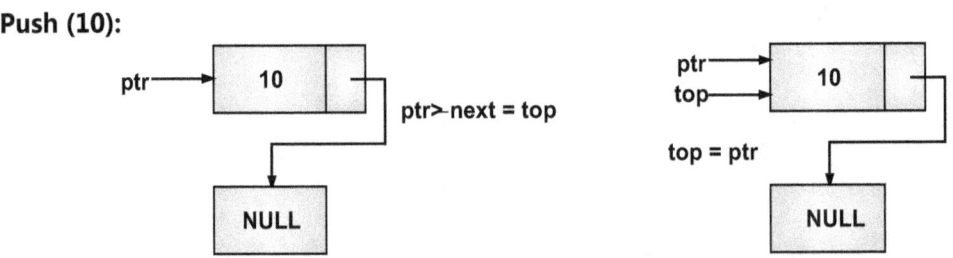

Fig. 2.6(a): Stack using linked list push (10)

Push (20):

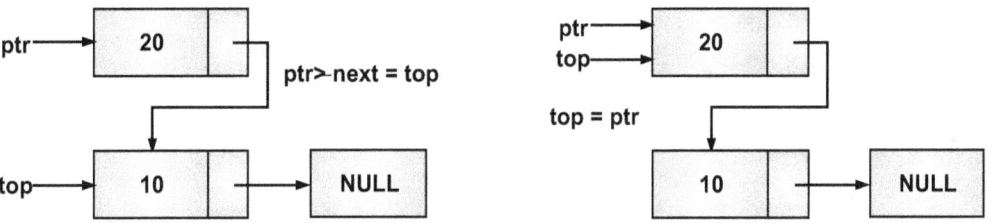

Fig. 2.6(b): Stack using linked list push (200)

Pop Operation:

Steps:

1. Make a pointer temp point to the top of the stack.
2. If it is NULL, then stack is empty.
3. If not, remove the data from this node then advance top.
4. De-allocate memory pointed by temp.

Following figures show this operation.

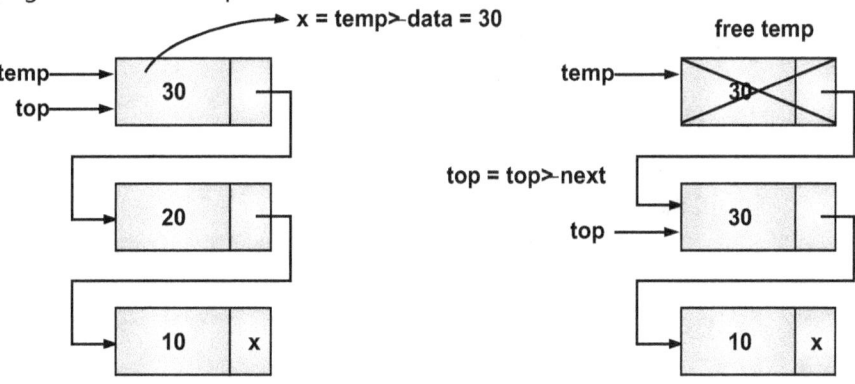

Fig. 2.7: Pop operation in stack using linked list

Following program implements stack using linked list. It has the function push and pop which has the-same prototype as that used in case of array. The function push accepts data, creates a node and puts it into a linked list. The function pop removes an element from the linked list and returns it.

Program 2.4: To implement stack using linked list.

```c
typedef struct node
{
    int data;
    struct node * next;
} NODE;
NODE *top = NULL;
void push (int);
int pop( );
void main( )
{
    int ch, x;
    do
    {
        clrscr( );
        printf(" 1. Push \n 2. Pop \n 3. Exit \n");
        printf("Enter your choice");
        scanf("%d", &ch);
        switch (ch)
        {
            case 1: printf("Enter a number \n");
                    scanf("%d", &x);
                    push (x);
                    break;
            case 2: x = pop( );
                    if (x!= -9999)
                        printf ("%d \n", x);
        }
        getch( );
    } while (ch!=3);
}
void push (int x)
{
    NODE *ptr;
    ptr = (NODE *) malloc (size of (NODE));
    if (ptr == NULL)
```

```
        printf("Insufficient memory");
    else
    {
        ptr->data = x;
        ptr->next = top;
        top = ptr;
    }
}
int pop( )
{
    NODE *temp; int x;
    temp = top;
    if (temp == NULL),
    {
        printf ("Stack empty");
        return (-9999);
    }
    else
    {
        x = temp->data;
        top = top->next;
        free (temp);
        return (x);
    }
}
```

2.4 APPLICATION OF STACK

Stack can be used in number of applications such as:
1. Conversion of expression.
2. Evaluation of expression.
3. Processing function calls.
4. Handling recursive function or removal of recursion.
5. Reversing a string.
6. Syntax checking e.g., parenthesis check.

2.5 ARITHMETIC EXPRESSION : POLISH NOTATION

This is the most important application of stack. When we write a program, we write number of expressions (arithmetic, logical, etc.) in it. The compiler has to interpret and convert these expressions into machine language.

An expression consists of operands and operators, e.g., the expression a + b has two operands a and b and one operator +. This is a very simple expression. Expression can be very complex consisting of number of operands and operators. While converting an expression into correct machine language format, compiler has to take care of the priority of the operators. It is very difficult to directly produce a code for evaluation of expression. The solution to this is, convert the expression into a form which will not require priority of operators and the expression can be directly evaluated.

An expression can be written in three different forms:
1. **Infix Expression:** Operator is in between the two operands, e.g., a + b.
2. **Postfix Expression:** Operator is after the two operands, e.g., ab+. It is called Reverse polish notation.
3. **Prefix Expression:** Operator is before the two operands, e.g., +ab. It is called Polish notation.

Suppose we have an expression in infix format a + b * c.
Its postfix is abc * +
and prefix is + a * be

If you observe postfix and prefix expression, we find that these expressions can be evaluated directly without knowing the priority of operators. Whereas for infix expression we have to find out priority and then evaluate.
Before we learn how to evaluate the postfix expression let us see how to convert an infix expression to postfix or prefix.
If we are given an infix expression the a + b * c steps for conversion will be as follows:
1. Write the expression with full parenthesized as per the priority of operators as
   e.g. (a + (b * c))
2. Replace the innermost parenthesized expression with e_1 as:
   exp = (a + e_1) where e_1 = b * c
3. Replace the next innermost parenthesized expression with e_2.
   i.e. exp = e_2 where e_2 = a + e:
   Continue till you get a single expression.

4. Now go in reverse direction replacing each expression with postfix or prefix.
   e.g., exp = ae_1 + or exp = + ae_1

   exp = abc* +   exp = + a * bc
   Hence the postfix expression is abc * +
   and the prefix expression is + a * be.

Example 1: Convert following expressions into postfix and prefix expressions.
1. a * b + c
2. a * b + c * d
3. a + b + c + d
4. a * b/c* d − e/f
5. a ** b * c ** d

Solution:

1.   exp = ((a * b) + c)

           = (e_1 + c) e_1 = a * b

           = e_2 e_2 = e_1 + c

       Postfix   **Prefix**

       exp = e_2 exp = e_2

             = e_1c +   = +e_1c

             = ab * c+   = +* abc

2.   exp = ((a *b) + (c * d))

           = (e_1 + e_2) e_1 = a * b e_2 = c * d

           = e_2 e_2 = e_1 + e_2

       Postfix   **Prefix**

       exp = e_2 exp = e_2

             = e_1 e_2 +   = +e_1 e_2

             = ab * cd * +   = + * ab * cd

3.   exp = (((a + b) + c) +d)

             = ((e_1 + c) + d) e_1 = a + b

             = (e_1 + d) e_2 = e_1 + c

             = e_3 e_3 = e_2 + d

       Postfix   **Prefix**

       exp = e_3 exp = e_3

             = e_2d +   = +e_2d

             = e_1c + d+   = ++$e_1$cd

             = ab + c + d+   = +++ abcd

4. $\quad \exp = a*b/c*d - e/f$

$\quad\quad\quad = ((((a*b)/c)*d) - (e/f)$

$\quad\quad\quad = (((e_1/c)*d) - e_2) \quad\quad e_1 = a*b \quad\quad\quad e_2 = e/f$

$\quad\quad\quad = ((e_3*d) - e_2) \quad\quad\quad e_3 = e_1/c$

$\quad\quad\quad = (e_4 - e_2) \quad\quad\quad\quad\quad e_4 = e_3*d$

$\quad\quad\quad = e_5 \quad\quad\quad\quad\quad\quad\quad\quad e_5 = e_4 - e_2$

Postfix $\quad\quad\quad\quad\quad\quad\quad\quad$ **Prefix**

$\exp = e_5 \quad\quad\quad\quad\quad\quad\quad \exp = e_5$

$\quad = e_4 e_2 - \quad\quad\quad\quad\quad\quad = -e_4 e_2$

$\quad = e_3 d * e_2 - \quad\quad\quad\quad\quad = -*e_3 d e_2$

$\quad = e_1 c/d * e_2 - \quad\quad\quad\quad = -*/e_1 c d e_2$

$\quad = ab*c/d*ef/- \quad\quad\quad\quad = -*/*abcd/ef$

5. $\quad \exp = a**b*c**d - e$

where ** is raised to operator

$\quad\quad\quad = (((a**b)*(c**d)) - e)$

$\quad\quad\quad = ((e_1 * e_2) - e) \quad\quad e_1 = a**b \quad\quad e_2 = c**d$

$\quad\quad\quad = (e_3 - e) \quad\quad\quad\quad\quad e_3 = e_1 * e_2$

$\quad\quad\quad = e_4 \quad\quad\quad\quad\quad\quad\quad\quad e_4 = e_3 - e$

Postfix $\quad\quad\quad\quad\quad\quad\quad\quad$ **Prefix**

$\exp = e_4 \quad\quad\quad\quad\quad\quad\quad \exp = e_4$

$\quad = e_3 e - \quad\quad\quad\quad\quad\quad\quad = -e_3 e$

$\quad = e_1 e_2 * e - \quad\quad\quad\quad\quad = -e*e_1 e_2$

$\quad = ab**cd***e- \quad\quad\quad\quad = -e***ab**cd$

2.5.1 Evaluation of Postfix Expression

Now let us see how we can evaluate a postfix expression. If we are given a postfix expression the expression is scanned from left till we come across an operator. The operator corresponds to previous two operands hence operate on the operand and result is an operand for next operator. Like this go on scanning till the end of the expression.

e.g. Suppose we have the expression 456 * +

1. The first operator is *. It will operate on 5 and 6 to give 30. The resultant expression is 430 +.

2. Next operator is +. It will operate on 4 and 30 to give the result is 34.

When we scan the expression and come across an operator we take latest two operands hence we can use a stack to store the operands, so that latest two operands can be accessed. Hence, the procedure for evaluation of postfix expression will be as follows:

1. Scan the expression.
2. In case of operand.
     push the operand on stack.
3. In case of operator
     Pop two operands from stack
     Do the operation
     Push the result on stack.
4. Repeat 2 and 3 till the end of expression.

The expression can be stored in a string and can be scanned character by character. The procedure is illustrated with example below:
Suppose we have the expression 456 * +.

Expression character	Action	Stack content
4	push	4 ...
5	push	4 5 ...
6	push	4 5 6 ...
*	pop 6	
	pop 5	
	push (5 * 6)	4 30 ...
+	pop 30	
	pop 4	
	push (30 + 4)	34 ...

Fig. 2.8: Evaluation of postfix expression 456*+

The detailed algorithm and program is:
Algorithm 2.1:
1. Read expression in string expr[ ]
2. i=0
3. while (expr [i] !='\0')   // while it is not end of string
    {
        if(expr[i] is operand)
            push (expr[i])

```
        else
        {
            op1 = pop( )
            op2 = pop( )
            v = op1 (operator in expr[i]) op2
            push (v)
        }
        i++;
    }
4.  result = pop( )
5.  print result
```

Program 2.5: To evaluate postfix expression.

```c
#define MAX 10
int stk [MAX];
int top = -1;
void push (int);
int pop( );
void main
{
    char expr[40];
    int i, op1, op2;
    clrscr( );
    printf("Enter expression \n");
    gets (expr);
    i=0;
    while (expr[i] != '\0')
    {
        if (isdigit(expr[i]))
            push (expr[i] -'0');
        else
        {
            op2 = pop( );
            op1 = pop( );
            switch (expr[i])
            {
                case '+':  push (op1 + op2);
                           break;
                case '-':  push (op1 - op2);
```

```
                    break;
         case '*':   push (op1 * op2);
                    break;
         case '/':   push ((op1 / op2));
                    break;
            }
        }
        i++;
    }
    result=pop( );
    printf("The result is %d", result);
    getch( );
}
void push (int x)
{
    if (top == MAX -1)
        printf("Stack is full")
    else
    {
        top ++;
        stk [top] = x;
    }
}
int pop( )
{
    int x;
    if (top == -1)
    {
        print("Stack is empty \n");
        return (-9999);
    }
    else
    {
        x = stk [top];
        top --;
        return (x);
    }
}
```

2.5.2 Conversion of Infix Expression to Postfix

The evaluation of postfix expression requires stack and the priority of operators need not be considered for evaluating the expression. Normally, we write the expression in infix format. It needs to be converted into postfix format. The procedure for conversion is as follows.

A stack is used this time to store operators. The infix expression is scanned from left to right. Incase of operands, the operands are directly copied to postfix expression. In case of operators, either of two decisions is taken.

(i) If priority of operator is greater than operator on top of stack, the operator is pushed on stack.

(ii) If priority of operator is less than operators on stack, the operators on stack are popped and copied into the output expression and the operator is pushed on to the stack.

Following examples illustrate the process of conversion of infix to postfix.

Example 1: a+b*c

Incoming character	Action	Postfix	Stack Contents
a	Copy to output	a	
+	Push	a	+ ...
b	Copy to output	ab	
*	Priority more than +, Push *	ab	+ * ...
c	Copy to output	abc	
c	Pop all operators copy to output	abc*+	

Fig. 2.9: Conversion of infix to postfix

Example 2: a*b+c

Incoming character	Action	Postfix	Stack Contents
a	Copy to output	a	
*	Push	a	* ...
b	Copy to output	ab	
+	Priority less than *, pop *, copy to output, push +	ab*	+ ...
c	Copy to output	ab*c	
End of expression	Pop all operators copy to output	ab*c+	

Fig. 2.10: Conversion of infix to postfix

Example 3: a + b * c / d - e

Incoming character	Action	Postfix	Stack Contents
a	Copy to output	a	
+	Push	a	+ ...
b	Copy to output	ab	
*	Priority more than +, push	ab	+ * ...
c	Copy to output	abc	
/	Priority equal to *, pop *, copy to output, push /	abc*	+ / ...
d	Copy to output	abc*d	
-	Priority less than /, pop /, copy to output	abc*d/	
	priority equal to +, pop +, copy to output, push -	abd*d/+	- ...
e	Copy to output	abc*d/+e	
End of expression	Pop all operations copy to output	abc*d/+e-	

Fig. 2.11: Conversion of infix to postfix

The algorithm for conversion of infix to postfix is:

Algorithm 2.2: To convert infix expression to postfix.
1. Read infix expression
2. i=0, j=0
3. while (infix[i] != '\0')
   {
       if (infix[i] is operand)
       {
           postfix[j] = infix[i];
           j++;
       }
       else
       {
           if (stack empty)
               push (infix[i]);
           else

```
            {   if (priority (infix [i])>priority (stack[top]))
                    push (infix[i]);
                else
                {
                    do
                    {
                        postfix[j] = pop( );
                        j++;
                    } while (priority (infix[i])<=priority(stk[top])&& (!stack_empty);
                    push (infix[i]);
                }
            }
        }
        i++;
    }
4.  while (!stack_empty)
    {
        postfix[j] = pop( );
        j++;
    }
5.  postfix[j] = '\0';
6.  print postfix
7.  stop.
```

For implementation of above algorithm following consideration are required.
1. A stack of characters need to be defined along with the operations push and pop.
2. A function called priority needs to be defined which will return address of operator passed to it.
3. Two string variables will be required one for storing infix expression and other for postfix expression.
4. So as to make the program simple, the stack is implemented using array and it is declared globally along with the top of stack, so that we can directly access it in main function.
5. Only four operators +, −, *, / are taken for the conversion. Otherwise the program will be bit complex since apart from priority; associativity of operators also plays an important role in the conversion.
6. The expression is assumed to have variable with single character or digit e.g. a + b * c and not like sum = n1 + n2.

Program 2.6: To convert infix expression to postfix
```
#define MAX 50
char stk[MAX];
int top = -1;
void push (char);
char pop( );
int priority (char);
void main( )
{
    char infix[MAX], postfix[MAX];
    int i, j;
    clrscr( );
    printf("Enter infix expression \n");
    gets (infix);
    i=0; j=0;
    while (infix [i]!='\0')
    {
        if (isalpha(infix[i]) || isdigit(infix [i]))
        {
            postfix [j] = infix [i];
            j++;
        }
        else
        {
            if(top == -1 || priority(infix[i])>priority(stk[top]))
                push (infix[i]);
            else
            {
                do
                {
                    postfix[j] = pop( );
                    j++;
                } while (priority (infix [i])<=priority(stk[top]) && top!=-1);
                push (infix[i]);
            }
        }
        i++;
    }
```

```c
        while (top!=-1)
        {
            postfix[j] = pop( );
            j++;
        }
        postfix[j] = '\0';
        printf("%s", postfix);
}
void push (char x)
{
    if(top!=MAX-1)
    {
        top ++;
        stk [top] = x;
    }
}
char pop( )
{
    char x;
    if (top!=-1)
    {
        x = stk[top];
        top --;
    }
    return(x);
}
int priority (char ch)
{
    switch (ch)
    {
        case '*' :
        case '/' : return (2);
                    break;
        case '-' :
        case '+':  return (1);
    }
}
```

Note: If at all you want to include the raised to operator ($ or ^) you can assign priority 3 (highest) to it.

2.6 INTRODUCTION OF QUEUE

Queue is a linear data structure in which the first element inserted is taken out first. Thus, Queue is a first in first out (FIFO) type of a list where all insertions are made at one end called rear end and all deletions-are made at other end called front end. It is just like queue for railway reservation or buses. The first person in the queue will be first to go out.

Queue can be implemented using:
1. Arrays.
2. Linked lists.

Following four operations can be done on a queue.
1. **Insert operation:** In this, an element is stored at a location indicated by rear.
2. **Delete operation:** In this operation, the element at the front is removed.
3. **Queue Full:** When all the locations reserved for queue are occupied, we can't insert any more elements. This condition is queue_full condition.
4. **Queue empty:** When there is no element stored in a queue, we can't delete any more element. This condition is called as queue_empty.

2.7 QUEUE USING ARRAY

To represent a queue using array we require an array of some size to be declared say int a[4]. This will create a space for storing elements of queue. The size of the queue is 4. We will require two more variables say front and rear which will be indices to the front and rear element of the queue. Initially, the queue is empty. The variables front and rear will be initialized to −1.

Insert operation:

Now if we want to store a number 10 on the queue, we can increment rear and the element 10 will be stored at location a[0].

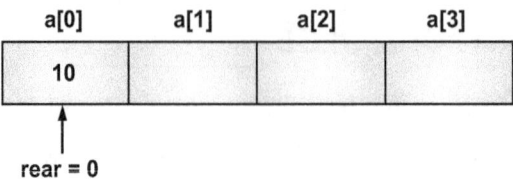

Fig. 2.12(a): Insertq (10)

Next we store a number 20 on the queue, rear will be incremented to 1 and element 20 will be stored at location a[l].

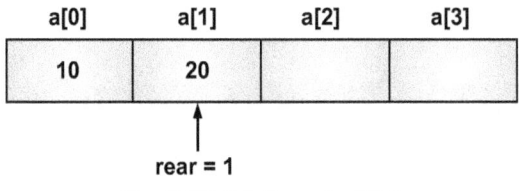

Fig. 2.12(b): Insertq (20)

Next we store a number 30 on the queue, rear will be incremented to 2 and element 30 will be stored at location a[2].

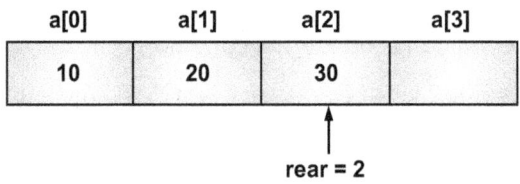

Fig. 2.12(c): Insertq (30)

Next we store a number 40 on the queue, rear will be incremented to 3 and element 40 will be stored at location a[3].

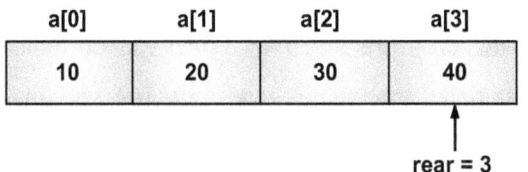

Fig. 2.12(d): Insertq (40)

Now there is no space left on the queue hence, the queue is full. The condition for queue_full is rear becomes equal to maximum size of array −1.

Delete operation:

Now suppose we want to remove an element from the queue. We can access element at the front which is given by the index value in front. Consider the queue where we have already inserted four elements. If we want to carry out delete operation, front is incremented to 0 and element at the front 10 will be accessed.

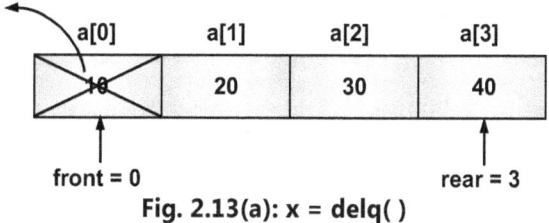

Fig. 2.13(a): x = delq( )

The next delete operation will increment front to 1 and remove 20 from the queue.

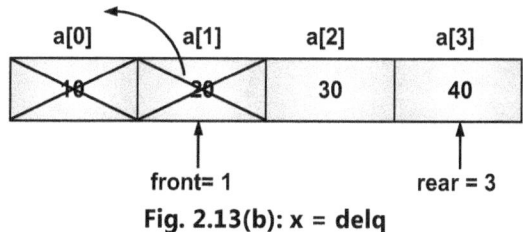

Fig. 2.13(b): x = delq

Another delete operation will increment front to 2 and remove 30 from the queue.

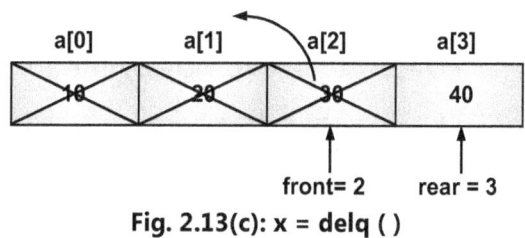

Fig. 2.13(c): x = delq ( )

If the operation is carried out again, element 40 will be removed and front becomes 3 equal to rear.

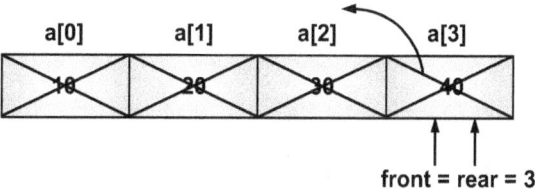

Fig. 2.13(d): x = delq( )

Then we can't remove any more elements because queue is empty. The condition for queue_empty is front == rear.

The disadvantage of linear queue is when rear reaches the value MAX-1, queue full condition occurs. Now if we remove some elements from front end of the queue, we will not be able to store or insert element in these locations as rear remains MAX-1.

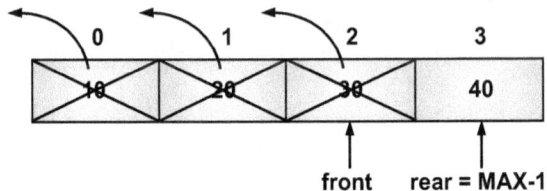

Fig. 2.14: Problem with insert operation even if queue is not full

The program for implementation of queue will require the two functions insertq and delq whose algorithms are as follows:

1. **Insertq (x)**
    1. If rear == MAX -1
         print "queue full"
    2. else
         rear ++;
         a [rear] = x;
    3. stop.

Every time we do insertq operation, we need to increment rear and store the data at the location given by rear in the array a. But before we do this operation, we have to check whether the queue is full or not. Hence, the condition rear==MAX-1.

II. **x = delq( )**
    1. If front == rear
         return -9999
    2. else
         front++
         x = a [front]
         return x

Every time we do a delq operation, we increment front and remove an element. But before we do this operation, we have to check whether the queue is empty or not. Hence the condition front == rear. Note that we are returning −9999 when queue is empty. This is an indication for the calling function so that it takes appropriate action when the queue is empty. The complete program for queue implementation is as follows:

Program 2.7: To implement queue using array.

```
#define MAX 4
int a[MAX];
int front = -1, rear = -1;
void insertq(int);
int delq( );
void main( )
{
    int ch;
    do
    {
        clrscr( );
        printf 1. Insert \n 2. Delete \n 3. Exit \n");
        printf ("Enter your choice");
        scanf ("%d", &ch);
        switch (ch)
        {
            case 1 : printf ("Enter data \n");
                     scanf ("%d", &x);
                     insertq (x);
                     break;
            case 2 : x = delq( );
                     if (x!=-9999)
                         printf ("%d \n", x);
                     break;
        }
        getch( );
    } while (ch!=3);
}
void insertq (int x)
{
    if (front == MAX -1)
```

```
        front = rear = (-1);
    if (rear == MAX -1)
        printf ("Queue full");
    else
    {
        rear ++;
        a[rear] = x;
    }
}
int delq( )
{
    int x;
    if (front ==rear)
    {
        printf ("Q is empty");
        return (-9999);
    }
    else
    {
        front ++;
        x=a[front];
        return (x);
    }
}
```

We can implement separate functions for queue_full and queue_empty conditions as:

```
int q_full( )
{
    if (rear==MAX -1)
    {
        printf("Queue full");
        return (1),
    }
    else
        return (0);
}
```

The function returns 1, when queue is full; otherwise 0.

```
int q_empty( )
{
    if (front == rear)
    {
        printf("Quede is empty");
        return (1);
    }
    else
        return (0);
}
```

The function returns 1, when queue is empty, otherwise 0.

These functions can be used in functions 'insertq' and 'delq' as:

```
void insertq (int x)
{
    if (front == MAX -1)
    front = rear = -1
    if(!q_full( ))
    {
        rear ++;
        a[rear] = x;
    }
}
int delq( )
{
    int x;
    if (!q-empty( ))
    {
        front ++;
        x = a[front];
        return (x);
    }
}
```

The queue consists of an array, front and rear. If multiple queues are to be implemented in single program, we need to define separate arrays, font and rear for each queue. Instead, we can define a structure variable for a queue which combines array, front and rear together. The structure definition for queue is

    typedef struct queue
    {
        int a[MAX];
        int front, rear;
    } Q;

Now if we declare a variable Q q1; it consists of an array, front and rear as:

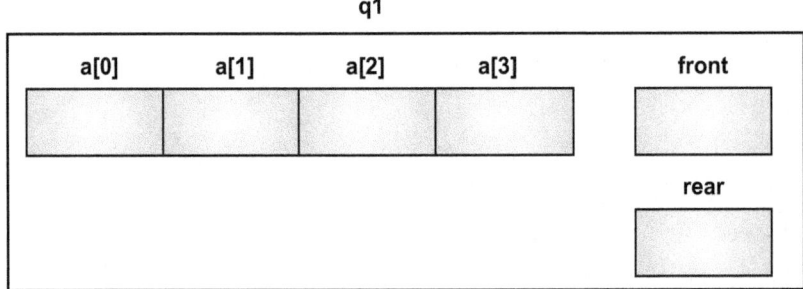

Fig. 2.15: Queue using structure

The elements in the queue can be accessed using dot operate, e.g., if front of the queue is to be initialized we can write q1.front = −1 or if 10 is to be stored at the rear end of the queue we can write q1.a [q1.rear] = 10. But the major advantage of this struct type queue will be, when more than one queue is to be implemented. The insertq and delq. functions require the queue variable to be passed to them. Since, these functions are going to modify the contents of the queue variable; we have to pass it by address. Hence, the function parameter will be pointer to a structure.

The insertq function will have prototype as,
$$\text{void insertq (Q*, int)}$$
The first argument is pointer to the queue in which we are going to store the element and second argument is the integer number to be stored on the queue.
The delq function will have prototype as,
$$\text{int delq (Q *)}$$

The argument is pointer to the queue from which number returned will be popped. A complete program using this is given as follows:

Program 2.8: Implementation of queue using structure

```
#define MAX 5
typedef struct queue
{
    int a[MAX];
    int front, queue;
} Q;
void insertq (Q*, int);
int delq (Q*
main( )
{
    Q q 1, q2;
    q1.front = q1.rear = q2.front = q2.rear=(-1);
    insertq(&q1, 10);
    insertq(&q1, 20);
    insertq(&q2, 100);
    insertq(&q2, 200);
    x = delq(&q1);
    printf("%d \n", x);
    x = delq(&q1);
    printf ("%d \n", x);
    x = delq (&q2);
    printf ("%d \n", x);
    x = delq (&q2);
    printf ("%d \n", x);
}
void insertq (Q *q, int x)
{
    if (q->front == MAX-1)
        q->front = q->rear=-1;
    if (q->rear == MAX-1)
        printf("Queue is full");
    else
```

```
        {
            (q->rear) ++;
            q->a[q->rear]=x;
        }
}
int delq (Q *q)
{
    int x;
    if (q->front == q->rear)
    {
        printf("Queue empty");
        return (-9999);
    }
    else
    {
        (q->front) ++;
        x = q->a [q->front];
        return (x);
    }
}
```

2.7.1 Queue Using Linked List

The array implementation of queue is not efficient from the view point of memory utilization. The fixed size of array is required and it remains allocated for the entire duration of the program. Linked list implementation will have advantage over the array implementation because we can allocate memory as and when it is required and memory can be deallocated (free) when not in use.

The queue using linked list consist of nodes having data and address of next node.

The node definition will be
```
    typedef struct node
    {
        int data;
        struct node *next;
    } NODE;
```

Two pointers called front and rear can be declared (NODE *front, *rear) which will point to the front and rear end of the queue. The operations insert and delete will be implemented as follows:

Steps for insert operation:
1. Create a node and store data in the node.
2. Link rear node to new node, if it is not first node.
3. Point rear to the recently created node.
   Following figures show this operation.
   Initially, front = rear = NULL

1. **Insertq (10)**

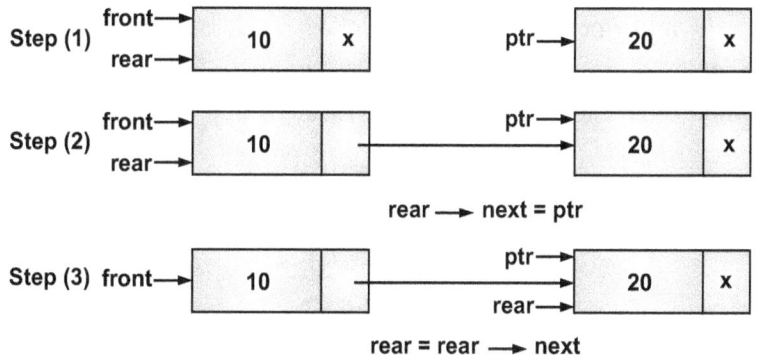

Fig. 2.16(a): Insertq (10) in queue using linked list

2. **Insertq (20)**

Fig. 2.16(b): Insertq (20) in queue using linked list

Steps for delete operation:
1. Make a pointer temp point to the front end of the queue.
2. If it is NULL, then queue is empty..
3. If not, remove the data from this node and advance front.
4. De-allocate memory pointed by temp.

Following figures show this operation.

1. **x = delq**

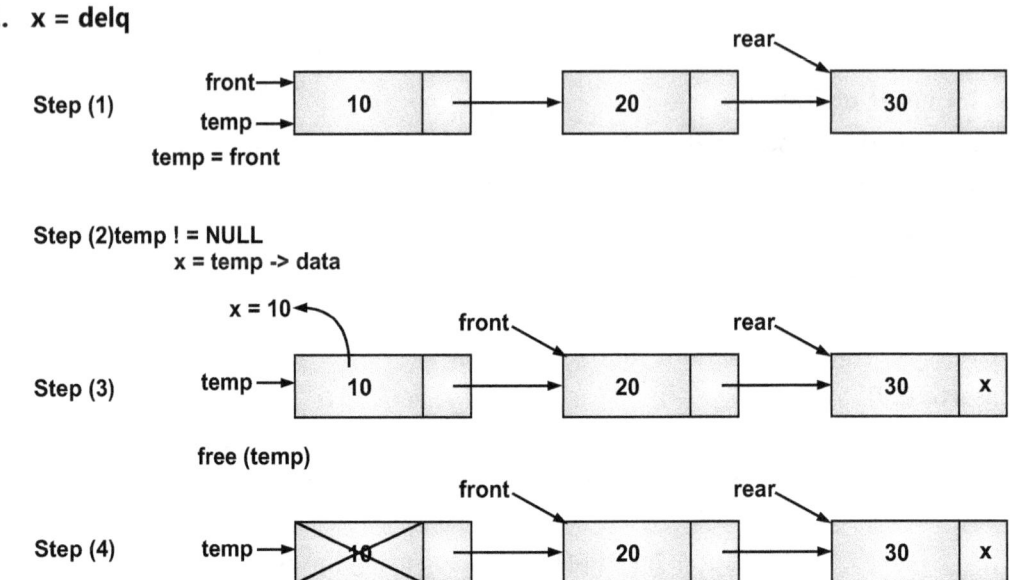

Fig. 2.17: Delete operation in queue using linked list

Following program, implements queue using linked list. It has the function push and pop which have the same prototype as that used in case of array. The function push accepts data, creates a node and puts it into linked. list. The function pop removes an element from the linked list and returns it.

Program 2.9: Implementation of queue using linked list.

```
typedef struct node
{
    int data;
    struct node*next;
} NODE;
NODE*front=NULL, rear=NULL;
void insertq (int x)
{
    NODE*ptr;
```

```
        ptr = (NODE.*)malloc(sizeof(NODE));
        if (ptr == NULL)
            printf("Insufficient memory");
        else
        {
            ptr->data = x;
            ptr->next = NULL;
            if (rear == NULL)
                front = rear = ptr;
            else
            {
                rear->next = ptr;
                rear = ptr;
            }
        }
    }
    int delq
    {
        NODE = temp, int x;
        temp = front;
        if (temp == NULL)
        {
            printf("Queue empty");
            return(-9999);
        }
        else
        {
            x = temp->data;
            front = front->next;
            free (temp);
            return (x);
        }
    }
```

In order to implement queue using linked list you can use two pointers front and rear. Front will point to first node and rear to the last node. Whenever insert operation is done a new node is created, it is attached to the last node in the list and the pointer rear points to this new node. Whenever delete operation is done an element from front end is accessed, front is advanced to next node and the node is deleted.

2.8 QUEUE AS AN ABSTRACT DATA TYPE (ADT)

```
//Queue data definition
typedef struct queue
{
    <datatype> data;
    struct queue*front, *rear;
}Q;
```

```
//Operation definition
initializeq(Q);              // Initialize front and rear
insertq(Q, x);               // Insert into Q
x = delq(Q);                 // Remove x from Q
int qempty(Q)                // If Q is empty return 1 else return 0
int qfull(Q)                 // If Q is full return 1 else return 0
```

The above data definition can be written as
```
typedef struct queue
{
    <data type> data [size]
    int front, rear;
} Q;
```

2.9 CIRCULAR QUEUE

The disadvantage of linear queue is that, even if some locations are available for storage, we will not be able to use them when rear becomes MAX −1. Hence, when rear reaches MAX −1, we should be able to come back to location 0 in case it is empty. Hence, rear ++ can be replaced by rear = (rear + 1) % MAX.

Similarly, when front reaches MAX-1 we should be able to come back to location 0 which is done using front = (front + 1) % MAX. This implementation is called circular queue. In order to handle queue full and queue empty conditions, one more variable called counter will be required. The counter c is incremented whenever insert operation is performed and decremented when delete operation is performed. The program for circular queue is as follows:

Program 2.10: To implement circular queue.

```
#define MAX 5
int a[MAX];
int front = 0, rear = -1, c = 0;
void insertq (int);
int delq( );
void main( )
{
    int ch;
    do
    {
        clrscr( );
        printf ("1. Insert \n 2. Delete \n 3. Exit \n");
        printf ("Enter your choice");
        scanf("%d", &ch);
        switch (ch)
        {
            case 1 : printf ("Enter data \n");
                     scanf ("% d". &x),
                     insertq (x);
                     break;
            case 2 : x = delq( );
                     if (x!=-9999)
                         printf ("%d \n", x);
                     break;
        }
        getch( )
    }while (ch!=3);
}
void insertq (int x)
{
    if (c==MAX)
```

```
        printf("Q is full");
    else
    {
        rear = (rear + 1) % MAX;
        q[rear] = x;
        c++;
    }
}
int delq( )
{
    int x;
    if (c == 0)
    {
        printf("Q is empty"),
        return(-9999);
    }
    else
    {
        x = q[front];
        front = (front + 1) % MAX;
        c --;
        return (x);
    }
}
```

Explanation:

1. Let us assume queue size 5. Initially when queue is empty
   front = 0   rear = −1   c = 0

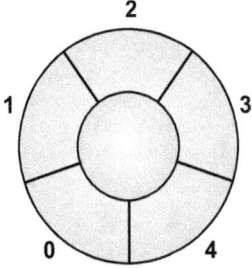

Fig. 2.18(a): Circular queue

2. Insert(10) operation
   front 0
   rear = 0   c = 1

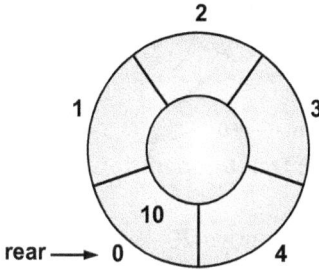

Fig. 2.18(b): Insert (10)

3. Insert(20) operation
   front = 0   rear = 1   c = 2

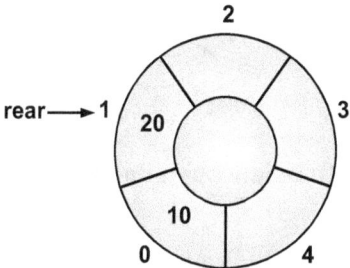

Fig. 2.18(c): Insert (20)

4. Like this if we insert 30, 40, 50
   front = 0   rear = 4   c = 5
   The queue is full i.e., c=MAX=5

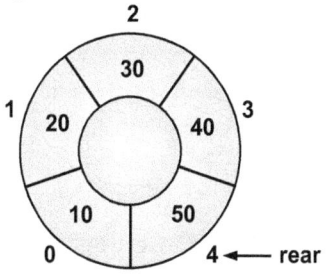

Fig. 2.18(d): Insert (30), Insert (40), Insert (50)

5. Now if delete operation is performed, 10 will removed,
   Before delete, front = 0   rear = 4   c = 5
   After delete, front = 1   rear = 4   c = 4

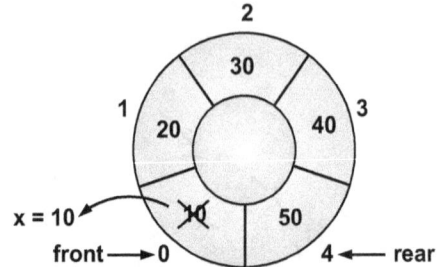

Fig. 2.18(e): Delete operation in circular queue

6. One more delete operation will remove 20
   Before delete; front = 1   rear = 4   c = 4
   After delete,   front = 2   rear = 4   c = 3

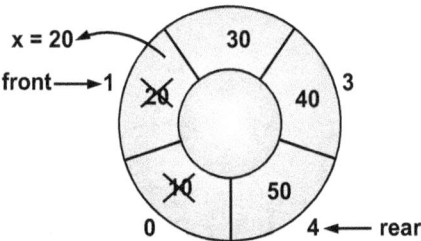

Fig. 2.18(f): Delete operation in circular queue

Now if we want to insert say 60,

rear = (rear + 1)% MAX.= (4 + 1)% 5 = 0 and we can store/insert the element at location 0.

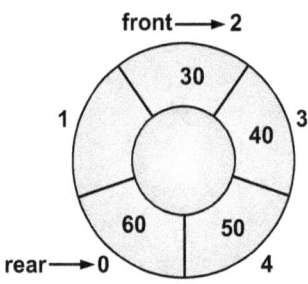

Fig. 2.18(g): Insert operation

Thus, we are able to insert the element in the queue at location 0 even if rear has reached value MAX−1.

Note: If we don't use counter, the implementation becomes slightly complex, we have to keep one location empty in the queue.

Circular queue using linked list

A circular queue can also be implemented using circular linked list. This implementation will most efficient than array implementation. We can use two pointers front and rear. In fact a single pointer to last element will also be sufficient. We can access the front element with this pointer as list is circular.

2.10 PRIORITY QUEUE

The priority queue is a data structure in which the ordering of elements decides the two operations insert and delete. The elements from the priority queue are removed as per their priority. There are two types of priority queues:

1. Ascending order Priority Queue,
2. Descending order Priority Queue.

1. **Ascending order Priority Queue:** It is collection of elements into which the elements are stored or inserted in any order but the smallest element can be removed.
2. **Descending order Priority Queue:** It is collection of elements into which elements are inserted at any order but only larger element can be removed. The other operations on priority queue will be queue empty and queue full. There are several implementations of priority queues.

The priority queue can be implemented in number of ways. One method can be:
(i) When insert operation is done, the element is stored in an array in the continuous locations.
(ii) But when the element is removed, we have to search for maximum in case of descending priority queue or minimum in case of ascending priority queue.
(iii) In place of deleted element an invalid element (say −1) is stored.

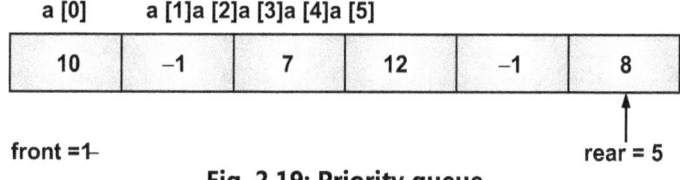

Fig. 2.19: Priority queue

(iv) When an element is inserted, we can increment rear but if rear reaches maximum size, we can do compaction i.e. rearrange the array to remove invalid elements as shown in Fig. 2.20.

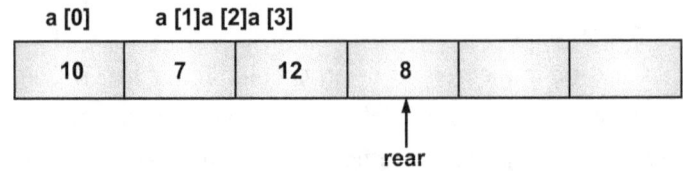

Fig. 2.20: Priority queue after compaction

Second method can be
(i) Instead of maintaining the priority queue as an unordered list of elements, we can maintain it as an ordered (sorted) list of elements but then this will require more work while inserting the element in the queue.
(ii) The delete operation will be simple as the minimum or maximum element is available as front end of queue.

The priority queue is used for scheduling of jobs by operating system programs. The priority queue can be used in job scheduling where the execution of job is required to be done based on the priorities. The jobs will be kept in a queue along with their priority numbers. Whenever a new job is to be executed, the job with highest priority will be taken up from the queue.

2.11 APPLICATIONS OF QUEUE

Applications of Queues:
There are several applications of queues in real world. Some of these applications are:
(i) Railway/Bus/Airplane Reservations.
(ii) Processing of customer requests.
(iii) Processing of online applications.
(iv) In a computer system processing of jobs such as print spool (printing of multiple files/pages).
(v) In a operating system scheduling of jobs as per their priority in multitasking operating system.
(vi) Categorizing of data can be useful in many problems.
(vii) Queue simulation can be used to study performance of any application involving queue like situation.

Categorizing Data:
We need to organize the data into groups. For example, if we have a list records having empno, name and age and we may want to group them as per their age as 21-30, 31-40, 41-50, 51-60 etc. While rearranging these records into groups, the original order is to be maintained.

The following algorithm implements categorizing of data into four groups of 1-10, 11-20, 21-30 and 31-40.

Algorithm 2.3: The algorithm reads integers between 1-40 and inserts them into four queues.

Step 1: Read n   // Number of data items
Step 2: i=1
Step 3: while(i<n)
```
        {
            Read x                          // Enter data
            if(x<=10)
                insertq (&q1, x)
            if(x>10 && x<=20)
                insertq(&q2, <=30)
            if(x>21, &&xx<=30)
                insert(&q3, x)
            if(x>31 && x<=40)
                insert(&q4, x)
            j=x+1
        }
```
Step 4: Stop

The complete program is given below.

/*Program for categorizing data
Input is a list of integers between 0-39
output is four groups (queues)*/

```c
#include <stdio.h>
#include <conio.h>
#include <stdlib.h>
#define MAX 5
typedef struct queue
{
    int ar [MAX];
    int front, rear;
}Q;
void insertq (Q*, int);
```

```c
int deleteq (Q*);
void main( )
{
    Q q[4];
    int x, i, n;
    clrscr( );
    for(i=0;i<4;i++)
        q[i].front=q[i].rear=-1;
    printf("How many numbers\n");
    scanf("%d",&n);
    i=0;
    randomize( );
    while(i<n)
    {
        //printf("Enter number between 1-40\n");
        //scanf("%d",&x);
        x=rand( )%100;
        if (x>=0 && x<40)
        {
            insertq(&q[x/10],x);
            i++;
        }
        else
            printf("Invalid number\n");
    }
    printf("\nThe categorised data is\n");
    i=0;
    while(i<4)
    {
        printf("\nData between %d to %d is \n", 10*i, 10*i+9);
        while (1)
        {
            x=deleteq(&q[i]);
            if(x!=-9999)
                printf("%d\t",x);
            else
                break;
```

```
            }
            printf("\n");
            i++;
        }
    }
    void insertq (Q *q, int x)
    {
        if(q->front == MAX-1)
            q->front = q->rear = -1;
        if (q->rear == MAX-1)
            printf("queue is full");
        else
        {
            (q->rear) ++;
            q->ar[q->rear] = x;
        }
    }
    int deleteq (Q *q)
    {
        int x;
    if (q->front == q->rear)
    {
        //printf("queue empty"); return (-9999);
    }
    else
    {
        (q->front) ++;
        x = q->ar [q->front];
        return (x);

    }
}
```

Simulation of Queues:

Any real life application involving queue like activity can be simulated and the performance of the system can be analysed under different conditions. Thus, we can create a model of the real life application.

Suppose a shop is open for 8 hours a day for 6 days in a week. The shop activity can be studied in different situations i.e. busy day, average day, busy hours etc. We need to simulate the activities of the shop as queue. The events that can take place are as below:
(i) A customer arrives.
(ii) The counter is free.
(iii) The customer is served.

When the customer arrives and counter is not free he waits in a queue. Hence, we need to create a queue of customers.

When the counter becomes free to serve next customer, we need to start a timer to find out how much time is taken by each customer. When a customer is served we should count time taken by the server, waiting time for the customer in queue etc. This can be used to find average taken to serve each customer, average waiting time for each customer etc.

We can use random numbers to generate the inputs such waiting time for a customer, time taken to serve a customer etc.

Job Scheduling:

The operating system programs like Window, Unix etc, which are multitasking operating systems, execute number of programs simultaneously. It is required to do scheduling of executions of these programs. There are number of techniques for scheduling some of them are:
   (i) First Come First Serve (FCFS)
   (ii) Round - Robin Technique.

Both these technique uses queues for the implementation of scheduling program execution.

First Come First Serve (FCFS): The FCFS technique stores the programs in the queue on first come first serve basis. The program which comes first will be executed first. This technique is useful for scheduling of print jobs in a print server.

The disadvantages is, if one of the job in queue takes more time the other jobs have to wait for a long time.

Round Robin Technique: In this technique, the programs to be executed are stored in a queue. But each program is given a fix time slot for execution. If execution is over in time slot allotted, the program is removed otherwise the program is kept in the rear end of queue so that it gets another turn. The next program in the queue will be given its turn of execution for the next time slot as shown in Fig. 2.21.

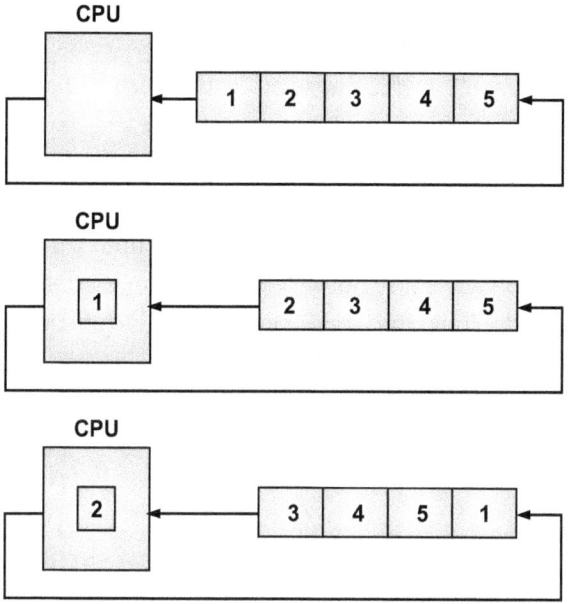

Fig. 2.21 (a): Round Robin technique

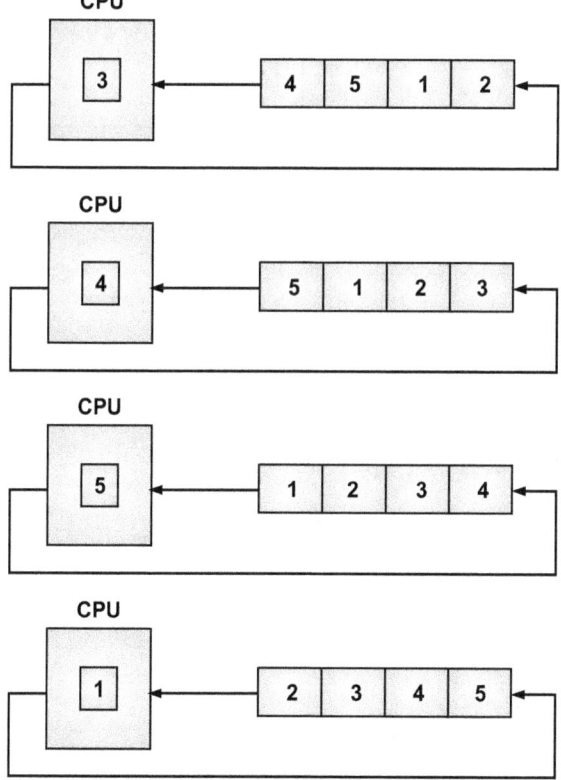

Fig. 2.21 (b): Round Robin technique

2.12 PROCESSING OF FUNCTION CALLS

One natural application of stacks, which arises in computer programming, is the processing of function calls and their terminations. The program must remember the place where the call was made; so that it can returns there after the function is complete. Suppose we have three functions say A, B and C and one main program. Let main invokes A, A invokes B and B in turn invokes C. Then B will not have finished its work until C has finished and returned. Similarly main is the first to start work, but it is last to be finished; not until sometime after A has finished and returned. Thus the sequence by which function actively proceeds are summed up as the property Last In First Out or First In Last Out as shown in Fig. 2.23 below :

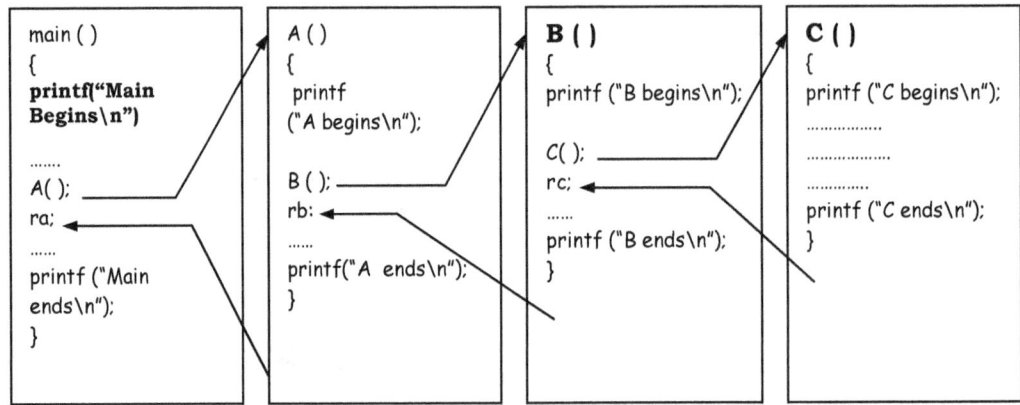

Fig. 2.22: Processing of function calls

The output will look like as shown below:

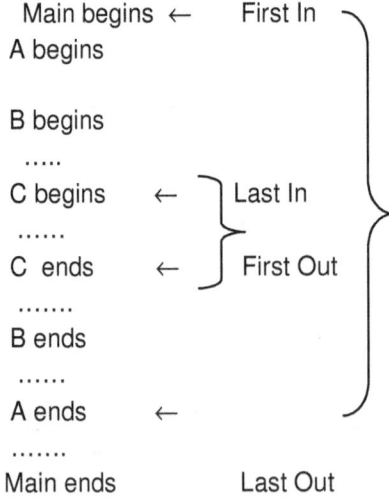

Fig. 2.23: Output

From the above output it can be observed that the main program is invoked first but finished last while function C is invoked last but finished first. Hence to keep track of return addresses ra, rb, and rc the only data structure required here is the **stack** as follows.

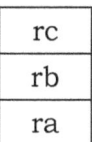

Stack of return address

2.13 RECURSION

Definition:

Recursion is a way of specifying a process by means of itself **or** a function is recursive if the definition includes a call to itself. We already know that, some languages also provide the ability of a function to call **itself**. This is called Recursion. In C, a function can call itself, that is, one of the statements of the function is a call to itself. Such functions are called recursive functions and can be used to implement recursive problems in an elegant manner.

To solve a recursive problem using functions, the problem must have a end condition that can be stated in non-recursive terms. As an example, in the case of factorials, we know that 1! = 1. If no such condition exists, then the recursive calls will indefinitely continue until the computer runs out of program is terminated by the operating system. Consider the recursive implementation of factorial given that :

$$1! = 1, \text{ and } n! = n * (n - 1)!$$

The recursive function in C is as :

```
long int factorial (unsigned int n)
    {
       if (n<=1)
          return (1);
                else
          return (n*factorial (n - 1));
    }
```

As we can see, the C function represents the recursive mathematical definition of n!. In order to see how it works, consider the computation of 5!

The function calls will proceed as follows :

factorial (5)   = 5 * factorial (4)
              = 5 * (4* factorial (3))
              = 5 * (4* (3* factorial (2)))

= 5 * (4 *(3* (2* factorial (1))))

= 5 * (4* (3* (2* 1)))

= 5 * (4* (3* 2))

= 5 * (4* 6)

= 5* 24

= 120

The important thing to remember when creating a recursive function is to give an **'end condition'**. We don't want the function to keep calling itself forever. Somehow, it should know when to stop. There are many ways of doing this. One of the simplest is by means of an 'if condition' statement, as above

As the starting number is not 1, the function calls itself with the value 5 – 1, that is, 4. Therefore, the original function call is kept incomplete and pending and a second call is kept incomplete and pending and a second call is made to factorial with a value 4. This process continues until the fifth call is made, with the value 1. In this call, the function terminates without any further recursion and returns the desired value of 1!, which is 1. Subsequently, each of the pending function calls are completed upto the original factorial (5) function call, which returns the computed value as 120. In the preceding piece of code parenthesis have been used to show how the recursive calls proceed from left to right and the computations are made from right to left. A program to print the first 15 factorials is given in the code below : Program to print the First 15 numbers Factorials :

```
#include <stdio.h>
    void main (void)
    {
      int i;
      for (i=1;i≤15;i++)
          printf ("\n The factorial of %d is \t %d", i , factorial (i));
    }
```

2.13.1 The Stack in Recursion

The Stack is an special area of memory in which temporary variables are stored. The Stack acts on the LIFO (Last In First Out) principle, which is the same principle involved in, say, the stacking of cardboard boxes one atop the other, where the topmost box, which was the last box stacked (Last In), will the first to be removed (First Out). Thus, if the values 9, 3, 2, 4 are stored (Pushed) on the Stack, they will be retrieved (Popped) in the order 4, 2, 3, 9. In order to understand how recursive functions use the Stack, we will walk through the second algorithm:

```
if(N<=1) return 1;
else return N*Factorial(N-1);
```

Let us assume we want to find the value of 3!, which is 3 × 2 × 1 = 6. The first time the function is called, N holds the value 3, so the *else* statement is executed. The function knows the value of N, but not of factorial (N-1), so it pushes N (value=3) on the stack, and calls itself for the second time with the value 2. This time the *else* statement is executed, and N (value=2) is pushed on the stack as the function calls itself for the third time with the value 1. Now the *if* statement is executed as n==1, so the function returns 1. Since the value of factorial (1) is now known, it reverts back to it's second execution by popping the last value (2) from the stack and multiplying it by 1. This operation gives the value of factorial (2), so the function reverts to it's first execution by popping the next value (3) from the stack, and multiplying it with factorial, giving the value 6, which is what the function finally returns.

From the above example, we see that:

- The function runs three times, out of which it calls itself two times. The number of times that a function calls itself is known as the **recursive depth** of that function.
- Each time the function calls itself, it stores one or more variables on the Stack. Since the Stack holds a limited amount of memory, functions with a high recursive depth may crash because of non-availability of memory. Such a condition is known as **Stack Overflow**.
- Recursive functions usually have a **terminating condition** (end condition). In the above example the function stops calling itself when n==1. If this condition were not present, the function would keep calling itself with the values 3, 2, 1, 0, −1, −2... and so on for infinity. This condition is known as **Endless Recursion**.
- All recursive functions go through two distinct phases. The first phase, **Winding**, occurs when the function is calling itself and pushing values on the Stack. The second phase, **Unwinding**, occurs when the function is popping values from the stack.

The recursive function in C is as :

```
long int factorial (unsigned int n)
    {
      if (n<=1)
         return (1);
      else
         return (n*factorial (n - 1));
    }
```

Simulation of recursive factorial function using stack

```
int factorial(int n)
{
    int fact;
    while (n>1)
    {
      PUSH(n);
      n- -;
    }
    fact=1;
    while (!isEmpty())     // till not empty pop each value of n and calculate fact
    {
      fact=fact * POP();
    }
    return fact;
}
```

Consider that a call as factorial (4) that is n is 4
Now, it is executed as follows

1. $n = 4$
   Hence recursive call is executed as 4 * fact(3)
   Push (4) on the stack.

4				

   top

2. $n = 3$
   Hence recursive call is executed as 3 * fact(2)
   Push (3) on the stack

4	3			

        top

3. $n = 2$
   Hence recursive call is executed as 2 * fact(1)
   Push (2) on the stack

4	3	2		

            top

4. $n = 1$
   Hence execute statement return (1).

5. Now POP the contents and n = 2 the expression = 2 * 1

6. n = POP( ) = 3
   the expression = 3 * 2 * 1

7. n = POP( ) = 4
   the expression = 4 * 3 * 2 * 1 = 24

8. n = POP( )
   The stack is empty hence stop.
   The answer 4! = 24.

When recursive function is written then
a) If the stack is empty then execute a normal return.
b) Otherwise POP the stack contents and set the values as parameters, local variables
c) jump to return address which is stored in stack.
d) Repeat the above steps till stack is empty

2.13.3 Simulating Recursion

Recursion is a technique that allows us to break down a problem into one or more sub problems that are similar in form to the original problem. As recursive programs are most inefficient as far their name and space complexities are concerned. Hence there is a need to convert them into iterative ones. To convert recursive programs into non-recursive ones, one has to use stacks.

2.14 TOWERS OF HANOI

In tower of Hanoi problem, we are given 'n' disks and three towers. We are to move the disks stacked on tower 1 to tower 2, one disk at a time, such that:
   (a) No disk is on the top of a smaller one.
   (b) Only the top disk on any tower can be moved to any other tower.

A very elegant solution to this problem results from the use of recursion. Thus, we reduce the problem into following steps:
   (i) Move top (n – 1) disks from tower 1 to tower 3. (Here, we need tower 3 as an auxiliary tower).
   (ii) Move top disk from tower 1 to tower 2.
   (iii) Move top (n – 1) disks from tower 3 to tower 1.

So, we define a procedure as:
   towerofhanoi (n, st, aux, end)
which moves top 'n' disks from initial tower (st) to final tower (end) using auxiliary tower (aux).

Algorithm: towerofhanoi (n, st, aux, end)
1. if n = 1, then
   (a) (Move top disk from st → end).
       print st → end
   (b) Return
       (end of if structure)
2. call tower_of hanoi (n – 1, st, end, aux).
3. print st → aux.
4. Call towerofhanoi (n – 1, aux, st, end).
5. Return.

SUMMARY

- Stack is a linear data structure where all additions and deletions are made only at one end called top.
- The operations performed on stacks are:
  (i) Push, (ii) Pop, (iii) Stack-empty, (iv) Stack full.
- Stack can be implemented using array or linked list.
- Stack can be used for expression conversion and evaluation, handling recursion, reversing a string, language processing applications, etc.
- An expression can be written in infix, postfix and prefix format.
- Postfix and prefix expressions are easier to evaluate than infix since priority of operators need not be considered.
- Queue is a linear data structure in which all insertions are made at rear end deletions are made at the other end called front end.
- Queue can be' implemented using array or linked list.
- The four operations done on queue are:
  (i) Insert, (ii) Delete, (iii) Queue full, (iv) Queue empty.
- Linear queue has the advantage that when queue becomes full, rear reaches end of queue and even if we remove some elements we cannot insert elements in it.
- Circular queue is used to avoid disadvantage of linear queue stated above. We can go to the front end of queue and insert the elements if it is empty in circular queue.
- In priority queue, the elements are stored as per the priority. The priority queue can be ascending or descending.
- Queue can be used in scheduling techniques like First Come First Serve or Round Robin Technique.

SOLVED PROBLEMS

1. **Write a program to reverse string using stack.**

Solution:
```
#define MAX 80
int top=-1;
char stk[MAX];
void main( )
{
    char s [MAX];               // String variable
    int i;
    printf("Enter a string \n");
    gets(s);                    // Accept a string
    i=0;
    while(s[i] !='\0')          // while it is not end of string
```

```
        {
            push(s[i]);              // Push character on stack
            i++;
        }
        i=0;
        while(top!=-1)               // while stack is not empty
        {
            s[i]=pop( );             // Pop a character from stack
            i++;
        }
        printf("Reversed string is %s", s);
    }
    void push (char x)
    {
        if(top!=MAX-1)
        {
            top ++;
            stk [top] = x;
        }
    }
    char pop( )
    {
        char = x;
        if(top!=-1)
        {
            x = stk [top];
            top --;
        }
    }
```

2. Write necessary 'C' functions to implement stack of characters using array.

Solution:

```
#define MAX 10
char s[MAX];
int top=-1;
void push (char x)
{
    if(top == MAX-1)
        printf("Stack full");
    else
```

```
    {
        top ++;
        s[top] = x;
    }
}
char pop( )
{
    char x;
    if(top == -1)
        printf("Stack full");
    else
    {
        x = s[top];
        top --;
    } return (x);
}
```

3. **Modify program 2.6 to incorporate bracketed expression e.g. (a*(b+c)).**

Hint: Assign lowest priority (say 0) to opening bracket `(`. Whenever there is opening bracket push it on the stack. Whenever there is closing bracket pop all the operators and copy them in output, till you get an opening bracket in the stack. The procedure for expression (a + (b * c / d) – e) is as follows:

Incoming character	Action	Postfix	Stack Contents
(	Push		(
a	Copy to output	a	
+	Priority more than (, push)		(+
(	Push		(+(
b	Copy to output	ab	
*	Priority more than (, push	ab	(+(*
c	Copy to output	abc	
/	Priority equal to *, pop*, copy to output, push/		
d	Copy to output	abc*d	
)	Pop /, copy to output, Pop (	abc*d/	(+
–	Priority equal to +, pop +, copy to output push-	abc*d/+	(–
e	Copy to output	abc*d/+e	
)	Pop-, Copy to output	abc*d\+e-	
End of expression		abc*d\+e-	

4. **Evaluate the following postfix expression using stack.**
   623 +− 382/+*2$3+

Incoming character	Action	Stack
6	Push	6
2	Push	6, 2
3	Push	6, 2, 3
+	Pop 3, 2 Push 2 + 3 = 5	6, 5
−	Pop 5, 6 Push 6 − 5 = 1	1
3	Push	1, 3
8	Push	1, 3, 8
2	Push	1, 3, 8, 2
/	Pop 2, 8 Push 8/2 = 4	1, 3, 4
+	Pop 4, 3 Push 3 + 4 = 7	1, 7
*	Pop 7, 1 Push 1 * 7 = 7	7
2	Push	7, 2
$	Pop 2, 7 Push 7^2 = 49	49

3		Push	49, 3
	+	Pop 3, 49	
		Push 49 + 3 = 52	52

∴ result = 52

5. **Convert following expression into prefix and infix.**
   (a + b * c) / (x + y / z)
   Solution:

   Postfix = (a + b * c) (x + y/z) /
   = (a + (bc *)) (x + (yz/))/
   = abc*+xyz/+/

   Infix = / (a + b * c) (x + y/z)
   = / (a + (* bc) (x + (/ yz))
   = / + a * bc + x / yz

6. **What is stack? Explain how stack is used to check validity of parenthesis with suitable example.**
   Solution: (Refer Section 2.1 for definition of stack)

   Validity of parenthesis using stack:
   1. Stack can be used to check validity of parenthesis.
   2. For example, if you are given an expression ((a + (b + c / d)) – e), we can scan the expression from left to right.
   4. We can create a stack of characters and as- and when we came across a (opening parenthesis) we push it on stack and whenever we get (closing parenthesis)) an opening parenthesis w be popped!
   5. At the end of the expression, if the stack is empty it means we have equal number of opening and closing parenthesis otherwise the expression is invalid.

   The algorithm for the same is given as follows:

   1. Input exp
   2. i=0;
   3. while (exp[i]!='\0')
      {   65
          if(exp[i] == '(')
              push('(')
          if(exp[i] == ')')
              pop( );
      }
   4. if(stack_empty( ))
          print "Valid expression"
      else
          print"Invalid expression"

7. **Consider infix expression.**
   a + (c / d) * (e * f)
   Convert it into postfix and prefix. Evaluate postfix expression for a = 2, c = 4, d = 2, e = 3, f = 5.

Solution:

   Given: a + (c / d) * (e * f)

   $$\text{expr} = (a + ((c/d) \quad * \quad (e * f)))$$
   $$\downarrow \qquad \downarrow$$
   $$= a \quad cd\backslash \quad ef ** +$$

   Hence, postfix is acd \ef ** +

   $$\text{expr} = (a + ((c/d) * (e * f)))$$
   $$= +a * / cd * ef$$

   Prefix is a * / cd * ef

Evaluation: acd \ ef ** +

Incoming character	Action	Stack
a	Push a = 2	2
c	Push c = 4	2, 4
d	Push d = 2	2, 4, 2
/	Pop 2, 4	
	Push 4/2 = 2	2, 2
e	Push e = 3	2, 2, 3
f	Push f = 5	2, 2, 3, 5
*	Pop 5, 3	
	Push 3 * 5 = 15	2, 2, 15
*	Pop 15, 2	2, 2, 15
	Push 15 * 2 = 30	2, 30
+	Pop 30, 2	
	Push 2 + 30 = 32	32

∴ result = 32

8. **Convert the following expression in other two forms where $ stands for unary minus.**

   (i) ab + cd - *
   (ii) $a + (b − c) ↑ d
   (iii) /- * abc + ef
   (iv) $a + p ↑ q ↑ r

Solution:

(i) ab + cd - *

The expression is postfix.

$$\begin{aligned}
\exp &\to ((ab\ +)\ (cd\ -)\ *) \\
&\to (((a + b) * (c - d))) \qquad \text{Infix} \\
&\to *\ +\ ab\ -\ cd \qquad \text{Prefix}
\end{aligned}$$

(ii) $a + (b − c) ↑ d

The expression is infix.

$$\begin{aligned}
\exp &\to \$a + (b - c) \uparrow d \\
&\to (\$a) + ((b - c) \uparrow d) \\
&\to +\ \$a \uparrow -\ bc\ d \qquad \text{Prefix} \\
&\to a\$\ bc - d \uparrow + \qquad \text{Postfix}
\end{aligned}$$

(iii) /- * abc + ef

The expression is prefix.

$$\begin{aligned}
\text{expr} &\to (/\ (-\ (*\ a\ b)\ c) + (ef)) \\
&\to ((a * b) - c) / (e + f) \qquad \text{Infix} \\
&\to ab * c - ef +/ \qquad \text{Postfix}
\end{aligned}$$

(iv) $a + p ↑ q ↑ r

The expression is infix.

$$\begin{aligned}
\text{expr} &\to \$a + p \uparrow q \uparrow r \\
&\to (\$a) + ((p \uparrow q) \uparrow r) \\
&\to a\$\ pq \uparrow r \uparrow + \qquad \text{Postfix} \\
&\to +\ \$a \uparrow\uparrow pqr \qquad \text{Prefix}
\end{aligned}$$

9. **Explain the necessity of representing expression in prefix and postfix. Evaluate the following expression. Show stepwise stack contents.**

$$ABC * DEF \wedge \backslash G * - H +$$

A = 6, B = 1, C = 4, D = 16, E = 2, F = 3, G = 2, H = 5.

Solution:

Incoming character	Action	Stack
A	Push A = 6	6
B	Push B = 1	6, 1
C	Push C = 4	6, 1, 4
*	Pop 4, 1 Push 4	6, 4
D	Push D = 16	6, 4, 16
E	Push E = 2	6, 4, 16, 2
F	Push F = 3	6, 4, 16, 2, 3
^	Pop 3, 2 Push 2 ^ 3 = 8	6, 4, 16, 8
/	Pop 8, 16 Push 16/8 = 2	6, 4, 2
G	Push 4 = 2	6, 4, 2, 2
*	Pop 2, 2 Push 2 * 2 = 4	6, 4, 4
-	Pop 4, 4 Push 4 − 4 = 0	6, 0
H	Push 5	6, 0, 5
*	Pop 5, 0 Push 5 * 0 = 0	6, 0
+	Pop 0, 6 Push 6 + 0 = 6	6

Result = 6

10. Convert the following expression into postfix. Show all steps.
Solution:

a + b * c / d − e

Incoming character	Action	Stack	Output
a	Print		a
+	Push	+	
b	Print	+	ab
*	Push	+ *	a
c	Print	+ *	abc
/	Pop Push /	+ /	abc*
d	Print	+ /	abc*d
−	Pop / Pop + Push	−	abc*d/+
e	Print		abc*d/+e
\0	Pop −		abc*d/+e−

Postfix is abc*d/+e−

11. Explain the application of stack to check the validity of parentheses in the expression. Also write the pseudo code for the same.
Solution:
(a) We can use stack to check validity of parentheses.
(b) The opening parentheses can be pushed into stack and as soon as a closing parenthesis comes, one parenthesis is popped. In the end, if the stack is empty there will be equal number of opening and closing parentheses.

(c) Pseudo-code will be as below:
1. Read expr
2. i=0
3. while expr[i] != '\0'
   {
       if(expr [i] == '(')
           push('(');
       if(expr [i] == ')')
           pop( );
   }
4. if(stack_empty( ))
     print "Valid"
   else
       print "Invalid"

12. Write a program to reverse a queue using stack.

Solution:
```
#define MAX 5
int q[MAX];
int front = 1, rear = -1;
void insertq (int);
int delq( );
int front -1, rear -1;
int stk[MAX]
int top =-1;
void main( )
{
    int i, x, n;
    printf ("Enter n \n")
    scanf("%d", &n);
    for(i=0; i<n; i++)
    {
        scanf("%d", &x);
        insertq(x);
    }
    while(front!=rear)
```

```
        {
            x=delq( );
            push(x);
        }
        while(top!=-1)
        {
            x=pop( );
            insertq(x);
        }
    }
    void insert q (int x)
    {
        if (front == MAX -1)
        front = rear = -1;
        if (rear = MAX -1)
            printf ("Queue full");
        else
        {
            rear ++;
            q[rear] = x;
        }
    }
    int delq( )
    {
        int x;
        if (front == rear)
        {
            printf ("Q is empty");
            return (-9999);
        }
        else
        {
            front ++;
            x = q [front];
            return (x);
        }
```

```
}
void push (int x)
{
    if(top == MAX-1)
        printf("Stack is full");
    else
    {
        top ++;
        stk [top] = x;
    }
}
int pop( )
{
    int x;
    if (top == -1)
    {
        print ("Stack is empty \n");
        return (-9999);
    }
    else
    {
        x = stk [top];
        top- -;
        return (x);
    }
}
```

13. Differentiate between circular and linear queue.

Solution:

No.	Linear queue	Circular queue
1.	When rear becomes MAX −1, we cannot insert elements at front end even if space is available.	When rear becomes MAX −1, we can continue adding elements at front end if space is available.
2.	Counter is not required to check Q full or Q empty.	Counter is required to check Q full or Q empty.
3.	Easy implementation.	Difficult implementation.

EXERCISE

1. Write 'push' and 'pop' functions in C to implement stack in an array.
2. Explain the of stack with the help of suitable example. Also write the pseudo-code for the operations performed cm stack.
3. Write necessary 'C' functions to implement stack using array.
4. Write functions in 'C' for push, pop is empty for stack using linked list. Give declaration in 'C' for implementing above functions for stack.
5. Write a program to perform following operations:
   (i) Push 10 and 20 on first stack.
   (ii) Push 100 and 200 on second stack.
   (iii) Pop all elements from both stacks one by one and display.
6. Write an ADT for stack.
7. What do you mean by ADT? Write an ADT for stack.
8. Define ADT. Write down ADT of stack.
9. Write necessary 'C' functions to implement stack using linked list.
10. Write all the necessary functions to represent stack using linked list. Write a C function using stack to determine whether the given string is palindrome or not.
11. Give a 'C' declaration to define a node structure for a stack using linked list.
12. Write function in 'C' to 'push' and 'pop' an item from a stack using linked list.
13. Explain how stack is implemented using linked list.
14. Write a 'C' function for push, pop, is stack empty using linked list.
15. Explain the necessity of representing expression in prefix and postfix notation. For the given postfix expressions, evaluate it for the values given. Show stepwise stack contents.

    A B C * D E F ^ / G * −1 * +

    A = 61 B = 1, C = 4, D = 16, E = 2, F = 3, G = 2, 1+= 5

    where ^ = exponential operator
16. Write pseudo C algorithm for postfix evaluation.
17. Give an algorithm for evaluation of a postfix expression.
18. Write a function in 'C' to evaluate postfix expression and explain with suitable example.
19. Write pseudo C algorithm for infix to postfix conversion.
20. Write an algorithm to convert infix expression to postfix. Convert the following infix expression to postfix using stack.

    A / B $ C + D * E − A * C where $ is an exponentiation. Show stepwise conversion.
21. Write pseudo-C algorithm to convert infix expression to postfix using stack.

22. Write an algorithm to convert infix expression to postfix.
23. Give the postfix and prefix forms of the infix expression given below. Also write an algorithm or pseudo 'C' code to evaluate a postfix expression.

    infix expression - (a + b * c) / (x + y/2).
24. Convert the following expressions into other two forms:
    (i) ((A – (B + C)) * D) $ (E + F) where $ = exponentiation
    (ii) /m n $ q p $ y $ /-r s * +
25. Convert following infix expression into postfix using stack. Show all steps.

    A/B**C+D*E-A*C where ** is exponentiation.
26. Explain the concept of queue with suitable example. Also explain any one application of queue with Pseudo-Code.
27. What is queue? Explain circular queue and priority queue with suitable example.
28. Explain concept of queue with suitable example. Also explain any one application of queue with pseudo code.
29. Write a menu driven program for implementation of queue using structure.
30. Write necessary 'C' functions to implement Queue using array.
31. Write necessary functions to implement queue using array.
32. How can queue be implemented using array and linked list? Explain.
33. Explain array and linked list implementation of queue.
34. Explain array and linked list implementation of queue.
35. Write necessary 'C' functions to implement Queue using linked list.
36. Write 'insert' and 'delete' operations to implement a linked queue.
37. Compare linear and circular queue representations using arrays. Give a node structure in 'C' to define a queue using linked list. Also write a function to add an item into a queue using linked list.
38. Write necessary 'C' functions to implement Circular Queue using array.
39. Write necessary functions in C to implement circular queue in all array. Assume rear=front=0 initially.
40. How circular queue is advantageous over sequential queue? Explain with an example.
41. Differentiate between linear and circular queue when represented using array.
42. Implement the following functions in 'C' to implement circular queue using array.
    (i)   Insert an element,
    (ii) Delete an element,
    (iii) Queue full,
    (iv) Queue empty.

    Assume data elements to be integer.

43. Explain advantages of circular queue over linear queue.
44. What is circular queue? Explain insert and delete operations in circular queue.
45. Explain the concept of priority queue with suitable example. Explain one application of Priority queue.
46. Explain the concept of priority queue with suitable example.
47. What is Priority Queue? Write Pseudo 'C' function to insert and delete item from Priority Queue.
48. Why do we need priority Queue? Explain with appropriate data structure, the implementation of priority queue.
49. What do you mean by priority queue? Explain any one application of priority queue with suitable example.
50. Explain priority queue and give application for the same.
51. What do you mean by priority queue? Explain any one application in detail.
52. Explain the term priority queue and give the application for the same.
53. What is priority queue? What are the applications of priority queue? Write a 'C' function to perform insertion and deletion on priority queue.
54. What is priority queue? Explain how insert and delete operations are implemented in it.
55. Compare circular and linear queue.
56. Write applications of queue.
57. Discuss in brief use of stacks in processing of subroutine calls.
58. Explain the use of stack in recursion using a suitable example.
59. Write a short note on 'Recursion in C'.
60. Write a recursive C function to find a factorial of a given number. Simulate the working of this function using stack.

UNIT III

LINKED LISTS

3.1 INTRODUCTION

A list consists of set of data items. Storage, retrieval, processing of the list is a major task required to be performed on computer. In the previous chapter, we have seen how can we store and process these lists using array. Though, it is easy to use array for storing the lists, there are two disadvantages of arrays.

(i) We cannot increase or decrease the size of the array as per our requirement during program execution.
(ii) The insert and delete operations are computationally complex.

Another way of storing a list is using linked organisation. We can store the data items alongwith address or link to the next data items. It is called linked list. Since linked lists allow us to allocate memory dynamically, we can increase or decrease the size of the list as per the number of elements to be stored. The linked lists make it easy to insert or delete the elements.

We summarize below the difference between arrays and linked lists.

Arrays	Linked Lists
1. Size of array needs to be mentioned while writing program. Hence fixed memory location are assigned for storage of data items.	1. Memory is allocated as and when it is required for storing data items in the linked list.
2. Data items are stored in contiguous (adjoining) memory locations.	2. Data items not in contiguous memory locations.
3. No overhead of storing address of another node.	3. Overhead of storing address of another node/structure.
4. Element in the array is difficult to insert or delete.	4. It becomes very easy to insert or delete.
5. Random access of any data element in an array is possible.	5. To access an element in linked list we have to traverse the list from beginning.
6. When an items is not required its space cannot be utilised by another variable.	6. When an item is no longer needed its space can be returned to the system which can be used by another variable.

Thus, the advantages of using linked lists are:
1. Linked list is a dynamic data structure which allows usage of memory as per requirement.
2. It is easy to perform insert and delete operations.
3. The deleted data items memory can be de-allocated.

The disadvantages are:
1. It is complex to implement.
2. Extra memory required for next field.
3. Random access not possible.

3.2 SINGLY LINKED LIST: CONCEPT

A singly linked list (SLL) is a linear collection of nodes, which consists of data item and the address of next node. Thus, each node is the SLL consists of two parts, data field and link field. Fig. 3.1 shows a linked list of integers.

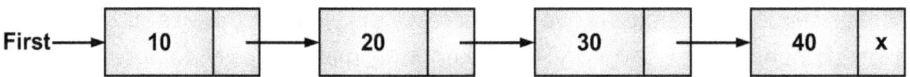

Fig. 3.1: Linked list of integers

Similarly, we can have a list of real numbers, list of names, list of records represented in Fig. 3.2.

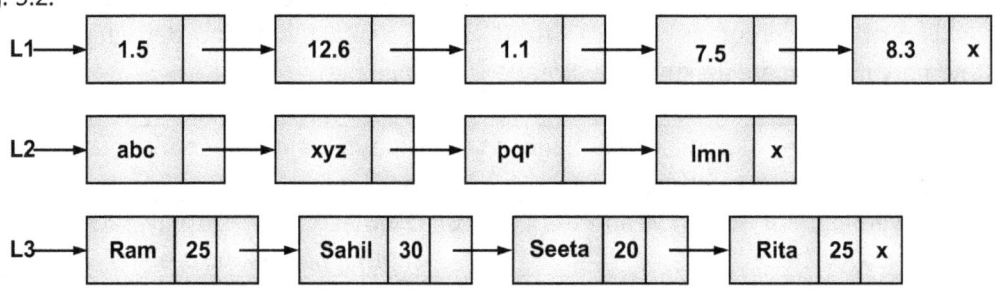

Fig. 3.2: Linked lists

It can be seen that the last node's link field contains nothing, hence it is filled with NULL (denoted as X). The first node in the list is the access point of the list, hence its address is stored in a variable called list pointer variable (For example, first L1, L2, L3 shown in the figures).

Example 3.1:

Suppose, we have a list of numbers to be stored using linked list. We want the numbers to be stored in sorted order, then the storage of number can be done alongwith its address of successor as below.

First → 3

Location number	Data	Next
0	-	-
1	20	6
2	40	4
3	10	1
4	50	NULL
5	-	-
6	30	2

Linked list of numbers

It can be seen that the address (location number) of first element in the list is in first. The address of second number is next field of 10 i.e. 1 and so on. The next field of last element is NULL.

3.2.1 Linked List as ADT List

Linked list can be used to implement an ADT list. Linked list can be used to implement a linear or non-linear structures.

A linear list consists of link to every element except the last node which has NULL pointer.

A non-linear list can have two or more links.

A list can be empty list with NULL which is called NULL list pointer.

3.3 REPRESENTATION OF LINKED LIST IN MEMORY

To maintain a linked list in memory two linear arrays will be required. One array contains information and second array will store links to the next node. A list will also have a variable say first which stores location of first node in the list. The last node in the list will have NULL or in its link field.

Suppose we want to store two lists in memory consisting of students having two elective subjects SUB1 and SUB2. Then the list can be maintained in memory as shown below.

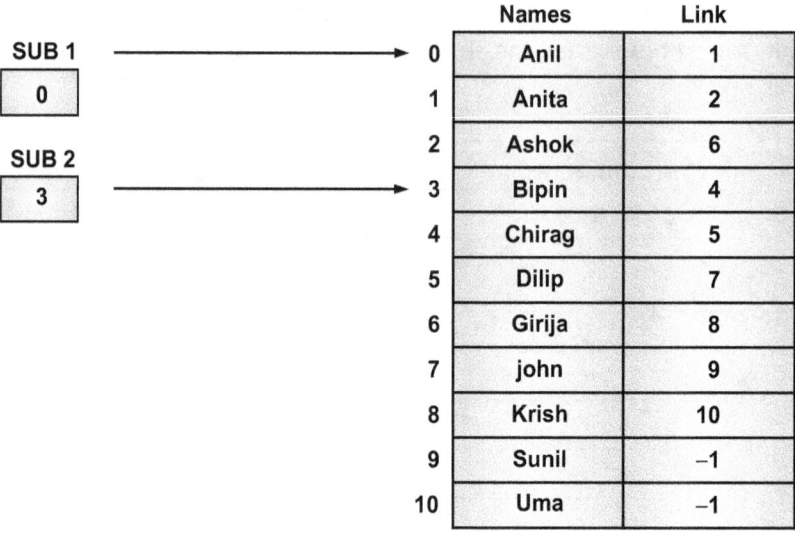

Fig. 3.3

Logically, the two lists will be represented as below:

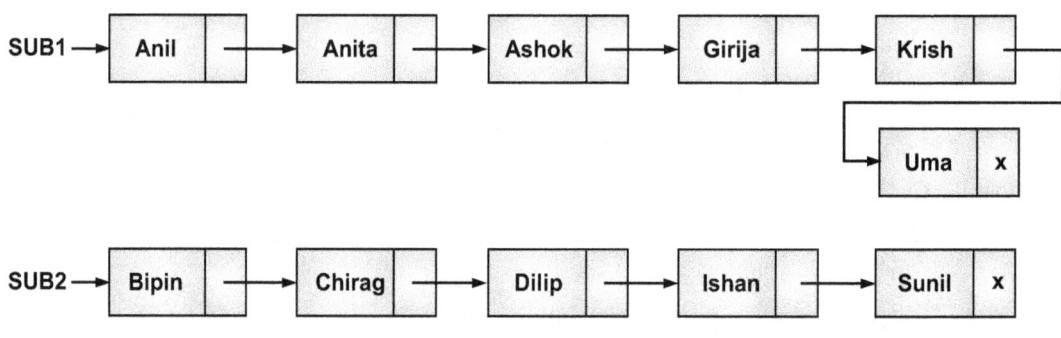

Fig. 3.4

The linked list can be implemented using static representation i.e. array or using dynamic representation i.e. pointer. Let us first see how can we store the linked list using array and traverse.

Let us consider a list shown in Fig. 3.3.

Two arrays namely DATA[ ] and NEXT[ ] will be used. A variable FIRST will store location number of first element in the list. A variable PTR will be used to store the location of mode currently being processed. Thus, we have,

FIRST=3

DATA[1]=20   NEXT[1]=6
DATA[2]=40   NEXT[2]=4
DATA[3]=10   NEXT[3]=1
DATA[4]=50   NEXT[4]=NULL
DATA[6]=30   DATA[6]=2

Note: The location number 0 and 5 are not used.

The algorithm for traversal of the linked list will be as below.

Algorithm 3.1: Traversing a linked list

Step 1:   Set PTR=FIRST
Step 2:   Repeat steps 3 and 4 while PTR != NULL
Step 3:   Display DATA[PTR]
Step 4:   Set PTR=NEXT [PTR]
Step 5:   Stop.

Similarly, we can write algorithms to perform various operations on the list such as insert, delete, search etc. The above implementation uses static memory allocation and hence is not efficient. The same concept can be used in implementation using dynamic memory allocation. Hence, we will discuss in detail the implementation of linked list using self-referential structure and pointers.

3.4 SINGLY LINKED LIST OPERATIONS

Linked list is a set of structures (called nodes) having one of the fields as pointer to similar structure. (nodes)

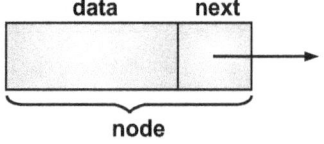

Fig. 3.5: Node in a linked list

The data field can be integers/real/string/record and next field is a pointer containing address of similar node.

A linked list is represented as:

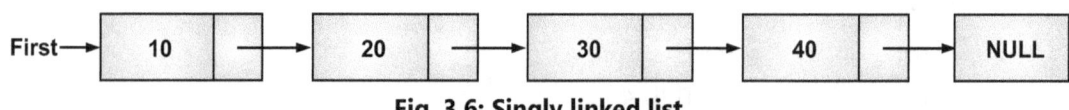

Fig. 3.6: Singly linked list

Here, first is a pointer containing address of first node of the linked list.

Also note that the last node has next field pointing to NULL means it is referring nowhere.

Before we go into details of linked list we discuss some basic concepts.

1. **Static Variable:** These variables are declared and named while writing program For example,

    int a, b;

the space allotted to these variables exists as long as program is running.

2. **Dynamic Variables:** They are created during program execution as and when required. These variables are accessed using pointers. They can be destroyed when they are not required.

3. **Defining a node in linked list:** Suppose that we have to store a list of integer numbers in a linked list following structure variable can be defined.

    struct node
    {
        int data;
        struct node *next;
    };

Here we are declaring a structure called as node. It has two fields data and next; data to store integer number and next to store address of another similar structure. (This is called as self referential structure),

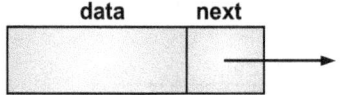

Fig. 3.7: Self referential structure

If we declare a pointer variable

    struct node *ptr;

It means a pointer called ptr is declared which is of type struct node i.e. ptr can store address of a variable of type struct node.

If we want to store a list of persons having name and age. The node can be defined as

    struct node
    {
        char name [25];
        int age;
        struct node *next;
    };

4. How to Allocate and Deallocate Memory?

To allocate memory to a dynamic variable we use malloc function as

    ptr = (struct node*) malloc (sizeof (struct node));

when we do this a block of memory of the size of struct node is allocated to ptr. i.e. ptr starts pointing to the node as shown in Fig. 3.8.

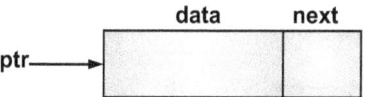

Fig. 3.8: Pointer to a node

Thus, ptr has address of the node.

If we have to assign the data to this structure pointed by ptr, we can write

    ptr->data=x;

where, x is an integer number.

To de-allocate the memory allocated to ptr we can write

    free (ptr);

The memory allocated to ptr will be returned back to system so that system can reuse it.

Note: When malloc fails to allocate memory, it returns NULL.

5. **Some linked list related statements:** Let us consider that we have pointers, *ptr1, *ptr2, *ptr3 of the type struct node

The following statements will result into the 3 pointers pointing to 3 locations (Structures) as shown in Fig. 3.8.

    ptr1=(struct node*)malloc(sizeof (struct node));
    ptr2=(struct node*)malloc(sizeof (struct node));
    ptr3=(struct node*)malloc(sizeof (struct node));

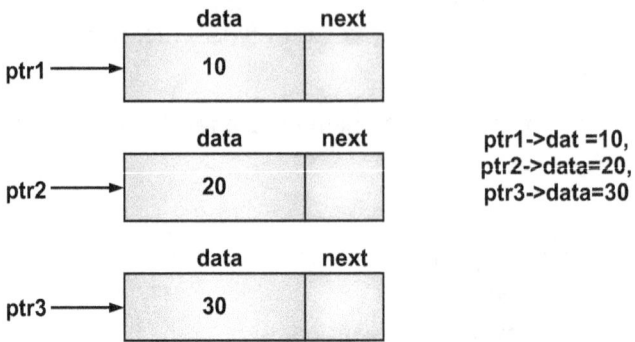

Fig. 3.9: Memory allocation and data storage

Now if we write

(a) ptr1->next=ptr2

We are storing address of second node (pointed by ptr2) in the next field of first node (pointed by ptr1). You can read this as ptr1's next will start pointing to a place where ptr2 is pointing.

i.e.

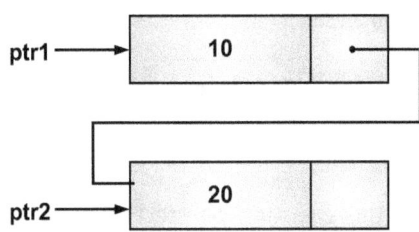

Fig. 3.10: Linking two nodes

(b) temp=ptr1;

temp will no longer point to current location. It will start pointing to a node pointed by ptr1. You can read this as temp will start pointing to a place where ptr1 is pointing

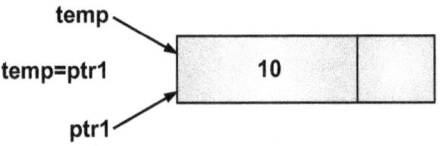

Fig. 3.11: Another pointer to a node

(c) The following statements will result in creation of a linked list.
  1. ptr1->next=ptr2;
  2. ptr2->next=ptr3;

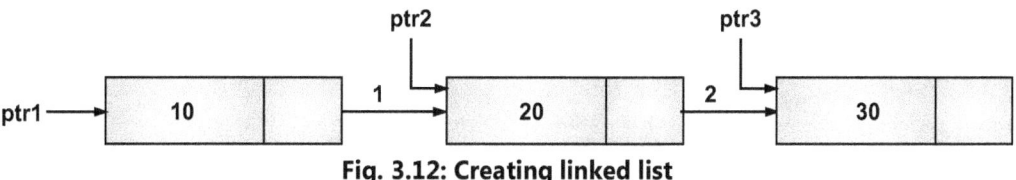

Fig. 3.12: Creating linked list

(d) If we write temp=ptr1->next, temp will start pointing to a place where ptr1-> next is pointing.

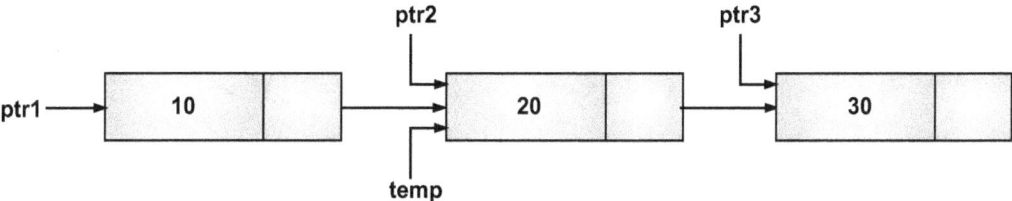

Fig. 3.13: Pointer to a next node

(e) ptr1->next=ptr->3
It will make ptr1->next point to the node pointed by ptr2->next. It will stop pointing to the node pointed by ptr2.

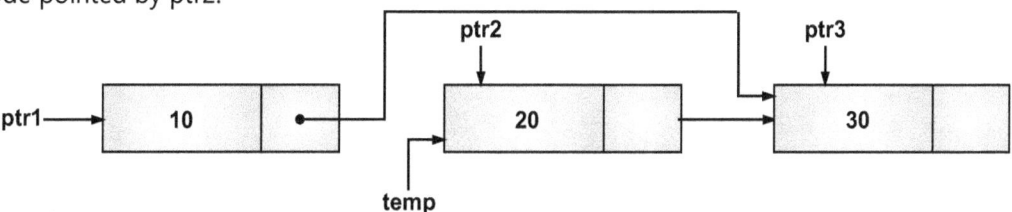

Fig. 3.14: Eliminating a node

Now let us write a simple program to create a linked list and display the elements in it.

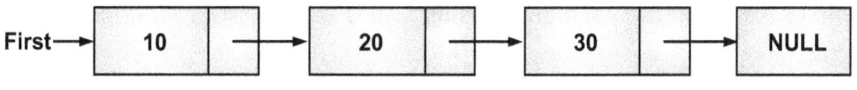

Fig. 3.15: Singly linked list

Program 3.1: A linked list of three elements.

```
#include<stdio.h>
#include<conio.h>
void main( )
{
    struct node
```

```
{
    int data;
    struct node *next;
};
struct node *ptr1, *ptr2, *ptr3, *temp;
ptr1=(struct node*)malloc(size of (struct node));
ptr1->data=10;
ptr2=(struct node*)malloc(size of (struct node));
ptr2->data=20;
ptr3=(struct node*)malloc(size of (struct node));
ptr3->data=30;
ptr1->next=ptr2;
ptr2->next=ptr3;
ptr3->next=NULL;
temp=ptr1;
while (temp!=NULL)
{
    printf("%d\n", temp->data);
    temp=temp->next;
}
}
```

Explanation:

1. In the first seven statements, memory is allocated to ptr1, ptr2, ptr3 and data is stored in the data fields.

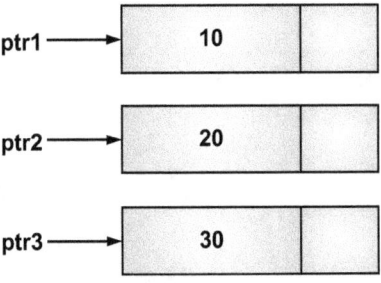

Fig. 3.16: Memory allocation and storage in nodes

2. ptr1->next=ptr2
    and ptr2->next=ptr3
        ptr3->next=NULL;
will create a linked list and the various pointers will be pointing as below.

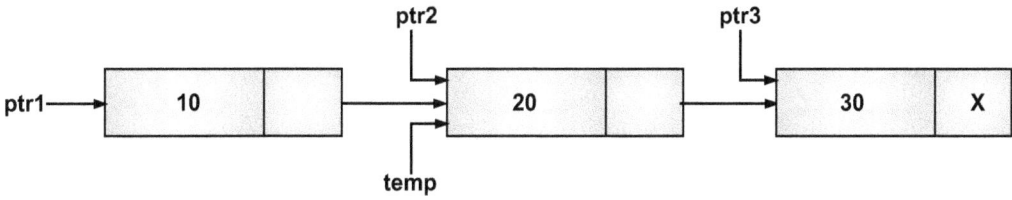

Fig. 3.17: Linking nodes

3. Next, to display the elements in the list we point temp to ptr1 and go on advancing the pointer while displaying the data in each node.

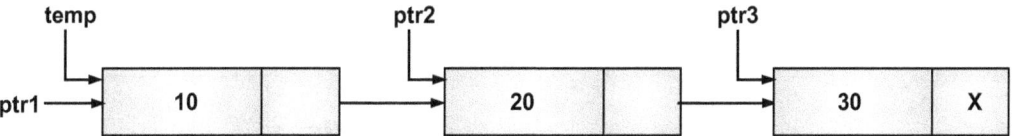

Fig. 3.18: Pointer to a first node

Above program is very elementary. Now let us write a program to create a linked list of n elements (i.e. generalized linked list). To create a list of integer numbers, we first read number of elements in the list. Then we go on allocating memory for each node and establishing link between them. Following is the program which creates and displays the linked list.

Program 3.2: To create and display a linked list.

```c
#include<stdio.h>
#include<conio.h>
void main( )
{
    struct node
    {
        int data
        struct node *next;
```

```
};
struct node *first, *temp, *ptr;
int i, n, x;
clrscr( );
printf("Enter how many elements\n");
scanf("%d", &n);
for(i=1;i<=n;i++)
{
    printf("Enter data\n");
    scanf("%d", &x);
    ptr=malloc(size of (struct node));
    ptr->next=x;
    ptr->next=NULL;
    if (first==NULL)
    {
        first=ptr;
        temp=ptr;
    }
    else
    {
        temp->next=ptr;
        temp=ptr;
    }
}
temp=first;
while (temp!=NULL)
{
    printf("%d->", temp->data);
    temp=temp->next;
}
printf("NULL");
getch( );
}
```

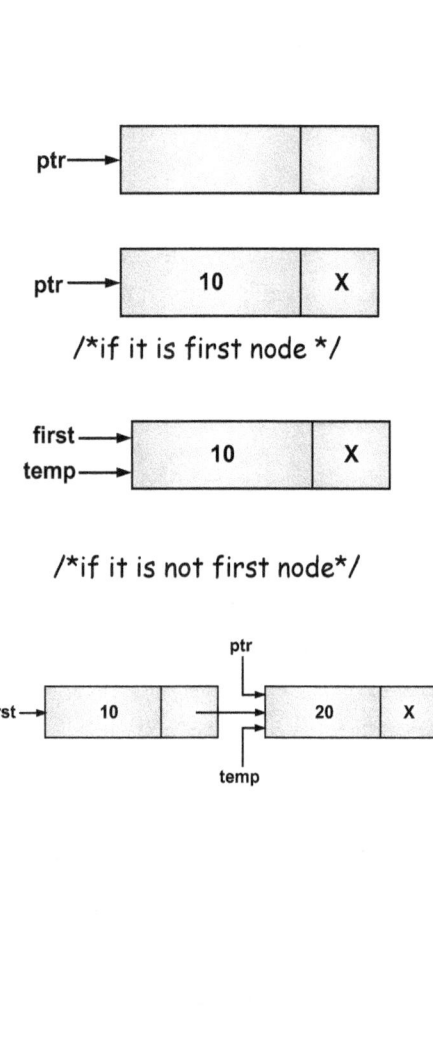

/*if it is first node */

/*if it is not first node*/

Explanation:
1. We read number of elements in the list in variable n.
2. We go on reading data in x. Allocate memory for ptr, store the data in x in the data field of ptr. If we are storing first element the condition first==NULL will be true. We should point the pointer first to this node (if part).
   Otherwise we link previous node with current and advance the pointer temp (else part).
3. To display the elements in the linked list we first point the pointer temp to first node. Access data and advance temp to next node. We continue this till temp doesn't reference to NULL.

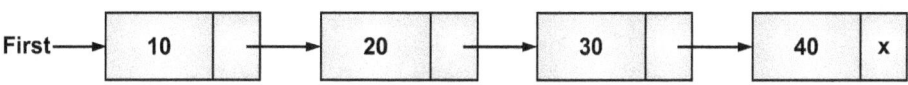

Fig. 3.19: Singly linked list

Now let us write separate functions for create and display the linked list:

Program 3.3: To create linked lists.

```
NODE *create( )
{
    NODE *first, *ptr, *temp;
    int i, x, n;
    printf("Enter number of elements \n");
    scanf("%d", &n);
    first=NULL;
    for(i=1;i<=n;i++)
    {
        printf("Enter data \n")
        scanf("%d"; &x);
        ptr=(NODE *)malloc(size of (NODE));
        ptr->data=x;
        ptr->next=NULL;
        if(first==NULL)
            first=ptr;
        else
            temp->next=ptr;
```

```
                    temp=ptr;
            }
            return(first);
    }
    void disp(NODE *temp)
    {
            while (temp!=NULL)
            {
                    printf("%d->", temp->data);
                    temp=temp->next;
                    printf("NULL \n");
            }
    }
    void main( )
    {
            NODE *l1, *l2;
            l1=create( );
            l2=create( );
            disp (l1);
            disp (l2);
    }
```

Explanation:

1. The create function when called from main function creates a linked list which is pointed by first pointer. The address in linked list in pointer first is return back in the main function to a pointer variable say l1 or l2. The pointer variable l1 and l2 in a main function now as address of linked list created by the create function.
2. The function disp displays the elements in the linked list, it required the address of linked list to be passed to it. The pointer variable temp collects this address and traverses the list sequentially.

3.4.1 Insert Operation

To insert an element in the linked list, the pointer (say temp) is advanced to the node after which the new element is to be inserted. A new node is created and it is inserted with the help of the pointer temp. The procedure is shown in Fig. 3.20.

(1) Get a pointer (temp) to a node after which element is to be inserted.
(2) Create a new node store the data.
(3) ptr->next=temp->next;
(4) temp->next=ptr;

It means we have to establish two new links and one link will be removed during insert operation in SLL. If the node is to be inserted before first node, then following steps will be performed.

(1) ptr->next=first
(2) first=ptr

In this case only one new link will be established.

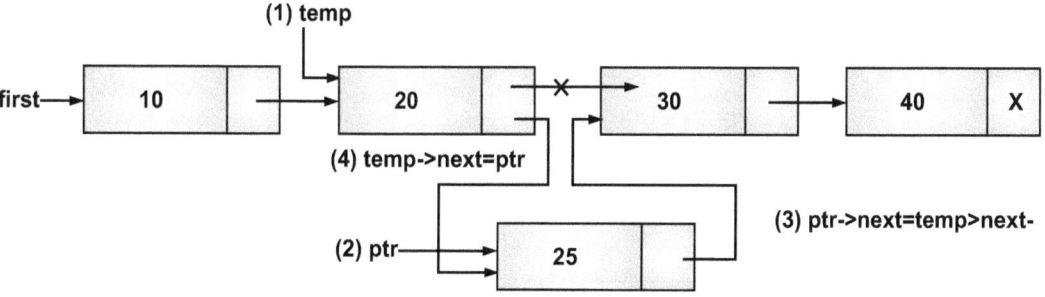

Fig. 3.20: Insert operation in SLL

The detailed algorithm is given as follows.

Algorithm 3.2: Insert an element in SLL

The detailed algorithm is given as follows:

```
(1) Read position p;
(2) temp=first;
(3) i=1;
(4) while (i<p&&temp!=NULL)
    {
        temp=temp->next;
        i++;
    }
(5) if (temp!=NULL)
    {
        ptr=malloc(sizeof(NODE));
```

```
            ptr->data=x;
            if(p==0)                    // inserting before first node;
            {
                ptr->next=first;
                first=ptr;
            }
            else                        // otherwise insert after any node
            {
                ptr->next=temp->next;
                temp->next=ptr;
            }
        else
            printf("Invalid position");
(6)  stop.
```

3.4.2 Delete Operation

To delete an element in the linked list, the pointer (say temp) in advanced to the node which is to be deleted. One more pointer (say prev) is required just before the node to be deleted. The procedure is shown in Fig. 3.21.

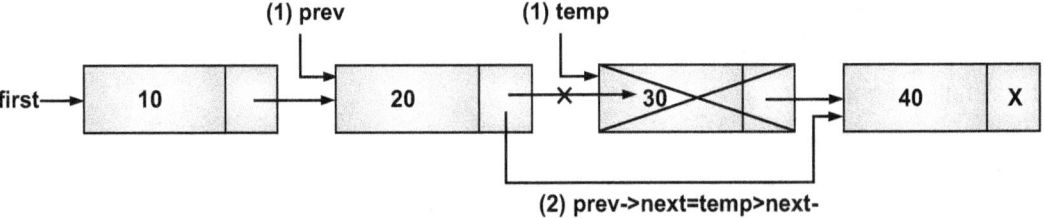

Fig. 3.21: Delete operation

(1) Let a pointer temp point the node to be deleted and pointer prev to the previous node.

(2) prev->next=temp->next.

(3) free (temp)

It means one new link will be established and two links will be removed during delete operation in SLL.

If the node to be deleted is the first node in the linked list, first has to be advanced to the second position and then it is deleted.

(1) first=first->next.

(2) free (temp);

In this case only one link will be removed.

Algorithm 3.3: Delete an element in the linked list.

(1) Read position p;

(2) i=i; temp=first;

(3) while (i<p&&temp!=NULL)
    {
        prev=temp;
        temp=temp->next;
        i++;
    }

(4) if (temp!=NULL)
    {
        if(p==1)   // node to be deleted is first node
        {
            first=first->next;
            free (temp);
        }
        else   // any other node than first
        {
            prev->next=temp->next;
            free (temp);
        }
    }
    else
        printf("Invalid position");   //list is empty or p specified is more

(5) stop.

3.4.3 Search Operation

To search an element in the linked list, we start with a pointer (say temp) to the first node and keep on advancing it till we find the required data in the linked list at a particular node. The algorithm will be as below.

Algorithm 3.4: Search an element in the linked list.

(1) Input x. (data to be searched)

(2) temp=first

(3) while(temp->data!=x&&temp!=NULL)

    temp=temp->next;

(4) if (temp==NULL)

    printf("Found");

else

    printf("Not found");

3.4.4 Implementation of SLL

Now we can write a complete menu driven program to implement operations viz. create, display, search, insert, delete in a linked list. For this we have to write separate function for these operations.

Program 3.4: Implementation of singly linked list with operations create, display, insert, delete and search.

```
#include<stdio.h>
#include<conio.h>
typedef struct_node
{
    int_node;
    struct node *next;
} NODE;
NODE *create( );
void disp (NODE *);
int search (NODE*, int);
```

```c
NODE *insert (NODE*, int, int);
NODE *del (NODE *, int);
void main( )
{
    NODE *first=NULL;
    int x, p, ch
    do
    {
        clrscr( );
        printf ("1.create\n, 2. Display\n, 3. search\n, 4. Insert\n,
        5. Delete\n, 6. Exit \n");
        printf("Enter your choice\n");
        scanf("%d", &ch);
        switch(ch)
        {
            case 1:  first=create( );
                     break;
            case 2:  disp (first);
                     break;
            case 3:  printf("Enter number to be searched \n");
                     scanf("%d", &x);
                     p=search (first, x);
                     if (p>0)
                         printf("found at %d", p);
                     else
                         printf("Not found");
            case 4:  printf("Enter data & position \n");
                     scanf(%d %d", &x, &p);
                     first=insert (first, x, p);
            case 5:  printf("Enter node number \n");
                     scanf("%d", &p);
                     first=del (first, p);
```

```c
            }
            getch( )
    } while (ch!=6);
}
NODE *create( )
{
    NODE *first, *ptr, *temp;
    int i, x, n;
    printf("Enter number if elements \n");
    scanf("%d", &n);
    first=NULL;
    for(i=1;i<=n;i++)
    {
        printf("Enter data \n");
        scanf("%d", &x);
        ptr=(NODE*)malloc(sizeof(NODE));
        ptr->data=x;
        ptr->next=NULL;
        if(first==NULL)
            first=ptr;
        else
            temp->next=ptr;
        temp=ptr;
    }
    return(first);
}
void disp (NODE *temp)
{
    while (temp!=NULL)
    {
        printf("%d->", temp->data);
        temp=temp->next;
```

```
        }
    }
    int search (NODE *first, int x)
    {
        Node *temp;
        int c=1;
        temp=first;
        while (temp->data!=x&&temp!=NULL)
        {
            temp=temp->next;
            c++;
        }
        if (temp!=NULL)
            return (c);
        else
            return (-1);
    }
    NODE *insert (NODE *first, int *x, int p)
    {
        NODE *temp, *ptr;
        int i;
        temp=first; i=1;
        while (i<p&&temp!=NULL)
        {
            temp=temp->next;
            i++;
        }
        if (temp!=NULL)
        {
            ptr=(NODE *)malloc(sizeof (NODE));
            ptr->data=x;
            ptr->next=NULL;
```

```c
            if (p==0)
            {
                ptr->next=first;
                first=ptr;
            }
            else
            {
                ptr->next= temp->next;
                temp->next=ptr;
            }
        }
        else
            printf("Invalid position");
        return (first);
}
Node *del (NODE*first, int p)
{
    NODE *temp, *prev;
    int i;
    temp=first; i=1;
    while (i<p&&temp!=NULL)
    {
        prev=temp;
        temp=temp->next;
        i++;
    }
    if (temp!=NULL)
    {
        if (p==1)
        {
            first=first->next;
            free (temp);
```

```
            }
            else
            {
                    prev->next=temp->next;
                    free (temp);
            }
        }
        else
            printf ("Invalid position");
        return (first);
}
void insert (NODE *first, int p, int x)
{
        NODE *ptr, *temp;
        temp=first;
        i=1;
        while (i<p&&temp!=NULL)
        {
            temp=temp->next;
            i++;
        }
        if (temp!=NULL)
        {
            ptr==(NODE *)malloc(sizeof (NODE));
            ptr->data x;
            if (p==0)                    // inserting before the first node;
            {
                    ptr->next=first;
                    first=ptr;
            }
            else                         // otherwise
            {
                    prev->next=temp->next;
```

```
                    temp->next=ptr;
                }
            }
            else
                printf ("Invalid position");
            return (first);
        }
```

3.5 MEMORY ALLOCATION; GARBAGE COLLECTION

The insert operation in linked list requires new memory location to be allocated and the delete operation makes the nodes free. The operating system has to allocate memory to new nodes when malloc requests for it. For this the operating system should know which location is available for allocation. For this system has to detect and reclaim the free nodes. This process is called garbage collection. Since these memory locations are scattered, the system has to maintain a list of available free nodes. For this the system has to periodically collect all the deleted locations free nodes.

The garbage collection is performed in two steps through a operating system routine called garbage collector.

(I) The system finds out all the nodes/cells which are currently in use and tags them. This phase is called marking phase.

(II) The entire memory is scanned and all the untagged spaces are collected and maintained under free storage list. This phase is called collection phase.

The garbage collection takes place under following circumstances.

(i) When there is minimum amount of space or no space available in the free storage list.

(ii) When CPU is idle and has time to do the garbage collection.

Whenever garbage collector is called, all user processing is stopped therefore, garbage collector has to be called under above circumstances.

3.5.1 Overflow and Underflow

When insert operation is performed and there is no space available, i.e. the free storage list is empty, overflow occurs. For example, during insert operation if malloc function fails to allocate memory, it returns NULL value. The programmer can display an error message indicating the overflow.

Similarly, during delete operation if there is no data in the list, it is called underflow. The programmer can print an error message when the pointer "first" is NULL.

3.5.2 Garbage Compaction

Though the method of garbage collection makes efficient use of memory, the available free list may not be usable, this is because the available memory is fragmented and may exist in the blocks of different sizes. If a programmer requires memory in large block sizes then some of the locations in the available free list may not be useful. For example, suppose all the even locations in memory are occupied and request for storing records of size more than one comes. This request will be rejected because the odd numbered location are of size one unit. The solution to this problem is to move all used (tagged) nodes to one end of memory and all the free nodes to the other. This process is called compaction.

The process of compaction requires all the pointers to be updated whenever a block is moved. This is required because the next element of the current node will be moved to a new location and this happens for every node.

3.6 HEADER LINKED LIST

Sometimes it is desirable to keep an extra node in front or at the end of a linked list. This node will not store any data but it will be a dummy node and it is called as 'header node' or 'list header'. The data field can be used to store some information about the list, For example, number of nodes in the list. A list with header node is shown in Fig. 3.22.

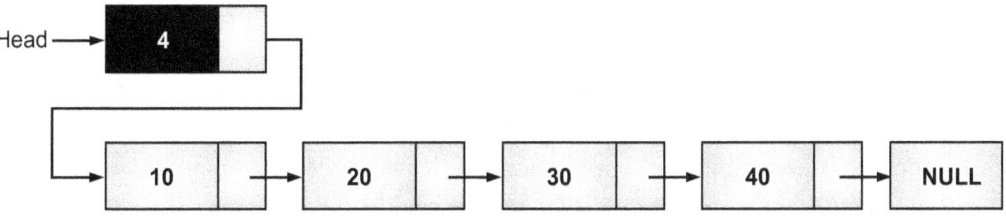

Fig. 3.22: Header node in linked list

This kind of head node will be useful in circular linked list where there is no fixed first node. Instead of a pointer to last node we can have a header node at the front end. The algorithms will be required to be modified to accommodate this change.

3.7 APPLICATIONS OF LINK LIST MANIPULATION

3.7.1 Polynomial Manipulation

A polynomial can be represented in an array or in a linked list by simply storing the coefficient and exponent of each term. However, for any polynomial operation, such as addition or multiplication of polynomials, you will find that the linked list representation is easier to deal with. First of all note that in a polynomial all the terms may not be present, especially if it is going to be a very high order polynomial. Consider,

$$5x^{12} + 2x^9 + 4x^7 + 6x^5 + x^2 + 12x$$

Now this 12th order polynomial does not have all the 13 terms (including the constant term). It would be very easy to represent the polynomial using a linked list structure, where each node can hold information pertaining to a single term of the polynomial. Each node will need to store the variable x, the exponent and the coefficient for each term. It often does not matter whether the polynomial is in x or y. This information may not be very crucial for the intended operations on the polynomial. Thus we need to define a node structure to hold two integers, viz. exponent and coefficient, For example, a polynomial $3x^4 + 5x^3 + 6x$ is represented in a linked list as,

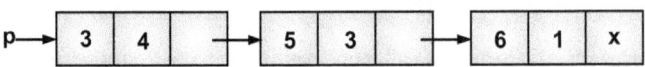

Fig. 3.23: Polynomial representation using SLL

3.7.2 Addition of Two Polynomials

Consider addition of the following polynomials,
$$5x^{12} + 2x^9 + 4x^7 + 6x^6 + x^3$$
$$7x^8 + 2x^7 + 8x^6 + 6x^4 + 2x^2 + 3x + 40$$

The resulting polynomial is going to be,
$$5x^{12} + 2x^9 + 7x^8 + 6x^7 + 14x^6 + 6x^4 + x^3 + 2x^2 + 3x + 40$$

Now notice how the addition was carried out. Let us say the result of addition is going to be stored in a third list. We started with the highest power in any polynomial. If there was no item having same exponent, we simply appended the term to the new list and continued with the process. Wherever we found that the exponents were matching, we simply added the coefficients and then stored the term in the new list. If one list gets exhausted earlier and the other list still contains some lower order terms, then simply append the remaining terms to the new list. Now we are in a position to write our algorithm for adding two polynomials. Let a, b and c represent the pointers of the three lists under consideration. Let each node contain two integers exponent and coefficient. Let us assume that the two linked lists already contain relevant data about the two polynomials. Also assume that we have got a function insert to insert a new node at the end of the given list. Let us consider two polynomials as,
$$3x^3 + 5x^2 + 7$$
$$3x^4 + 5x^3 + 6x$$

Following linked list pointed by a and b will be created using create function. The terms in a polynomial can be stored sequentially using a linked list as shown. The coefficient and power of each term is stored in -the nodes of linked list. The process of addition of two polynomials consists of testing each term power sequentially. The resultant polynomial will be pointed by c and is shown in Fig. 3.24.

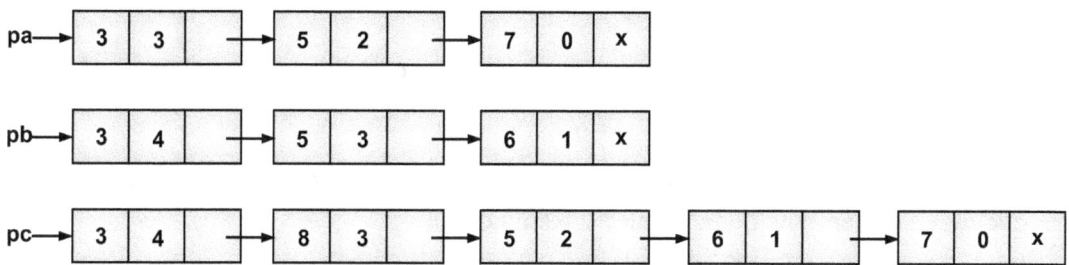

Fig. 3.24: Additional of two polynomials

Algorithm 3.4:

The algorithm to add two polynomials using linked list will be as follows:

1. Create first polynomial. Let, a be pointer to it.

    a=create( )

2. Create second polynomial. Let, b be pointer to it.

    b=create( )

3. Let, pa=a pb =b pc=NULL
4. while (pa !=NULL&&pb!=NULL)

    {

    if(pa->power==pb->power)

    {

        c=pa->coeff + pb->coeff;

        p=pa->power;

        pa=pa->next; ph=pb->next;

    }

    else

        if(pa->power>pb->power)

        {

            c=pa->coeff;

            p=pa->power;

            pa=pa->next;

        }

        else

        {

            c=pb -> coeff;

            p=pb -> power;

```
            pb=pb -> next;
        }
    }
    insert (pc, c, p); i.e. create new node with c and p (coeff and power of terms to be
    added) and insert the node in third linked list pc.
    }
5.  while (pa!=NULL)                    // Remaining terms of first polynomial.
    {
        c=pa->coeff;
        p=pa->power;
        insert (pc, c, p);
    }
6.  while (pb!=NULL)                    // Remaining terms of second polynomial
    {
        c=pb->coeff;
        p=pb->power;
        insert (pc, c, p);
    }
7.  Display third polynomial terms.
```

To write a program for addition of two polynomials we require four functions viz.

1. create( )
2. disp( )
3. addpoly( )
4. insert( )

Program 3.5: Addition of two polynomials using linked list.

```
    typedef struct node
    {
        int coeff, pow;
        struct node *next;
    } NODE;
NODE *create( );
void disp(NODE *);
```

```
NODE *addpoly (NODE NODE *);
NODE *insert(NODE *, int, int);
void main( )
{
    NODE *a, *b, *c;
    a=create( );
    b=create( );
    c=addpoly(a, b);
    disp (c);
}
NODE *create( )
{
    int i, n;
    NODE *first, *temp, *ptr;
    int c, p;
    printf("Enter number of terms \n");
    scanf("%d", &n);
    first=NULL;
    for(i=1;i<n;i++)
    {
        printf ("Enter coefficient and power \n");
        scanf("%d %d", &c, &p);
        ptr=(NODE *) malloc (sizeof (NODE));
        ptr->coeff=c;
        ptr->pow=p;
        ptr->next=NULL;
        if (first==NULL)
            first=ptr;
        else
            temp->next=ptr;
        temp=ptr;
    }
```

```c
        return (first);
}
void disp (NODE*first)
{
    NODE *temp;
    temp=first;
    while (temp!->next=NULL)
    {
        printf ("%dx^ %d+", temp->coeff, temp->power);
        temp=temp->next;
    }
    if(temp->power!=0)
        printf("%dx^ %d+", temp->coeff, temp->power);
    else
        printf("%d", temp->coeff);
}
NODE *addpoly(NODE *pa, NODE *pb)
{
    NODE *pc=NULL;
    int c, p;
    while (pa!=NULL&&pb!=NULL)
    {
        if (pa->power==pb->power)
        {
            c=pa->coeff + pb->coeff;
            p=pa->power;
            pa=pa->next; pb=pb->next;
        }
        else
        {
            if(pa->power > pb->power)
            {
```

```
                c=pa->coeff;
                p=pa->power;
                pa=pa->next;
            }
            else
            {
                c=pb->coeff;
                p=pb->power;
                pb=pb->next;
            }
        }
        pc=insert (pc, c, p);
    }
    while (pa!=NULL)
    {
        c=pa->coeff;
        p=pa->power;
        pa=pa->next;
        pc=insert (pc, p, c);
    }
    while (pb!=NULL)
    {
        c=pb->coeff;
        p=pb->power;
        pb=pb->next;
        pc=insert (pc, p, c);
    }
    return (pc);
}
NODE *insert (NODE *first, int c, int p)
{
    NODE *temp, *ptr;
```

```
        ptr=(NODE*) malloc(sizeof (NODE));
        ptr->coeff=c;
        ptr->power=p;
        ptr->next=NULL;
        if(first==NULL)
            first=ptr;
        else
        {
            temp=first;
            while (temp->next!=NULL)
                temp=temp->next;
            temp->next=ptr;
        }
        return (first);
}
```

Explanation:

1. The function create( ) creates a linked list of polynomial and returns address of the linked list. The create function is called twice in main to create and store two polynomials in linked lists a and b.

2. The addpoly( ) function adds the two polynomials and returns the address of third polynomial. For this we take three pointers pa, pb and pc; each points to the three linked lists of polynomials a, b and c (initially pc will be NULL). We start comparing the terms of first and second polynomial copy the terms in third polynomial as per the conditions mentioned and advance the pointers to next terms. To copy the term in third polynomial insert function is used.

3. The disp( ) function displays the polynomial stored in the linked list.

3.8 CIRCULAR LINKED LIST (CLL)

In singly linked list we can access the data only in forward direction. Given a pointer to a node in a singly linked list, we can access all the node which follow that node. But we can not access the previous node.

In circular linked list, we store the first node's address in the next field of last node, so that the list becomes circular. In this case, given a pointer to any node we can access all the nodes in the list.

Truly speaking circular linked list does not have first or last node. Any node can be treated as a first node and the node before it can be last. But as a convention and convenience we can have pointer to last node and the next will be first node.

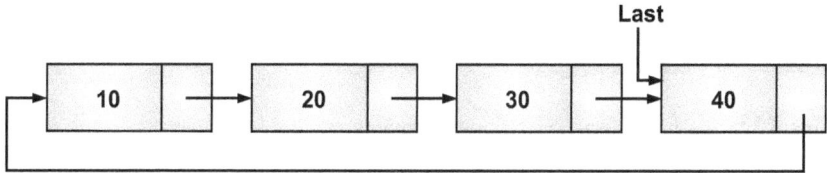

Fig. 3.25: Circular Linked List

Some of the algorithms where we need to frequently move in the forward or backward direction are easily implemented using circular linked list.

There can be different ways of implementation of CLL

Following program implements a circular linked list. The circular linked list is created in such a way that at every stage, the list will be circular, i.e., right from insertion of first node, the list will be circular. The rest of the operations insert, delete, search etc. will be similar to singly linked list.

Program 3.6: To implement Circular Linked List.

```
typedef struct node
{
    int data;
    struct NODE *next;
}   NODE;
NODE *create( )
{
    NODE *last, *ptr, *temp;
    int i, x, n;
    printf("Enter number of elements \n");
    scanf("%d", &n);
```

```
        last=NULL;
        for(i=1;i<n;i++)
        {
            printf("Enter data");
            scanf("%d", &x);
            ptr=(NODE *) malloc(sizeof (NODE));
            ptr->data=x;
            ptr->next=NULL;
            if(last==NULL)
                last=ptr;
            else
                last->next=ptr;
            ptr->next=last;
                last=ptr;
        }
        return (last);
}
void disp (NODE *last)
{
    NODE *temp;
    temp=last->next;
    while (temp!=last)
    {
        printf ("%d->", temp->data);
        temp=temp->next;
    }
    printf("%d", temp->data);          // Last element
}
void main( )
{
    NODE *last;
    last=create( )
    disp (last);
}
```

Explanation:
1. The pointer 'last' points to the last node in the list.
2. To create a list we start with last=NULL.
   Data is accepted stored in a node ptr.
   If it is first element last will point to it.
   Second element onward the node is linked to last and the next field is linked to first node which is nothing but
   last->next and the new node is made last.
3. To display, we start with first node (i.e. last->next) and advance till we reach the last node.

3.9 DOUBLY LINKED LIST

A doubly linked list is a set of linked nodes in which each node stores data as well as address of next and previous nodes. In singly linked list we can move only in forward direction. Doubly linked list allows us to move in both directions. Hence, given pointer to a node we can access any element which is either after the node or before the node. Some of the algorithm can be implemented with better time complexity using doubly linked list. But this list requires additional space in each node for storing previous node address. The implementation of the list is complex compared to singly linked list.

A node in the doubly linked list can be defined as below:

```
typedef struct node
{
    int data;
    struct node *next, *prev;
} NODE;
```

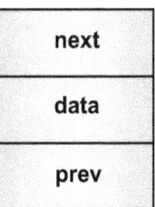

Fig. 3.26: NODE in a doubly linked list

The field data stores data element. The field next stores address of the next node and the field prey stores address of the previous node. A doubly linked list of integers is shown in Fig. 3.27.

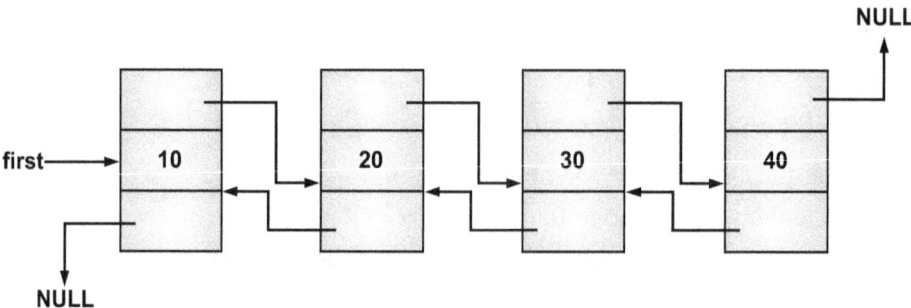

Fig. 3.27: Doubly linked list

Now let us discuss various operations on doubly linked list.
The node definition will be as follows:

```
typedef struct node
{
    int data;
    struct node *next, *prev;
}   NODE;
```

1. **Create:**

```
NODE *create( )
{
    NODE *first, *temp, *ptr;
    int i, n, x;
    first=NULL;
    printf("How many elements \n");
    scanf("%d", &n);
    for(i=1;i<=n;i++)
    {
        printf("Enter data \n");
        scanf("%d", &x);
        ptr=(NODE*)malloc(sizeof (NODE));  // Create a node
        ptr->next=ptr->prev NULL;
        ptr->data=x;  // Store data in node
        if (first==NULL)
            first=ptr;                    // if it is first node point first to it
```

```
        else
        {
            temp->next=ptr;     // Link previous node with new node (forward link)
            ptr->prev=temp;     // Link new node with previous node (backward link)
        }
        temp=ptr;               // Advance temp
    }
    return (first);
}
```

The process is shown in Figure 3.28.

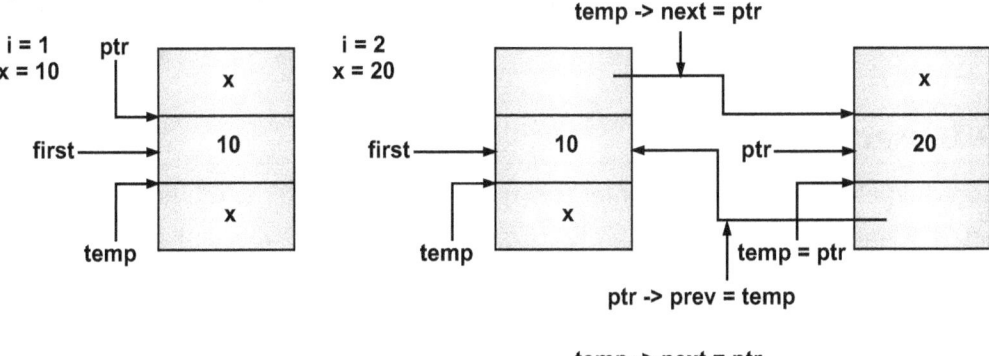

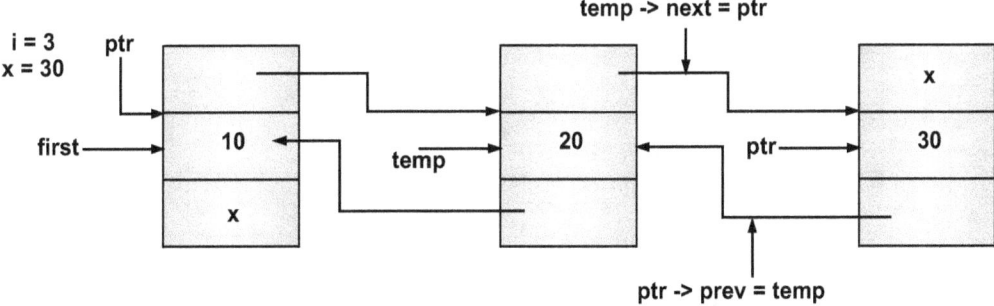

Fig. 3.28: Create procedure of DLL

2. **Display:**

```
void disp (NODE *first)
{
    NODE *temp;
    temp=first;
    printf("DLL in forward direction \n");
    while (temp->next!=NULL)
    {
```

```
            printf("%d->", temp->data);
            temp=temp->next;
    }
    printf("%d \n", temp->data);
    printf("DLL in reverse direction \n");

    while (temp!=NULL)
    {
            printf("%d<-", temp->data);
            temp=temp->prev;
    }
}
```

3.9.1 Insert Operation

To insert an element we get a pointer (say temp) to a node after which new element to be inserted. Then the new node (say ptr) links to temp in backward direction and the next node after temp in forward direction. It is shown in figure 3.29, where 30 is inserted in between 20 and 40.

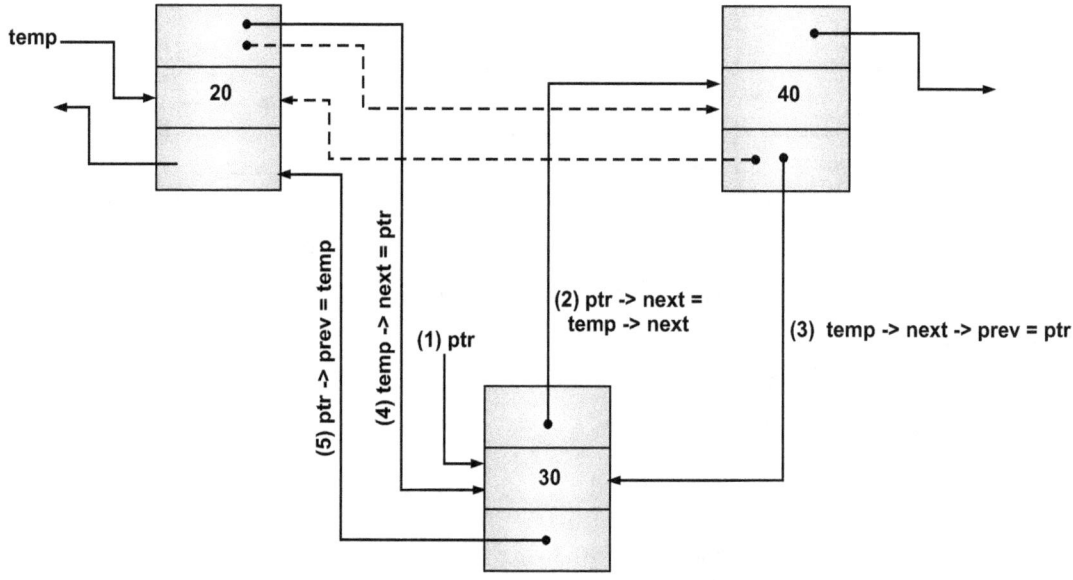

Fig. 3.29: Insert operation in DLL

It means during insert operation in DLL, four new links are created and two links are deleted. If we are inserting before first node, only two new links are established.

Algorithm 3.5: To insert a node in DLL.
1. Read p position where new node is to be inserted.
2. i=1;
3. temp= first;
4. while (i<p&&temp!= NULL)
   {
       temp=temp->next;
       i++;
   }
5. if (temp!=NULL)
   {
       Read x;
       ptr=malloc (sizeof (NODE))
       ptr->data=x;
       ptr->next=ptr->prev=NULL;
       if (p==0)   // Insertion before first node
       {
           ptr->next=temp;
           temp->prev=ptr;
           first=ptr;
       }
       else   // Insertion after first node
       {
           ptr->next=temp->next;
           temp->next->prev=ptr;
           temp->next=ptr;
           ptr->prev = temp;
       }
   }
   else
       printf("Invalid position");
6. stop.

3.9.2 Delete Operation

To delete node in DLL we get a pointer (say temp) to a node to be deleted. With the help of this pointer a node previous to temp and next to temp are linked to each other and temp is eliminated from the list. The operation is shown in figure 3.30.

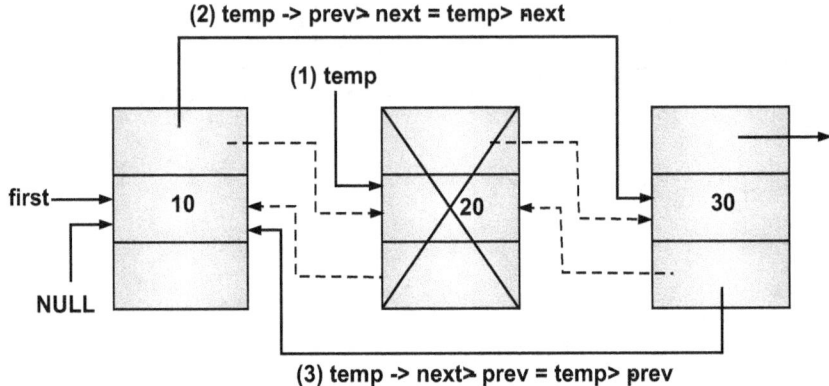

Fig. 3.30: Delete operation

It means during delete operation in DLL, two new links are established and four links are removed. If we are deleting first node, only two links are deleted.

Algorithm 3.6: To delete a node in DLL.
1. Read p
2. i=1.
3. temp=first
4. while (i<p&&temp!= NULL)
   {
       temp=temp->next;
       i++;
5. if (temp!==NULL)
   {
       if (p==1)   // First node
       {
           first=first->next;
           first->prev=NULL;

```
                free (temp);
        }
        else                                    // Any other node after first
        {
                temp->prev->next=temp->next;
                temp ->next->prev=temp->prev;
                free (temp);
        }
    }
    else
        printf("Invalid position");
6. stop.
```

3.9.3 Search Operation

To search an element, we start from the first node and keep on advancing in the list till we get the data at a particular node.

Algorithm 3.7: To search data in DLL.
1. Read s (data to be searched)
2. temp=first;
3. while (temp->data!=s&&temp!=NULL)
        temp=temp->next;
4. if (temp!=NULL)
        printf("Found");
   else
        printf("Not found");

3.9.4 Implementation of DLL

Now let us write a complete program to implement a DLL. The functions used in the program are:

1. **Create:** Creates a DLL and returns the address of first node.
   node *create_dll( );

2. **Display:** Displays the list in forward and reverse direction.
   void disp_dll(NODE*);
3. **Insert:** Inserts a new node in DLL and returns the address of first node.
   NODE *insert_dll(NODE*, int, int);
4. **Delete:** Deletes a node in DLL and returns the address of first node.
   NODE *del_dll(NODE*, int);
5. **Search:** Finds a node with given data and returns position of the node.
   int *search_dll(NODE*, int);

Program 3.7: To implement various operations on DLL.

```
typedef struct node
{
    int data;
    struct node *next, *prev;
}   NODE;
NODE *create_dll( );
void disp_dll(NODE *);
int search_dll(NODE*, int);
NODE *insert_dll (NODE*, int, int);
NODE *del_dll (NODE*, int);
void main( )
{
    NODE *first;
    int ch, x, p;
    do
    {
        clrscr( );
        printf 1. Create \n 2. Display \n 3. Search \n 4. Insert \n 5. Delete \n 6. Exit \n");
        printf ("Enter your choice \n");
        scanf("%d", &ch);
        switch (ch)
        {
            case 1:  first=create_dll( );
                     break;
            case 2:  disp_dll (first);
                     break;
```

```
            case 3:  printf("Enter number to be searched \n");
                     scanf("%d", &x);
                     p=search_dll (first, x);
                     if (p>0)
                         printf(Found at %d", p);
                     else
                         printf("not found");
            case 4:  printf("Enter data and position \n");
                     scanf("%d %d", &x, &p);
                     first=insert_dll (first, x, p);
            case 5:  printf("Enter node number \n");
                     scanf("%d", &p);
                     first=del_dll (first, p);
        }
        getch( );
    } while (ch!=6);
}
NODE *create_dll( )
{
    NODE *first, *temp, *ptr;
    int i, n, x;
    first=NULL;
    printf("How many elements? \n");
    scanf("%d", &n);
    for(i=1;i<=n;i++)
    {
        printf("Enter data \n"),
        scanf("%d", &x);
        ptr=(NODE*) malloc(sizeof (NODE));
        ptr->data=x;
        if (first==NULL)
            first=ptr;
        else
        {
            temp->next=ptr;
            ptr->prev=temp;
```

```
            }
            temp=ptr;
        }
        return (first);
}
void disp_dll(NODE *first)
{
    NODE *temp;
    temp=first;
    printf("DLL in forward direction \n");
    while (temp->next!=NULL)
    {
        printf("%d->", temp->data);
        temp=temp->next;
    }
    printf("%d \n", temp->data);
    printf("DLL in reverse direction \n")
    while (temp!=NULL)
    {
        printf("%d<-", temp->data);
        temp=temp->prev;
    }
}
int search_dll(NODE *first, int x)
{
    NODE *temp;
    int i=1;
    temp=first;
    while (temp->data!=x&&temp!=NULL)
    {
        temp=temp->next;
        i++;
    }
    if (temp!=NULL)
        return (i);
    else
```

```
        return (-1);
}
NODE *insert_dll(NODE first, int p, int x)
{
    NODE *temp, *ptr;
    int i;
    i=1;
    temp=first;
    while (i<p&&temp!=NULL)
    {
        temp=temp->next;
        i++;
    }
    if (temp!=NULL)
    {
        ptr=(NODE*) malloc (sizeof (NODE));
        ptr->data=x;
        ptr->prev=ptr->next=NULL;
        if (p==0)
        {
            first->prev ptr;
            ptr->next=first;
            first=ptr;
        }
        else
        {
            ptr->next=temp ->next;
            temp->next->prev=ptr;
            temp->next=ptr;
            ptr->prev=temp;
        }
    }
    else
        printf("Invalid position");
    return (first);
}
```

```c
NODE *delete_dll(NODE *first, int p)
{
    NODE *temp, *ptr;
    int i;
    i=1;
    temp=first;
    while (i<p&&temp!=NULL)
    {
        temp=temp->next;
        i++;
    }
    if (temp!=NULL)
    {
        if (p==1)
        {
            first=first->next;
            first->prev=NULL;
        }
        else
        {
            temp->prev->next=temp->next;
            temp->next->prev=temp->prev;
            free (temp);
        }
    }
    else
        printf("Invalid position");
    return (first);
}
```

3.10 COMPARISON OF SINGLY LINKED, CIRCULARLY LINKED AND DOUBLY LINKED LIST

Singly linked list	Doubly linked list	Circular linked list
1. It consist of nodes having single link to next data.	1. It consist of nodes having double link one to next node and other to previous node.	1. It consists of last node whose next field stores address of first node.
2. Given a pointer p to a node one can only traverse in forward direction.	2. Given a pointer p to a node one can traverse in both forward and backward direction.	2. Given pointer P to a node one can access node.
3. Implementation is simple.	3. Implementation is complex.	3. Implementation is complex compared to SLL.
4. Delete operation requires two pointers.	4. Delete operation requires one pointer.	4. Delete operation requires two pointers.
5. Used in application where you need to access elements sequentially.	5. Used in application where traversal in both direction is required.	5. Used in application where nodes may be traversed frequently.

3.11 GENERALISATION LINKED LIST

A Generalization Link List is a list of elements $G_1, G_2, G_3, \ldots G_n$. Where $n >= 0$ and G_1 is either an element or a sublist. It is denoted by G. The length of list is n if there are n elements.

Suppose we are given a list G = (a, b, (c, d), e). The question is how to represent this list using linked list? We have to think of a node structure to store the elements in the list at the same time we should be able to distinguish the sublists in the list. Following is representation of the list;

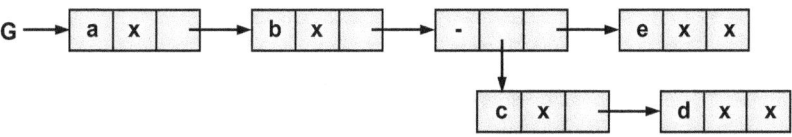

Fig. 3.31: Generalized linked list G = (a, b, (c, d), e)

Thus, each node in the above list consists of three fields:
1. **Data field:** To store data.
2. **Down pointer:** To store address of sublist.
3. **Next pointer:** To store address of next element.

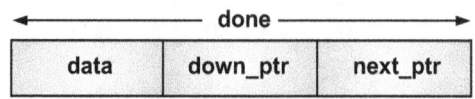

Fig. 3.32: Node in GLL

Note that in the above list, the field down ptr can be shared with data field because when we are using data field down ptr is NULL and when down ptr is used data field is blank. Hence, above list representation can be optimized as,

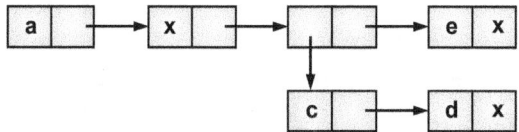

Fig. 3.33: Generalised linked list G = (a, b, (c, d), e)

The node definition for this list will be as follows:

typedef struct node
{
   union un
   {
      char data;
      struct node *down_ptr;
   }u1;
   struct node *next_ptr;
}NODE;

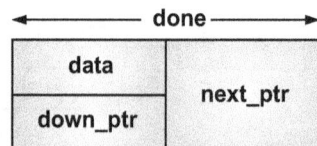

Fig. 3.34: Node in GLL with sharing of fields

Note that we are using union to share the fields data and down_ptr.

3.11.1 Representation of Polynomials

One of the usages of generalized linked list is representation of polynomials in several variables. We have seen that a polynomial with single variable can be represented using singly linked list. Similarly, a polynomial with multiple variables can be represented using GLL.

Consider a polynomial given below:
$$p(x, y, z) = 4x^3 + y^2z + 5x^3y^2z^2 + 6x^3yz$$

This polynomial is required to be rearranged as below:
$$p(x, y, z) = x^3 [4y^2z + 5y^2z^2 + 6yz]$$
$$= x^3 [y^2 (4z + 5z^2) + y (6z)]$$

This suggests that the list in which above polynomial is to be stored will have 3 levels. First level will represent terms containing x, second level will have terms containing y and the third level will have terms containing z.

The node structure will consist of the following fields:
1. **Variable / coefficient:** To store variable name or coefficient.
2. **Exponent (power):** To store power of corresponding variable.
3. **Down ptr:** To store address of sublist.
4. **Next ptr:** To store address of next item.

The Polynomial will be represented as follows:

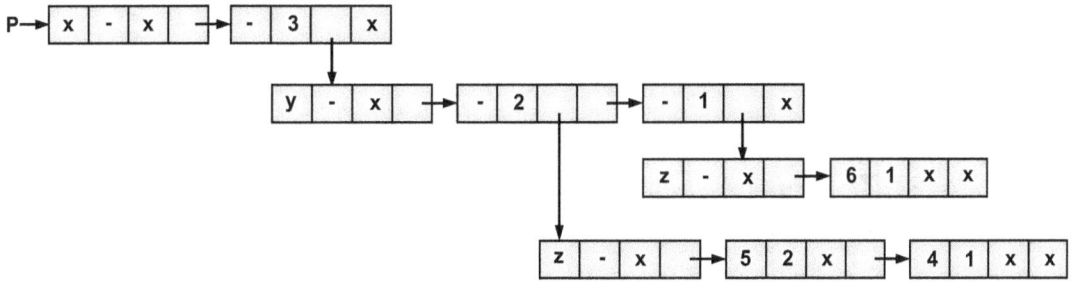

**Fig. 3.35: Polynomial representation using GLL P(x, y, z) = x^3 (y^2 (4z + 5z^2) + y (6z)]

The first level has nodes containing variable x (i.e. x^3). The second level has nodes containing variable y (i.e. y^2 and y). The third level has terms containing variable z (i.e. 6z associated with y and $5z^2$ and 4z associated with y^2).

In the above representation, only the first field is shared by variable and coefficient. Some of the fields in above representation can be shared, e.g. variable and power and coefficient and down_ptr. But then we should have a mechanism to identify the field usage for a particular node. Hence, we can add one more field called tag and the new node structure will be as shown in figure 3.36.

Tag	Variable	Coefficient	next_ptr
	Power	down_ptr	

Fig. 3.36: Node in GLL for Polynomial

       Tag = 0   when coefficient is used.
and Tag = 1   when down_ptr or next_ptr is used.

The node definition will be as:
```
struct node
{
    int tag;
    union vp
    {
        char var;
        int power;
    }u1;
    union cd
    {
        int coeff;
        struct node *down_ptr;
    }u2;
    struct node*next_ptr;
}NODE;
```

The revised GLL representation will be as shown in figure 3.37.

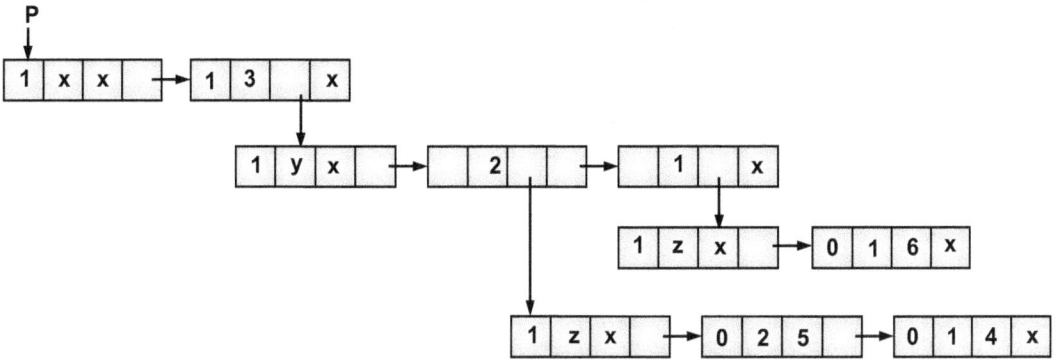

Fig. 3.37: Polynomial representation using GLL
with tag field $p(x, y, z) = x^3 [y^2 (4z + 5z^2) + y (6z)]$

Example:

Draw the generalised linked list for following polynomial.

$3x^{10}y^3z^2 + 5x^8y^3z^2 + 7x^8y^2z^2 + x^4y^4z + 6x^3y^4z + 9yz$

Solution: Given:

$$p(x, y, z) = 3x^{10}y^3z^2 + 5x^8y^3z^2 + 7x^8y^2z^2 + x^4y^4z + 6x^3y^4z + 9yz$$
$$= z^2 (3x^{10}y^3 + 5x^8y^3 + 7x^8y^2) + z (x^4y^4 + 6x^3y^4 + 9y)$$

$\therefore \quad p(x, y, z) = z^2 [y^3 (3x^{10} + 5x^8) + y^2 (7x^8)] + z [y^4(x^4 + 6x^3) + y (9x^0)]$

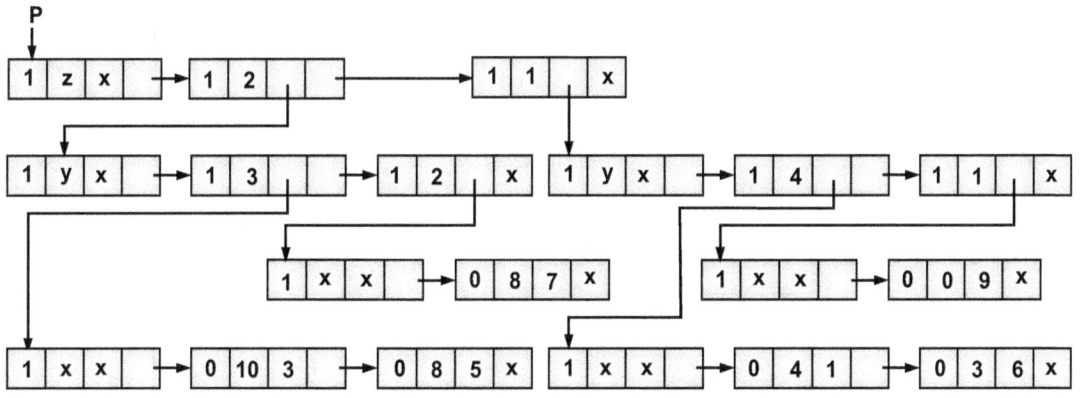

Fig. 3.38: Polynomial representation using
GLL $p(x, y, z) = z^2 [y^3 (3x^{10} + 5x^8) + y^2 (7x^8)] + z [(y^4 (x^4 + 6x^3) + y (9x^0)]$

Note: You can exclude the tag field and draw the linked list.

Example: Represent following polynomial using GLL and give node structure also.

$$[(x^{12} + 2x^9) y^4 + (4x^9) y^2] z^3 + [(x^5 + 6x^3) y^5 + 3y] z$$

Solution: The node structure will be as shown in Fig. 3.36.

```
struct node
{
    int tag;
    union vp
    {
        char var
        int power;
    }u1;
    union cd
    {
        int coeff;
        struct node *down_ptr;
    }u2;
    struct node*next_ptr;
}NODE;
```

The GLL representation will be as shown in Fig. 3.39.

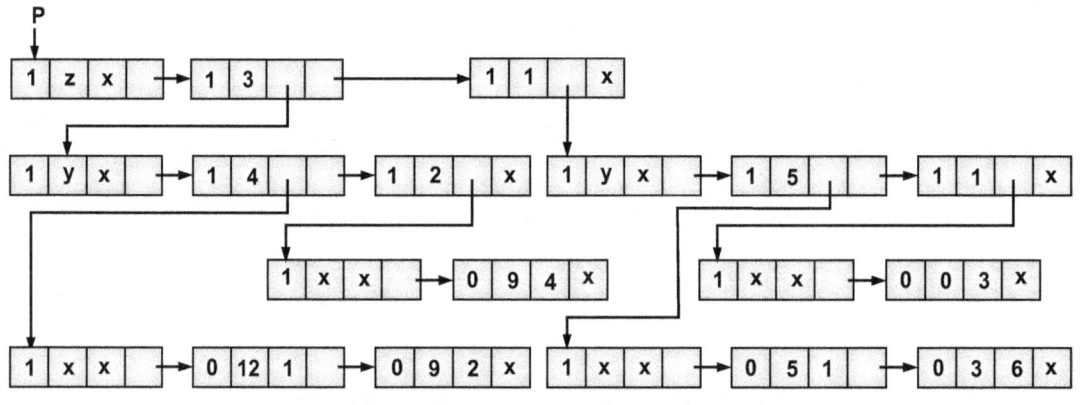

Fig. 3.39: Polynomial representation using
GLL $[(x^{12} + 2x^9) y^4 + (4x^9) y^2] z^3 + [(x^5 + 6x^3) y^5 + 3y]z$

Example: Represent the following using GLL. Explain the node structure of GLL.

$3x^2y^2z + 8xyz + 5x^2yz^2 + 8xyz^2 + 3x^2y^2z^2$.

Solution: $x^2 (y^2 (3z + 3z^2) + y (5z^2)) + x (y (8z + 8z^2))$

Hence, the representation will be,

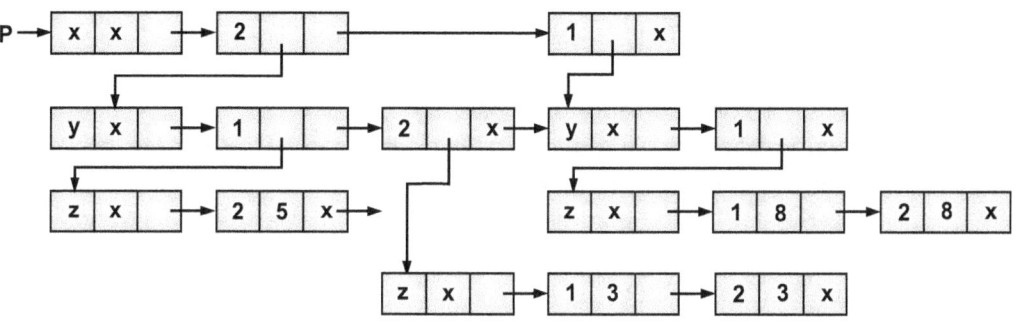

Fig. 3.40

Example: Represent the following polynomial using GLL

$x^2 [y^2 (3z + 5)] + x[y^3 (4z)]$

Solution:

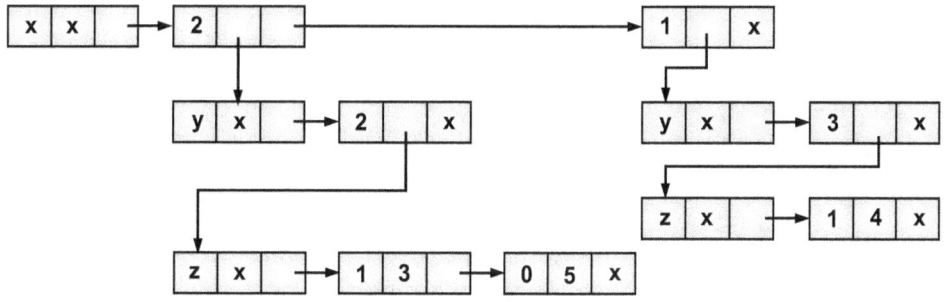

Fig. 3.41

SUMMARY

- Linked list is linear, dynamic data structure in which elements are stored in nodes which are connected to each other. Each node in the linked list consists of data field and address field.
- Singly linked list (SLL) consists of set of nodes which have single address field which stores the address of next node. SLL can be traversed in forward direction only.
- Doubly linked list (DLL) consists of set of nodes with two address fields for string address of previous and next node. The DLL can be traversed in both directions.
- A polynomial can be stored in linked list with coefficient and power of each term being stored in each node along with address of next node.
- Addition of two polynomials stored in two linked lists can be carried out by accessing each term in the linked lists sequentially.
- A Circular Linked List (CLL) stores address of first node in the next field of last node.
- Linked list can be used for information storage and retrieval, storage management and implementation of stacks and queues etc.
- A Generalized Linked List (GLL) consists of elements which themselves can be sub-list.
- A Generalized Linked List (GLL) can be used to store polynomial with multiple variables.

SOLVED PROBLEMS

1. **Write a function to reverse a Singly Linked List without creating new node or swapping data.**

Solution:

```
NODE *reverse(NODE *first)
{
    NODE *p1,*p2,*p3;        // Take three pointers to point to 3 successive nodes
    p1=NULL;
    p2=first;                // Initialize
    p3=first->next;
    while(p2!=NULL)          // while it is not end of list
    {
        p2->next=p1;         // link middle's next to first
        p1=p2;               // advance first to middle.
        p2=p3;               // advance middle to last
        if(p3!=NULL)
            p3=p3->next;     // advance p3 to next node
    }
    return(p1);
}
```

2. **Write a function to merge two Singly Linked Lists.**
Solution:
```
NODE *merge(NODE *p, NODE *q)
{
    NODE *pc NULL, *temp;
    if(p!=NULL)
    {
        temp=pc=p;
        p=p->next;
    }
    else
    {
        if(q!=NULL)
        {
            temp=pc=q;
            q=q ->next;
        }
    }
    while (p!=NULL&&q!=NULL)
    {
        temp->next=q;
        q=q->next;
        temp=temp->next;
        temp->next=p;
        p=p->next;
        temp=temp->next;
    }
    while (p!=NULL)
    {
        temp->next=pa;
        p=p->next;
        temp=temp->next;
    }
    while (q!=NULL).
    {
        temp->next=q;
        q=q->next;
        temp=temp->next;
    }
    return(pc);
}
```

3. Write a C function to delete a node in DLL pointed by P.
Solution:
```
NODE *delete_dll(NODE *first, NODE *p)
{
    NODE *temp;
    temp=p;
    if(temp!=NULL)
    {
        if (temp==first)          // For first nude
        {
            first=first->next;
            first->prev=NULL;
        }
        else
        {
            temp->prev->next=temp->next;
            temp ->next->prev=temp ->prev;
            free (temp);
        }
    }
    else
        printf("List empty");
    return (first);
}
```

4. Write a C function to delete a node in DLL with value x.   [May 09]
Solution:
```
NODE *delete-dil(NODE *first, int x)
{
    NODE *temp;
    temp=first;
    while(temp->data!=x&&temp!=NULL)
        temp=temp->next;
    if(temp!=NULL)
    {
        if (temp==first)                  // For first node
        {
            first=first->next;
            first->Prev=NULL;
        }
```

```
        else
        {
            temp->prev->next=temp->next;
            temp->next->prev=temp->prev;
            free (temp);
        }
    }
    else
        printf("Data not found");
    return (first);
}
```

5. Create a linked list of person having name, age and salary.

Hint: The node definition will be as follows:

```
typedef struct node
{
    char name [20];
    int age;
    float sal;
    struct NODE*next;
}   NODE;
NODE *first;
```

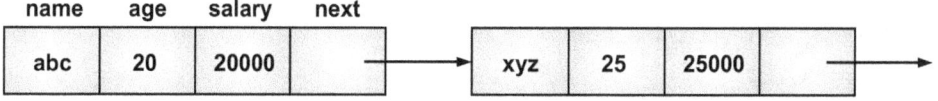

Fig. 3.42: Nodes in a linked list of records

6. Write a C function to delete all nodes in a SLL.
Solution:
```
void del_all(NODE *first)
{
    NODE *temp;
    temp=first;             // Start with first node
    while (temp!=NULL)      // not end of list
    {
        first=first->next;  // Advance first
```

```
            free (temp);        // delete node
            temp=first;         // Advance temp
        }
    }
```

7. **Write a 'C' function to add two binary numbers using doubly linked list (DLL).**

Solution:

```
NODE *add(NODE *l1, NODE *l2)
{
    int d1, d2, d3, c, r;
    NODE *l3=NULL, *ptr;
    while (l1->next!=NULL)      // go to LSB next;
        l1=l1->next;
    while (l2->next!=NULL)      //go to LSB
        l2=l2->next;
    c=0,
    while (l1 != NULL&&l2!= NULL)
    {
        d1=l1->data;
        l1=prev;
        d2=l2->data;
        l2=l2->prev;
        r=(d1 + d2 + c)/2;
        c=(d1 + d2 + c)/2;
        ptr=(NODE *)malloc(size of (NODE));
        ptr->data=r;
        ptr->next=ptr->prev=NULL;
        if(l3==NULL)
            l3=ptr;
        else
        {
            temp->prev=ptr;
            ptr->next=temp;
        }
        temp=ptr;
    }
    return (l3);
}
```

Explanation:

(a) The two binary numbers are stored in two DLL's *l*1 and *l*2.

(b) The two DLL's are traversed from last to first node adding each binary digit and storing the result in third DLL which gets created the same way a DLL is created but in reverse order (last node to first node).

(c) *l*3 points to the last node that is LSB.

8. Write a 'C' function to sort doubly linked list (DLL). Explain with example.

Solution:

```
NODE *sort(NODE *first)
{
    NODE *temp, *last;
    int t
    temp=first;
    while(temp->next!=NULL)
        temp=temp->next;
    last=temp;
    while(last!=first)
    {
        temp=first;
        while(temp!=last)
        {
            if(temp->data>temp->next->data)
            {
                t=temp->data,
                temp->data=temp->next->data
                temp->next->data=t;
            }
            temp temp->next;
        }
        last last->prev;
    }
    return (*first);
}
```

9. **Write a function in 'C' to delete the node of DLL with data value x.**

Solution:
```
NODE *del(NODE *first, int x)
{
    NODE *temp;
    temp=first;
    while(temp->data!=x&&temp NULL)
        temp=temp->next;
    if(temp != NULL)
    {
        temp->prev->next=temp->next;
        temp->next->prev=temp->prev;
        free(temp);
    }
    else
        printf("Not found");
}
```

10. **Give a node structure for singly linked list. Write a function in 'C' to add a node in SLL which is maintained in ascending order of numeric value. Function should handle:**
   (i)   Insertion at the beginning.
   (ii) Insertion at the end.
   (iii) Insertion in the middle.

Solution:
```
NODE structure
typedef struct node
{
    int data;
    struct node *next;
}   NODE;
NODE *insert(NODE *first, int x)
{
    NODE *temp, *ptr, *prev;
    temp=first;
```

```
        while(temp->data <- x)
        {
            prey=temp;
            temp=temp->next;
        }
        ptr=(NODE *)malloc(size of (NODE));
        ptr->data=x;
        ptr->next=NULL
        if(temp==first)                    // Insert at beginning
        {
            ptr->next=temp;
            first=ptr;
        }
        else                               // Insert in middle for end
        {
            ptr->next temp->next;
            prev->next=ptr
        }
        return(first);
    }
```

11. Write a function to delete a node pointed by p from DLL. Also write a function in 'C' to insert a new node after a node which is pointed by p.

Solution:
```
    void insert(NODE *p, NODE *q)
    {
        q->next p->next;
        p->next->prey=q;
        p->next q;
        q->prev p;
    }
```

12. Write a recursive function to count number of nodes in DLL or SLL.

Solution:
```
    int count(NODE *first)
    {
        if(first==NULL)
            return (0);
        else
            return(1+count (first->next));
    }
```

13. Write a C program to sort a given linked list and display the sorted linked list.
Solution:

```c
typedef struct node
{
    int data;
    struct node *next;
} NODE;
void main( )
{
    NODE *first, *temp, *ptr;
    int i, n, x;
    printf("Enter number of elements \n");
    scanf("%d", &n);
    first=NULL;
    for(i=1; i<n; i++)
    {
        printf("Enter data \n");
        scanf("%d", &x);
        ptr=(NODE *)malloc(size of (NODE));
        ptr->data=x;
        ptr->next=NULL;
        if(first==NULL)
            first=ptr;
        else
            temp->next=ptr;
        temp=ptr;
    }
    temp=first;
    for(i=1;i<=n-1;i++)
    {
        temp1=temp->next;
        for(j=i+1;j<=n;j++)
        {
            if(temp->data > temp1->data)
            {
                t=temp->data;
                temp->data=temp1->data;
                temp1->data=t;
```

```
            }
                temp1=temp1->next;
            }
            temp=temp->next;
        }
        printf("Sorted list is \n");
        temp=first;
        while(temp != NULL)
        {
            printf("%d->", temp->data);
            temp=temp->next;
        }
    }
```

14. Compare Singly liked list with Doubly linked list and Circular linked list.
Solution:

Singly linked list	Doubly linked list	Circular linked list
1. It consist of nodes having single link to next data.	1. It consist of nodes having double link one to next node and other to previous node.	1. It consists of last node whose next field stores address of first node.
2. Given a pointer p to a node one can only traverse in forward direction.	2. Given a pointer p to a node one can traverse in both forward and backward direction.	2. Given pointer P to a node one can access node.
3. Implementation is simple.	3. Implementation is complex.	3. Implementation is complex compared to SLL.
4. Delete operation requires two pointers.	4. Delete operation requires one pointer.	4. Delete operation requires two pointers.
5. Used in application where you need to access elements sequentially.	5. Used in application where traversal in both direction is required.	5. Used in application where nodes may be traversed frequently.

15. Write a C function to delete all nodes in SLL.
Solution:
```
    void del_all(NODE *first)
    {
        NODE *temp;
```

```
        temp=first;
        while(temp!=NULL);
        {
            first=first->next;
            free(temp);
            temp=first;
        }
    }
```

16. Write a C function to delete all nodes in SLL after the node pointed by p.
Solution:
```
    void del(NODE *p)
    {
        NODE *temp;
        temp=p;
        while(temp!=NULL);
        {
            p=p->next;
            free(temp);
            temp=p;
        }
    }
```

17. Write a function in 'C' to insert a node in sorted singly linked list, so that after insertion the list remains sorted. Consider all cases of insertion.
Solution:
```
    NODE *insert(NODE *first, int x)
    {
        NODE *ptr, *temp, *prey;
        ptr=(NODE *)malloc(size of(NODE));
        ptr->data=x;
        ptr->next=NULL;
        temp=first;
        if(temp==NULL)                       // If the list is empty
            first=ptr;
        else                                 // not empty
        {
            if(temp->data>x)   // if data at current node is greater
            {
                ptr->next=temp;
                first=ptr;                   // Insert
```

```
        }
        else
        {
            while(temp->data<=x)          // If data at current node is smaller
            {
                prev=temp;                // move forward
                temp=temp->next;
            }
            prev->next=ptr;               // Insert
            ptr->next=temp;
        }
    }
    return(first);
}
```

EXERCISE

1. Write a program to count number of nodes in a link list.
2. Write a program to sort the elements in a linked list.
3. Write a program to reverse a linked list.
4. Write difference between array and linked list.
5. What is the need of linked list? Explain any one application of DLL with suitable example.
6. Write a function for following operations in SLL.
   (i) Display the elements.   (ii) Search an element.
7. Write a C function to add a node in doubly linked list at any position.
8. Write a C function to delete a node from doubly linked list from any position.
9. Give a 'C' declaration for a node structure for declaring a DLL.
10. Write a function for following operations in DLL.
    (i) Display the elements.   (ii) Search an element.
11. Write a C function to delete a node from doubly linked list from any position.
12. Write a pseudo-code to delete a node in DLL at any position.
13. Write a function in 'C' to delete a node from DLL without using any additional pointer.
14. What are the different ways to represent polynomial in single variable?
15. Write a C function for insertion of a node in circular linked list at any position.
16. Explain what do you mean by circular linked list.

17. What is CLL? Explain any one application of CLL.
18. What is circular linked list? Explain any one application of CLL.
19. What is circular linked list? What are advantages of CLL?
20. What is CLL? Write a function to create a circular linked list.
21. Write a pseudo-c code for addition of two polynomials using SLL.
22. Write a function in 'C' to invert the singly linked list.
23. Write a C function to reverse a singly linked list.
24. Write a function in 'C' to invert SLL without creating new node and without swapping data. Assume the list contains numerical data.
25. Consider a linked list which is pointed by pointer P having nodes $P_1, P_2, \ldots P_n$. Consider another linked list pointed by pointer Q having nodes $Q_1, Q_2, \ldots Q_n$. Write a function in 'C' to merge the above two linked lists in the third list having nodes $P_1, Q_1, P_2, Q_2, \ldots P_n, Q_n$.

    No additional memory allocation should be done while merging. Size of 2 linked lists could be different.
26. Let p be a pointer to head node of one SLL and q be a pointer to head node of second SLL. Write a function in 'C' to merge the two SLL's as shown below.

    $p_1 \rightarrow q_1, p_2 \rightarrow q_2, \ldots, p_n \rightarrow q_n$
27. Write a function to merge two sorted, linked lists.
28. Write a C function to insert a node in DLL after the node pointed by p.
29. Write a function in 'C' to delete a node of doubly linked list where 'P' denotes the pointer to the node to be deleted.
30. Write a function in 'C' to delete a node of doubly linked list where 'P' denotes the pointer to the node to be deleted.
31. Write a function to delete a node in DLL pointed by p.
32. Write a non-recursive function in 'C' to delete all nodes in SLL pointed by p.
33. Write a function to create sorted linked list.
34. Write a program to sort the elements in a linked list.
35. Write a C function to create a SLL for storing list of persons with name and age. State the node structure also.
36. Write a short note on generalised linked list.

Unit IV
TREES

4.1 INTRODUCTION

Till now we have seen data structures such as arrays, linked lists, stacks, queues, etc. All these are linear data structures. The data is stored in sequential locations. In order to retrieve data, we have to traverse in sequence. For large amount of data this kind of access is not efficient because, time complexity of retrieval in such data structures will be poor, i.e. O(n).

If we arrange the data in hierarchical manner, we can have more than one successor of a data element as shown in Fig. 4.1.

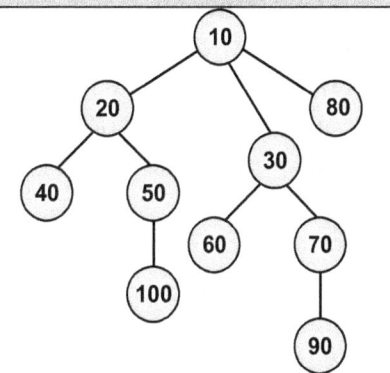

Fig. 4.1: Tree

Such a structure is called tree. There are number of applications in computer science where we can use this data structure. A tree can be defined in several ways.

Definition 1:

A tree (T) is a set of nodes. The set can be empty. If its nonempty set it consists of a specially designated node called root node and zero or more (sub) trees $T_1, T_2, T_3, \ldots, T_n$, each of whose roots are connected by a directed edge from the root of T.

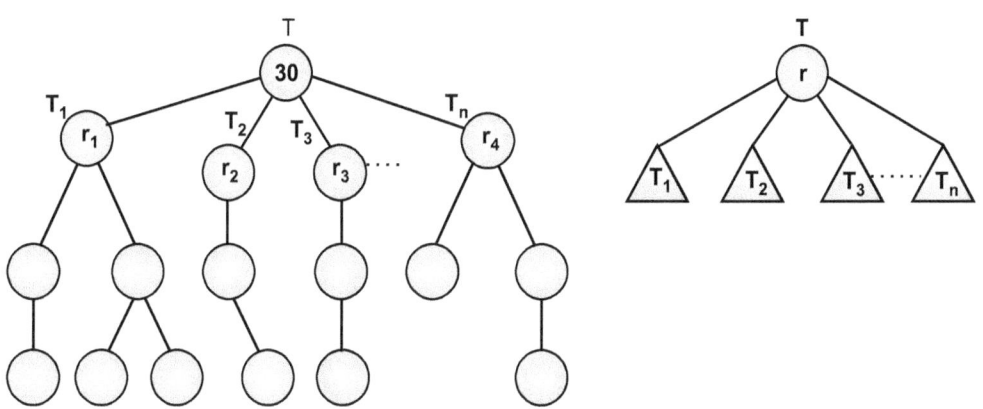

Fig. 4.2: Tree definition

Definition 2:
A tree consists of finite set of elements called nodes and a finite set of directed lines called branch edges that connect the nodes.

4.2 BASIC TERMINOLOGY

There are number of terms used with tree. Let us see the definition of each of them.
1. **Node:** It stands for item of information plus the branches to other items.
2. **Degree:** The total number of edges associated with a node is called degree of that node.
3. **Indegree:** The total number of edges converging a node is called indegree of the node. Root node will have indegree 0.
4. **Outdegree:** The total number of edges diverging from a node is called outdegree of the node.
5. **Leaf node or Terminal node:** The nodes that have outdegree zero are called leaf node or terminal node.
6. **Non-terminals:** The nodes which have nonzero outdegree are called nonterminals.
7. **Children:** The root nodes of the sub-tree of a node are called children of that node, i.e., they are immediate successors of node.
8. **Parent Node:** If A is child of B then B is the parent node of A, i.e., it is immediate predecessor of a node.
9. **Siblings:** Children of the same parent are called siblings.
10. **Degree of a tree:** It is maximum degree of a node in the tree.
11. **Ancestor nodes:** Ancestors of a node are all the nodes along the path from the root to that node.
12. **Level of a node:** Root node of a tree is said to be at level 1. Its children will be at level 2. In general, the node at level l will have its children at level $l + 1$.
13. **Height or depth of tree:** It is the maximum level of any node in the tree.
14. **Forest:** It is a set of disjoint trees, i.e., these trees will not have common node amongst them. Let us draw a tree and represent these terms.

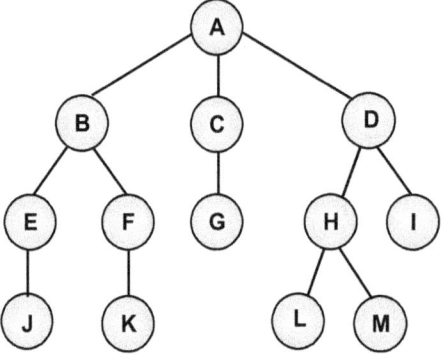

Fig. 4.3: Tree

Observation:

1. Total degree of A ⇒ 3
2. Indegree of H ⇒ 1
3. Out-degree of H ⇒ 2
4. Leaf nodes ⇒ J, K, G, L, M, I
5. Non-terminal ⇒ A, B, C, D, E, F, H
6. Children of B ⇒ E, F
7. Parent node of J ⇒ E
8. Siblings ⇒ {B, C,D}, {E, F}, {H, I} {L, M}
9. Ancestors of J ⇒ E, B, A
10. Degree of Tree ⇒ 3
11. Level of H ⇒ 3
12. Height of Tree ⇒ 4
13. Forest: if we remove root A of the tree we get set of three trees which is a forest.

The tree can be represented in a linked list format, where each node in the tree will be as:

Data	Link 1	Link 2	......	Link 4

For a general tree there are no restrictions on the number of sub-trees. The data field will store the information. The link fields will store the addresses of children of the node. Now the question is how many link fields should be defined? It is going to depend on maximum number of branches a node can have. Hence, it is very difficult to create a general tree. Binary trees are used in most of the applications where the number of branches will be fixed to 2. Hence, we will restrict our study to binary trees.

4.3 BINARY TREE

A binary tree is a tree in which no node has more than two sub-trees. It means any node can have at most two branches. i.e., there is no node with degree greater than two.

Definition:

A binary tree is a finite set of nodes which is either empty or consists of root and two disjoint binary trees called left sub-tree and right sub-tree.

Following are examples of binary trees.

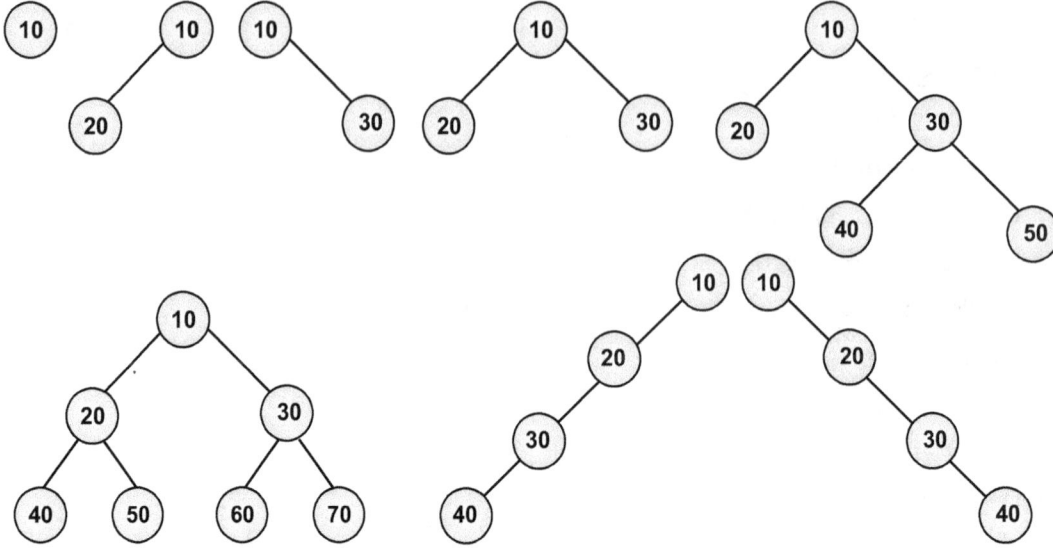

Fig. 4.4: Binary trees

The maximum number of nodes in a binary tree will be $2^h - 1$ where h is height of the tree. The number of leaf nodes in the binary tree will be 2^{h-1}.

Depending on how the nodes are placed in the binary, we can have following types of binary tree.

1. Complete binary tree:

If the height of binary tree is h and there are 2^{h-1} node at least level, then it is complete binary tree. Following are examples of complete binary tree. It is also called full binary tree.

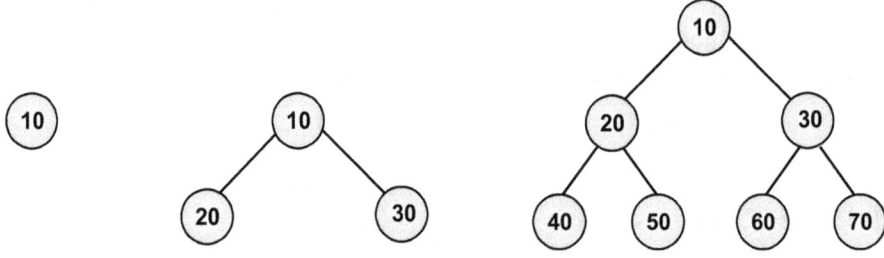

Fig. 4.5: Complete binary tree

2. Almost complete binary tree:
If the height of binary tree is h, then the binary tree is said to be almost complete if
  (i) The leaf nodes are at level h or h − 1.
  (ii) There is no leaf node at level h − 2 i.e., at h − 2 level every node has two children.
  (iii) At level h the leaf nodes are as far to the left as possible.

Following are examples of almost complete binary tree.

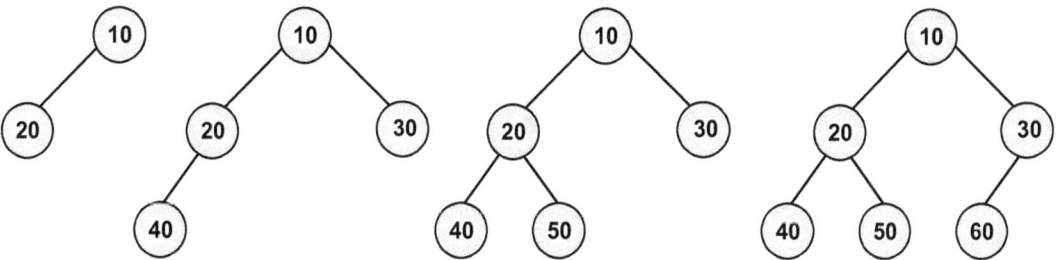

Fig. 4.6: Almost complete binary tree

3. Left skewed binary tree:

If the nodes in a binary tree have only left child it is called left skewed binary tree.

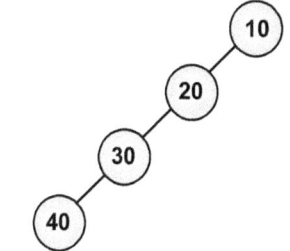

Fig. 4.7: Left skewed binary tree

4. Right skewed binary tree:

If the nodes in a binary tree have only right child it is called right skewed binary tree.

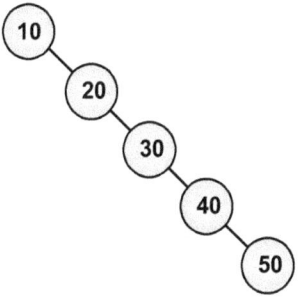

Fig. 4.8: Right skewed binary tree

5. Strictly binary tree:

It is a binary tree in which each node will have either two children or no child. Examples of strictly binary tree are shown in Fig. 4.9.

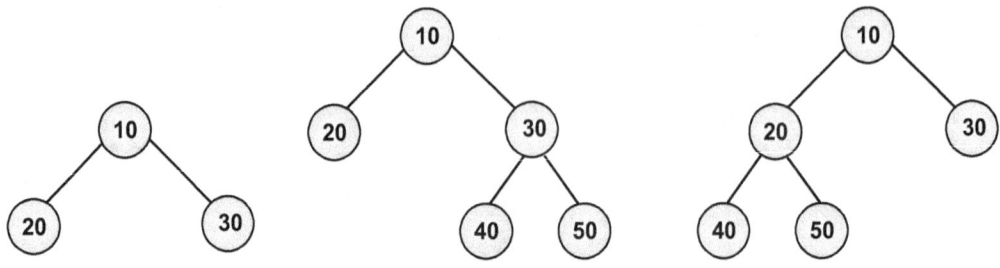

Fig. 4.9: Strictly binary tree

4.3.1 Representation of Binary Tree

A binary tree can be represented using arrays or linked lists.

The array representation of binary tree is very simple for implementations where each node in binary tree will be stored in the array sequentially. Consider a complete binary tree as shown in Fig. 4.10.

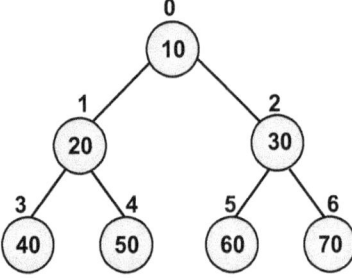

Fig. 4.10: Binary tree

The nodes are designated by numbers which can be used as location number of the element in the array for example, the element 30 will be stored a[2]. The array representation of above binary tree is shown in Fig. 4.11.

a[0]	a[1]	a[2]	a[3]	a[4]	a[5]	a[6]
10	20	30	40	50	60	70

Fig. 4.11: Array representation of binary tree in Fig. 4.10

Observe that if an element is at i^{th} location, its left child will be at $(2i+1)^{th}$ location and right child will be at $(2i+2)^{th}$ location.

But, if we have binary tree which is not complete binary tree or almost complete binary tree most of the space in the array will be unutilized. For example, if we have a binary tree as shown in Fig. 4.12.

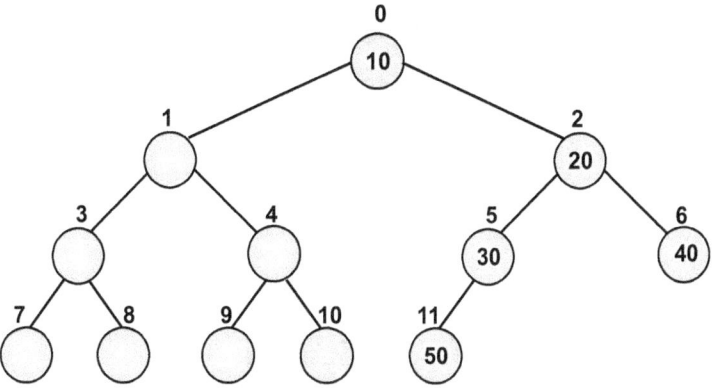

Fig. 4.12: Binary tree

Its array representation will be

a[0]	a[1]	a[2]	a[3]	a[4]	a[5]	a[6]	a[7]	a[8]	a[9]	a[10]	a[11]	a[12]
10	–	20	–	–	30	40	–	–	–	–	50	–

Fig. 4.13: Array representation of binary tree in figure 4.12

It is not only wastage of space, the insertion or deletion of node is also going to cause lot of movements. These problems can be eliminated using linked representation.

In linked representation, each node will be having three fields viz., data, lchild and rchild. The data field is information to be stored. It can be int, float, char, array or records. The two field's lchild and rchild will be pointers storing the addresses of left sub-tree and right sub-tree.

The node structure can be defined as

    typedef struct node
    {
        int data;
        struct node *lchild, *rchild;
    } NODE;

The node will be as shown in Fig. 4.14.

Fig. 4.14: Node in a binary tree

The binary tree in node structure will be as shown in Fig. 4.15.

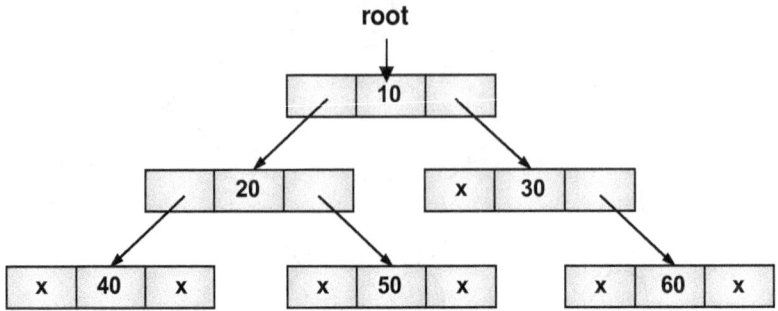

Fig. 4.15: Linked list representation of binary tree

4.3.2 Binary Tree Traversal

Once a binary tree is created the major operation that we will be required to do will be traversal of the tree. Traversing a tree means, visiting each node in the tree exactly once.

While traversing a binary tree, if we are at-a particular node there are six different ways in which we can move. They **LVR, VLR, LRV, RVL, VRL** and **RLV**. Where **V** is visit the node or access data, **L** move to left and **R**-move to right. There is a standard conversation that we should move to left first before right. Hence, there are only three standard traversals **LVR, VLR** and **LRV**.

LVR is called in order traversal where left sub-tree is processed first then root and finally right sub-tree. **VLR** is called preorder traversal where root is processed first followed by left sub-tree the right sub-tree.

LRV is called post order traversal where left sub-tree is processed first then right and finally root node.

Let us consider a binary tree.

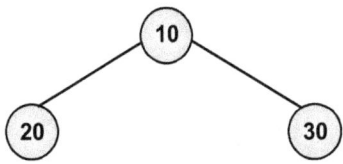

Fig. 4.16: Binary tree

Inorder traversal for Fig. 4.16, is shown in Fig. 4.17.

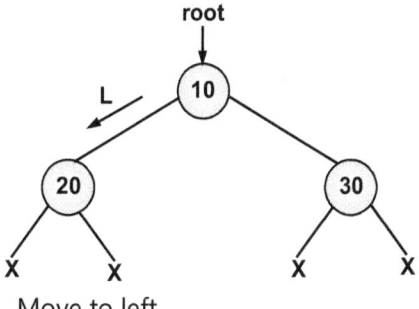
Move to left

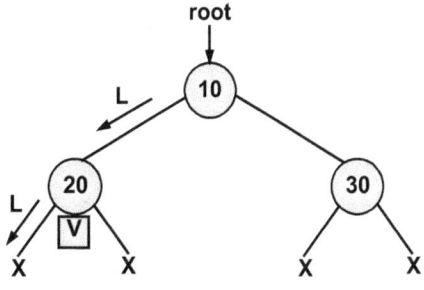
Move to left
left sub-tree of 20 is Null
Hence, visit node 20

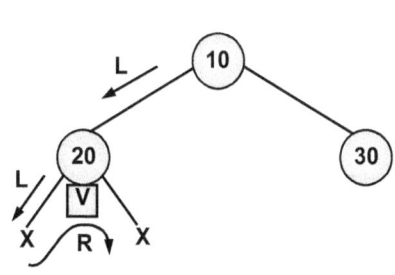
Move to right
Right sub-tree of 20 is Null
LVR for 20 is order
Go back to previous node

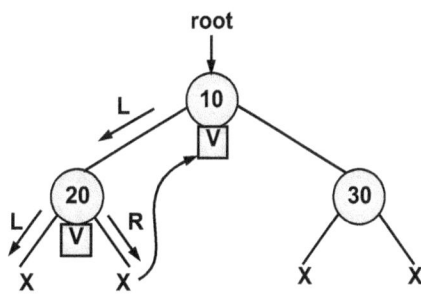
Left sub-tree of 10 is over
Visit the node 10

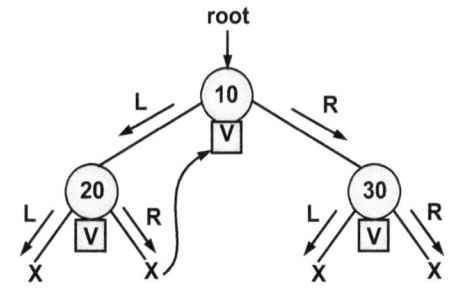
Move to right
Move to left, it is NULL
Visit 30
Move to right, it is Null
LVR for 30 is over, Go back to 30

Go back to root
LVR for 10 is over

Fig. 4.17: Inorder traversal of binary tree

Hence, inorder traversal is 20 10 30.

Similarly, preorder traversal will be as shown in Fig. 4.18.

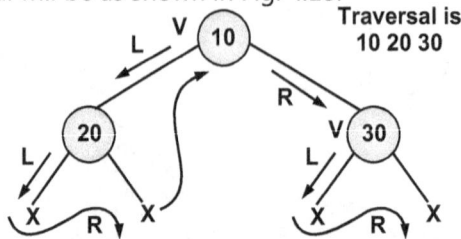

Fig. 4.18: Preorder traversal

Postorder traversal will be as shown in Fig. 4.19.

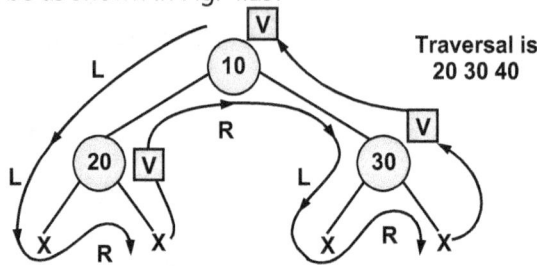

Fig. 4.19: Postorder traversal

Let us consider another example.

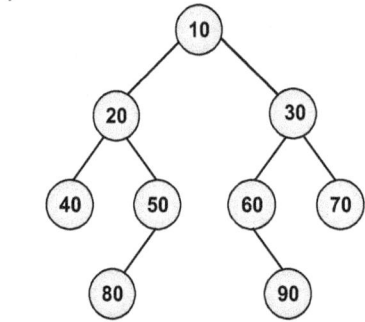

Fig. 4.20: Inorder traversal

Inorder traversal:

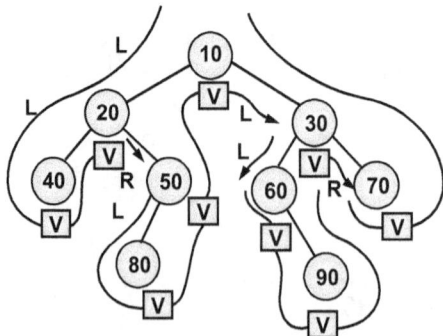

Fig. 4.21: Inorder traversal

Traversal is 40 20 80 50 10 60 90 30 70.

Preorder traversal:

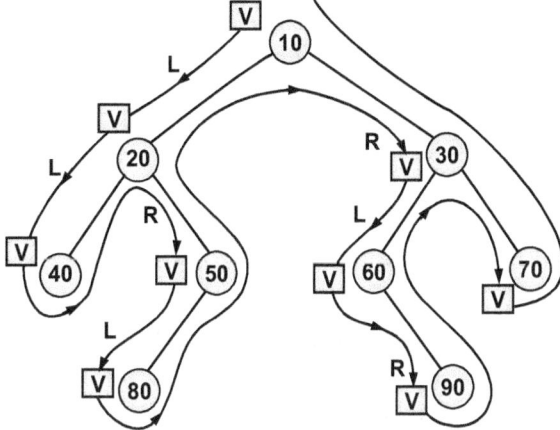

Fig. 4.22: Preorder traversal

Traversal is 10 20 40 50 80 30 60 90 70

Postorder traversal:

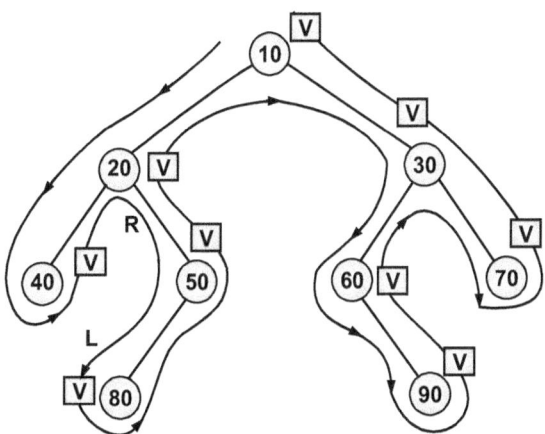

Fig. 4.23: Postorder traversal

Traversal is 40 80 50 20 90 60 70 30 10

Observation:
1. In inorder traversal, the root element is in between the left sub-tree and right sub-tree.
2. In preorder traversal, root element is at the beginning.
3. In postorder traversal, root element will be at the end.
4. If we are given any two traversals of a tree we can draw the tree diagram.

Example: Let us take up the same traversals of Figs. 4.21 and 4.22.
    Inorder: 40 20 80 50 10 60 90 30 70
    Preorder: 10 20 40 50 80 30 60 90 70

Step 1: From preorder, we find that root is 10. Hence the right and left sub-tree elements will be as shown in Fig. 4.24 (a).

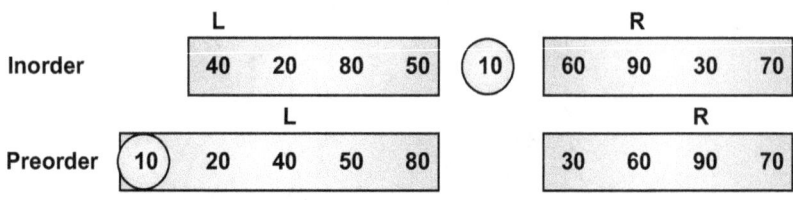

Fig. 4.24 (a): Binary tree from traversal

Step 2: Left sub-tree has root 20 (first element of pre-order).
Right sub-tree has root 30 (first element of pre-order).
Hence, the division will be as shown in Fig. 4.24 (b).

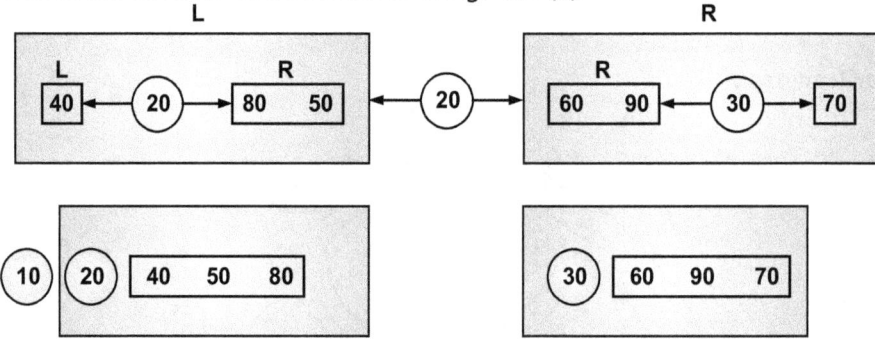

Fig. 4.24 (b): Binary tree from traversal

Step 3: Continuing on the same lines.

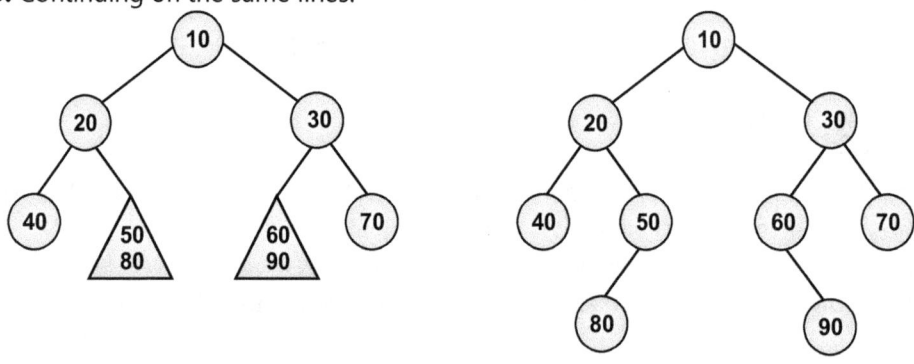

Fig. 4.24 (c): Binary tree from traversal

4.4 BINARY SEARCH TREE (BST)

Binary search tree as the name suggests, is used for storing the data mainly for searching applications. We have seen that nonlinear data structures are used for speeding up the process of searching. If we store the data in binary tree in a particular way, we will be able to improve the efficiency of searching to the order of $\log_2 n$ similar to binary search. In fact, **BST** implements the same principle as that of binary search,

Definition 1:
A binary search tree is a binary tree that is either empty or has each node that can satisfy following conditions.
(i) All the elements in left sub-tree of the root precede the element in the root.
(ii) All the elements in the right sub-tree of the root succeed the element in the root.
(iii) Left and right sub-trees are again binary search tree.

Definition 2:
A binary search tree is a binary tree in which for each node the left sub-tree elements are less than the node element and right sub-tree elements are greater than the node element or vice versa.

The example of BST is shown in Fig. 4.25.

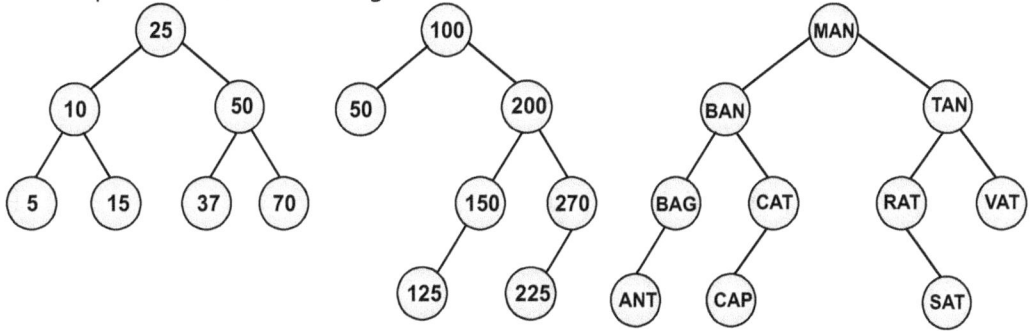

Fig. 4.25: Binary search tree

4.5 OPERATIONS ON BINARY SEARCH TREE

We can use the traversals discussed earlier for the binary search trees. For example for first tree the traversals will be as:

Inorder	:	5 10 15 25 37 50 75
Preorder	:	25 10 5 15 50 37 75
Postorder	:	5 15 10 37 75 50 25

Note that inorder traversal of BST will result into ascending order.
We can store the elements in BST in reverse order also. i.e., smaller element on right side and larger element on left side of root. In that case, the inorder traversal will result into descending order of the elements in the tree.
The main operation that we need to do on binary search tree is searching an element. Consider tree as shown in Fig. 4.26.

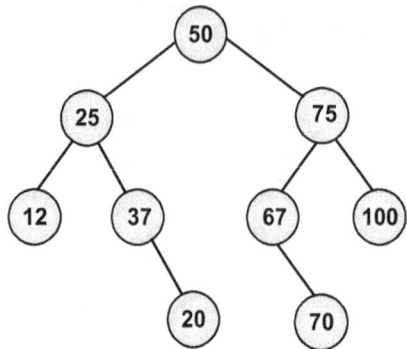

Fig. 4.26: Binary search tree

Suppose we want to search 37 in the tree. We start from the root node and move to left or right side depending on whether the number is smaller or greater.

Step 1: Compare whether element at current node is 37. The answer is no. Now since 37 < 50 we move to the left side.

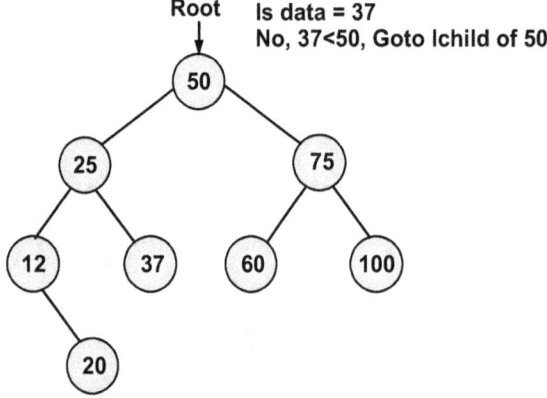

Fig. 4.27 (a): Search operation

Step 2:

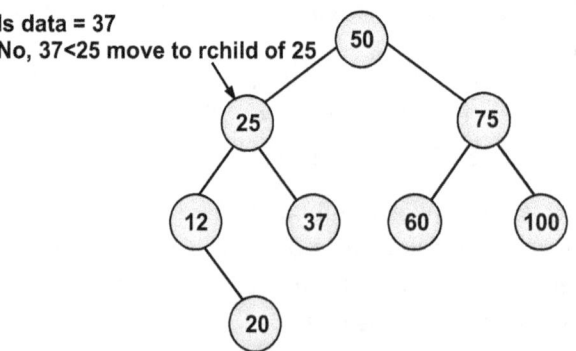

Fig. 4.27: (b) Search operation

Step 3:

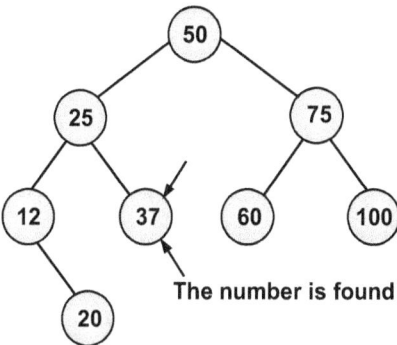

Fig. 4.27 (c): Search operation

If the number to be searched is not there in the BST, we will reach the end of BST (i.e. Leaf node).

There are various operations that can be performed on BST viz., create, search and traverse. Let us write the algorithms for various operations on BST.

4.5.1 Creating BST

1. Read n {Number of elements}
2. root=Null
3. Repeat Steps 4 to 11 n times.
4. Read x
5. Create a node ptr
6. ptr->data=x
7. ptr->lchild=ptr->rchild=Null
8. temp = root
9. if (temp==NULL) root=ptr
10. while (temp!=NULL)
    {
        prev=temp;
        if (temp->data>x)
            temp=temp->lchild; flag=1;
        else
            temp= temp->rchild; flag=0;
    }

11.   if (flag==1)
                prev->lchild = ptr;
        else
                prev->rchild=ptr;

Explanation:
1. n is number of elements to be stored in BST.
2. The root pointer points to root node which is initially null.
3. Every time we accept the data, we create a new node ptr, store the data in it and this node is to be placed in the BST.
4. When first node is created it will be pointed by root.
5. Whenever a new node is created we start from root node and find a position for this node in BST. For this we compare the element in the tree with current element and move to right or left side. Before we move, pointer prev is kept behind so that we can connect new node to the current node, in case its lchild or rchild becomes null.
6. The movement of pointer temp before it becomes null gives location where new node is to be inserted. It is tracked with the help of flag.

4.5.2 Searching in BST

1. Read s
2. temp=root
3. while (temp!=NULL)
   {
       if (temp->data ==s)
       {
           printf("Found");
           break;
       }
       if (temp->data>s)
           temp=temp->lchild
       if (temp->data <s)
           temp=temp->rchild
   }
4. if (temp==NULL)
       printf("Not found");

DATA STRUCTURES (SE – COMP./IT. – NMU)

Explanation:
1. The element to be searched is s.
2. We start from the root and move into the tree either on left or right side depending on data at current node,
3. If we find the data at a particular node, we exit.
4. If we don't find the data, temp will finally become null.

4.5.3 Tree Traversal Operations

We can use recursive functions as:
Inorder (temp)
1. {
2.   if(temp!=NULL)
    {
3.   inorder (temp- >lchild)
4.   print temp->data
5.   inorder (temp->rchild).
    }
}

Explanation:
Let us take a BST as shown in figure 4.28 for this.

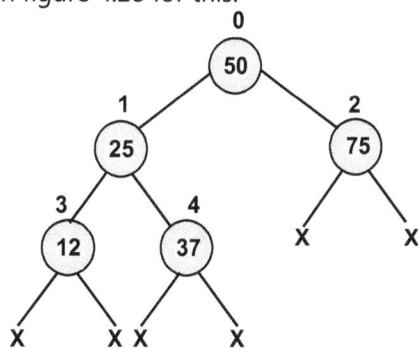

Fig. 4.28: Binary search tree

Let 0, 1, 2, 3, 4 be the addresses of there nodes.
The function will be called as
    inorder (root)
The function gets address of root which is assumed to be 0. Temp is assigned this address. The following table shows how the function gets called recursively. Follow the numbered lines in that sequence.

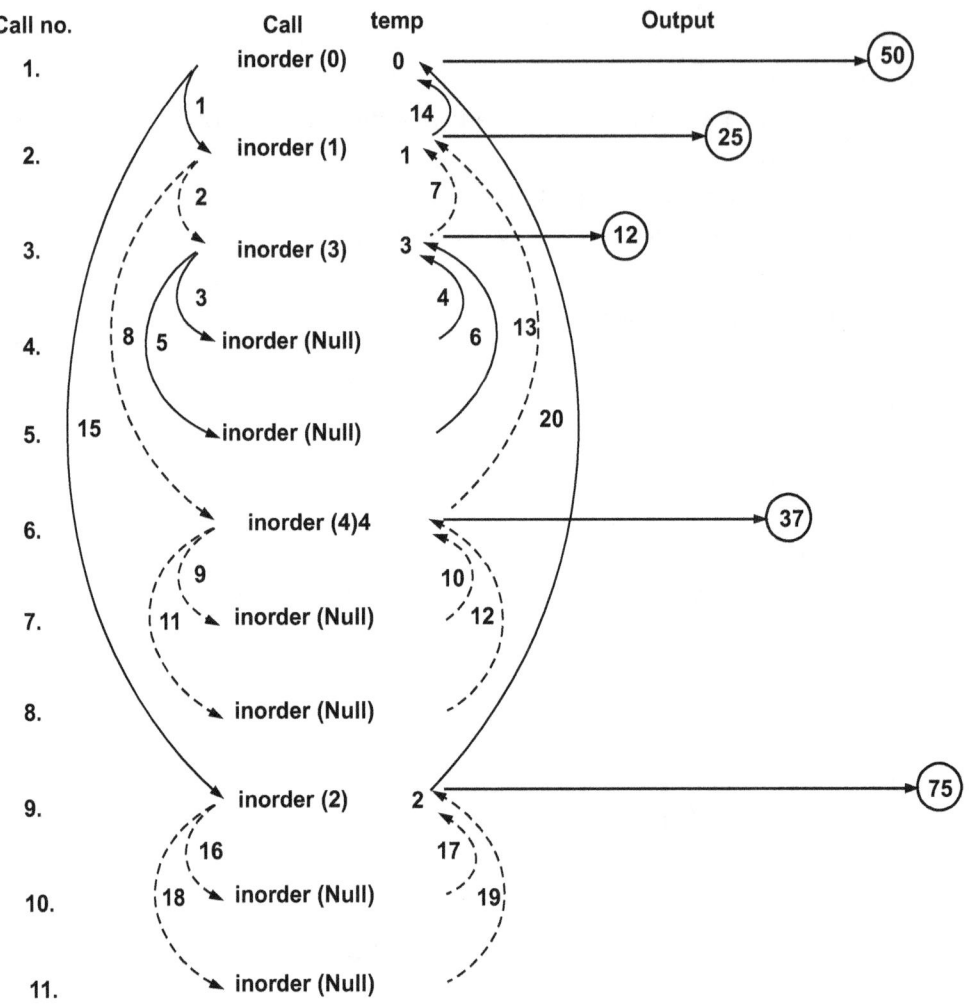

Fig. 4.29: Recursive inorder traversal function trace

The other two traversal functions are as follows:

```
preorder (temp)
{
    if (temp!=Null)
    {
        print temp->data
        preorder(temp->lchild)
        preorder(temp->rchild)
    }
}
```

```
}
postorder (temp)
{
    if(temp!=Null)
    {
        postorder(temp->lchild)
        postorder(temp->rchild)
        print temp->data
```

4.5.4 Delete Operation

Deleting a node in BST is a complex operation because we need to readjust the nodes in the tree. There are four different situations in the BST for deleting a node. They are,
(i)   The node to be deleted is leaf node.
(ii) The node has right child only.
(iii) The node has left child only.
(iv) The node has both children.
Let us find out how to deal with these four cases with example

Case 1:

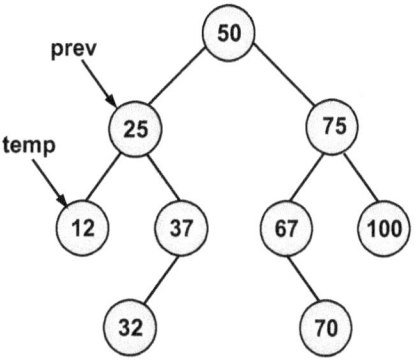

Fig. 4.30 (a): Delete operation leaf node

Suppose, the node to be deleted is 12, we need two pointers one at 12 (temp) other at its parent node i.e. 25 (prev). We need to check whether the node to be deleted (temp) is connected to *l*child or rchild of prev.
    if   prev->*l*child=temp make prev-*l*child=Null
    if   prev->rchild=temp make prev->rchild=Null
    and then free (temp)

Case 2:

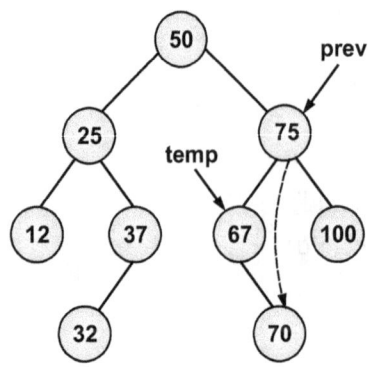

Fig. 4.30 (b): Delete operation node with rchild

Suppose, the node to be deleted has right child as shown in Fig. 4.30 (b). In this case, since 67 is to be deleted, its successor 70 is to be made *l*child of its parent i.e. 75. The node to be deleted might be right child of its parent or left child. Hence, we have to determine this first. The code will be:

```
if (temp->rchild != NULL &&temp->lchild == NULL)
{
    if(prev-lchild==temp)
        prev-lchild=temp->rchild
    else
        prev->rchild=temp->rchild;
}
```

Case 3:

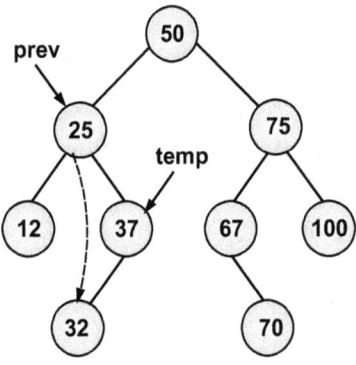

Fig. 4.30 (c): Delete operation node with *l*child

If the node to be deleted has left child as shown in figure 4.30(c). If 37 is deleted, its successor should be made right child of 25. We can have the node to be deleted as right or left child of its parent node. Hence, we will have two options.'

```
if (temp->rchild==NULL &&temp->lchild!=NULL)
{
    if (prev->lchild==temp)
        prev->lchild=temp->lchild;
    else
        prev->rchild=temp->lchild;
}
```

Case 4: The node to be deleted has both children as shown in Fig. 4.30(d).

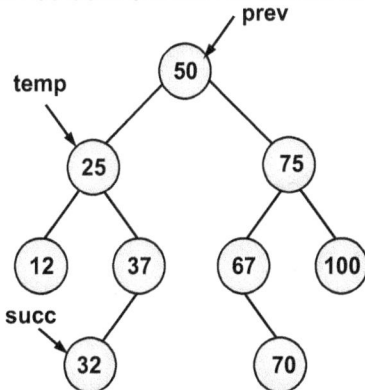

Fig. 4.30 (d): Delete operation node with *lchild* and *rchild*

Let us say we want to delete 25. The inorder successor of 25 is 32. We can copy 32 in place of 25 and delete 32. Hence, the process is to find inorder successor of the node. Copy the successor in its place and delete the inorder successor node.

```
if (temp->lchild!=NULL, &&temp->rchild!=NULL)
{
    succ= temp;
    x=temp->rchild;
    while(x!=NULL)
    {
        prev=succ;
        succ=x;
        x=x->lchild;
    }
    temp->data=succ->data;
    temp=succ;
}
```

This will copy the value of inorder, successor into the node to be deleted. Now, that we have a pointer temp to the inorder successor node and prev to its parent node, this node will fall into one of the 3 cases considered earlier. If we write the cases after this case, automatically one of them will get executed and the-node will be deleted.

4.5.5 Insert Operation

If new data is to be inserted in already existing BST, the position for this new data has to be located. It will be inserted as a leaf node in the BST. The algorithm will be as follows:
1. Read x (Data to be added)
2. Create a new node ptr and store the data in it
3. temp=root
4. while(temp!=NULL)
   {   prev=temp;
        if(temp->data>x)
            temp=temp->lchild; flag=1;
        else
            temp=temp->rchild; flag=0;
   }
5. if (flag==1)
        prev->lchild=ptr;
   else
        prev->rchild=ptr;

Explanation:
1. The new data to be inserted is accepted and stored into a new node ptr.
2. Start from root node till you go bottom of tree. Compare at each node and move to left or right. Before we move to left or right keep a pointer prev to previous node so that if you fall into null, we have a pointer to the node on whose left or right side new node is to be attached. The decision of whether the new node will be attached to right or left will be made from the value of flag.
   Now let us write a menu driven program to implement all these operations.
   The functions that we are going to write are
   (i)   Create   : Creates a binary search tree and returns address of root node,
   (ii) Search   : Searches an element in BST.
   (iii) Inorder   : Display inorder traversal.

(iv) Preorder : Display preorder traversal.
(v) Postorder : Display postorder traversal.
(vi) Delete : Deletes a node.
(vii) insert : Inserts a new node.

Program 4.1: To create and implement binary search tree

```c
#include <stdio.h>
#include <conio.h>
typedef struct node
{
    int data;
    struct node *lchild,*rchild;
}NODE;
NODE*create( );
int search (NODE*, int);
void inorder (NODE*);
void preorder (NODE*)
void postorder (NODE*);
NODE*del(NODE*);
NODE* insert (NODE*);
void main( )
{
    int ch, s;
    NODE*root=NULL;
    do
    {
        clrscr( );
        printf("1.Create \n 2.Search \n 3.Inorder \n 4.Preorder \n 5.Postorder \n 6.Delete \n 7.Insert \n8.Exit \n");
        printf("Enter your choice \n");
        scanf("%d", &ch);
        switch(ch)
        {
            case 1 :  root=create( );
                      break;
            case 2 :  printf("Enter number to be searched \n");
```

```
                        scanf("%d", &s);
                        search(root, s)
                        break;
            case 3 :    inorder(root);
                        break;
            case 4 :    preorder(root);
                        break;
            case 5 :    postorder(root);
                        break;
            case 6 :    root=del(root)
                        break;
            case 7 :    root=insert(root);
                        break;
        }
        getch();
    }while(ch!=8);
}
NODE *create( )
{
    int x, i, n, flag;
    NODE *root, *ptr, *temp, *prev;
    root=NULL;
    printf("How many elements? \n");
    scanf("%d", &n);
    for(i=1;i<=n;i++)
    {
        printf("Enter the number");
        scanf("%d", &x);
        ptr=(NODE*)malloc(sizeof(NODE));
        ptr->data=x;
        ptr->rchild=ptr->lchild=NULL;
        if (root==NULL)
            root=ptr;
        else
        {
            temp=root;
```

```
                while (temp!=NULL)
                {
                    prev=temp;
                    if (temp->data>x)
                    {
                        temp=temp->lchild;
                        flag=1;
                    }
                    else
                    {
                        temp=temp->rchild;
                        flag=0;
                    }
                }
                if (flag==1)
                    prev->lchild=ptr;
                else
                    prev->rchild=ptr;
        }
    }
    return (root);
}
int search (NODE *root, int x)
{
    NODE *temp;
    temp=root;
    while (temp!=NULL && temp->data!=x)
    {
        if(temp->data>x)
            temp=temp->lchild;
        else
            temp=temp->rchild;
    }
    if (temp!= NULL)
        return (1);
    else
```

```c
            return (0);
}
void inorder (NODE *temp)
{
    if (temp!= NULL)
    {
        inorder (temp->lchild);
        printf("%d \n", temp->data);
        inorder(temp->rchild);
    }
}
void preorder (NODE *temp)
{
    if (temp!=NULL)
    {
        printf("%d \n", temp->data);
        preorder(temp->lchild);
        preorder(temp->rchild);
    }
}
void postorder (NODE *temp)
{
    if (temp!=NULL)
    {
        postorder(temp->lchild);
        postorder(temp->rchild);
        printf("%d \n", temp->data);
    }
}
NODE *del(NODE*root)
{
    NODE *temp, *prev, *x, *succ;
    int s;
    printf("Enter data to be deleted \n");
    scanf("%d", &s);
    temp=root;
```

```
        prev=temp;
        while(temp!=NULL)
        {
            if (temp->data==s)
                break;
            prev=temp;
            if(temp->data>s)
                temp=temp->lchild;
            else
                temp=temp->rchild;
        }
        if(temp==NULL)
        {
            printf("Not in the BST \n");
            exit(0);
        }
        if(temp->lchild!=NULL &&temp->rchild!=NULL)
        {
            succ=temp;
            x=temp->rchild;
            while(x!=NULL)
            {
                prev=succ;
                succ=x;
                x=x-Achild;
            }
            temp->data=succ->data;
            temp=succ;
        }
        if(temp->rchild== NULL & temp->lchild!=NULL)
        {
            if(prev->lchild == temp)
                prev->rchild=temp->lchild;
            else
                prev->rchild=temp->lchild;
        }
```

```
        if(temp->rchild!=NULL &&temp->lchild==NULL)
        {
            if(prev->lchild==temp)
                prev->lchild=temp->rchild;
            else
                prev->rchild=temp->rchild;
        }
        if(temp->lchild == NULL &&temp->rchild == NULL)
        {
            if(prev->lchild==temp)
                prev->lchild=NULL;
            else
                prev->rchild=NULL;
        }
        free(temp);
        return(root);
}
NODE *insert(NODE *root)
{
    NODE *temp, *prev, *ptr;
    int x, flag;
    printf("Enter data to be inserted \n");
    scanf("%d", &x);
    ptr =(NODE*)malloc(sizeof(NODE));
    ptr->data=x;
    ptr->lchild=ptr->rchild=NULL;
    temp=root;
    while (temp!=NULL)
    {
        prev=temp;
        if(temp->data>x)
        {
            temp=temp->child;
            flag=1;
        }
        else
```

```
            {
                    temp=temp->rchild;
                    flag=0;
            }
        }
        if(root==NULL)
            root=ptr;
        else
        {
        if(flag==1)
            prev->lchild=ptr;
        else
            prev->rchild=ptr;
        }
        return (root);
}
```

4.6 OPERATIONS ON BINARY TREE

We have seen Binary search tree and operations on it. The BST was relatively easy to implement along with the operations such as create, insert, delete traversals, etc. It was because of the relation that exists among the elements in BST. Now, if you are given a binary tree and asked. to create it as it is, we will have to ask the user to manually enter the data and their positions in the tree. The operators that we can have on this tree are insert, traversals (all three). The algorithms of these operations are as follows.

4.6.1 Creating a binary tree

1. Read n
2. root=Null
3. for (i=1;i<=n;i++)
   {
4.   Read x
      Create a new node ptr
      store x in ptr->data
5.   if(root==NULL)
         root=ptr
      else

```
6.          temp=root;
7.          while(temp!=NULL)
            {
                prev=temp;
                read side
                if(side=='l')
                    temp=temp->lchild
                else
                    temp=temp->rchild;
            }
8.          if(side=='l')
                prev->child=ptr
            else
                prev->rchild=ptr
        }
    }
9. Stop
```

Explanation:
1. Read number of nodes (n) in the tree.
2. root=NULL.
3. Repeat for each element the following process
4. Read data and store it in a node ptr.
5. If it is first node let it be pointed by root.
6, 7. If it is not first node, start from root node and traverse in the tree every time asking the user about which side of current node the new node is to be added.
8. When temp becomes NULL, prev will be at a node in the tree on whose left or right side new node is to be inserted. Insert the node accordingly.

4.6.2 Traversal Operation

The inorder, preorder and postorder traversals can be implemented in the same way as discussed in BST.

4.6.3 Insert Operation

It will be similar to create operation except that the process is to be carried out only once.

Program 4.2: To implement a binary tree

```
typedef struct node
{
    int data;
    struct node *lchild, *rchild;
} NODE;
NODE *create( );
void    inorder(NODE*);
void    preorder (NODE*);
void    postorder(NODE*);
NODE *insert(NODE*);
void main( )
{
    int ch;
    NODE *root;
    root=NULL;
    do
    {
        printf("1.Create \n2. Inorder \n3. preorder \n4. Postorder \n5. Insert \n6. Exit \n");
        printf("Enter your choice \n");
        scanf("%d", &ch);
        switch(ch)
        {
            case 1 :  root=create( );
                      break;
            case 2 :  inorder(root);
                      break
            case 3 :  preorder(root);
                      break;
            case 4 :  postorder(root);
                      break;
```

```
                    case 5 : root=insert(root);
            }
            getch( );
        } while(ch!=6);
}
NODE *create( )
{
    NODE *ptr, *temp, *prev;
    int x; n, i;
    char ch;
    printf("Enter number of nodes \n");
    scanf("%d",&n);
    root=NULL;
    for(i=1;i<=n;i++)
    {
        printf("Enter data \n");
        scanf("%d", &x);
        ptr=(NODE*) malloc(sizeof (NODE));
        ptr->lchild=ptr->rchild=NULL;
        if(root == NULL)
            root=ptr;
        else
        {
            temp=root;
            while(temp!=NULL)
            {   prev=temp;
                printf("which side of %d? (l/r) \n", temp->data);
                ch=getch( );
                if(ch=='l' || ch=='L')
                    temp=temp->lchild;
                else
                    temp=temp->rchild;
            }
            if(ch=='l' || ch=='L')
                prev->child=ptr;
            else
```

```
                prev->rchild=ptr;
            }
        }
        return (root);
}
void inorder(NODE*root)
{   NODE *temp;
    temp=root;
    if (temp!=NULL)
    {
        inorder(temp->lchild);
        printf("%d \n", temp->data);
        inorder(temp->rchild);
    }
}
void preorder(NODE*root)
{   NODE *temp;
    temp=root;
    if (temp!=NULL)
    {
        printf("%d \n", temp->data);
        preorder(temp->lchild);
        preorder(temp->rchild);
    }
}
void postorder(NODE*root)
{
    NODE*temp;
    temp=root;
        if(temp!=NULL)
        {
            postorder(temp->lchild);
            postorder(temp->rchild);
            printf("%d \n", temp->data);
        }
}
```

```
NODE *insert(NODE*root)
{
    NODE *temp,*ptr, *prev;
    int x;
    char ch;
    printf("Enter data \n");
    scanf("%d", &x);
    ptr=(NODE*)malloc(sizeof(NODE));
    ptr->data=x;
    ptr->lchild=ptr->rchild=NULL;
    if (root==NULL)
        root=ptr;
    else
    {
        temp=root;
        while(temp!=NULL)
        {
            printf("which side of %d (l/r) \n", temp->data);
            ch=getch( );
            if(ch=='l' || ch=='L')
                temp=temp->lchild;
            else
                temp=temp->rchild;
        }
        if(ch=='l' || ch=='L')
            prev->lchild=ptr;
        else
            prev->rchild=ptr;
    }
    return(root);
}
```

4.6.4 Non-Recursive Traversal

The recursive inorder, preorder and postorder traversals use the program's recursion stack. The recursion can be removed by implementing user defined stack. Let us see, how we can write inorder and preorder traversals using stack.

1. Inorder traversal

Algorithm: Inorder traversal
1. temp=root
2. do
    {
        while(temp!=NULL)
        {
            push(temp);
            temp=temp->lchild;
        }
        temp=pop( );
        print temp->data
        temp=temp->rchild;
    }while(stack is not empty OR temp!=NULL);
3. Stop.

Explanation:
1. Start with root node.
2. Traverse on left side while storing the address of each node on stock.
3. Pop the address of a node from stack (it will be left most node). Display the data.
4. Move to right side.
5. Repeat above till all nodes are traversed.
6. The stack will be stack of pointers as it has to store addresses of nodes.

Consider a binary tree as:

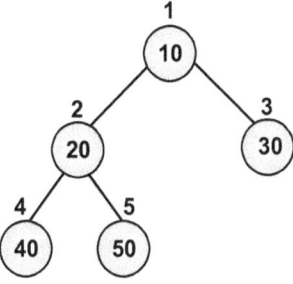

Fig. 4.31(a): Binary tree

Let 1, 2, 3, 4, 5, be the addresses of the nodes.
1. We start with root node and move to left pushing every time address of node on the stack. At the end of inner while, the stack will be

Fig. 4.31(b): Stack contents for non-recursive inorder traversal

2. temp=pop( ) will pop node 4.
     data at node 4 i.e. 40 will be displayed.
3. temp will be Null as rchild of 4 is Null.
   Since temp is NULL, 2 is poped.
   Data at 2 i.e. 20 is displayed.
   temp will move to rchild of 2.
   Hence, 5 will be pushed and stack will be

Fig. 4.31(c): Stack contents for non-recursive inorder traversal

4. 5 is popped and data at 5 is displayed i.e. 50.
   Since temp is NULL
   1 is popped and data 1 is displayed i.e. 11.
   temp will move to rchild 3.
   3 is pushed and stock will be'

Fig. 4.31(d): Stack contents for non-recursive inorder traversal

   3 is popped data at 3. i.e. 30 displayed.
   stack becomes empty and temp is null hence the function gets over.

2. Preorder traversal: For preorder traversal (VLR) we used to make only one change the print statement will be written before left move as follows:
1. temp=root
2. do
   {   while(temp!=NULL)
       {

```
                print temp->data
                push(temp);
                temp=temp->lchild;
            }
            temp=pop( );
            temp=temp->rchild;
        } while (stack is not empty OR temp!=NULL)
```
3. Stop

4.7 THREADED BINARY TREE

Almost every operation performed on binary tree requires traversing a binary tree. We have seen recursive traversals are not that efficient. It is because the recursive calls take place even for NULL values of leaf nodes.

Another problem with binary tree is that, the lchild and rchild of leaf nodes store nothing. The space of lchild and rchild is wasted. If the height of tree is more this is a serious issue because there will be more number of leaf nodes.

Both these problems have a single solution and it is threaded binary tree i.e. we can utilize the space of lchild and rchild of leaf nodes and speedup the traversal by eliminating recursion.

The idea of threaded binary tree is to replace NULL links with addresses of the nodes in the binary tree itself.

Now which node's address is to be stored in the NULL field? We can store the address of the node which is next node in inorder traversal For example, for inorder traversal, we will be storing the inorder successor's addresses in rchild. Such a pointer is called thread. The tree so designed is called right-in-threaded binary tree.

If the NULL pointer in lchild is replaced by the pointers to inorder predecessor then the tree is called left-in-threaded binary tree.

If both NULL pointers in lchild and rchild are replaced by pointers to inorder predecess or and successor respectively, it is called in-threaded binary tree or inorder-threaded binary tree.

If the NULL pointer in lchild and rchild are replaced by pointers to preorder predecessor and successor respectively, then it is called pre-threaded or preorder thereaded binary tree.

If the NULL pointers in lchild and rchild are replaced by pointers to postorder predecessor and successor respectively, then it is called post-threaded or post-order threaded binary tree.

Now one important point about the threaded binary tree is how to distinguish between the thread and normal pointers? Because threads are not the natural pointers in the binary tree, they are created and are to be distinguished in traversal algorithms from normal pointers. For this, an extra field is added in each node to indicate whether the rchild or lchild is a thread or not. For these two threads we will require two logical fields say rt and lt. The values of rt and lt will be equal to 1 if the lchild or rchild is thread otherwise it will be 0.

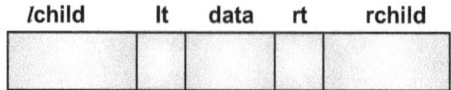

Fig. 4.32: Node in a threaded binary tree

The node structure for threaded binary tree will be as follows:
```
typedef struct node
{
    int data;
    int rt, lt;
    struct node *lchild, *rchild;
}NODE;
```

Following figures show some threaded binary trees.

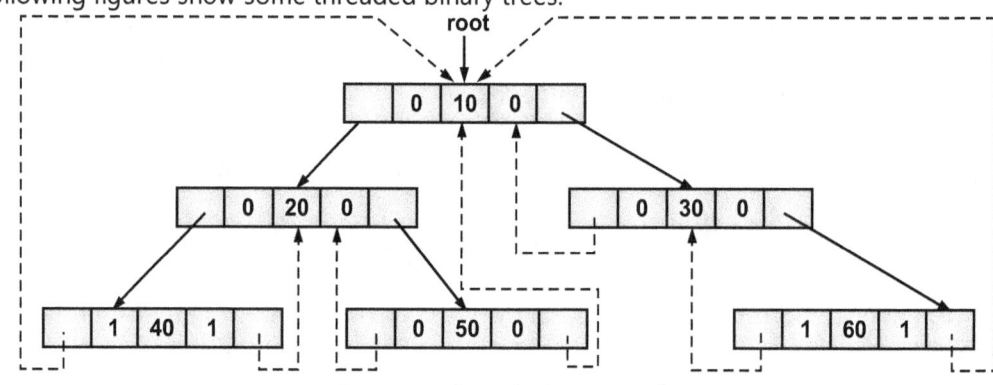

Fig. 4.33: Threaded binary tree

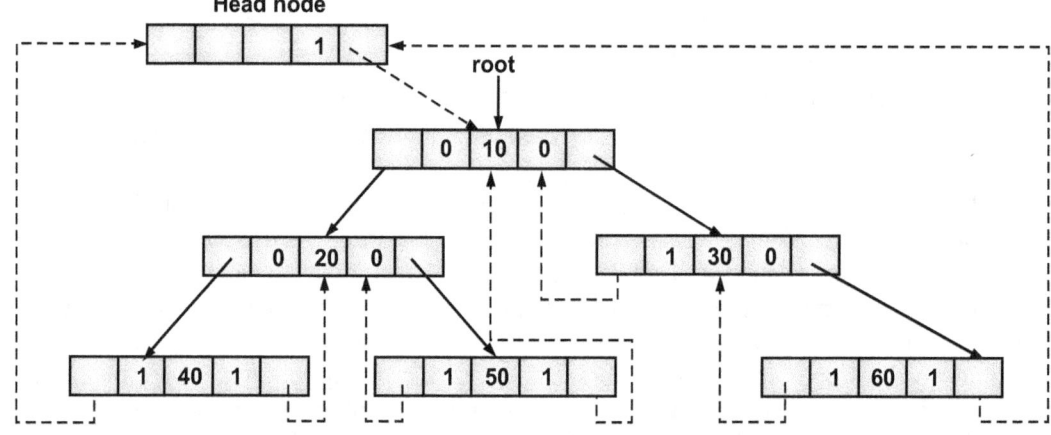

Fig. 4.34: Threaded binary tree with header node

Note: Threads are shown with dotted lines.

Some more threaded binary trees are as shown in Figs. 4.35, 4.36, 4.37.

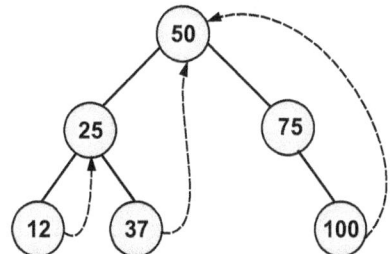

Fig. 4.35: Right-in-threaded binary search tree

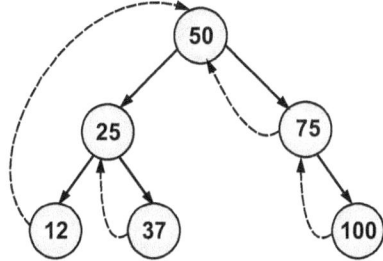

Fig. 4.36: Left-in-threaded binary search tree

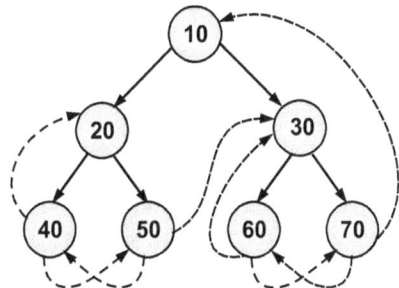

Fig. 4.37: Pre-threaded binary tree

Note: To draw a threaded binary tree.
1. Write the traversal For example in pre-threaded binary tree above, preorder traversal is 10 20 40 50 30 60 70.
2. Find predecessor and successors of nodes whose lchild or rchild is NULL and draw the threads For example preorder successor of 40 is 50 and predecessor is 20.
   Hence, threads from 40 are going to 50 and 20.
   Now, let us consider the operations on threaded binary tree. For this we consider only inorder threaded binary tree. The primitive operations are create, insert and traversals.

4.7.1 Create/Insert Operation

Suppose we are given elements to be stored in a threaded binary tree as 10 20 30 40 50 60
The steps will be as follows:

Step: 1

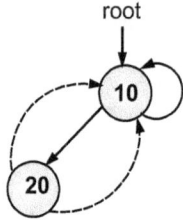

Step: 2

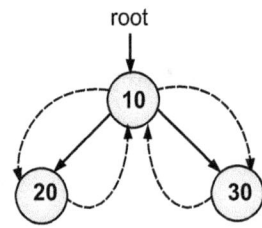

Step: 3

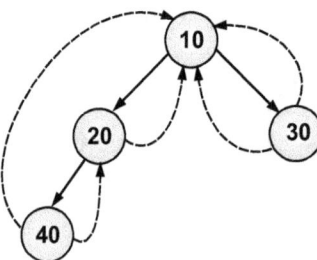

Step: 4

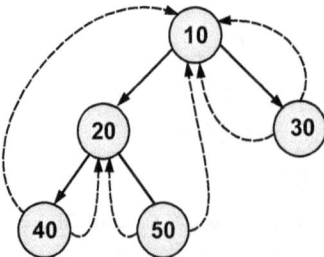

Step: 5

Step: 6

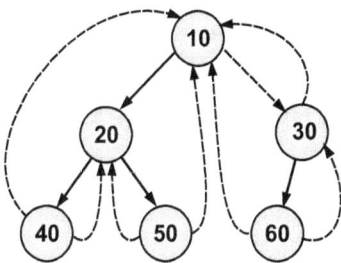

Fig. 4.38: Create/Insert operation in threaded binary tree

When new node is added threads are constructed as follows:
If the new node is added in left sub-tree of a node, point rchild to that node (parent) and point *l*child to a place where *l*child of parent was pointing earlier. Make *l*t and rt fields of the new node 1. Make It field of parent 0.
When new node is to be added in the right sub-tree of a node, point left child to that node (parent) and right child to a place where right child of parent was pointing earlier. Make lt and rt field of new node 1 and rt field of parent 0.

4.7.2 Non-recursive Traversals

The advantage of threaded binary tree is that, we don't have to use stack for traversing the tree. Let us look into non-recursive inorder and preorder traversals for in-threaded binary tree.

Algorithm: Inorder traversal of in-threaded binary tree.
1. temp=root
2. curr=root
3. do
   {
4.   if (temp!=root)
         temp=curr->rchild
5.   if(curr->rt==0)
      {
        while(temp->*l*t==0)
          temp=temp->*l*child;
      }
6.   if (temp!=root)
         print temp ->data
7.   curr=temp
   } while (temp!=root)
8. stop.

Explanation:

1,2. Two more pointers are used curr and temp.
3. The process (steps 4, 5, 6, 7) of traversal continues until we come back to root.
4. Except for the first time (when temp=root) more to right (R of LVR).
5. If previous node was not thread (rt=0) then more to left side (L of LVR) till there is no left child.
6. Print the data (V of LVR).
7. Make it current node.

Algorithm: Preorder traversal of in-threaded binary tree.
1. temp=root, curr=root
2. do
     {
3.   if (curr->rt==0)
        {
4.   while (temp->lt==0)
           {
               printf("%d \n", temp->data);
               temp=temp->lchild;
           }
5.   printf("%d \n", temp->data);
        }
6.   curr=temp;
7.   temp=curr->rchild
     } while(temp! =root)
8. stop

Explanation:

1. Start with two pointers, curr and temp at root.
2. Repeat the process of traversal until we come back to root.
3,5. If the current node has right child then till we get a thread move to left and display the data.
6,7. Move to the right side and repeat.

4.8 HEIGHT BALANCE TREE (AVL TREE)

A binary search tree (BST) is used to store and retrieve data. The maximum number of comparisons required for searching in a binary search tree depends on how data is stored in a tree. If tree is well balanced as shown figure 4.39, the number of comparisons will be minimum.

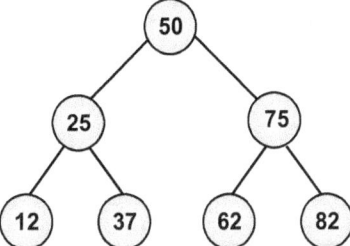

Fig. 4.39: Balanced binary tree

If the tree is right or left skewed it will require same number of comparison as that of sequential search.

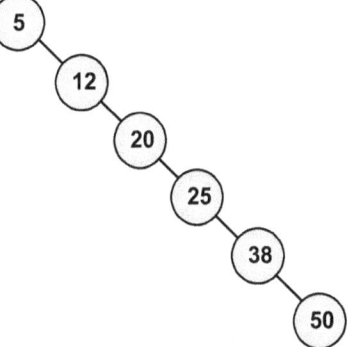

Fig. 4.40: Unbalanced binary tree

Imagine a situation where the BST is dynamic means the elements of the tree are getting deleted or new elements getting added to it. Average and maximum search time will be minimized, if tree is maintained as complete binary tree at all times. It will require restructuring of tree to accumulate new entry, so that both average and worst case search time will be $O(\log_2 n)$ for the tree of n nodes.

Adelson-Velskii and *Landis* (AVL) in 1962 introduced a Binary Tree that is balanced with respect to height of sub-trees.

Definition: An empty tree is height balanced. If T is non-empty binary tree with T_l and T_r as left and right sub-tree, then T is said to be height balanced iff.
1. T_l and T_r is height balanced.

2. $|h_l - h_r| \le 1$.

Where, h_f and h_r are heights of T_l and T_r.

The tree in Fig. 11.39 is height balanced.

Restructuring of BST is done so that tree becomes height balanced. When we add a node to a particular tree its height may change. This change can disturb the balancing also. In order to verify whether a tree is height balanced or not, we need to find out balance factor of every node.

Balanced factor:

Balance factor of a node is defined as $h_l - h_r$ where h_l and h_r are heights of T_l and T_r.

When a new node is added in BST one of the four types of situations can arise in the tree. In other words, there are 4 ways in which rebalancing can be done. These are called Rotations. They are RR, LL, RL, LR rotations.

1. **RR rotation:** If the newly inserted node (say Y) is in right sub-tree of right sub-tree of the nearest ancestor (say A) whose | balance factor | >= 2.

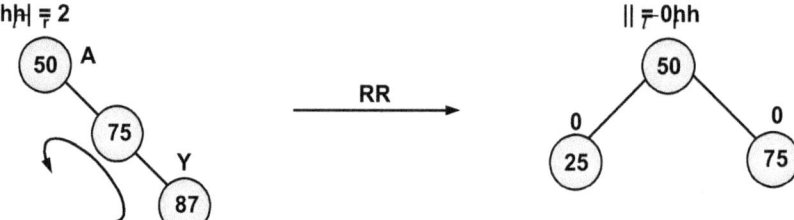

Fig. 4.41: RR rotation

2. **LL rotation:** The newly inserted node Y is the left sub-tree of left sub-tree of A.

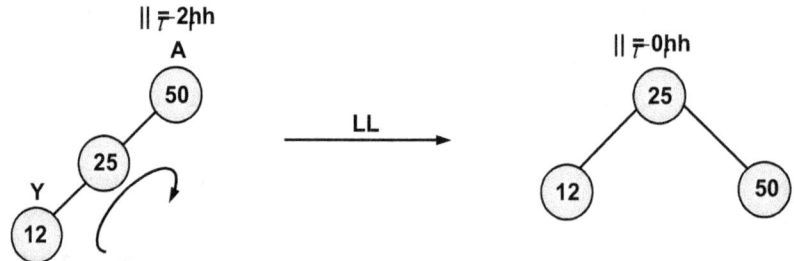

Fig. 4.42: LL rotation

3. **LR rotation:** Y is inserted in right sub-tree of left sub-tree of A.

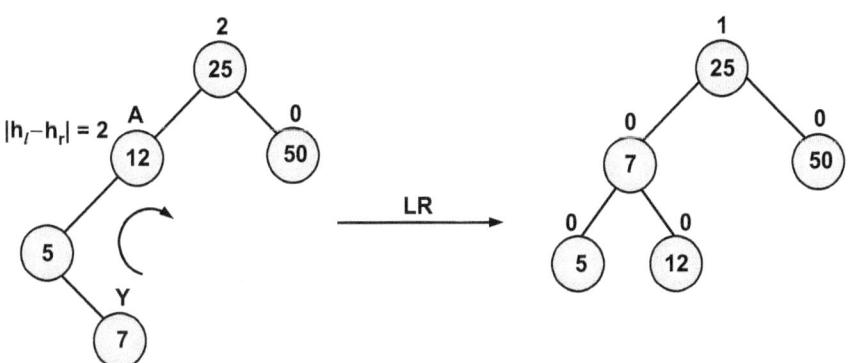

Fig. 4.43: LR rotation

4. **RL rotation:** Y is inserted in left sub-tree of right sub-tree of A.

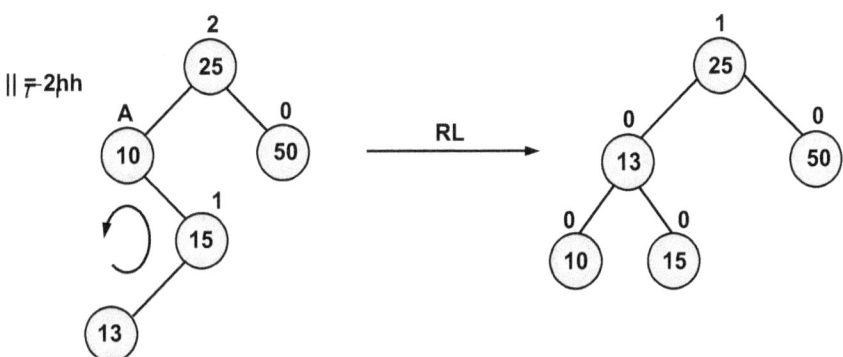

Fig. 4.44: RL rotation

Let us look into some more examples. Each rotation type has two different situations. First is the simple and the other is complex.

Case I: LL rotation
Situation 1

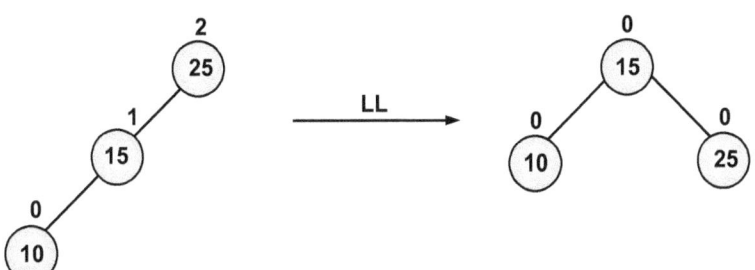

Fig. 4.45 (a): LL rotation

Situation 2

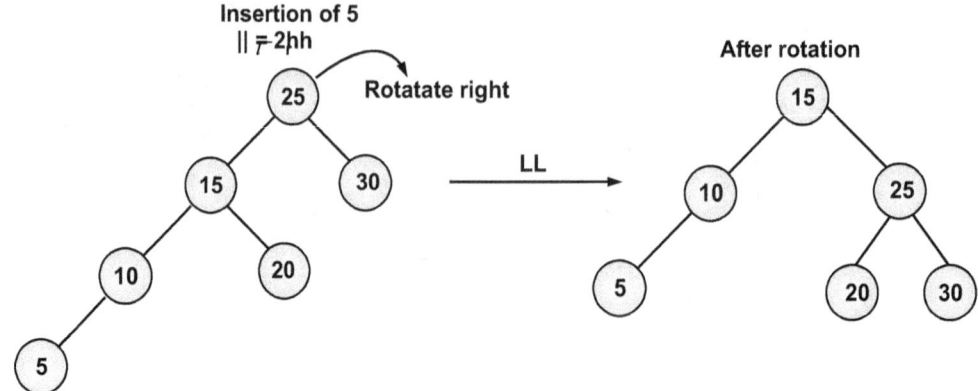

Fig. 4.45 (b): LL rotation

Case II: RR rotation
Situation 1

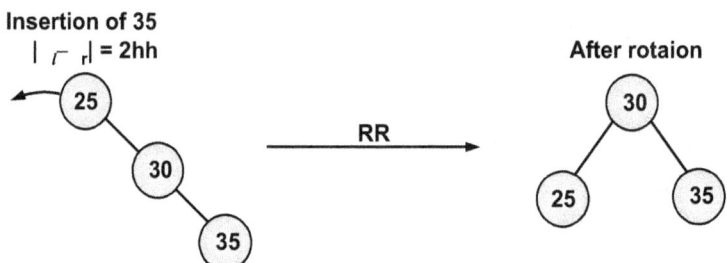

Fig. 4.45 (c): RR rotation

Situation 2

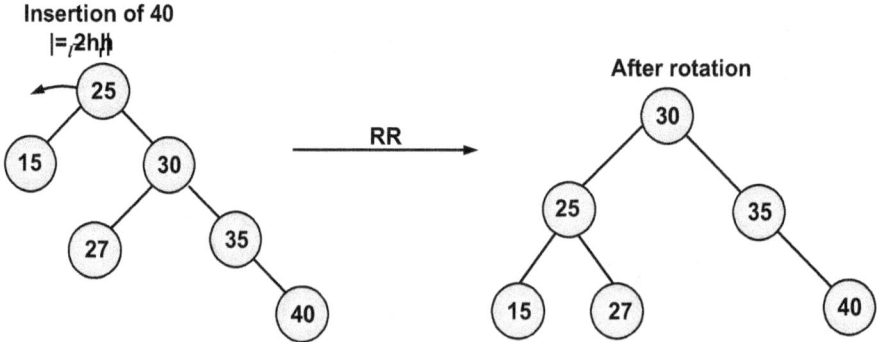

Fig. 4.45 (d): RR rotation

Actually, the RL and LR rotations are carried out in two steps. Following examples illustrate how exactly these rotations are done.

Case III: LR rotation
Situation 1

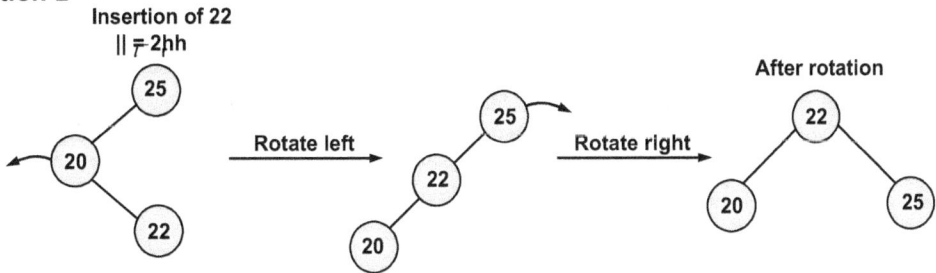

Fig. 4.45 (e): LR rotation

Situation 2

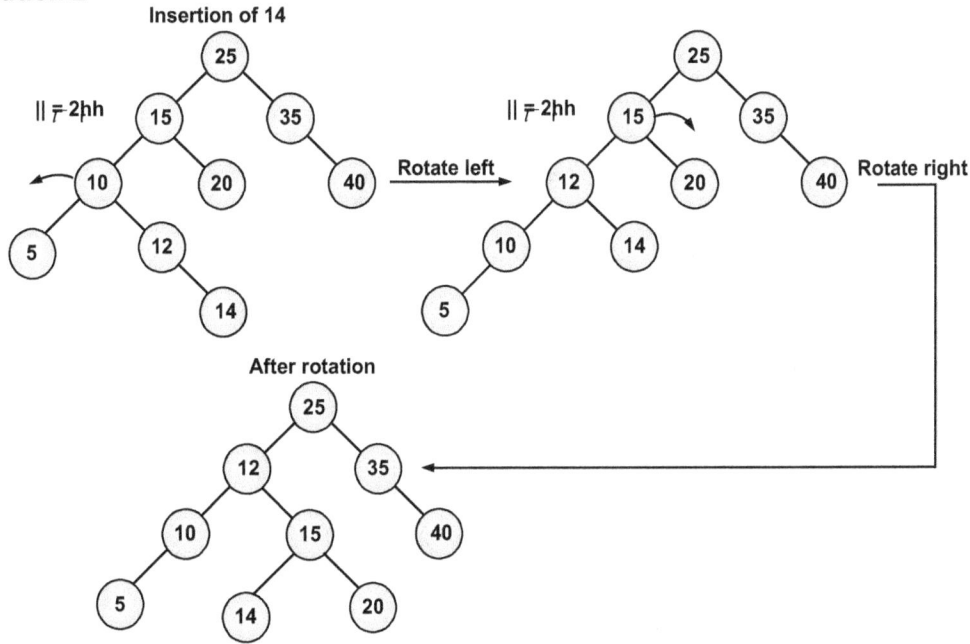

Fig. 4.45 (f): LR rotation

Case IV: RL rotation
Situation 1

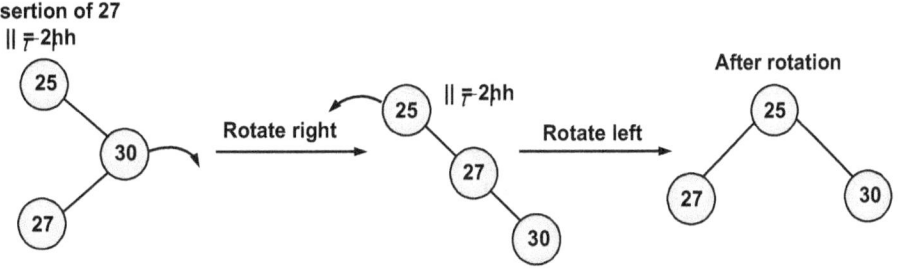

Fig. 4.45 (g): RL rotation

Situation 2

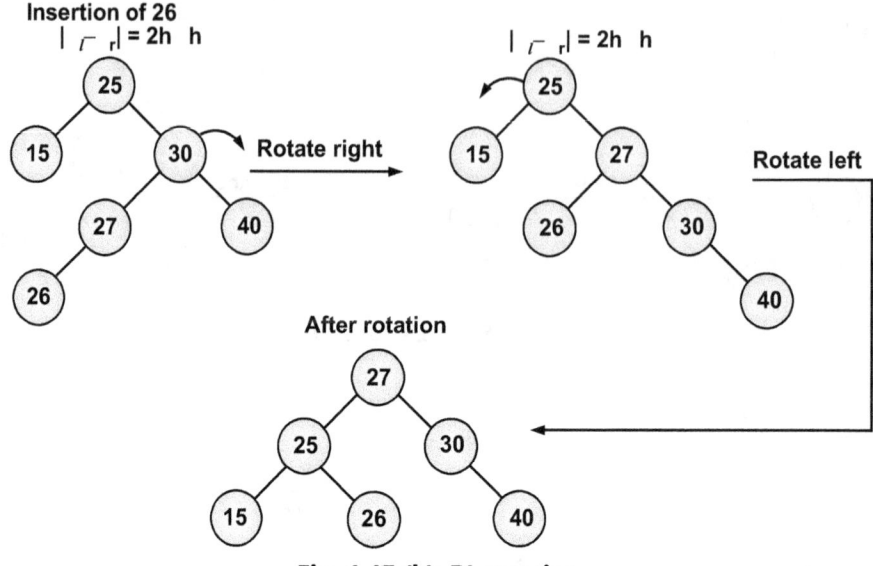

Fig. 4.45 (h): RL rotation

Example 1: Create AVL tree for the following elements:

Solution:

Note: The figures shown in nodes are balance factors

1.
2.
3.
4.

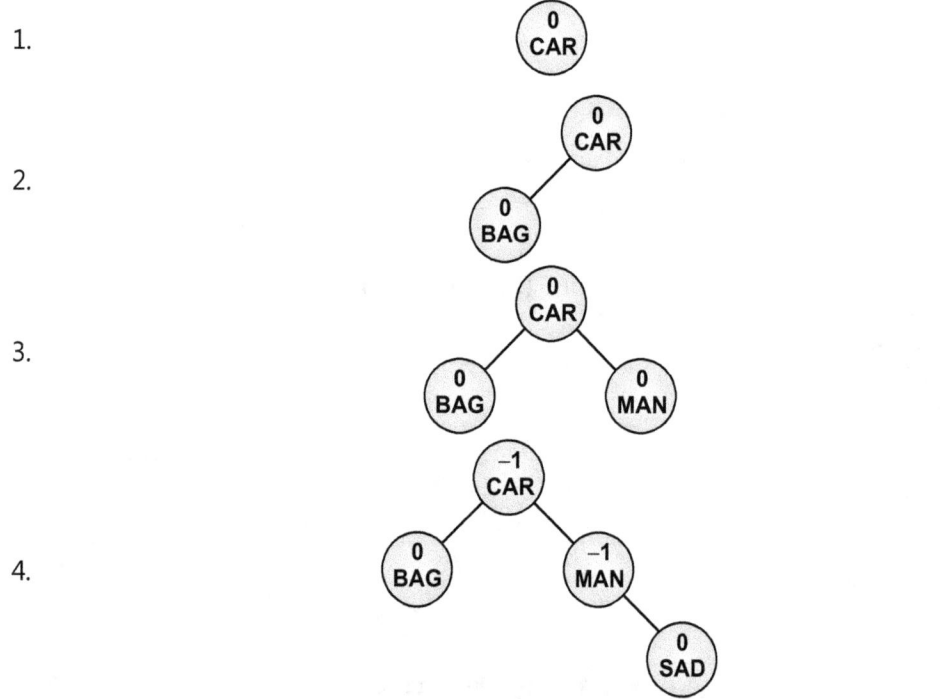

5.

6.

7.

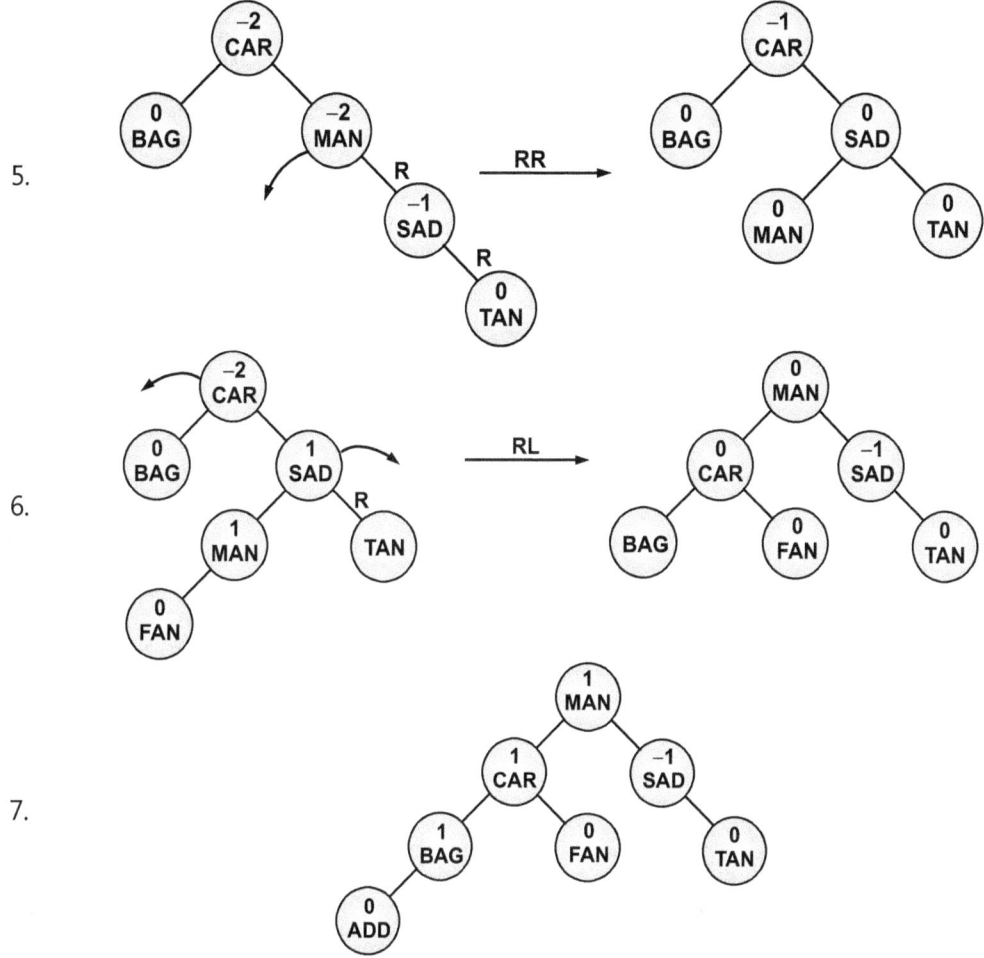

Fig. 4.46: Creating height balance (AVL) binary tree

Example 2: Create AVL tree for the following elements:
MAR MAY NOV AUG APR JAN DEC JUL FEB

Solution:
Note: The figures shown in nodes are balance factors.

1.

2.

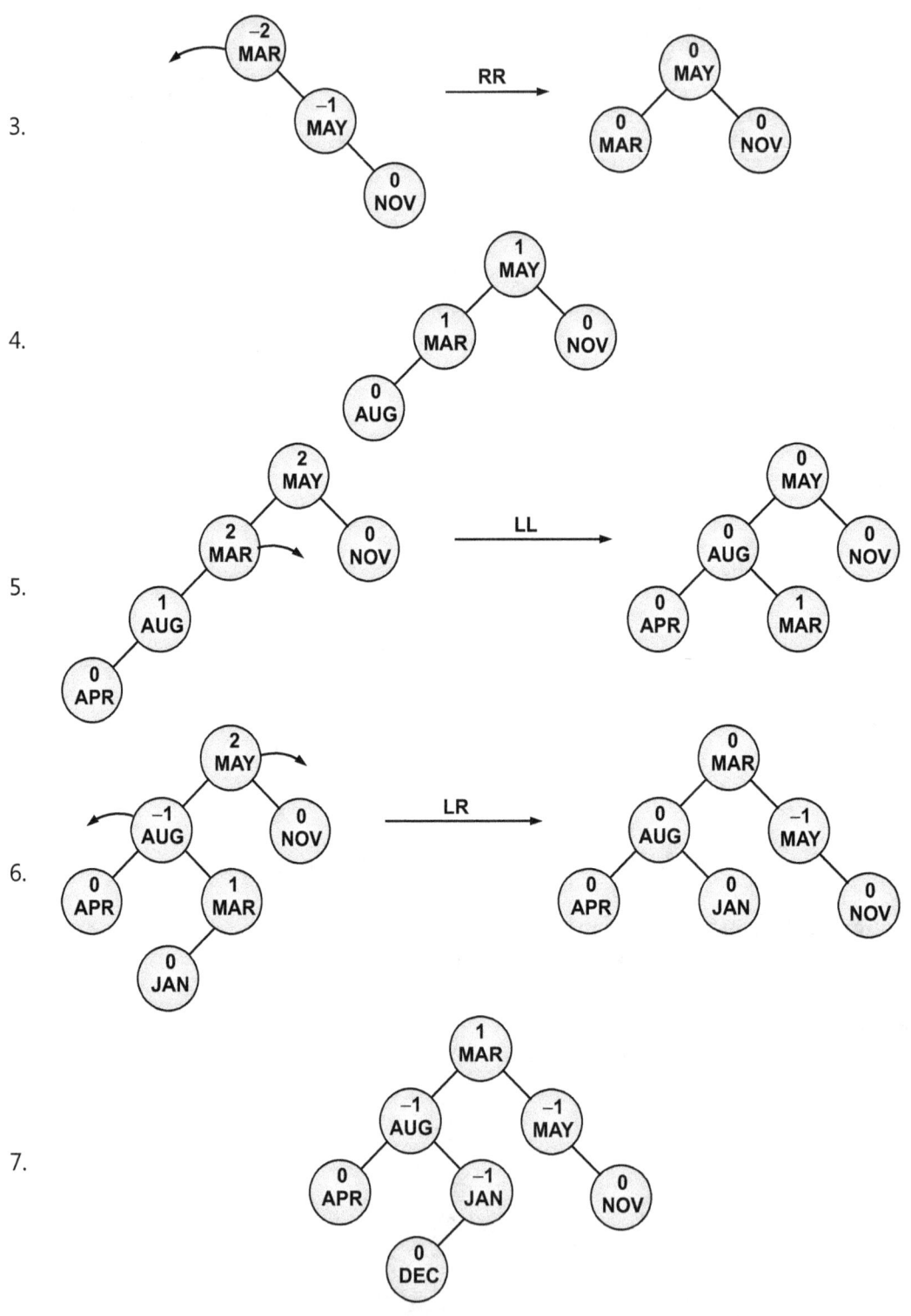

8.

9.

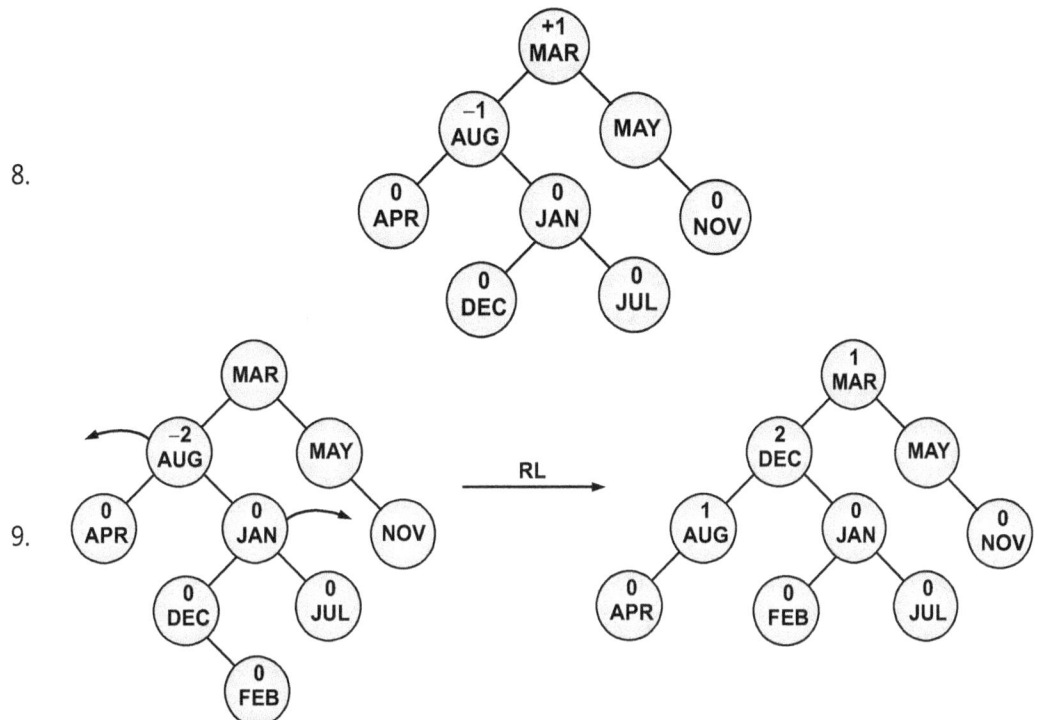

Fig. 4.47: Creating height balance (AVL) binary tree

4.9 APPLICATIONS OF TREES

In computer science, trees have number of applications because they are most efficient for searching the data. Hence, they are used to store large databases. Some of the applications are as below.

1. **Expression Tree**

The compilers and interpreters evaluate the expression based on the precedence of operators. Any arithmetic expression can be represented using binary tree. The evaluation of the expression becomes convenient with such representation. For example, the expression a + b * c/d can be represented as below:

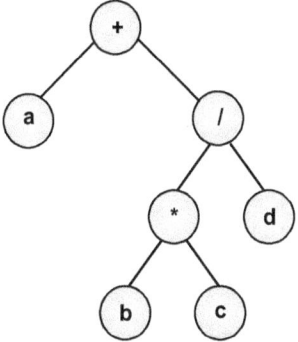

Fig. 4.48: Expression tree for a + b * c/d

The expression 3 * 4 + (8 + 7) can be represented as

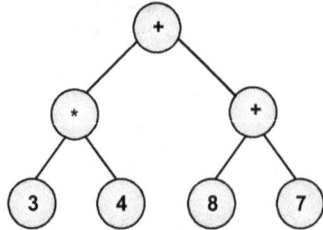

Fig. 4.49: Expression for tree 3*4+(8+7)

Inorder traversal of tree will result into evaluation of the expression. Some more examples are as below.
d=a * b/d − 4.

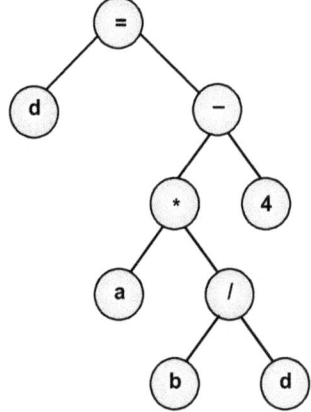

Fig. 4.50: Expression tree for d = a*b/d−4

x=4 * 5 + 6 * 7 − 3/2

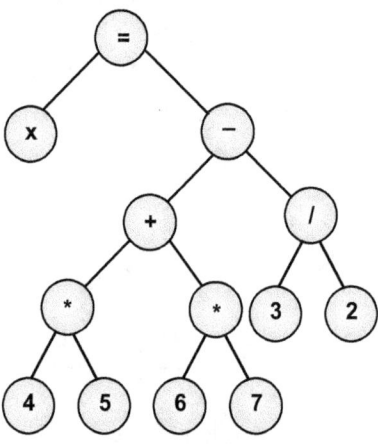

Fig. 4.51: Expression tree for x = 4*5+6*7−3/2

2. Game Trees

The trees can be used in many gaming applications. The different moves in the game can be represented using trees. From a given board position, we can represent all possible moves so that we can select best possible move.

Consider the problem of implementing a computer program to play a game. To simplify things a bit, we will only consider games with the following two properties:

(i) Two player - we do not deal with coalitions etc.
(ii) Zero sum - one player's win is the other's loss; there are no co-operative victories

Examples of these kinds of games include many classic board games, such as tic-tac-toe, chess, checkers, and go. For these types of games, we can model the game using what is called a *game tree*.

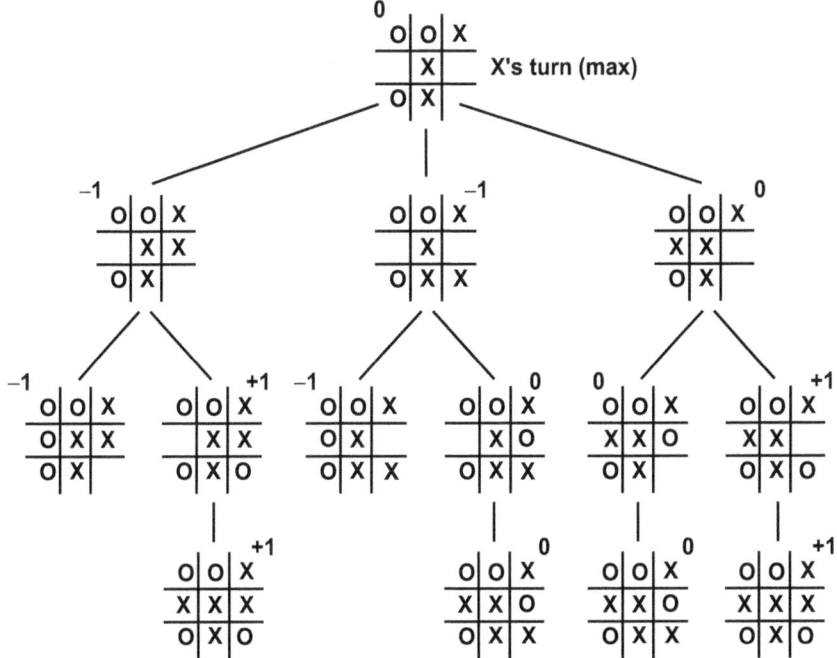

Fig. 4.52: Game tree

Fig. 4.52 shows a section of a game tree for tic-tac-toe. Each node represents a board position, and the children of each node are the legal moves from that position. To score each position, we will give each position which is favorable for player 1 a positive number (the more positive, the more favorable). Similarly, we will give each position which is favorable for player 2 a negative number (the more negative, the more favorable). In our tic tac toe example, player 1 is 'X', player 2 is 'O', and the only three scores we will have are +1 for a win by 'X', −1 for a win by 'O', and 0 for a draw. Note that scores of current positions can only be calculated. To calculate the scores for the other positions, we must look ahead a few moves, by using tree traversal algorithms.

4.10 HUFFMAN CODING

Huffman coding is a lossless data compression algorithm. The idea is to assign variable length codes to input characters, lengths of the assigned codes are based on the frequencies of corresponding characters. The most frequent character gets the smallest code and the least frequent character gets the largest code.

The variable-length codes assigned to input characters are Prefix Codes, means the codes (bit sequences) are assigned in such a way that the code assigned to one character is not prefix of code assigned to any other character. This is how Huffman Coding makes sure that there is no ambiguity when decoding the generated bit stream.

Let us understand prefix codes with a counter example. Let there be four characters a, b, c and d, and their corresponding variable length codes be 00, 01, 0 and 1. This coding leads to ambiguity because code assigned to c is prefix of codes assigned to a and b. If the compressed bit stream is 0001, the de-compressed output may be "cccd" or "ccb" or "acd" or "ab".

There are mainly two major parts in Huffman Coding
1. Build a Huffman Tree from input characters.
2. Traverse the Huffman Tree and assign codes to characters.

4.10.1 Steps to build Huffman Tree

Input is array of unique characters along with their frequency of occurrences and output is Huffman Tree.

1. Create a leaf node for each unique character and build a min heap of all leaf nodes (Min Heap is used as a priority queue. The value of frequency field is used to compare two nodes in min heap. Initially, the least frequent character is at root)
2. Extract two nodes with the minimum frequency from the min heap.
3. Create a new internal node with frequency equal to the sum of the two nodes frequencies. Make the first extracted node as its left child and the other extracted node as its right child. Add this node to the min heap.
4. Repeat steps#2 and #3 until the heap contains only one node. The remaining node is the root node and the tree is complete.

Let us understand the algorithm with an example:

Character	Frequency
a	5
b	9
c	12
d	13
e	16
f	45

Step 1: Build a min heap that contains 6 nodes where each node represents root of a tree with single node.

Step 2: Extract two minimum frequency nodes from min heap. Add a new internal node with frequency 5 + 9 = 14.

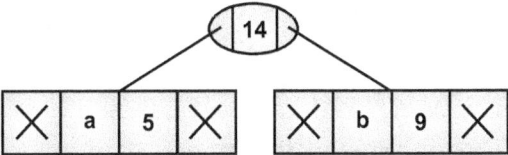

Fig. 4.53

Now min heap contains 5 nodes where 4 nodes are roots of trees with single element each, and one heap node is root of tree with 3 elements

Character	Frequency
c	12
d	13
Internal Node	14
e	16
f	45

Step 3: Extract two minimum frequency nodes from heap. Add a new internal node with frequency 12 + 13 = 25.

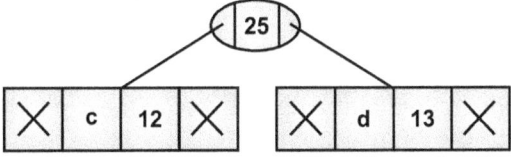

Fig. 4.54

Now min heap contains 4 nodes where 2 nodes are roots of trees with single element each, and two heap nodes are root of tree with more than one nodes.

Character	Frequency
Internal Node	14
e	16
Internal Node	25
f	45

Step 4: Extract two minimum frequency nodes. Add a new internal node with frequency 14 + 16 = 30.

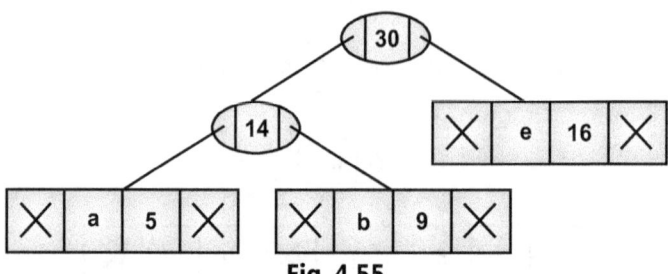

Fig. 4.55

Now min heap contains 3 nodes.

Character	Frequency
Internal Node	25
Internal Node	30
f	45

Step 5: Extract two minimum frequency nodes. Add a new internal node with frequency 25 + 30 = 55.

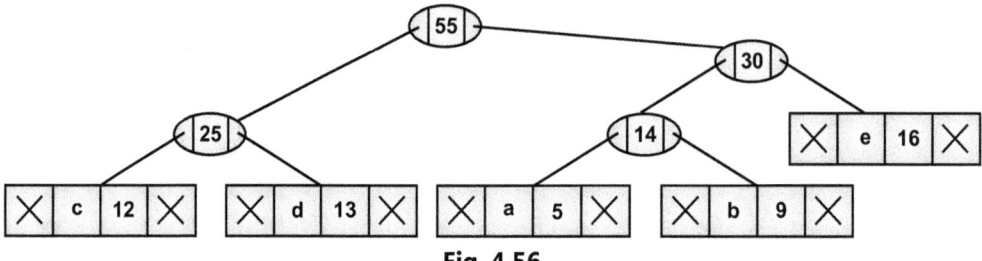

Fig. 4.56

Now min heap contains 2 nodes.

Character	Frequency
f	45
Internal Node	55

Step 6: Extract two minimum frequency nodes. Add a new internal node with frequency 45 + 55 = 100.

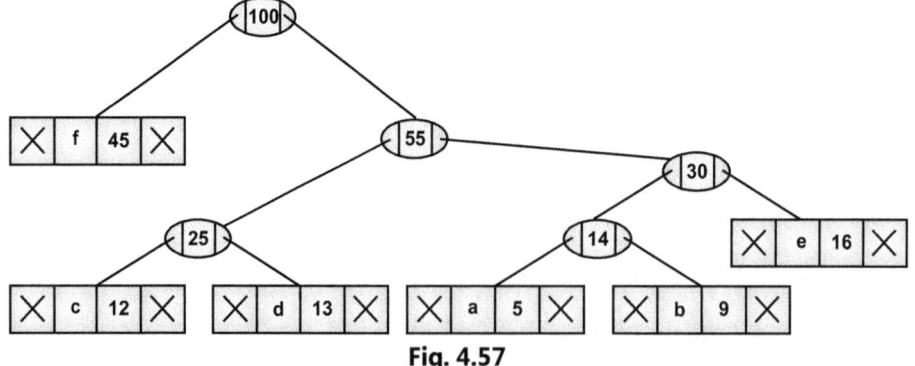

Fig. 4.57

Now min heap contains only one node.

Character	Frequency
Internal Node	100

Since the heap contains only one node, the algorithm stops here.

4.10.2 Steps to Print Codes from Huffman Tree

Traverse the tree formed starting from the root. Maintain an auxiliary array. While moving to the left child, write 0 to the array. While moving to the right child, write 1 to the array. Print the array when a leaf node is encountered.

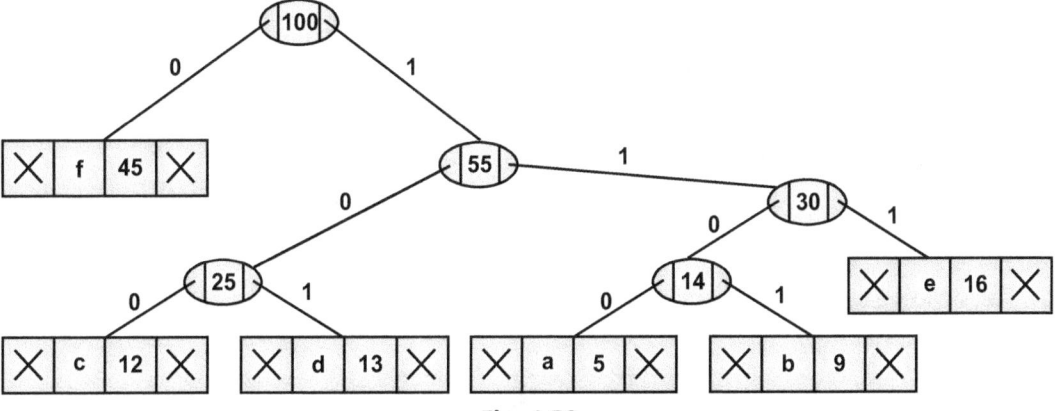

Fig. 4.58

The codes are as follows:

Character	Codeword
f	0
c	100
d	101
a	1100
b	1101
e	111

SUMMARY

- Tree is a nonlinear data structure used for efficient access or retrieval of elements.
- A tree (T) is a set of nodes. The set can be empty. If it is non-empty set, it consists of a specially designated node called root node and zero or more sub-trees ($T_1, T_2, ..., T_n$) each whose roots are connected by a directed edge from the root of T.
- Binary tree is a tree in which no node has more than two sub-trees.

- A binary tree can be represented using array or linked representation.
- A binary tree can be traversed in three different ways inorder (LVR), preorder (VLR) and postorder (LRV).
- A Binary Search Tree (BST) is used to store data for searching applications. A binary search tree is a binary tree in which for each node, the left sub-tree elements are less than the node elements and right sub-tree elements are greater than the node element.
- If binary search tree is height balanced, the time complexity of search is $O(\log_2 n)$.
- The traversals of binary tree can be implemented using recursive or non-recursive ways.
- A threaded binary tree makes use of NULL fields in the nodes of binary tree for spreading up the operations on binary tree.
- A height balanced or AVL tree is a binary tree with T_l and T_r as left and right sub-trees having heights h_l and h_r such that $|h_l - h_r| \leq 1$.
- In order to make a binary tree height balanced, we can use one of the four rotations LL, RR, LR or RL.
- Trees can be used for expression storage and evaluation and gaming applications.

SOLVED PROBLEMS

1. Write a recursive function to print leaf nodes of binary tree.

Solution:

```
void leaf node_check(NODE *temp)
{
    printf("The leaf nodes are \n");
    if (temp!=NULL)
    {
        leaf-node-check (temp->lchild);
        if(temp->lchild==NULL && temp->rchild=NULL)
        {
            printf("%d \n", temp->data);
        }
        leaf_node_check(temp->rchild);
    }
}
```

2. **Write Inorder, Preoder and Postorder traversals for following tree.**

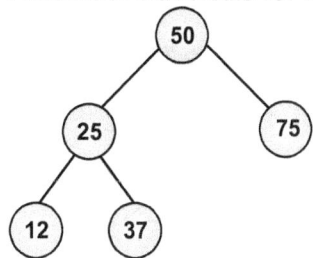

Fig. 4.59: Binary Tree

Solution:

Inorder	12 25 37 50 75
Preoder	50 25 12 37 75
Postorder	12 37 25 75 50

3. **For the following data draw a binary search tree. Show all steps.**

50 80 30 20 100 75 25 15 68

Solution: A binary search tree is shown in figure 4.60.

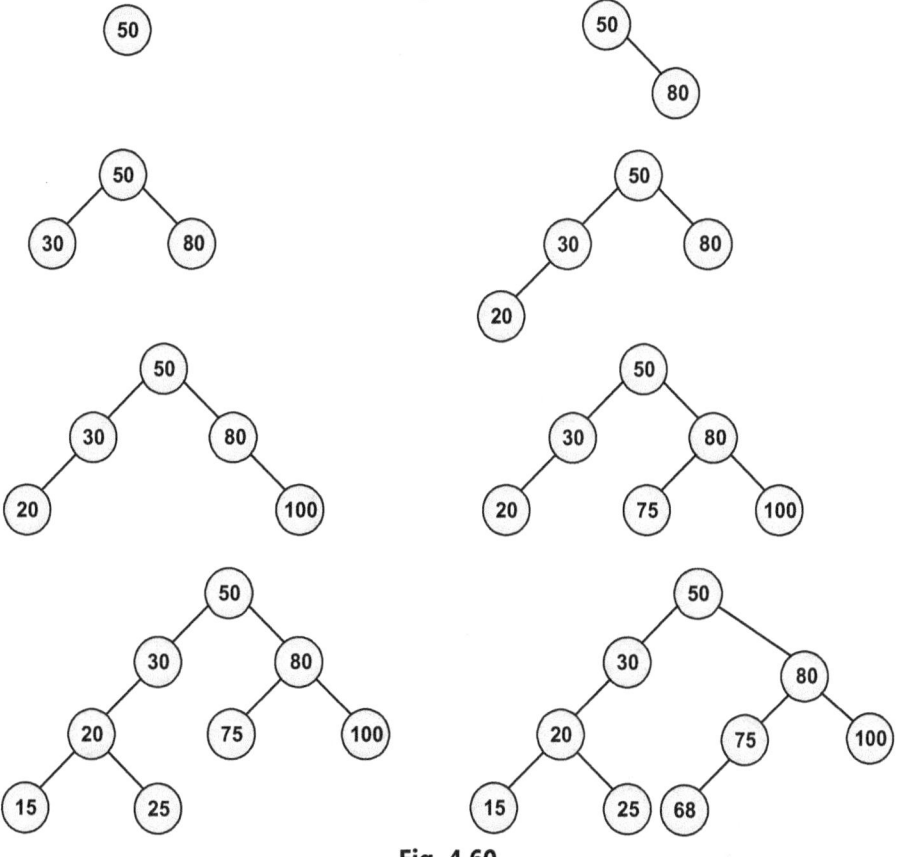

Fig. 4.60

4. Create an AVL tree for the following data.

40 20 10 30 70 60 55

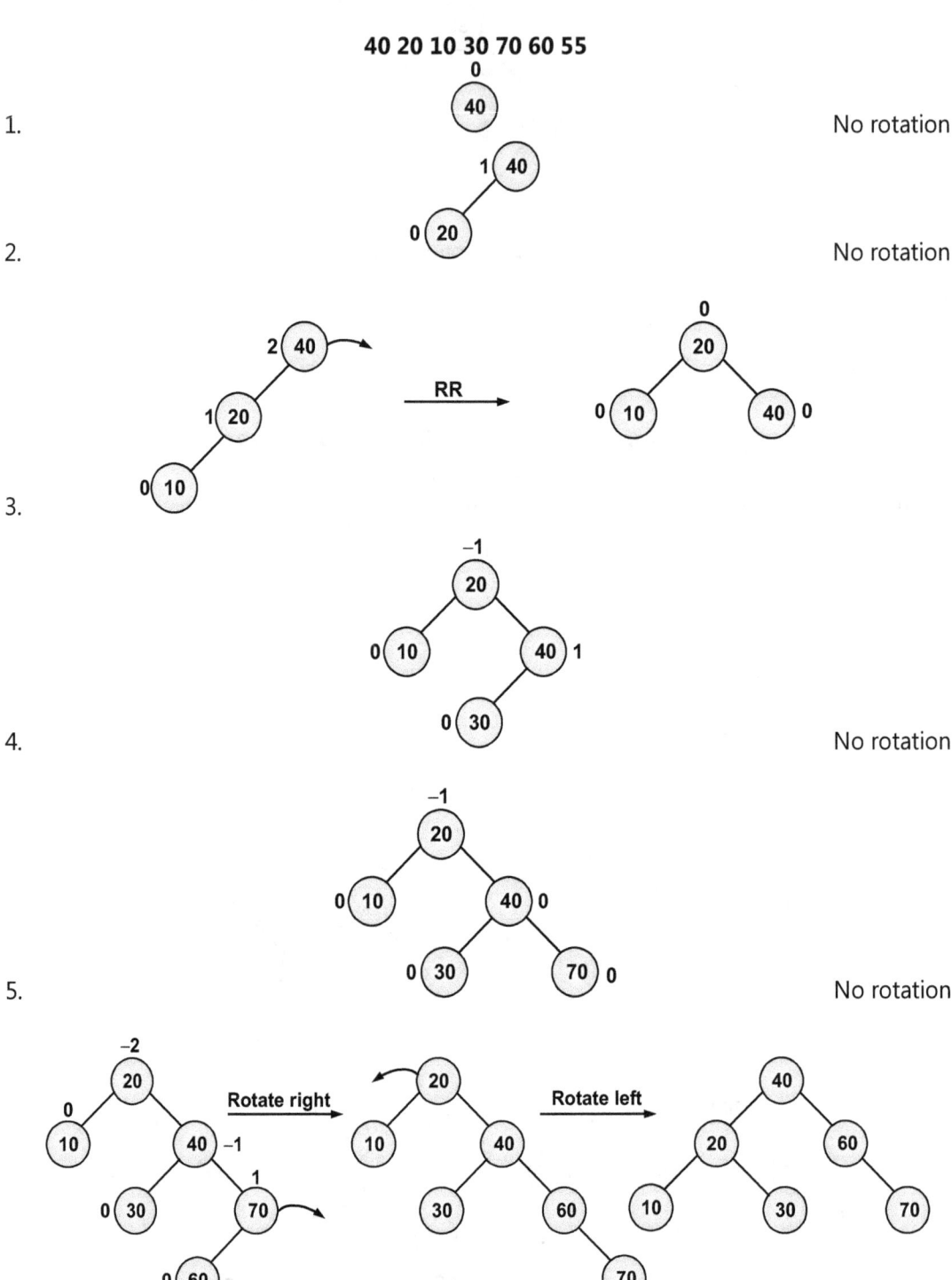

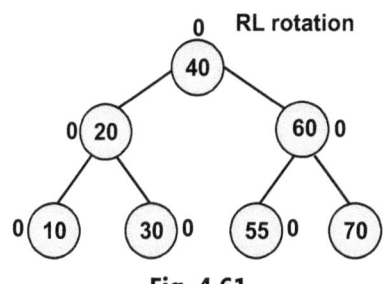

Fig. 4.61

RL rotation

No rotation

5. Write Inorder, Preoder and Postorder traversals for the following.
Solution:

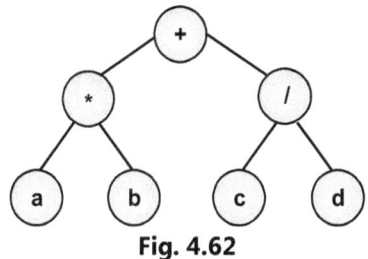

Fig. 4.62

Solution:
- Inorder   :   + *ab/cd
- Preoder   :   a * b + c/d
- Postorder :   ab * cd \+

6. Create an AVL tree for the following elements. Show all steps with rotation.

CAR BAG MAN SAD TAN FAN ADD

Solution:

1. 0
   CAR   No rotation

2. 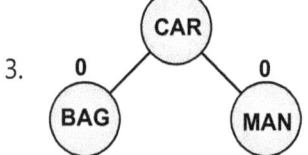   No rotation

3. BAG — CAR — MAN   No rotation

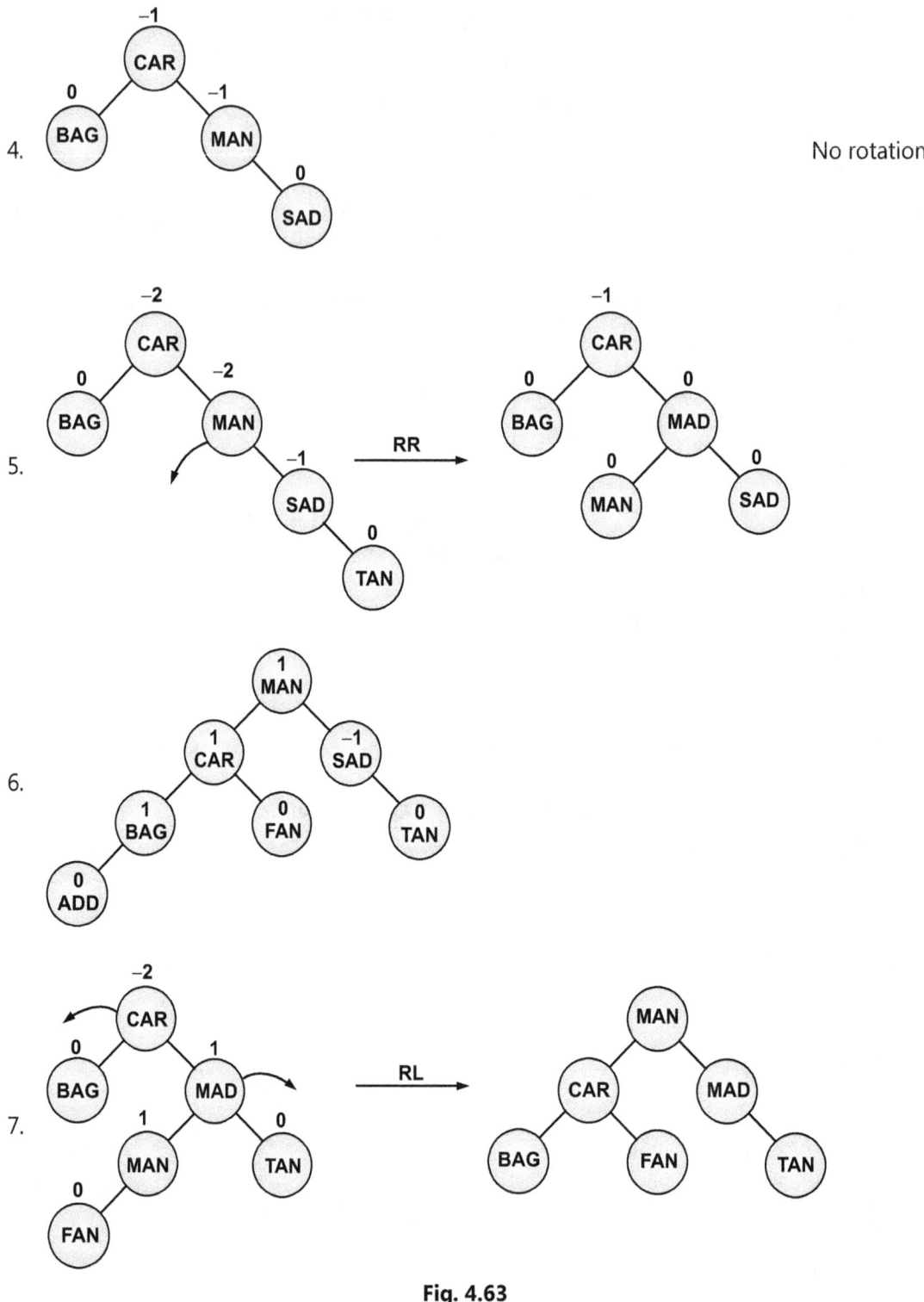

Fig. 4.63

7. **From gives traversal, construct the binary tree.**

   Inorder   : DBFEAGCLJHK

   Preorder : DFEBGLJKHCA

Solution:

Step I: From postorder we can see last element is root.

Hence, the left sub-tree and right sub-tree from inorder traversal is

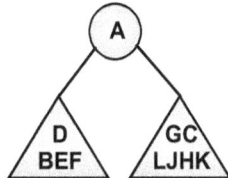

Step II:

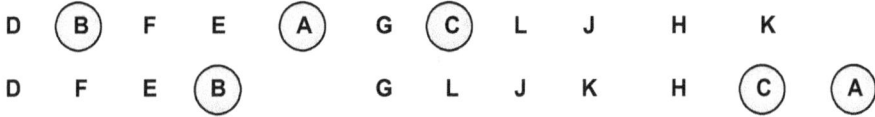

Step III:

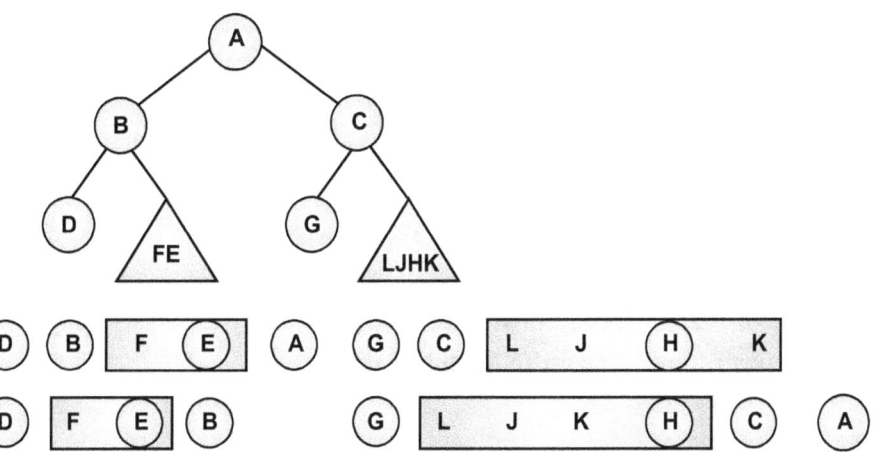

Step IV:

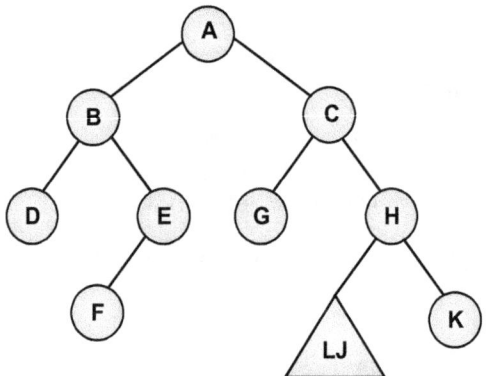

Step V:

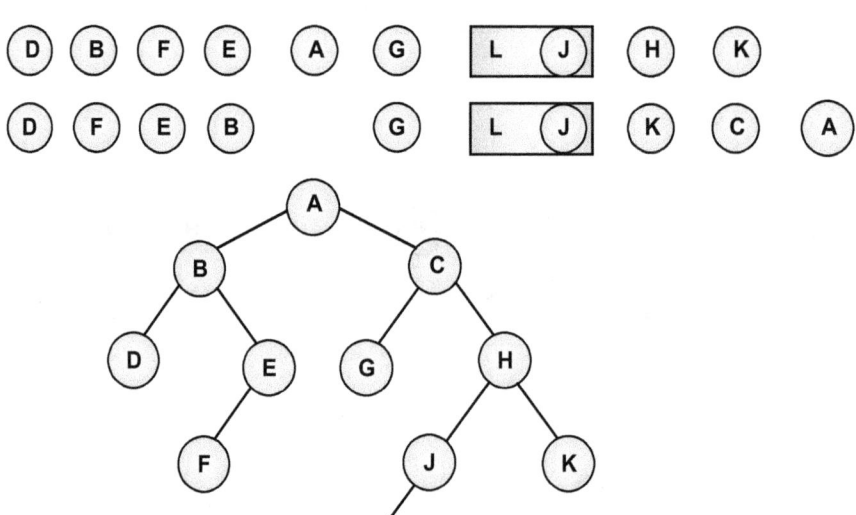

Fig. 4.64

8. **Define binary search tree. Construct binary search tree from following set of strings. Show all steps. Also write height of final tree.**

   JAN FEB MAR APR MAY JUN JUL AUG SEP OCT NOV DEC

   Solution: (Refer section 11.4 for definition)

Steps for creation of BST.

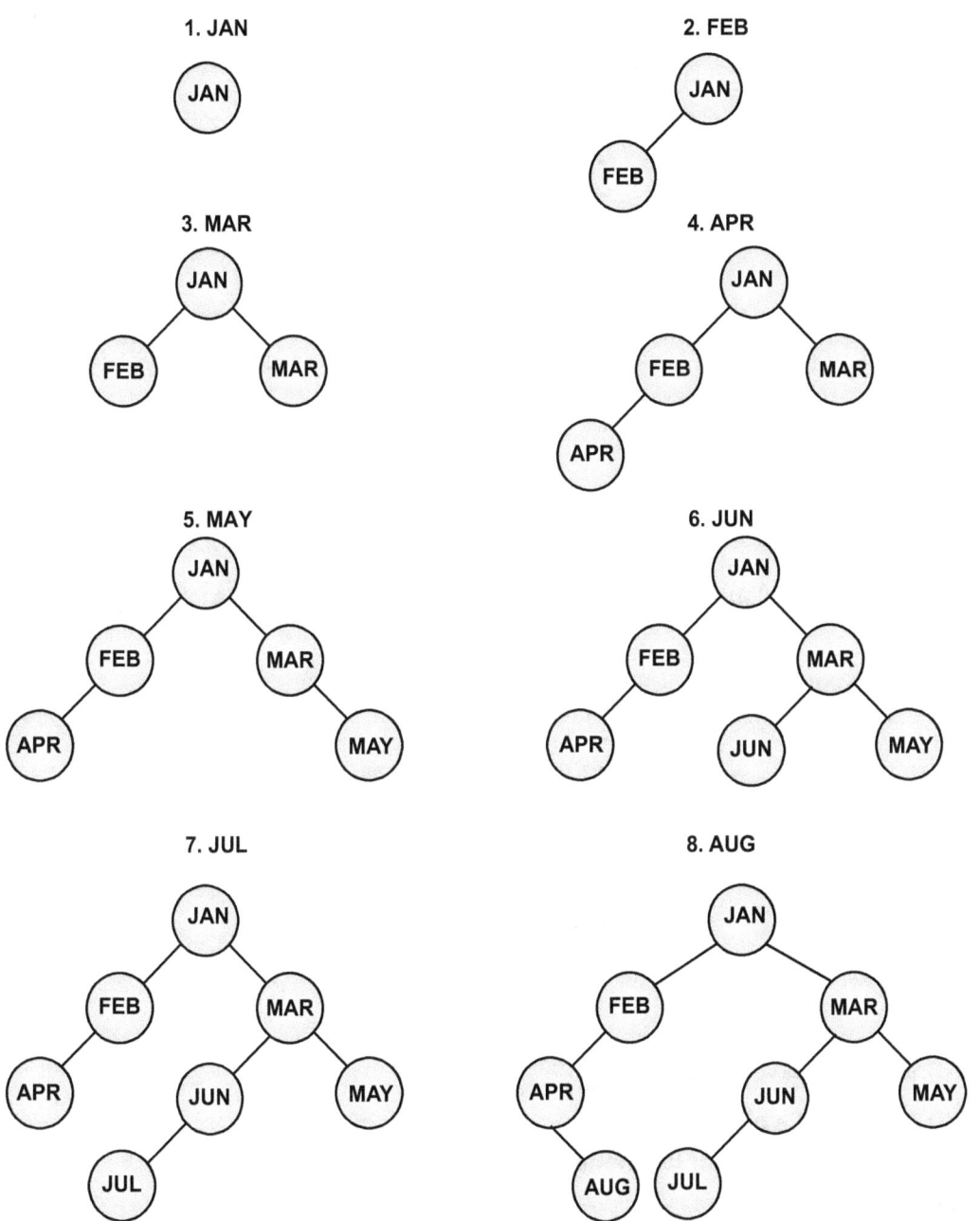

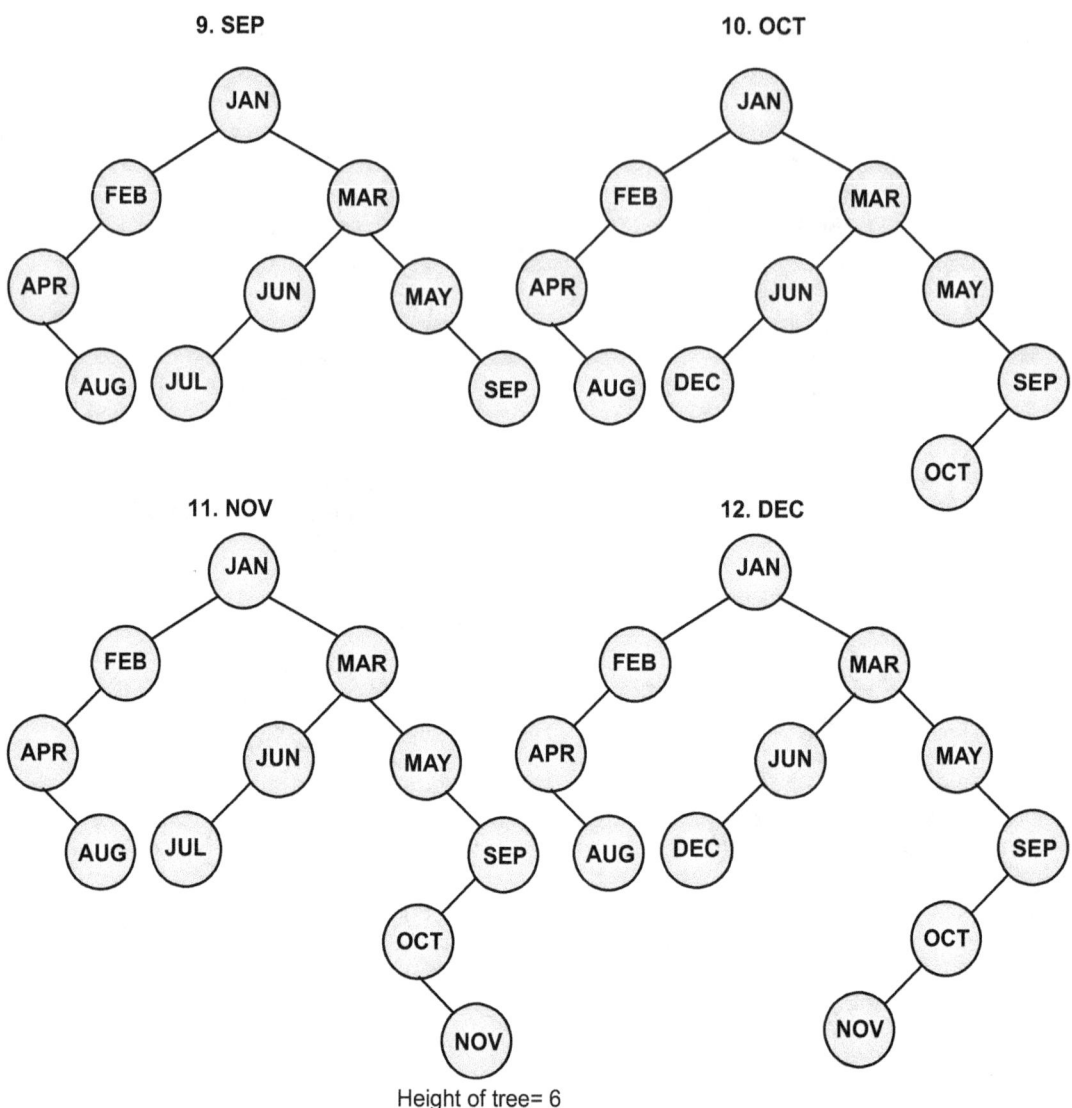

Fig. 4.65

9. Write a recursive function to find.
   (i) Height of a binary tree.
   (ii) To count and print leaf nodes of binary tree.

Solution:

(i) int height(NODE *root)
    {
        int c;

```
    if (root== NULL)
        return(0);
    if (root->lchild==NULL & root->rchild==NULL)
        return(0);
    hl=height(root->lchild);
    hr=height(root->rchild);
    if(hl>hr)
        return(1 + hl)
    else
        return(1 + hr);
}
```

(ii) Refer solved problem 3.

10. Give pseudo code to print the leaves of tree using any traversal.

Solution:

```
void print_leaves(NODE *root)
{
    if (root!=NULL)
        print_leaves(root->lchild);
    if (root->lchild == NULL & root->rchild == NULL)
        printf("%d \n", root->data);
    print_leaves(root->rchild);
}
```

11. Explain any one application of binary tree with suitable example.

Solution: There are two applications of binary tree that we can list out.

(i) Binary search tree.

(ii) Expression tree.

(i) Binary search tree:

We can use binary tree to store data in such a way that it will be easier to search required data. We can store the binary search tree such that at each node on the left side we will have smaller numbers and on right side we will have larger numbers than the data at node.

(ii) Expression tree:

Another application can be expression tree. We can store an infix expression into the binary tree so that we can have its prefix or postfix conversion using preorder or postorder traversal.

12. Write a non-recursive function to count number of leaf nodes in a binary tree.

Solution:

We can use non-recursive inorder traversal function. In place of print statement, we can use following statement.

```
if (temp->lchild==NULL&&temp->rchild==NULL)
    count=count + 1;


int count_leaves(NODE *root)
{   NODE *temp;  int count;
    temp=root;
    do
    {
        while(temp!=NULL)
        {
            push(temp);
            temp temp->lchild;
        }
        temp=pop( );
        if(temp-lchild==NULL && temp->rchild==NULL)
            count=count + 1;
        temp=temp->rchild;
    } while(!stack empty( ) || temp!=NULL);
    return(count);
}
```

13. Construct a threaded binary search tree for following set of elements. Show all steps.

100 50 200 300 20 150 70 180 120 30

Solution:

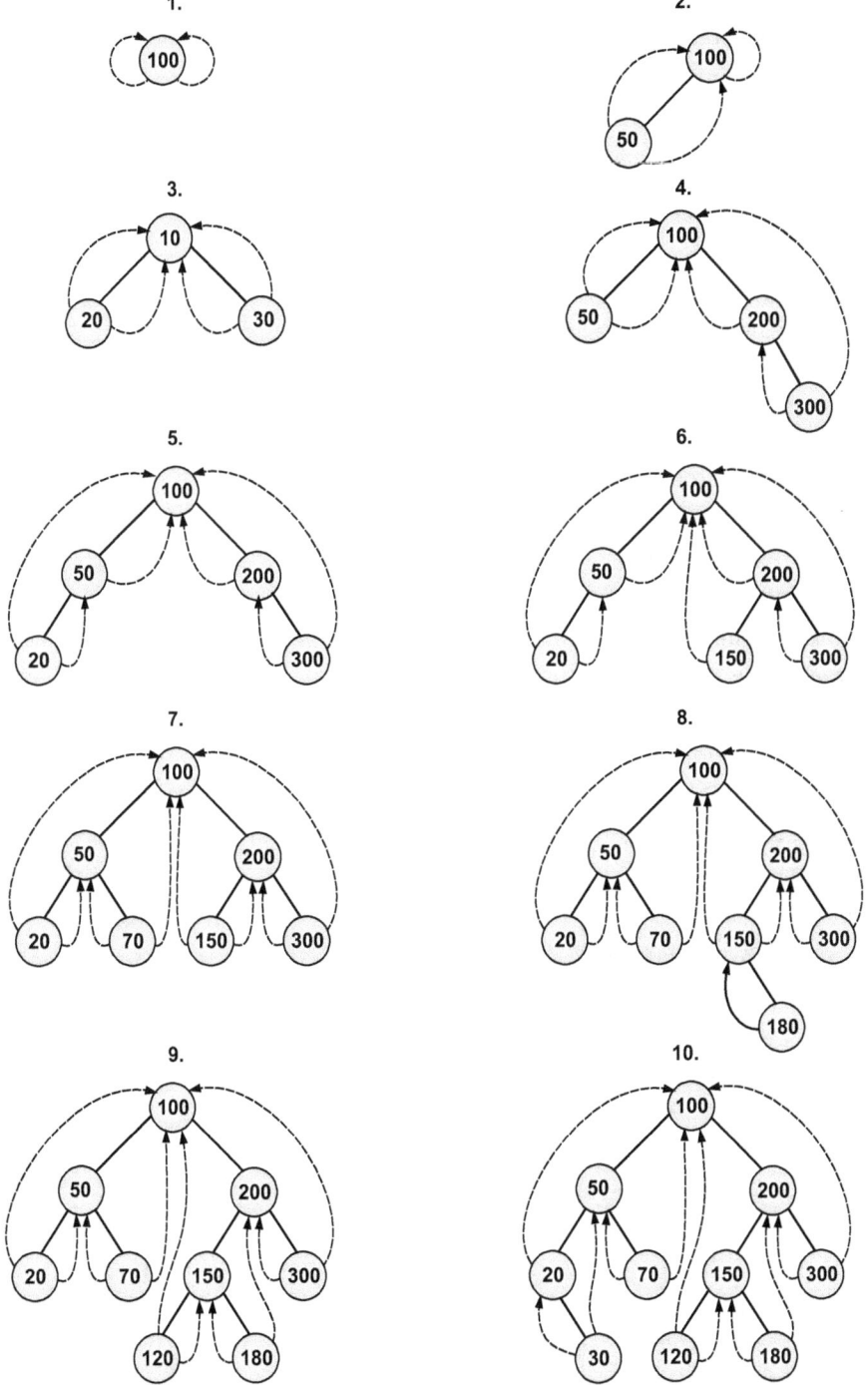

Fig. 4.66

EXERCISE

1. Define the following related to tree:
   1. Complete binary tree.
   2. Siblings.
   3. Non-terminals, (All non-leaf nodes are known as non-terminals).
   4. Forest.
   5. Height or Depth.
   6. Ancestors (All nodes on the path joining the current node and the root node are ancestors of the current node).
2. Define following terms with example.
   (i) Complete binary tree.
   (ii) Siblings.
   (iii) Height.
   (iv) Binary search tree.
   (v) Forest.
3. Define the following terms.
   1. Binary tree,
   2. Complete Binary tree,
   3. Threaded Binary Tree.
   4. What is binary tree?
5. Define the following:
   (a) Binary tree,
   (b) Complete binary tree,
   (c) Full binary, tree,
   (d) Sibling.
6. Define the following terms with respect to tree.
   (i) Complete binary tree.
   (ii) Forest.
   (iii) Height of binary tree.
   (iv) Skewed binary tree.
   (v) Full binary tree.
7. Explain the sequential representation of binary tree with example.
8. Define the term binary search tree. Give a 'C' declaration to define a node structure for the same. Write a function in 'C' to insert a node in a binary search tree.
9. What do you mean by binary search tree? Write a C function to search an element from a given binary search tree.
10. What is binary search tree? Explain its application.
11. What is binary search tree? Explain its application.

12. What is Binary search tree? Explain the application of BST.
13. Define binary search tree. Write a function to delete a node from a BST. Consider all possible cases.
14. Write necessary 'C' functions to search given data in BST.
15. Write a function to search an element in BST.
16. Traverse the tree built in Q. 47 in inorder, postorder and preorder and display the sequence of numbers.
17. Write a 'C' function (non-recursive) for deleting a node from binary search tree.
18. Write a C function to delete a node from binary search tree. Consider all cases.
19. Write necessary 'C' functions to delete a node in BST.
20. Write a non-recursive function to delete a node from BST. Explain all cases with suitable example.
21. Define binary search tree. Write a function to delete a node from BST.
22. Write a C function to insert a node in binary search tree.
23. Write a function to insert an element in BST.
24. Write necessary 'C' functions to implement inorder traversal in a binary tree non-recursively.
25. Write a non-recursive C function to traverse a binary tree in in-order traversal.
26. Write a non-recursive function in 'C' to perform a pre-order traversal on a binary tree.
27. Write necessary 'C' functions to implement preorder traversal in a binary tree non-recursively.
28. Write a pseudo code to traverse a given binary tree in preorder without recursion.
29. Write a non-recursive 'C' function to traverse binary tree in preorder. Explain with suitable example.
30. Explain non-recursive inorder traversal of binary tree.
31. Write an algorithm to implement non-recursive inorder traversal of binary tree.
32. Comment on "Threaded binary tree can be traversed without using stack".
33. What is threaded binary tree? State its advantage and disadvantages.
34. What is threaded binary tree? State its advantages and disadvantages.
35. State and explain the advantages of threaded binary tree.
36. Explain the term threaded binary tree. Give a 'C declaration to define the node structure of a threaded binary tree. What are the advantages of threaded binary trees over normal binary trees?
37. What do you mean by threaded binary tree? Also write pseudo code to perform non-recursive preorder traversal of TBT without using stack.
38. What is threaded binary tree? Explain its application.
39. What is threaded binary tree? Explain the application of threaded binary tree.
40. (i) Give declaration in 'C' for TBT.
    (ii) Write a function in 'C' to perform traversal of threaded binary tree.
    (iii) Compare traversal of TBT with binary tree.

41. List the advantages of using a threaded binary tree. Give node structure for defining a threaded binary tree. Write a function in 'C' to find the pre-order successor of any node pointed by P in a threaded binary tree.
42. List advantages of threaded binary tree. Give its node structure. Write a function in 'C' to find preorder successor of any node pointed by 7 in TBT.
43. What is threaded binary tree? Explain its advantages/applications.
44. Comment on "Threaded binary tree can be traversed without stack".
45. Write a non-recursive algorithm for pre-order traversal of a binary tree.
46. What is AVL tree? Explain RR and LL rotations with example.
47. Build a binary search tree from the following set of elements:
    100, 50, 200, 300, 20, 150, 70, 180, 120, 30
48. Construct binary search tree from the following set of strings:
    JAN, FEB, MAR, APR, MAY, JUN, JUL, AUG, SEP, OCT, NOV and DEC.
49. Construct Binary tree if following traversals are give.
    Inorder   :   D, F, E, G, A, H, I, C
    Postorder :   D, F, G, E, B, I, H, C, A
50. Construct BST from following elements:
    (i) MAT, TAN, BAN, BAT, SUN, CAT, RAT Show all steps.
    (ii) 100, 50, 200, 300, 20, 150, 70, 180, 120, 30
51. Construct binary search tree from the following set of strings:
    MAR, MAY, NOV, AUG, APR, JAN, DEC, JUL, FEB, JUN, OCT and SEP. Show all steps.
52. Create Binary Search Tree for the following data and print the tree using all tree traversals.
    MAR, OCT, JAN, APR, NOV, FEB, MAY, DEC, JUN, AUG, JUL, SEP.
53. Write a recursive function to count and print leaf nodes of binary tree.
54. Write a recursive function to find height of binary tree.
55. Write recursive functions to obtain:
    (i) Height of a binary tree,
    (ii) To count and print the leaf nodes of a binary tree.
56. Explain any one application of binary tree with suitable example.
57. Construct a threaded binary search tree for the following set of elements:
    100, 50, 200, 300, 20, 150, 150, 70, 180, 120, 30 show all steps
58. Write a short note on Huffman coding.

***

UNIT V

SEARCHING AND SORTING

5.1 COMPLEXITY OF ALGORITHM

Complexity of an algorithm is the function which gives the running time and space requirement of an algorithm in terms of size of input data. Frequency count refers to the number of times particular instructions executed in a block of code. Frequency count plays important role in the performance analysis of an algorithm. Each instruction in algorithm is incremented by one as its execution. Frequency count analysis is the form of priori analysis. Frequency count analysis produces output in terms of time complexity and space complexity.

- **Time complexity:** Time complexity is about to number of times compiler execute basic operations in instruction. That is because basic operations are so defined that the time for the other operations is much less than or at most proportional to the time for the basic operations. To determine time complexity user need to calculate frequency count and express it in terms of notations. Total time taken by program is the summation of compile time and running time. Out of these two main point to take care about is running time as it depends upon the number and magnitude of input and output.
- **Space complexity:** Space complexity is about to maximum amount of memory required for algorithm. To determine space complexity user need to calculate frequency count and express it in terms of notations.

Frequency count analysis for this code is as follows

Sr. No.	Instructions	Frequency count
1.	#include<stdio.h>	
2.	#include<conio.h>	
3.	void main() {	
4.	int marks;	
5.	printf("enter a marks");	add 1 to the time count
6.	scanf("%d",&marks);	add 1 to the space count
7.	printf("your marks is %d",marks);	add 1 to the time count
8.	getch(); }	

In the above example, for the first four instructions there is no frequency count. For data declaration and the inclusion of header file there is no frequency count. So, for this example has a frequency count for time is 2 and a frequency count for space is 1. So, total frequency count is 3.

Consider the following example

Sr. No.	Instructions	Frequency count
1.	#include<stdio.h>	
2.	#include<conio.h>	
3.	void main() {	
4.	int sum=0;	1
5.	for(i=0;i<5;i++)	6
6.	sum=sum+i;	5
7.	printf("Addition is %d",sum);	1
8.	getch(); }	

Explanation: In the above example, one is add to frequency count for instruction four and seven after that in fifth instruction is check from zero to five so it will add value six to frequency count. 'For' loop executed for five times so for sixth instruction frequency count is five. Total frequency count for above program is 1+6+5+1 =13.

Consider the following example

Sr. No.	Instructions	Frequency count
1.	#include<stdio.h>	
2.	#include<conio.h>	
3.	void main() {	
4.	int a[2][3],b[2][3],c[2][3]]	
5.	for(i=0;i<m;i++)	m+1
6.	{	
7.	for(j=0;j<n;j++)	m(n+1)
8.	{	
9.	c[i][j]=a[i][j]*b[i][j];	m.n
10.	}}	
11.	getch(); }	

Explanation: In the above example, in instruction five value of 'i' is check from 0 to 'm' so frequency count is 'm+1' for fifth instruction. In instruction five value of 'j' is check from 0 to 'n' so frequency count is 'n+1' but this instruction is in the for loop which execute for 'm' times, so for seventh instruction is m*(n+1). Ninth instruction is in the two for loops, out of which first for loop execute for m times and second 'for' loop execute for 'n' times. So for ninth instruction frequency count is m*n. The total frequency count for the above program is (m+1)+m(n+1)+mn=2m+2mn+1=2m(1+n)+1.

Consider the following example

Sr. No.	Instructions	Frequency count
1.	#include<stdio.h>	
2.	#include<conio.h>	
3.	void main() {	
4.	int a[2][3],b[2][3],c[2][3]]	
5.	for(i=0;i<m;i++)	m+1
6.	{	
7.	for(j=0;j<n;j++)	m(n+1)
8.	{	
9.	a[i][j]=n;	m.n
10.	for(k=0;k<n;k++)	mn(n+1)
11.	c[i][j]=a[i][j]*b[i][j];	m.n.n
12.	}}	
13.	getch(); }	

Explanation: For above program total frequency count

$$= (m+1)+m(n+1)+mn+mn(n+1)+mn$$
$$= m+1+mn+m+mn+mn^2+mn+mn^2$$
$$= 2mn^2+3mn+2m+1$$
$$= mn(2n+3)+2m+1$$

Consider the following example

Sr. No.	Instructions	Frequency count
1.	#include<stdio.h>	
2.	#include<conio.h>	
3.	void main() {	
4.	int n=1,m;	1
5.	do	
6.	{	
7.	printf("hi");	10
8.	if(n==10)	10

Sr. No.	Instructions	Frequency count
9.	break;	1
10.	n++;	9
11.	}	
12.	while(n<15);	10
13.	getch(); }	

Explanation: the above example, one is add to frequency count for instruction four. The loop will execute till value of n is incremented to 10 from 1, so for loop statements ie instructions seven and eight is execute for tem times. when the value of 'n' is ten then 'break' statement will execute for one time and it will skip the tenth execution of tenth instruction. Tenth instruction will add value nine to frequency count. Total frequency count for above program is 10+10+1+9+10 = 40.

5.2 NOTATIONS

To express the running time complexity of algorithm three asymptotic notations are available. Asymptotic notations are also called as asymptotic bounds. Notations are used to relate the growth of complex function with the simple function. Asymptotic notations have domain of natural numbers. These notations are as follows

    1. Big-oh notation: Big-oh notations can be express by using 'o' symbol. This notation indicates the maximum number of steps required to solve the problem. This notation expresses the worst case growth of an algorithm. Consider the following diagram in which there are two functions f(x) and g(x). f(x) is more complex than the function g(x).

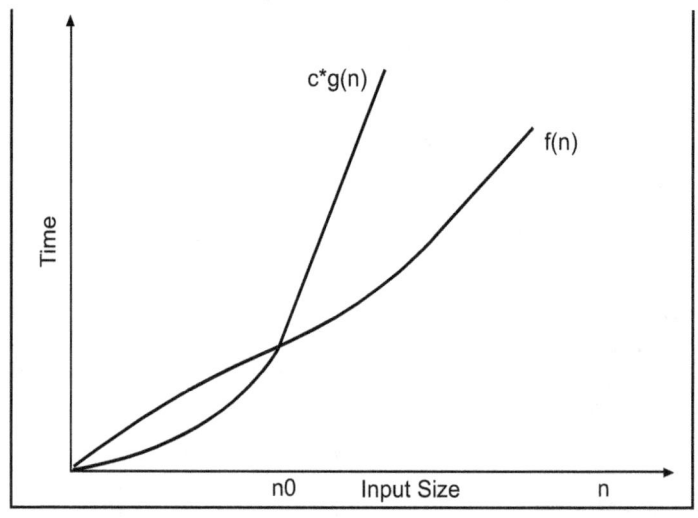

Fig. 5.1

In the above diagram out of two function f(n) and g(n), more complex function is f(n), so need to relate its growth as compare to simple function g(n). More specifically we need one constant function c(n) which bound function f(n) at some point n0. Beyond the point 'n0' function c*g(n) is always greater than f(n).

Now f(n)=Og(n) if there is some constant 'c' and some initial value 'n0'. such that f(n)<=c*g(n) for all n>n0

In the above expression 'n' represents the input size

f(n) represents the time that algorithm will take

f(n) and g(n) are non-negative functions.

Consider the following example

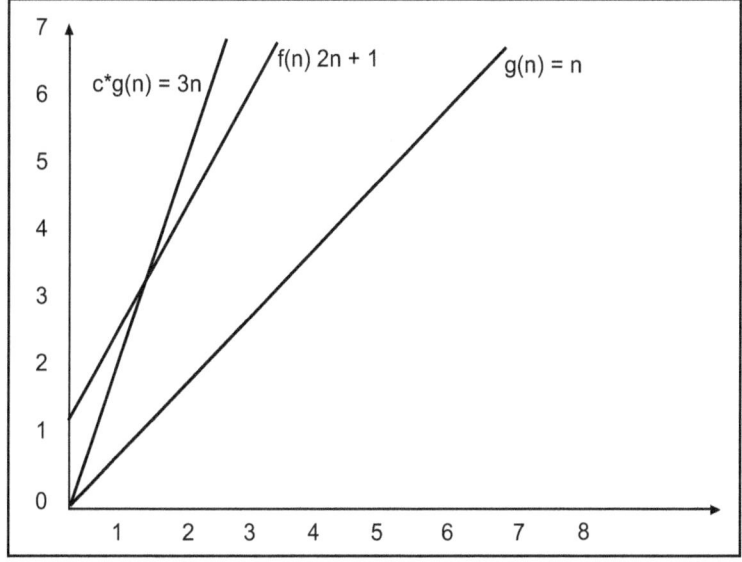

Fig. 5.2

In the above example g(n) is "n" and f(n) is '2n+1' and value of constant is 3. The point where c*g(n) and f(n) intersect is "n0". Beyond 'n0' c*g(n) is always greater than f(n) for constant '3'. We can write the conclusion as follows

f(n)=O g(n)   for constant 'c' =3 and 'n0'=1

such that f(n)<=c*g(n) for all n>n0

2. Big-omega notation: Big-omega notations can be express by using 'Ω' symbol. This notation indicates the minimum number of steps required to solve the problem. This notation expresses the best case growth of an algorithm. Consider the following diagram in which there are two functions f(n) and g(n). f(n) is more complex than the function g(n).

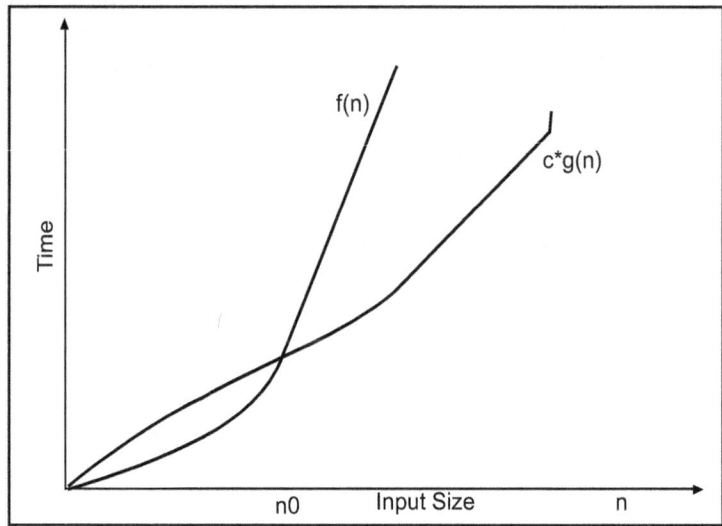

Fig. 5.3

In the above diagram out of two function f(n) and g(n), more complex function is f(n), so need to relate its growth as compare to simple function g(n). More specifically we need one constant function c(n) which bound function f(n) at some point n0. Beyond the point 'n0' function c*g(n) is always smaller than f(n).

Now f(n)=Ωg(n)if there is some constant 'c' and some initial value 'n0'. such that c*g(n) <= f(n)for all n>n0

In the above expression 'n' represents the input size

    f(n) represents the time that algorithm will take

    f(n) and g(n) are non-negative functions.

    Consider the following example

In the above example g(n) is '2n' and f(n) is '2n-2' and value of constant is 0.5. The point where c*g(n) and f(n) intersect is "n0'. Beyond 'n0' c*g(n) is always smaller than f(n) for constant '0.5'. We can write the conclusion as follows

    f(n) = Ω g(n)   for constant 'c' =0.5 and 'n0'=2

    such that c*g(n)<= f(n) for all n>n0

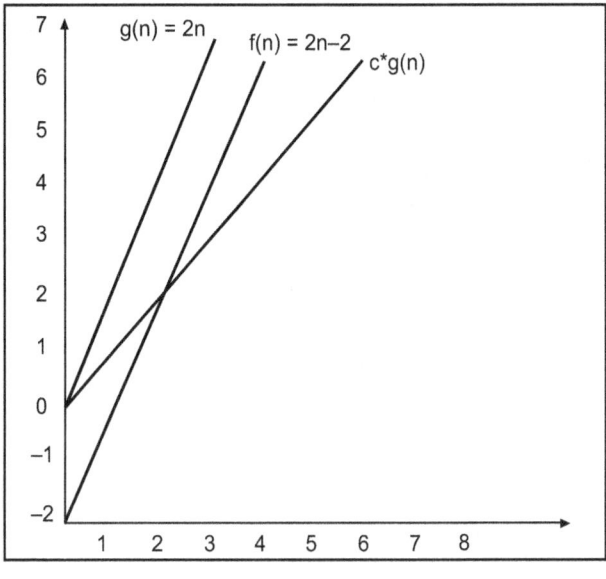

Fig. 5.4

Big-theta notation: Big-theta notations can be express by using 'Θ' symbol. This notation indicates the exact number of steps required to solve the problem. This notation expresses the average case growth of an algorithm. Consider the following diagram in which there are two functions f(n) and g(n). f(n) is more complex than the function g(n).

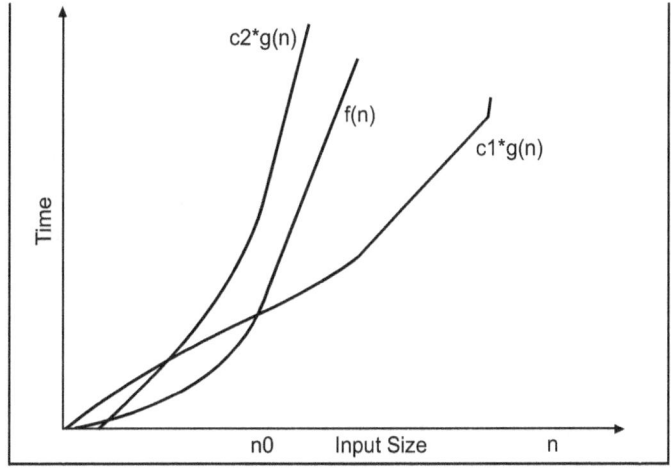

Fig. 5.5

In the above diagram out of two function f(n) and g(n), more complex function is f(n), so need to relate its growth as compare to simple function g(n). More specifically we need one constant function c1 and c2 which bound function f(n) at some point n0. Beyond the point 'n0' function c1*g(n) is always smaller than f(n) and c2*g(n) is always greater than f(n).

Now f(n) = θ g(n) if there is some constant 'c1 and c2' and some initial value 'n0' such that c1*g(n) <= f(n)<=c2*g(n)for all n>n0

In the above expression 'n' represents the input size
f(n) represents the time that algorithm will take
f(n) and g(n) are non-negative functions.
f(n) = θ g(n) if and only if f(n)=O g(n) and f(n)=Ω g(n)
Consider the following example

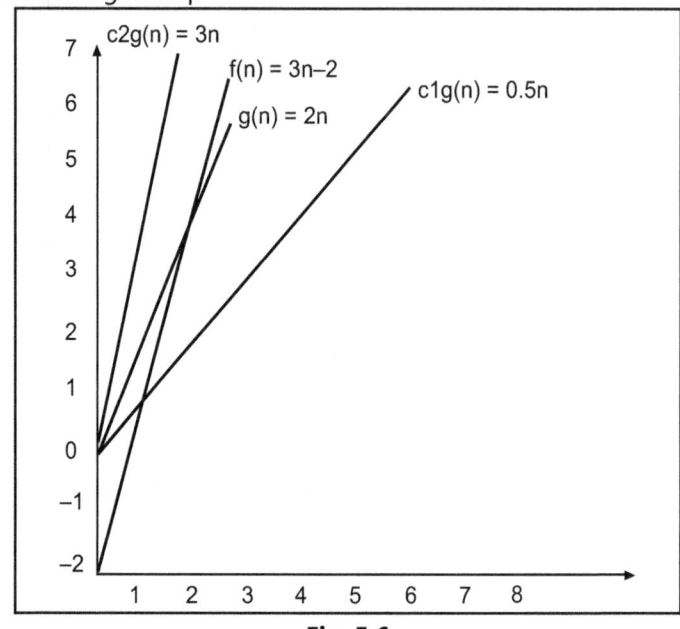

Fig. 5.6

In the above example g(n) is '2n' and f(n) is '3n-2' and value of constant c1 is 0.5 and c2 is 2. The point where c*g(n) and f(n) intersect is "n0". Beyond 'n0' c1*g(n) is always smaller than f(n) for constant '0.5' and c2*g(n) is always greater than f(n) for constant '2'. We can write the conclusion as follows

f(n)=Ω g(n) for constant 'c1' =0.5 , 'c2' = 2 and 'n0'=2
such that c1*g(n)<= f(n)<=c2*g(n) for all n>n0

5.3 ANALYSIS OF AN ALGORITHM

Analysis is the theoretical way to study performance of computer program. Analysis of an algorithm is helpful to decide the complexity of an algorithm. There are three ways to analyze an algorithm which are stated as below.

1. Worst case: In worst case analysis of an algorithm, upper bound of an algorithm is calculated. This case considers the maximum number of operation on algorithm. For example if user want to search a word in English dictionary which is not present in the dictionary. In this case user has to check all the words in dictionary for desired word.

2. **Best case:** In best case analysis of an algorithm, lower bound of an algorithm is calculated. This case considers the minimum number of operation on algorithm. For example if user want to search a word in English dictionary which is found at the first attempt. In this case there is no need to check other words in dictionary.

3. **Average case:** In average case analysis of an algorithm, all possible inputs are consider and computing time is calculated for all inputs. Average case analysis is performed by summation of all calculated value which is divided by total number of inputs. In average case analysis user must be aware about the all types of input so average case analysis are very rarely used in practical cases.

5.4 NEED OF SEARCHING AND SORTING

Sorting and Searching are fundamental operations in computer science. Sorting refers to the operation of arranging data in some given order. Searching refers to the operation of searching the particular record from the existing information.

Consider a database of banking system where information of all customers such as name, contact number, address and account number is stored. If a manager wants to search for a record of a particular customer, he has to look for that record from among all records that has been stored in a database. This process of looking up for a particular record in a database is referred as searching.

If records in a banking database are not ordered properly it will be very difficult for a manager to search for a specific record. On the contrary if all the records are arranged in order according to some criteria like names in alphabetical order or account numbers in ascending order, searching becomes easy and fast. The process of ordering the records in a data base is called sorting. Thus for efficient searching sorting is necessary.

5.5 CONCEPT OF INTERNAL AND EXTERNAL SORTING

Sorting Mechanism is generally categorized in two types.
1. Internal Sorting
2. External Sorting

5.5.1 Internal Sorting

The internal sorting methods are applied to small collection of data. As the entire collection of data to be sorted in internal sort is small enough, sorting can take place within main memory of a computer. Internal Sorting algorithms are of 7 types.

1. Insertion sort
2. Selection sort
3. Merge Sort
4. Radix Sort
5. Quick Sort
6. Heap Sort
7. Bubble Sort

5.5.2 External Sorting

The External sorting methods are applied when the number of data elements to be sorted is too large. These methods involve as much external processing as processing in the CPU. Hence this sorting requires auxiliary storage such as disk or tapes. Algorithms for External sort are

1. Merge sort
2. Replacement Sort

5.6 SORTING METHODS

Sorting is one of the most common data processing applications. Sorting is a process of arranging data according to their values. The data that we get after sorting is called ordered data. Ordered data will be useful in searching a particular data item.

Just like searching, sorting is classified as internal and external sort.

Internal sort is a sort in which all of the data is held in primary memory.

External sort uses primary memory for data being sorted currently and secondary storage for data that cannot fit into primary memory.

There are number of sorting techniques such as selection, bubble, insertion, quick sort, merge sort, heap sort, shell sort etc.

A sorting technique is said to be stable, if elements with equal keys/values maintain their relative input order in the sorted list also.

Data may be sorted in ascending or descending order. It is called sort order. If the order is not specified it is by default ascending.

Since, there are number of methods of sorting, efficiency of these methods should be known to the programmer. The efficiency considerations are nothing but Time and Space complexity also the implementation complexity. The time complexity of sorting algorithm is specified in terms of comparisons and exchanges required.

When elements in the list are sorted, we have to traverse the list. When we traverse the list once, it is called as one pass of the sort.

5.7 SELECTION SORT

In selection sort, successive elements are selected in order and placed into their proper sorted position.

One way of implementing this is, if you are given an array a[ ], find maximum of the elements in the list and interchange it with the last element. It means we are selecting largest element in the list and placing it in its position. Then reduce the size of list by 1 and repeat the process. This will be continued till the list size is reduced to 1.

Another way of implementing it is, find minimum of the elements in the list and interchange it with first element. Both versions are implemented below. Let us first write an algorithm for the first case.

Algorithm 5.1: Selection Sort
1. Read n
2. for(i=0; i<n−1;i++)
    Read a[i]
3. for (i=n-1;i>0;i--)
    {
        max = a[0];
        index = 0
        for(j=1;j<=i;j++)
        {
            if(a[j]>max)
            {
                max = a[j];
                index = j;
            }
        }
        a [index] = a [i]
        a[i] = max;
    }
4. for(i=0;i<k;i++)
        print a[i]
5. stop

Explanation:

1. Read number of element to be sorted.
2. Read the numbers and store them in an array a.
3. Repeat the process of selecting maximum element and placing it at the end, n − 1 times (corresponds to n − 1 passes).
4. Find maximum of the elements from j = 0 to i = 1 (meaning current list size i). The variable index stores the location of the element and max stores the maximum element.
5, Put i^{th} number (i.e., last number in current list of size i) in the location given by index and the maximum number in i^{th} location, i.e., at the end of current list.
6. Display the sorted list.

Example 5.1: Let us take, following 7 numbers to be sorted. Here, n = 7.

a[0]	a[1]	a[2]	a[3]	a[4]	a[5]	a[6]
5	8	6	3	11	35	15

Pass 1: i = n − 1 = 6; max = a[0] = 8

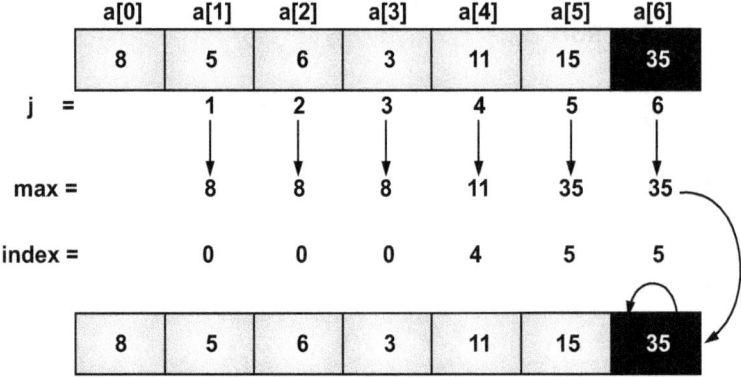

Pass 2: i = 5, max = a[0] = 8

Pass 3: i = 4; max = a[0] = 8

	a[0]	a[1]	a[2]	a[3]	a[4]	a[5]	a[6]
	8	5	6	3	11	15	35
j =		1	2	3	4	5	
max =		8	8	8	11		
index =		0	0	0	4		
	8	5	6	3	11	15	35

Pass 4: i = 3; max = a[0] = 8

	a[0]	a[1]	a[2]	a[3]	a[4]	a[5]	a[6]
	8	5	6	3	11	15	35
j =		1	2	3		5	
max =		8	8	8			
index =		0	0	0			
	8	5	6	3	11	15	35

Pass 5: i = 2; max = a[0] = 3

	a[0]	a[1]	a[2]	a[3]	a[4]	a[5]	a[6]
	3	5	6	8	11	15	35
j =		1	2				
max =		5	6				
index =		1	2				
	3	5	6	8	11	15	35

Pass 6: i = 1; max = a[0] = 3

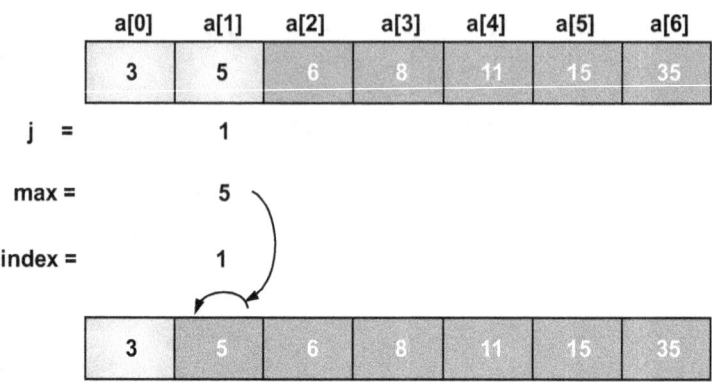

Analysis:

1. In the first pass, number of comparisons (a[j] > max) will be n − 1. In each successive pass, the number of comparisons reduces by 1. In the last pass, there will be only one comparison. Hence, the total number of comparisons will be,

   $(n - 1) + (n - 2) + (n - 3) + \ldots + 3 + 2 + 1$

   $= \dfrac{n(n-1)}{2} = O(n^2)$

   Hence, time complexity of the algorithm will be $O(n^2)$.

2. The number of interchanges will be (n − 1). Note that there are some interchanges with the elements itself.

3. There is no additional memory requirement except to hold the element temporarily like max, index, etc.

4. The number of comparisons and swaps required for this algorithm are as below:

(i) Number of comparisons

Best case $\dfrac{n(n-1)}{2}$ i.e. $O(n^2)$

Worst case $\dfrac{n(n-1)}{2}$ i.e. $O(n^2)$

(ii) Number of swaps

Best case n − 1 i.e. O(n)

Worst case n − 1 i.e. O(n)

Program 5.1: Selection Sort
```
#include <stdio.h>
#include <conio.h>
#define MAX 100
void main( )
{
    int a[MAX], i, j, n, index, max;
    clrscr( );
    printf ("Enter number of elements in the list \n");
    scanf ("%d", &n);
    printf ("Enter the number \n")
    for(i=0;i<n;i++)
        scanf("%d" , &a[i]);
    for(i=n-1;i>0;i--)
    {
        max = a[0];
        index = 0;
        for(j=1;j<=i;j++)
        {
            if (a[j]>max)
            {
                max = a[j];
                index = j;
            }
        }
        a[index] = a[i];
        a[i] = max;
    }
    printf ("Sorted list is \n");
    for(i=0;i<n;i++)
        printf("%d \n", a[i]);
}
```

Algorithm 5.2: Selection sort (version 2)

Another approach to selection sort can be find minimum number in the list and interchange the first location in the list with this number. Hence, step number 3 and 4 in above algorithm will be changed as follows:

3. for(i=0;i<n-1;i++)
    {
        min = a[i];

```
            index = i;
4.          for(j=i+1;j<n;j++)
            {
            if(a[j]<min)
            {
                min = a[j];
                index = j;
            }
            }
            a[index] = a[i];
            a[i] = min;
    }
```

There is one more way in which selection sort is implemented. We can start with, first number in the array. Compare it with all the elements one by one. If we find the number to be smaller than this number, we interchange them. In the next pass, we start the process from second number and so on. In this case, the number of swaps is more compared to the methods discussed earlier.

The algorithm is as follows:

Algorithm 5.3: Selection sort (version 3)

```
1.  Read n
2.  for(i=0;i<n;i++)
    Read a[i]
3.  for(i=0;i<n-1;i++)
    {
        for(j=i+1;j<n;j++)
        {
        if (a[i] > a[i])
        {
            temp = a[i];
            a[i] = a[j];
            a[j] = temp;
        }
        }
    }
3.  for (i=0; i<n; i++)
        print a[i]
4.  Stop
```

5.8 BUBBLE SORT

This technique is relatively easy to implement and understand. In bubble sort, we compare each element with its successor. If we find that the successor is smaller, then it is interchanged with its predecessor. By doing so, we will be shifting the smaller numbers one position up in every pass. The largest number will move to last location at the end of 1st pass. Then we again start from first location and repeat the process in 2nd pass. The second largest number will move to second last position. We continue this till n − 1 passes. The algorithm for bubble sort is as follows:

Algorithm 5.4: Bubble sort
1. Read n
2. for(i=0; i<n; i++)
   Read a[i]
3. for (i=0; i<n−1; i++)
   {
4.   for j=0; j<n−1−i; j++)
       {
       if (a[j] > a[j + 1]
           {
               temp = a[j];
               a[j] = a[j + 1];
               a[j + 1] = temp;
           }
       }
   }
5. for (i = 0; i<n; i++)
       print a[i]

Explanation:
1. Read number of element in the list (n).
2. Read the number and store them in the array a.
3. Repeat for n − 1 times i.e., i taking values from 0 to n − 2 (n − 1 passes).
4. In each pass, start with the first element in the array and go on comparing the adjacent elements a[j] and a[j + 1]. Interchange them if a[j] > a[j + 1], otherwise do not interchange. During pass 1, i = 0 and j starts with 0 and goes upto location (n − 1). Note that the inner for loop starts with j = 0 and goes upto n − 1 − i means, when i = 0 (1st pass) we go upto location n − 2 i.e., when i = 0 (1st pass) we go upto second last location. When i = 1, we go upto third location from last. When i = 2, we go upto 4th location from last and so on. Thus in every pass, largest number will go to down the list in its position.
5. The sorted numbers are displayed.

Example 5.2: Let the numbers to be sorted be 25 38 33 11 73 29. Here, n = 6.

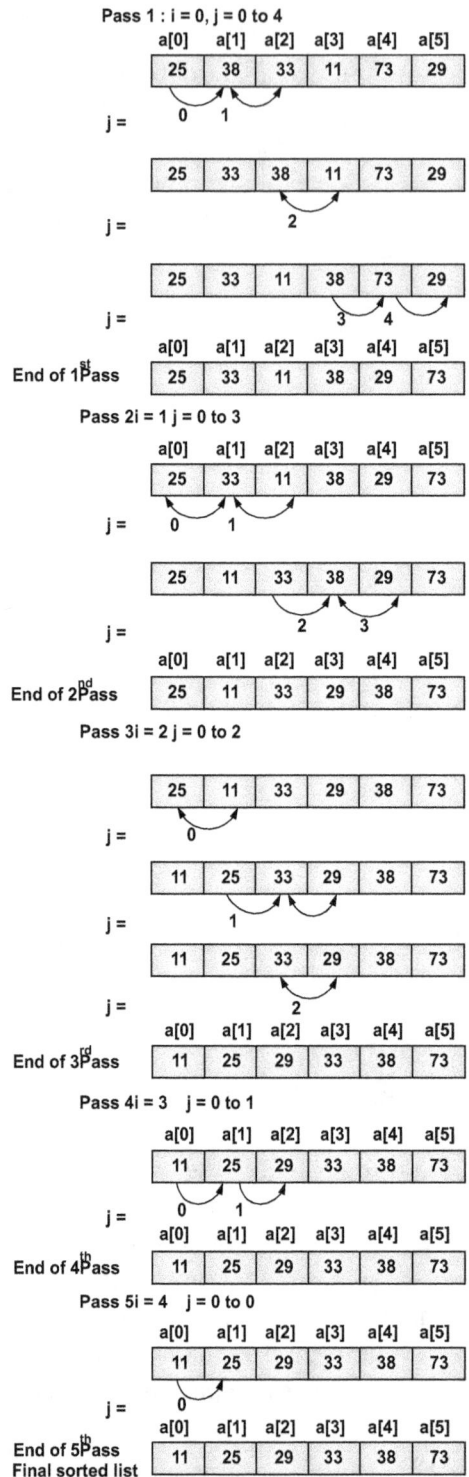

Analysis:

1. As indicated in the above example, the first pass will require n – 1 comparison and interchanges. The second pass will have n – 2, third pass n – 3 and so on. Hence, the total number of comparisons and interchanges will be,

   $(n - 1) + (n - 2) + (n - 3) + \ldots + 3 + 2 + 1$

   $= \dfrac{n(n-1)}{2} = O(n^2)$

   Hence, the time complexity of bubble sort will be $O(n^2)$.

2. This time complexity will be same, whatever may be the order of numbers i.e., even if the list is already sorted it will be $O(n^2)$.

3. There is no additional space required except the temp variable required for interchanging.

4. Thus, bubble sort algorithm will require number of comparisons and swaps as below.

   (i) Number of comparisons

   Best case: $\dfrac{n(n-1)}{2}$ i.e. $O(n^2)$

   Worst case: $\dfrac{n(n-1)}{2}$ i.e. $O(n^2)$

   (ii) Number of swaps

   Best case: n – 1 i.e. $O(n)$

   Worst case: $\dfrac{n(n-1)}{2}$ i.e. $O(n^2)$

Program 5.2: Bubble sort.

```c
#include <stdio.h>
#include <conio.h>
#define MAX 100
void main( )
{
    int a[MAX], i, j, n, temp;
    clrscr( );
    printf("Enter number of elements in the list \n");
    scanf("%d", &n);
```

```
    printf("Enter the number \n")
    for(i=0;i<n;i++)
    scanf("%d" , &a[i]);
    for(i=0;i<n-1;i--)
    {
    for(j=0;j<n-1-i;j++)
    {
        if(a[j]>a[j+1])
        {
        temp = a[j];
        a[j] = a[j + 1];
        a[j + 1] = temp;
        }
    }
    }
    printf("Sorted list is \n");
    for(i=0;i<n;i++)
    printf("%d \n", a[i]);
}
```

5.9 MERGE SORT

Combing the two lists is called as merging. For example A is a sorted list with r elements and B is a sorted list with s elements. The operation that combines the elements of A and B into a single sorted list C with n = r + s elements is called merging. After combing the two lists the elements are sorted by using the following merging algorithm.

Suppose one is given two sorted decks of cards. The decks are merged as in Fig. 5.7. That is, at each step, the two front cards are compared and the smaller one is placed in the combined deck. When one of the decks is empty, all of the remaining cards in the other deck are put at the end of the combined deck. Similarly, suppose we have two lines of students sorted by increasing heights, and suppose we want to merge them into a single sorted line. The new line is formed by choosing, at each step, the shorter of the two students who are at the head of their respective lines. When one of the lines has no more students, the remaining students line up at the end of the combined line.

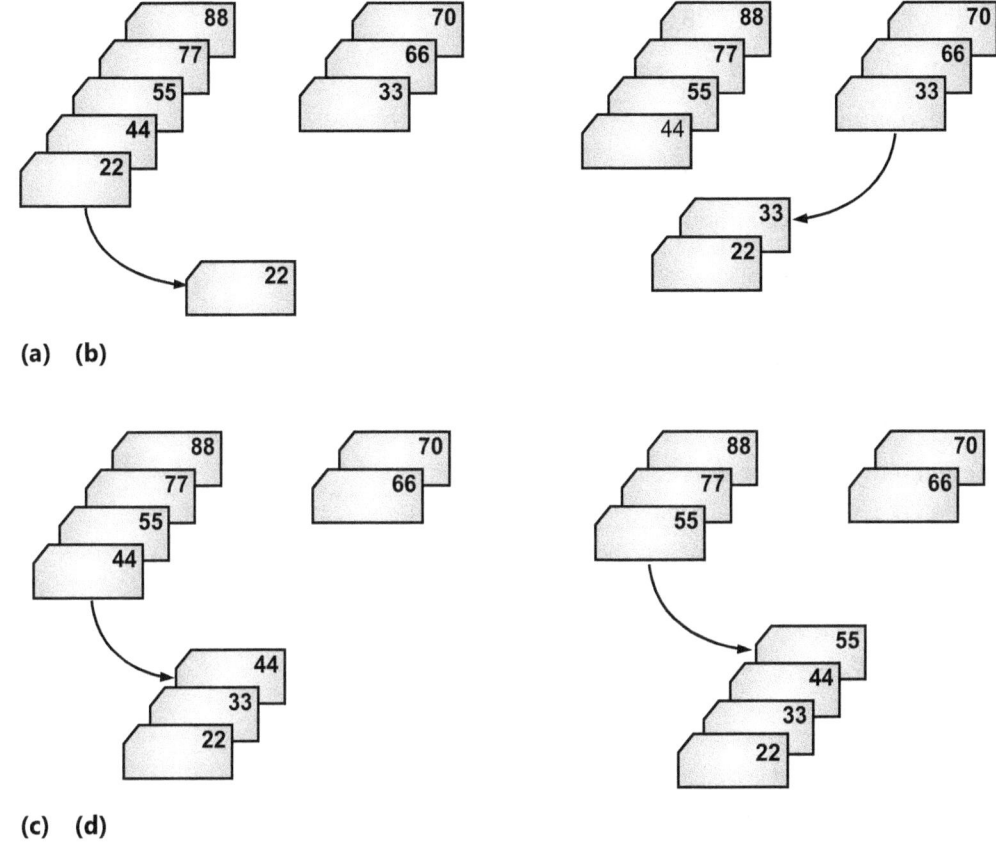

(a) (b)

(c) (d)

Fig. 5.7

The above discussion will now be translated into a formal algorithm which merges a sorted r-element array A and a sorted s-element array B into a sorted array C, with n = r + s elements. First of all, we must always keep track of the locations of the smallest element of A and the smallest element of B which have not yet been placed in C. Let NA and NB denote these locations, respectively. Also, let PTR denote the location in C to be filled. Thus, initially, we set NA : = 1, NB : = 1 and PTR : = 1. At each step of the algorithm, we compare A[NA] and B[NB] and assign the smaller element to C[PTR]. Then we increment PTR by setting PTR:= PTR + 1, and we either increment NA by setting NA: = NA + 1 or increment NB by setting NB: = NB + 1, according to whether the new element in C has come from A or from B. Furthermore, if NA> r, then the remaining elements of B are assigned to C; or if NB > s, then the remaining elements of A are assigned to C.

Algorithm 5.5

MERGING (A, R, B, S, C)

Let A and B be sorted arrays with R and S elements. This algorithm merges A and B into an array C with N = R + S elements.

1. [Initialize] Set NA := 1, NB := 1 AND PTR := 1
2. [Compare] Repeat while NA <= R and NB <= S

    If A[NA] < B[NB], then

       (a) [Assign element from A to C] set C[PTR] := A[NA]

       (b) [Update pointers] Set PTR := PTR +1 and NA := NA +1

    Else

       (a) [Assign element from B to C] Set C[PTR] := B[NB]

       (b) [Update Pointers] Set PTR := PTR +1 and NB := NB +1

    [End of loop]

3. [Assign remaining elements to C]

    If NA > R, then

    Repeat for K = 0, 1, 2, ..., S- NB

       Set C[PTR+K] := B[NB+K]

    [End of loop

    Else

    Repeat for K = 0, 1, 2, ..., R-NA

       Set C[PTR+K] := A[NA+K]

    [End of loop]

4. Exit

The total computing time = $O(n \log_2 n)$.

The disadvantages of using mergesort is that it requires two arrays of the same size and type for the merge phase

5.10 RADIX SORT

Radix sort is the method that many people intuitively use or begin to use when alphabetizing a large list of names. Specifically, the list of names is first sorted according to the first letter of each name. That is, the names are arranged in 26 classes, where the first class consists of those names that begin with "A," the second class consists of those names that begin with "B," and so on. During the second pass, each class is alphabetized according to the second letter of the name. And so on. If no name contains, for example, more than 12 letters, the names are alphabetized with at most 12 passes.

The radix sort is the method used by a card sorter. A card sorter contains 13 receiving pockets labeled as follows:

9, 8, 7, 6, 5, 4, 3, 2, 1, 0, 11, 12, R (reject)

Each pocket other than R corresponds to a row on a card in which a hole can be punched. Decimal numbers, where the radix is 10, are punched in the obvious way and hence use only the first 10 pockets of the sorter. The sorter uses a radix reverse-digit sort on numbers. That is, suppose a card sorter is given a collection of cards where each card contains a 3-digit number punched in columns 1 to 3. The cards are first sorted according to the units digit. On the second pass, the cards are sorted according to the tens digit. On the third and last pass, the cards are sorted according to the hundreds digit. We illustrate with an example.

Example 5.3:

Suppose 9 cards are punched as follows:

348, 143, 361, 423, 538, 128, 321, 543, 366

Given to a card sorter, the numbers would be sorted in three phases, as pictured in Fig. 6.

(a) In the first pass, the units digits are sorted into pockets. (The pockets are pictured upside down, so 348 is at the bottom of pocket 8.) The cards are collected pocket by pocket, from pocket 9 to pocket 0. (Note that 361 will now be at the bottom of the pile and 128 at the top of the pile.) The cards are now reinput to the sorter.

(b) In the second pass, the tens digits are sorted into pockets. Again the cards are collected pocket by pocket and reinput to the sorter.

(c) In the third and final pass, the hundreds digits are sorted into pockets.

Input	0	1	2	3	4	5	6	7	8	9
348									348	
143				143						
361		361								
423				423						
538									538	
128									128	
321		321								
543				543						
366										

DATA STRUCTURES (SE – COMP./IT. – NMU) SEARCHING AND SORTING

(a) First pass

Input	0	1	2	3	4	5	6	7	8	9
361							361			
321			321							
143					143					
423			423							
543					543					
366					543					
366							366			
348					348					
538				538						
128			128							

(b) Second pass

Input	0	1	2	3	4	5	6	7	8	9
321				321					348	
423					423					
128		128								
538										
143		143							538	
543									128	
348				348						
361				361						
366				366						

When the cards are collected after the third pass, the numbers are in the following order:

128, 143, 321, 348, 361, 366, 423, 538, 543

Thus the cards are now sorted.

The number C of comparisons needed to sort nine such 3-digit numbers is bounded as follows:

$$C \leq 9 * 3 * 10$$

The 9 comes from the nine cards, the 3 comes from the three digits in each number, and the 10 comes from radix d = 10 digits.

Complexity of Radix Sort

Suppose a list A of n items $A_1, A_2, \ldots, A_n$ is given. Let d denote the radix (e.g., d = 10 for decimal digits, d = 26 for letters and d = 2 for bits), and suppose each item Ai is represented by means of s of the digits:

$$A_i = d_{i1} d_{i2} \ldots d_{is}$$

The radix sort algorithm will require 5 passes, the number of digits in each item. Pass K will compare each d_{ik} with each of the d digits. Hence the number C(n) of comparisons for the algorithm is bounded as follows:

$$C(n) \leq d * s * n$$

Although d is independent of n, the number s does depend on n. In the worst case, s = n, so $C(n) = O(n^2)$. In the best case, s = $\log_d n$, so $C(n) = O(n \log n)$. In other words, radix sort performs well only when the number s of digits in the representation of the A_i's is small.

Another drawback of radix sort is that one may need d*n memory locations. This comes from the fact that all the items may be "sent to the same pocket" during a given pass. This drawback may be minimized by using linked lists rather than arrays to store the items during a given pass. However, one will still require 2*n memory locations.

5.11 QUICK SORT

As the name suggest is the fastest one. The quick sort is an in-place, divide-and-conquer, massively recursive sort. The algorithm is simple in theory, but very difficult to put into code. The purpose of the quick sort is to move a data item in the correct direction just enough for it to reach its final place in the array. The method, therefore, reduces unnecessary swaps, and moves an item a great distance in one move. A pivotal item near the middle of the array is chosen, and then items on either side are moved so that the data items on one side of the pivot are smaller than the pivot, whereas those on the other side are larger. The middle (pivot) item is now in its correct position. The procedure is then applied recursively to the two parts of the array, on either side of the pivot, until the whole of numbers.

The recursive algorithm consists of four steps:

1. If there is one or less element in the array to be sorted, return immediately.
2. Pick an element in the array to serve as a "pivot" point. (Usually the left-most element in the array is used.)
3. Split the array into two parts - one with elements smaller than the pivot and the other with elements larger than the pivot.
4. Recursively repeat the algorithm for both halves of the original array.

Quick Sort in details:

In this method an array a[1] ------- a[n] is sorted by picking some value in the array as a key element. We then swap the first element of the list with the key element so that the key will come in the first position. We then find out the proper place of key in the list.

The proper place is that position in the list where, if a key is placed, then all elements to the left of it are smaller than the key, and all the elements to the right of it a greater than the key.

To obtain the proper position of the key we traverse the list in both the directions using the indices i and j, respectively. We initialize i to that index which is one more than index of the key element, i.e. if the list to be sorted has the indices running from m to n, then the key element is the at index m, hence we initialize i to (m+l).

The index i is incremented till we get an element at the ith position greater than key value. Similarly, we initialize j to n and go on decrementing j till we get an element having the value less than the key value.

We then check whether i and j have crossed each other. If not then we interchange elements at the ith and j^{th} position, and continue the process of incrementing i and decrementing j till i and j cross each other. When i and j cross each other, we interchange the elements at the key position (i.e. at m^{th} position) and the elements at the jth position.

This brings the key element to the jth position, and we find that the elements to its left are less than it, and the elements to its right are greater than it. Therefore we can split the given list into two sub-lists. The first one made of elements from m^{th} position to the $(j-1)^{th}$ position, and the second one made of elements from the $(j+1)^{th}$ position to n^{th}, position, and repeat the same procedure with each of the sub-lists separately.

Choice of the key

We can choose any entry in the list as the key. The choice of the first entry is often a poor choice for key, since if the list is already sorted, then there will be no element less than the first element selected as key, and so one of the sub-lists will be, empty.

Hence we choose a key near the center of the list, in the hope that our choice will position the list in such a manner that about half come one each side of the key.

The choice of the key near the center is also arbitrary, and hence it is not necessary that it will always divide the list nicely in half. It may also happen that one sub-list is much larger than other. Hence some other method of selecting a key should be used. A good way to choose a key is to use a random number generator to choose the position of next key in each activation of quicksort.

Program 5.3: Quick Sort

```
#define MAX 10
void swap(int *x, int *y)
{
    int temp;
    temp = *x;
    *x = *y;
    *y = temp;
}
void qsort(int list[ ],int m,int n)
{
    int key,i,j,k;
    if(m<n)
    {
        k = (m+n)/2;
        swap(&list[m],&list[k]);
```

```
key = list[m];
i=m+1;
j=n;
while(i<=j)
{
    while((i<=n)&&(list[i] <= key))
        i++;
    while((j>=m)&&(list[j]>key))
        j--;
    if (i<j)
        swap(&list[i],&list[j]);
}
    swap(&list[m],&list[j]);
    qsort(list,m,j-l) ;
    qsort (list,j+1,n);
}
}
```

Consider the following list:

0	1	2	3	4	5	6
10	5	23	67	20	30	60

1. When qsort is called first time, key = 67, and i = 1, and j = 6, i is incremented till it becomes 7, because there is no element greater than key, j is not decremented, because at position 6, the value that we have is less than the key. Since i > j, we interchange the key element that is the element at position 0, with the element at position 6, and call qsort recursively with the left sub-list made of elements from position 0 to 5, and right sub-list which is empty is shown below :

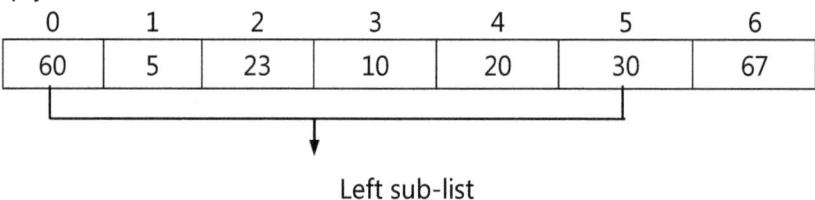

Left sub-list

Fig. 5.8

2. When qsort is called second time with left sub-list as shown above, key = 23, and i = 1, and j = 5. i is incremented till it becomes 2. Because the element at position 2 is greater than key, j is decremented to 4 because the value at position 4 is less than the key. Since I < j, the element at position 2 and 4 are swapped, i is then incremeneted to 4 and j is decremented to 3. Since i > j, we interchange the key element that is the element at position 0, with the

element at position 3, and call qsort recursively with the left sub-list made of elements from position 0 to 2, and right sub-list made of elements from position 4 to 5 as shown below.

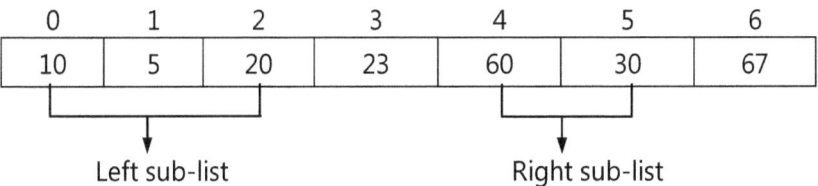

Fig. 5.9

3. By continuing in this fashion, finally we get the sorted list.
   Let us see details of all passes through following example.

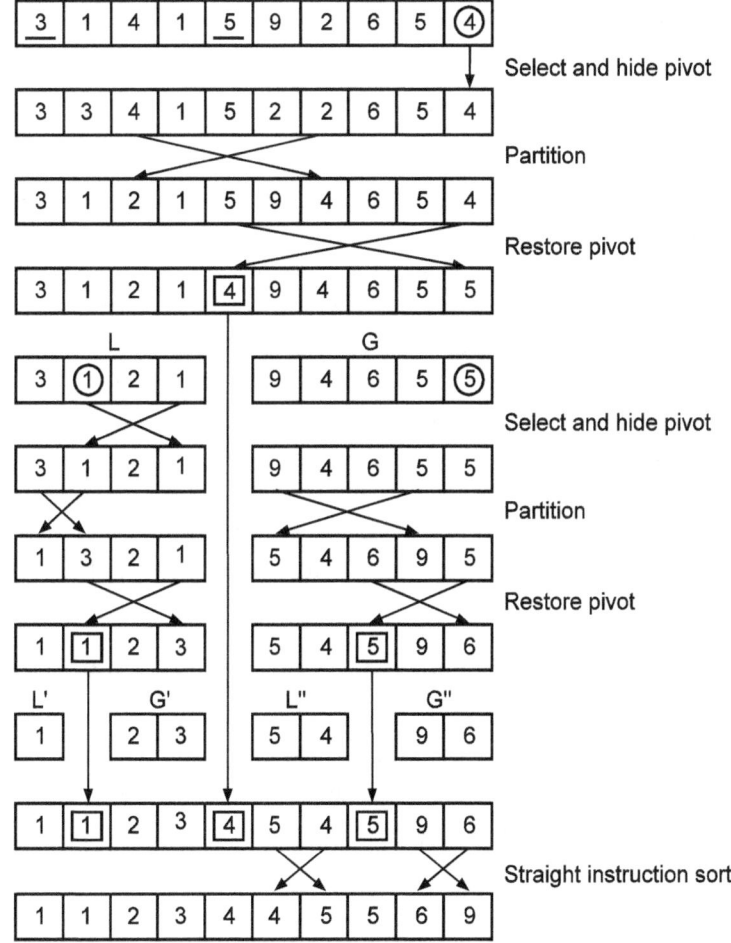

Fig. 5.10: Quick Sorting

The purpose of the quick sort is to move a data item in the correct direction just enough for it to reach its final place in the array. The method, therefore, reduces unnecessary swaps, and moves an item a great distance in one move.

Now, let us see the efficiency of quick sort. On the first pass, every element in the array is compared to the pivot, so there are n comparisons. The array is then divided into two parts each of size (n/2) approximately. (We assume that the array is divided into approximately one half each time). For each of these sub arrays, (n/2) comparisons are made and four sub arrays of size (n/4) are formed. So at each level, the number of sub arrays doubles. It will take up $\log_2 n$ divisions if we are dividing the array approximately one half each time. Therefore, quick sort is **O ($n\log_2 n$)** on the average.

If the original array is sorted and array[left] is chosen as a pivot, the quick sort turns out to be $O(n_2)$. Therefore, when we choose array[left] as pivot, quick sort works best for files that are completely unsorted and worst for files which are completely sorted. In the case of nearly sorted arrays choose a random element as a pivot value.

We assume that every time the list gets splitted into two approximately equal sized sub-lists. If the size of a given list is n, then it gets split into two sub-lists of size approximately n/2. Each of these sub-lists further gets split into two sub-lists of size n/4, and this is continued till the size becomes equal to 1. When the quick sort works with a list of size n, it places the key element (which we take the first element of the list under consideration) at its proper position in the list. This requires no more than n iterations. After placing the key element at its proper position in the list of size n, quick sort activates itself two times to work with left and right sub-lists, each assumed to be of size n/2. Therefore T(n) is the time required to' sort a list of size n. Since the time required to sort the list of size n is equal to the sum of the time required to put the key element at its proper position in the list of size n and the time required to the left and right sub-lists each assumed to be of size n/2, T(n) turns out to be :

$$T(n) = c*n + 2*T(n/2)$$

where, c is a constant and T(n/2) is the time required to sort the list of size n/2.

Similarly the time required to sort the list of size n/2 is equal to the sum of 1 time required to place the key element at its proper position in the list of size 2 and the time required to sort the left and right sub-lists each assumed to be of size n/4 T(n/2) turns out to be :

$$T(n/2)=c*n/2+-2*T(n/4)$$

where, T(n/4) is the time required to sort the list of size n/4.

∴ T(n/4) = c*n/4 + 2*T(n/8), and so on and finally we get T(1) = 1.

∴ T(n) = c*n + 2(c*n(n/2) + 2T(n/4)) '

∴ T(n) = c*n + c*n + 4T(n/4)) = 2*c*n +4T(n/4) = 2*c*n + 4(c*(n/4) + 2T(n/8))
∴ T(n) = 2*c*n + c*n + 8T(n/8) = 3*c*n + 8T(n/8).
∴ T(n) = (log n)*c*n + nT(n/n)= (log n)*c*n + nT(1) = n + n*(log n) *c
∴ T(n) = nlog(n)

Therefore we conclude that the average complexity of the quick sort algorithm is O(nlog n). But the worst-case time complexity is of the $O(n^2)$. The reason for this is in the worst case one of the two subsists wild always be empty, and the other will be of size (n-1), where n is the size of the original list. Therefore in the worst case, T(n) turns out to be
T(n) = c*n + T(n-1)
= c*n + c*(n-1) + T(n-2)
= 2*c*n - c + T(n-2)
= 2*c*n -c + c*(n-2) + T(n-3)
= 3*c*n - 3*c + T(n-3)
...
...
= n*c*n - n*c + T(1)
= n^2c-nc+l
Therefore the order is $O(n^2)$.

Space Complexity:
The average-case space complexity is $log_2 t$, because the space complexity depends on the maximum number of activations that can exist. We find that if we assume that every time the list gets split into approximately two equal-sized lists, the maximum number of activations that will exists simultaneously will be $log_2 n$.
In the worst case, there exist n activations because the depth of the recursion is n. Hence the worst case space complexity is O(n).

Pros and Cons of Quick Sort :
- Extremely fast.
- This quick sort can be implemented efficiently by using recursion; but
- Very complex algorithm, massively recursive.
- Gives good results when an array is in random order.
- Quick sort is O (nlog2n) on the average.

5.12 HEAP SORT

Heapsort is a sorting technique that sorts a list of length n with $O(n\ log_2(n))$ comparisons and movement of entries, even in the worst case.

Hence it achieves the worst-case bounds better than those of quicksort; and for the list it is better than mergesort, since it needs only a small and constant amount of space apart from the list being sorted.

Heapsort works in two steps. First all the entries in the list are arranged to satisfy heap property, and then the top of the heap is removed and another entry is promoted to take its place repeatedly. Therefore we need a function that builds an initial heap to arrange all the entries in the list to satisfy heap property. The function that builds an initial heap uses a function that adjusts its entry in the list whose entries at 2i and 2i + 1 positions already satisfy heap property in such a manner that the entry at i^{th} position in the list will also satisfy heap property.

In brief,

Algorithm

(I) Build a heap tree with a gives set of data.

(II) (a) Delete root node from heap

    (b) Rebuild the heap after deletion

    (c) Place the deleted node in the output

(III) Continue with step (II) until the heap tree is empty.

Program 5.4: Heap Sort

```c
#define MAX 10
    void swap(int *x,int *y)
    {
        int temp;
        temp = *x;
        *x = *y;
        *y = temp;
    }
    void Adjust( int list[ ],int i, int n)
    {
        int j,k,flag;
        k=list[i];
        flag=1;
        j = 2 * i;
```

```
            while(j<=n&&flag)
            {
              if(j<=n&&list[j]<list[j+1])
              j++;
              if(k>=list[j])
                  flag = 0;
              else
              {
                  list[j/2]=list[i];
              }
            }
        }
        list [j/2] = k;
}
void Build-Heap(int list[], int n)
{
    int i;
    for(i=(n/2);i>=0;i-)
        Adjust(list,i,n-1);
}
void HeapSort(int list[ ],int n)
{
    int i;
    Build_Heap(list,n);
    for(i=(n-2);i>=0;i-),
    {
        swap(&list[0], &list[i+1]);
        Adjust(list,i,n-i);
    }
}
void main( )
    {
    int list [MAX], n;
    .
    .
    .
    HeapSort (list,n);
    .
    .
    .
}
```

Let the elements of the list are:

1 11 12 21 34 42 56 66 87 90

In each pass of while loop in function Adjust (x, i, n), the position i is double hence the number of passes cannot exceed log(n/i). Therefore the computation time adjust is O(logn/i).

The function Build-Heap calls the Adjust procedure n/2 for values ranging from nl/2 to 0. Hence the total number of iterations will be:

= log (n) + log(n/2) + ... + log(n/n/2)

$$= \sum_{i=1}^{n/2} \log(n/i)$$

= n/2 1og(n) − log (in/2)

This turns out to be some constant times n. Hence the computation time of build_initial_heap is O(n). The heapsort function calls the adjust (x, 1, −i) (nod) times. Hence the total number of iterations made in the heapsort will be

log (i/1)

$$= \sum_{i=1}^{n-1} \log(i)$$

= log(1) + log(2) + ... + log(n − 1)

which turns out to be approximately nlogn. Hence the computing time of heap sort it is O(n log(n)) + O(n). The only additional space needed by heapsort is the space for one record to carry out swap.

5.13 SELECTION SORT

Assume we want to sort list in ascending order. Selection sort finds the smallest element from unsorted list and swap it with the element in first position. Then it finds second smallest element and swap it with element at second position. This process is repeated till entire list is sorted in ascending order. Each time we swap elements, we say that we have completed a sort pass. A list of n elements requires n–1 passes to completely rearrange the data.

Procedure for every pass is as follows.

Pass 1 : Find the position P of the smallest in the list of N elements A[l], A[2], . . . , A[N], and then interchange A[P] and A[1] . Then A[1] is sorted.

Pass 2 : Find the position P of the smallest in the sublist of N −1 elements A[2], A[3],..., A[N], and then interchange A[P] and A[2]. Then A[l], A[2] is sorted.

Pass 3 : Find the position P of the smallest in the sublist of N−2 elements A[3], A[4],..., A[N], and then interchange A[P] and A[3]. Then: A[l], A[2], A[3] is sorted.

Pass N −1 : Find the position P of the smaller of the elements A[N −1), A[N], and then interchange A[P] and A[N−1]. Then: A[l], A[2], ..., A[N] is sorted. Thus A is sorted after N −1 passes.

Example 1:

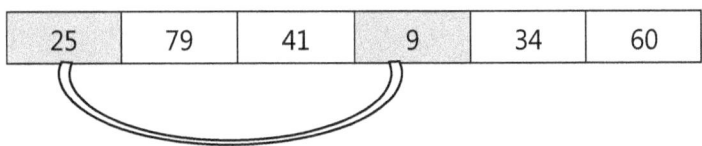

Fig. Original List

We will apply selection sort on this list.

Pass 1 :

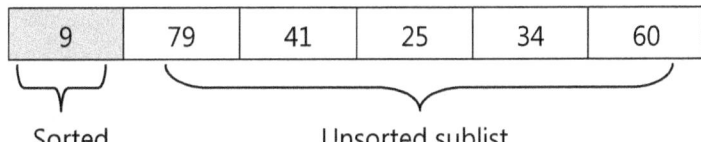

Here smallest element is 9 and 25 is located at first position. so we swap 9 with 25.

After Pass 1

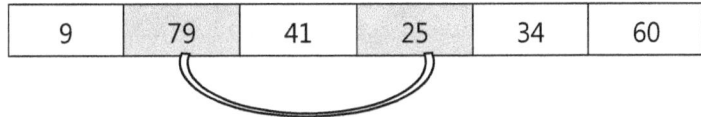

Now we find smallest element from unsorted sublist and place it in second position.

Pass 2:

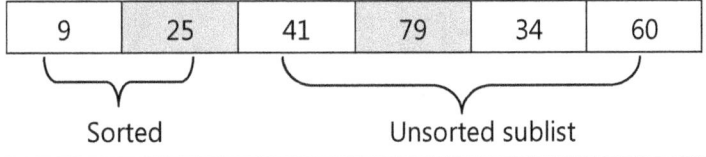

Unsorted sublist has 25 as a smallest element and 79 is located at second position. Hence we swap 25 and 79.

After Pass 2:

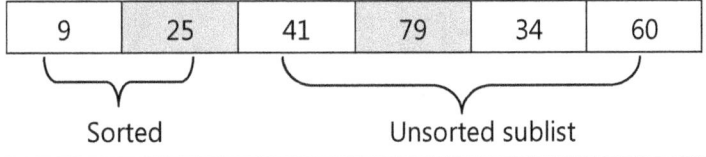

Pass 3:

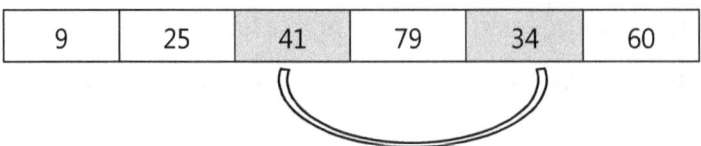

After Pass 3:

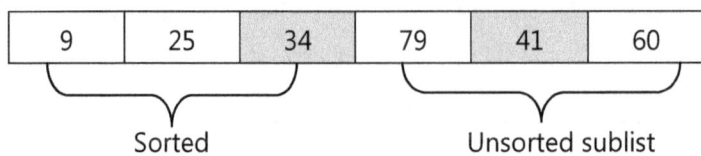

Pass 4:

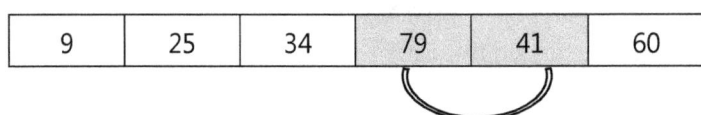

After Pass 4:

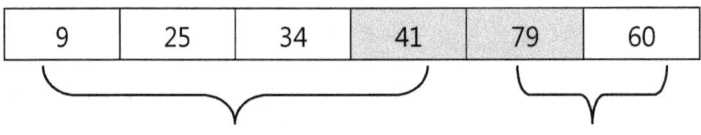

Pass 5:

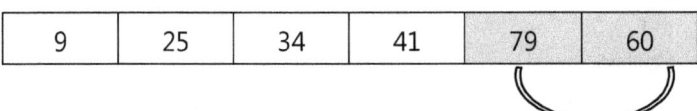

After Pass 5:

9	25	34	41	60	79

Thus list is sorted.

We will see one more example.

Apply selection sort on array A= {77,30,40,10,88,20,65,56}

Pass 1:

77	30	40	10	88	20	65	56

After Pass 1

10	30	40	77	88	20	65	56

Pass 2:

| 10 | 30 | 40 | 77 | 88 | 20 | 65 | 56 |

After Pass 2

| 10 | 20 | 40 | 77 | 88 | 30 | 65 | 56 |

Pass 3:

| 10 | 20 | 40 | 77 | 88 | 30 | 65 | 56 |

After Pass 3

| 10 | 20 | 30 | 77 | 88 | 40 | 65 | 56 |

Pass 4:

| 10 | 20 | 30 | 77 | 88 | 40 | 65 | 56 |

After Pass 4

| 10 | 20 | 30 | 40 | 88 | 77 | 65 | 56 |

Pass 5:

| 10 | 20 | 30 | 40 | 88 | 77 | 65 | 56 |

After Pass 5

| 10 | 20 | 30 | 40 | 56 | 77 | 65 | 56 |

Pass 6:

| 10 | 20 | 30 | 40 | 56 | 77 | 65 | 88 |

After Pass 6

| 10 | 20 | 30 | 40 | 56 | 65 | 77 | 88 |

Hence the list is sorted in ascending order by applying selection sort.

Function for Selection Sort

```
void selectionSort(int A[], int n)
{
int i, j, s, temp;
for (i= 0; i <= n; i ++)
{
s = i;
for (j=i+1; j <= n; j++)
if(A[j] < A[s])
s= j;
// Smallest selected; swap with current element
temp = A[i];
A[i] = A[s];
A[s] = temp;
}
```

Program 5.5: Selection Sort.

```
#include <stdio.h>
int main()
{
   int A[100], n, i, j, s, temp;
/* n=total no. of elements in array
     s= smallest element in unsorted array
     temp is used for swapping */
     printf("Enter number of elements\n");
     scanf("%d", &n);

     printf("Enter %d integers\n", n);
     for ( i = 0 ; i < n ; i++ )
         scanf("%d", &A[i]);
     for ( i = 0 ; i < ( n - 1 ) ; i++ )
```

```c
        {
            s = i;
            for ( j = i + 1 ; j < n ; j++ )
            {
                if ( A[s] > A[j] )
                    s = j;
            }
            if ( s != i )
    {
            temp = A[i];
            A[i] = A[s];
            A[s] = temp;
            }
        }
    printf("Sorted list in ascending order:\n");
    for ( i = 0 ; i < n ; i++ )
        printf("%d\n", A[i]);
    return 0;
    }
```

Output:
```
Enter number of elements
5
Enter 5 integers
4
1
7
5
9
Sorted list in ascending order
1
4
5
7
9
```

Complexity of Selection Sort:

In selection sort outer for loop is executed n–1 times. On the kth time through the outer loop, initially the sorted list holds k–1 elements and unsorted portion holds n–k+1 elements. In inner for loop 2 elements are compared each time.

Thus, 2*(n–k) elements are examined by the inner loop during the k th pass through the outer loop. But k ranges from 1 to n–1.

Total number of elements examined is:

$$T(n) = 2*(n-1) + 2*(n-2) + 2*(n-3) + .. + 2*(n-(n-2))$$
$$\qquad\qquad + 2*(n-(n-1))$$
$$= 2*((n-1) + (n-2) + (n-3) + ... + 2 + 1)$$

(or 2*(sum of first n–1 integers)

$$= 2*((n-1)*n)/2)$$
$$= n^2 - n, \text{ so complexity of algorithm is } O(n^2).$$

5.14 COMPARISON OF SORTING METHODS

	Bubble sort	Selection sort
Number of comparisons		
Best case	$\frac{n(n-1)}{2}$	$\frac{n(n-1)}{2}$
Worst case	$\frac{n(n-1)}{2}$	$\frac{n(n-1)}{2}$
Number of swaps/shifts		
Best case	n – 1	n – 1
Worst case	$\frac{n(n-1)}{2}$	n – 1
Overall time complexity		
Best case	$O(n^2)$	$O(n^2)$
Worst case	$O(n^2)$	$O(n^2)$
Average	$O(n^2)$	$O(n^2)$
Additional memory	Not required	Not required
	In place algorithm	In place algorithm
Implementation	Simple	Complex
Stability of algorithm	Stable	Stable

5.15 SEARCHING AND SORTING

Searching and sorting are the most common operations required to be performed in programs. Almost 90% of times in the programs these operations are used. Hence, it is important to study these techniques and their efficiency, their advantages, disadvantages etc. Though we will be concentrating on only single dimensional arrays of integer and real numbers, we can extend these techniques to strings, records, linked list as well.

5.16 SEARCHING TECHNIQUES

Searching is a process of finding the location of required data in the given list of objects. The algorithm used for searching depends on how data is organized in the list. But we will be studying only search operations with arrays. The two important techniques used for searching in an array are linear of sequential search and binary search. Apart from these two searching techniques indexed sequential search technique. Before we look into these techniques, let us define some terms.

1. **List:** It is an ordered set of data contained in main memory.
2. **Record:** It is collection of related fields.
3. **Table or file:** It is collection of ordered set of records.
4. **Key:** It is a field in the record used to differentiate each record.
5. **Search Algorithm:** It is an algorithm that accepts an argument (say s) and tries to find a record whose key is s.
6. **Retrieval:** Successful search is called retrieval.
7. **Internal Search:** The search operation in which entire table is constantly stored in main memory is called internal search.
8. **External Search:** The search operation in which part of the table is in secondary memory is called external search.

5.17 SEQUENTIAL SEARCH

It is also called linear search. It is simplest searching technique and can be applied to a table organised as an array or linked list. Sequential search can be used when the list is not ordered or ordered.

In sequential search, we start searching from first element in the list and continue until we find the element. If we don't find the element, we reach the end of list and stop.

Example 5.4: Suppose we have 6 elements stored in an array as shown and we want to search element 5 in the list (i.e. array).

The steps are shown in Fig. 5.11.

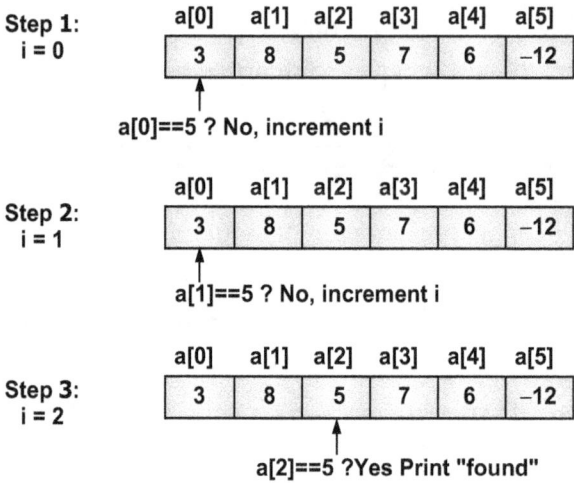

Fig. 5.11: Process of linear search

The algorithm for sequential search is as follows:

Algorithm 5.6: Sequential search or linear search.
Step 1:   Read n {Number of elements in list}
Step 2:   i=0
Step 3:   while i<n repeat step 4 and 5
Step 4:   Read a[i]
Step 5:   i=i+1
Step 6:   Read s {Number to be searched}
Step 7:   i=0; flag=1
Step 8:   While i<n repeat step 9 to 13
Step 9:   if a[i]==s execute step 10 to 12
Step 10: print "found" i+1
Step 11: flag=0;
Step 12: go to step 14
Step 13: i=i+1
Step 14: if flag==1 print "Not found"
Step 15: Stop

Explanation:

1. First we read number of element stored in the list (n).
2. We read the element in the list and store it in the array a.
3. Read the number to be searched (s).
4. Set initial value of i = 0 and flag = 1. Flag is used to indicate or sense whether the number is present in the list or not.
5. We repeatedly compare number in the ith location with s. If the number is found, we print the location number, make flag = 0 and exit. Otherwise we continue searching.
6. When we exit loop and find flag = 1, the number s will not be there in the list.
7. Stop.

Analysis:

1. While comparing, if we find the number s in the first location i.e., when i = 0 we exit. Hence, the minimum time required to search is 1. i.e., we require only one comparison. Hence, best case time complexity of the algorithm is 1. i.e., O(1).
2. If the element to be searched is at the end of the list or not there at all, we require to do n comparisons i.e., the loop, runs for n times. Hence, worst case time complexity is O(n).
3. On an average to find the element in the list, we will require (n+1)/2 comparisons. Hence, average case time complexity will be O(n), since (n+1)/2 = O(n).

    It can be found as below.

    If these are n numbers in the list, the number to be searched can be at any position from 1 to n.

    The probability of finding the number at a location will be 1/n. Hence average number of comparisons will be,

$$T(n) = 1 \times \frac{1}{n} + 2 \times \frac{1}{n} + 3 \times \frac{1}{n} + \ldots + n \times \frac{1}{n}$$

$$= \frac{1}{n}(1 + 2 + 3 + \ldots + n)$$

$$= \frac{1}{n} \frac{n(n+1)}{2}$$

$$= \frac{n+1}{2}$$

4. For large number of elements (n), this algorithm will be slow.

Program 5.6: To search a number in a list using sequential search.

```c
#include <stdio.h>
#include <conio.h>
# define MAX 100
void main( )
{
int a[MAX], i, s, n, flag;
printf ("Enter number of elements in the list \n");
scanf("%d", &n);
printf ("Enter the elements in the list \n");
for (i=0;i<n;i++)
    scanf ("%d", &a[i]);
printf("Enter the number to be searched \n");
scanf ("%d", &s);
flag = 1
i = 0;
while (i<n)
{
    if (a[i]==s)
    {
        printf("Found at location %d", i+1);
        flag = 0;
        break;
    }
}
if (flag==1)
    printf ("Not found");
getch( );
}
```

5.18 BINARY SEARCH

Sequential search is very slow for large n. We can make the searching process faster provided, we have the elements in the list in sorted order.

The binary search starts with the middle element of the list instead of first element. If the element to be searched is at the middle, we exit; otherwise we check whether the element in the middle location is smaller or greater than element to be searched. If it is greater, the number will be above this middle location and the second half need not be checked. If it is smaller, the number will be below the middle location and first half need not be checked. Hence, in the first comparison we eliminate half the numbers in the list. We repeat the same process for remaining half in which the number may be present. We continue this process till we find the target or determine that the number is not there in the list.

Example 5.5: Suppose we have 10 elements as shown and we want to search s = 70.

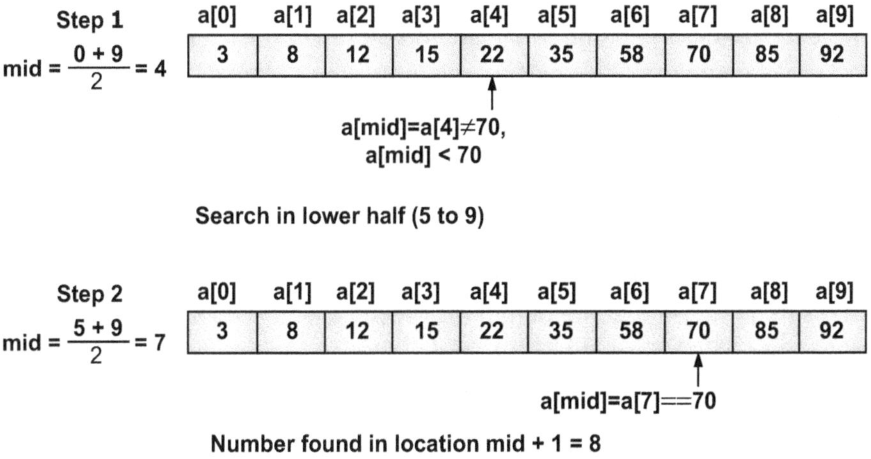

Step 1

$mid = \dfrac{0+9}{2} = 4$

a[0]	a[1]	a[2]	a[3]	a[4]	a[5]	a[6]	a[7]	a[8]	a[9]
3	8	12	15	22	35	58	70	85	92

a[mid]=a[4]≠70,
a[mid] < 70

Search in lower half (5 to 9)

Step 2

$mid = \dfrac{5+9}{2} = 7$

a[0]	a[1]	a[2]	a[3]	a[4]	a[5]	a[6]	a[7]	a[8]	a[9]
3	8	12	15	22	35	58	70	85	92

a[mid]=a[7]==70

Number found in location mid + 1 = 8

Fig. 5.12: Binary search process

As it can be seen above, number 70 is present at location 7. It is found in the second comparison only.

Algorithm 5.7: Binary Search

Step 1: Read n {Number of elements}
Step 2: i=0
Step 3: while i<n repeat step 4 and 5
Step 4: Read a[i]
Step 5: i=i+1

Step 6: Read s {Number to be searched}
Step 7: l=0, u=n-1; flag=1
Step 8: While (l=u) Repeat step 9 to 15
Step 9: mid=(l+u)/2
Step 10:   if a[mid]==s execute step 11 to 13
Step 11:   printf "found at" mid+1
Step 12:   flag=0
Step 13:   go to step 17
Step 14:   if a[mid] > s u=mid-1
Step 15:   if a[mid] < s l=mid+1
Step 17: if flag==1 print "Not found"
Step 18:   Stop

Explanation:
1. First we read number the number of elements stored in the list (n).
2. We read the element in the list and store it in the array a.
3. Read the number to be searched.
4. Set $l = 0$ (location of first element in the list) $u = n - 1$ (location of last element in the list) and flag=1 to determine whether the number is present in the list or not.
5. While ($l \leq u$) means the list to be checked has more than 1 element. We go to the middle location in the list and check whether number is present. If yes, we print the location and exit after setting flag = 0. If the number is greater than number to be searched, we have to check upper half. Hence, make u = mid − 1 and keeping and same for the new list. If the number is less than number to be searched, we have to check lower half. Hence, make l = mid + 1 keeping u same for new list.
   We repeat the process till the list to be checked has more than or equal to 1 element.
6. If we exit above loop with flag = 1, it means we did not find the number.

Analysis:
1. When we enter the loop (statement 5) and find the number is in the mid-locations, then we exit. Only 1 comparison will be required. Hence, the minimum time required to search is 1. Hence, best case time complexity is O(1).
2. If the element to be searched is not there in the table, we will keep on dividing the list into two parts and search in one half. The process is continued till there is single element left out finally. Suppose we have 32 element in the list i.e., n = 32, first comparison will reduce the list to 16 element, second comparison to 8, third to 4, fourth to 2 and fifth comparison will reduce to 1 element. Hence, the maximum number of comparison will be 5, which is $\log_2 32$. In general, sappose we have n elements, after first

comparison the number elements will reduce to n/2. The second comparison will leave n/4 elements. Comparison number x will leave $n/2^x$ elements. Hence, maximum number of comparisons × x = $\log_2 n$. Hence, worst case time complexity of the algorithm is $O(\log_2 n)$.

3. On an average, the number of comparisons to find and element of the algorithm is $O(\log_2 n)$.
4. Compared to linear search, this algorithm is faster for example, sequential search has time complexity 1000 whereas, binary search $\log_2 n = \log_2 1000 = 10$

Program 5.7: Binary Search */

```
#include <stdio.h>
#include <conio.h>
#define MAX 100
void main
{
int a[MAX], i, n, s, mid, l, u, flag,
clrscr( );
printf ("Enter number of element in the list \n")
printf ("%d", &n);
printf ("Enter the element in the list \n")
for (i=0;i<n;i++)
    scanf ("%d", &a[i]);
printf ("Enter number to be searched \n")
scanf ("%d", &s);
flag = 1; l=0; u = n - 1;
while (l<=u)
{
    mid=(l + u)/2;
    if (a[mid]==s)
    {
        printf("Number found at location %d", mid + 1);
        flag = 0;
        break;
    }
    if (a[mid]>s)
        u = mid - 1;
    if (a[mid]<s)
        l = mid + 1;
```

```
}
if (flag==1)
    printf ("Not found");
}
```

5.19 COMPARISON OF SEARCHING METHODS

No.	Parameter	Sequential search	Binary Search
1.	Time complexity	Best case: O(1) Worst case: O(n)	Best case: O(1) Worst case: $O(\log_2 n)$
2.	Prerequisite	No prerequisite of elements to be in sorted order	Element are to be in sorted ordered
3.	Performance	Works better for small n and slow for large n	Works better for large n
4.	Application	Can be used when the list is dynamic (i.e. changing)	Can be used when the list is not changing (i.e. fixed).

SUMMARY

- Efficient and reliable data processing depends upon sorted data.
- The internal and external sorting methods each have their relative efficiencies in different applications.
- It should be clear that no single sort is best for all applications. Certain properties such as the number, size, distribution and order of keys of a given key set plays an important role in determination of sorting technique which should be used for that particular application.
- If the number of entries in the array is small, the simpler bubble sort or selection sort as well and sometimes better and they require relatively little programming effort to write and maintain. If n is larger and the keys are short, the radix sort can perform well. For large n with long keys, we can use quick sort, heap sort or a merge sort.
- The order of the original data is an important consideration in choosing a sort algorithm. If the data are already sorted, quick sort should be avoided. If keys are uniformly distributed, address-calculation sort is the best choice.

- It appears that the quick sort is faster, and handle arrays of heterogeneous data fairly efficiently. The shell short is more efficient than the bubble sort, selection sort, and insertion sort.
- Sorting of larger files that cannot fit in main memory is best accomplished by external sorting techniques such as the merge sort.

SOLVED PROBLEMS

1. Sort Following numbers using bubble, Selection and Insertion. Show all steps. How many swaps and comparisons are required for each method?

10 30 20 40 60 50

Solution:

i) Bubble Sort...

List after Pass 1...

10 20 30 40 50 60

List after Pass 2...

10 20 30 40 50 60

List after Pass 3...

10 20 30 40 50 60

List after Pass 4...

10 20 30 40 50 60

List after Pass 5...

10 20 30 40 50 60

Sorted list is...

10 20 30 40 50 60

Number of comparisons = 15

Number of swaps = 2

ii) Selection Sort...

List after Pass 1

10 30 20 40 50 60

List after Pass 2

10 30 20 40 50 60

List after Pass 3

10 30 20 40 50 60

List after Pass 4

10 20 30 40 50 60

List after Pass 5

10 20 30 40 50 60

Sorted list is...

10 20 30 40 50 60

Number of comparisons = 15

Number of swaps = 5

2. Sort Following numbers uning bubble, Selection. Show all steps. How many swaps and comparisons are required for each method?

50 40 30 20 10

Solution:

i) Bubble Sort...

List after Pass 1...

40 30 20 10 50

List after Pass 2...

30 20 10 40 50

List after Pass 3...

20 10 30 40 50

List after Pass 4...

10 20 30 40 50

Sorted list is...

10 20 30 40 50

Number of comparisons = 10

Number of swaps = 10

ii) Selection Sort...

List after Pass 5

10 40 30 20 50

List after Pass 4

10 20 30 40 50

List after Pass 3

10 20 30 40 50

List after Pass 2

10 20 30 40 50

Sorted list is...

10 20 30 40 50

Number of comparisons = 10

Number of swaps = 4

3. Sort Following numbers uning bubble, Selection. Show all steps. How many swaps and comparisons are required for each method?

10 20 30 40 50

Solution:

(i) Bubble Sort...

List after Pass 1...

10 20 30 40 50

List after Pass 2...

10 20 30 40 50

List after Pass 3...

10 20 30 40 50

List after Pass 4...

10 20 30 40 50

Sorted list is...

10 20 30 40 50

Number of comparisons = 10

Number of swaps = 0

(ii) Selection Sort...

List after Pass 5

10 20 30 40 50

List after Pass 4

10 20 30 40 50

List after Pass 3

10 20 30 40 50

List after Pass 2

10 20 30 40 50

Sorted list is...

10 20 30 40 50

Number of comparisons = 10

Number of swaps = 4

4. Sort Following numbers uning bubble, Selection. Show all steps. How many swaps and comparisons are required for each method?

15 3 18 7 21 10

Solution:

(i) Bubble Sort...

List after Pass 1...

3   15   7   18   10   21

List after Pass 2...

3   7   15   10   18   21

List after Pass 3...

3   7   10   15   18   21

List after Pass 4...

3   7   10   15   18   21

List after Pass 5...

3   7   10   15   18   21

Sorted list is...

3   7   10   15   18   21

Number of comparisons = 15

Number of swaps = 6

(ii) Selection Sort...

List after Pass 6

15 3   18 7   10 21

List after Pass 5

15 3   10 7   18 21

List after Pass 4

7   3   10 15 18 21

List after Pass 3

7   3   10 15 18 21

List after Pass 2

3   7   10 15 18 21

Sorted list is...

3   7   10 15 18 21

Number of comparisons = 15

Number of swaps = 5

5. Sort Following numbers using bubble, Selection. Show all steps. How many swaps and comparisons are required for each method?

100 50 70 40 30

Solution:

(i) Bubble Sort...

List after Pass 1...

50 70 40 30 100

List after Pass 2...

50 40 30 70 100

List after Pass 3...

40 30 50 70 100

List after Pass 4...

30 40 50 70 100

Sorted list is...

30 40 50 70 100

Number of comparisons = 10

Number of swaps = 9

(ii) Selection Sort...

List after Pass 5

30 50 70 40 100

List after Pass 4

30 50 40 70 100

List after Pass 3

30 40 50 70 100

List after Pass 2

30 40 50 70 100

Sorted list is...

30 40 50 70 100

Number of comparisons = 10

Number of swaps = 4

EXERCISE

1. Write algorithms for
   (i) Bubble sort
   (ii) Insertion sort
   (iii) Selection sort
2. Compare the sorting methods.
   Bubble sort, Selection sort.
3. Modify the programs for sorting to display output after each pass.
4. What are the different searching techniques? Compare them on the basis of time complexity?
5. Give the algorithm for searching any elements using binary search method. Comment on complexity.

www.ingramcontent.com/pod-product-compliance
Lightning Source LLC
Chambersburg PA
CBHW080422230426
43662CB00015B/2188

CONTENTS

Foreword..xi
Preface..xiii

Part A Academic Writing

1 Writing Assignments..3
   Plan Your Essay..3
      Understanding the Question..................................3
      Sourcing Relevant Information...............................4
   Write Your Essay...5
      The Introduction..5
      The Conclusion..6
      The Body..7
   Summary..8

2 Scholarly Writing..9
   Some Thoughts about Structure..................................9
      Triads..9
      Headings...11
      Bridging and Summarising...................................12
      Footnotes..13
   A Few Tips concerning Style...................................14
   General Advice about Presentation.............................15
   Summary...17

3 In-Text Citations...19
   The Advantages of In-Text Citations...........................19
   The Elements of In-Text Citations.............................19
   How to Add an In-Text Citation................................20
   How to Handle Variations on the Main Elements.................21
      Problems Related to the *Author*...........................22
      Problems Related to the *Date*.............................23
      Problems Related to the *Page*.............................25
   Some Loose Ends...26
      How to Cite Scripture......................................26
      How to Order Groups of Citations...........................26
      How to Punctuate In-Text Citations.........................27
      How Often to Repeat an In-Text Citation....................27
   Summary...29

4	Footnote Citations	31
	Two Types of Footnotes	31
	Advantages of Footnote Citations	31
	Principles of Footnote Citation	32
	Examples of Common Footnote Citations	33
	Footnotes for Books	34
	Footnotes for Articles	36
	Footnotes for Electronic Resources	38
	Footnotes for Other Resources	39
	Multiple Citations in One Footnote	39
5	The Bibliography	41
	Types of Bibliographies	41
	How to Compose a Bibliography Entry	42
	Examples of Common Bibliography Entries	42
	Bibliography Entries for Books	43
	Bibliography Entries Articles	47
	Bibliography Entries for Electronic Resources	50
	Bibliography Entries for Other Sources	51
	Punctuation in a Bibliography	52
	How to Order the Works in a Bibliography	53
	Summary	54
6	Plagiarism	55
	Defining Plagiarism	55
	Dealing with Plagiarism	57
	Avoiding Plagiarism	57
	Recognising Plagiarism	58
	Undermining Research	59
	Challenging Plagiarisers	59
7	Formatting an Academic Paper	61
	The Cover Page	61
	The Declaration and Dedication (only for theses)	62
	Abstract	62
	Table of Contents	62
	Normal Pages	63
	Headers and Footers	64
	The First Page	64
	Numbered and Bulleted Lists	65
	Tables and Figures	65
	Bibliography	66

| 8 | Software for Bible Study | 77 |

- The Benefits of Software 77
- The Limitations of Software 78
- The Categories of Software 79
- Free Online Applications 79
    - New Testament and Greek 80
    - Old Testament and Hebrew 82
- Commercial Software Programmes 85

Part B Theological Research

| 9 | Thesis Requirements | 93 |

- Bachelor's Level 94
- Master's Level 94
- Doctoral Level 95
- Summary 96

| 10 | The Research Proposal | 97 |

- The Value of a Research Proposal 97
- The Elements of a Research Proposal 98
    - Part 1: The Research Problem 98
    - Part 2: The Research Plan 100
- The Preparation of a Research Proposal 101
- Summary 102

| 11 | The Research Problem | 105 |

- The Process at a Glance 105
- The Research Idea 107
- The Preliminary Literature Review 108
- The Main Problem 109
- The Key Questions 112
- Fleshing out the Problem 113
    - The Hypotheses 114
    - The Delimitations 114
    - The Definitions 116
    - The Presuppositions 117
    - The Value 118
- Summary 118

| 12 | The Research Plan | 121 |

- The Design 121
- The Methodology 124
    - The Tools 124

	The Data	126
	The Presentation	127
	The Bibliography	127
13	**Biblical Exegesis**	**131**
	Presuppositions of Evangelical Exegesis	131
	Design for an Exegetical Study	132
	Section 1: The Introduction	132
	Section 2: The Context	133
	Section 3: The Meaning	133
	Section 4: The Significance	135
	Section 5: The Conclusion	135
	Writing Up an Exegetical Study	136
	The Commentary Structure	136
	The Topical Structure	137
	Summary	137
14	**Systematic Theology**	**139**
	Presuppositions of Evangelical Theology	139
	Steps in Evangelical Theology	140
	Step 1: Identify All the Scriptures That Address the Topic	140
	Step 2: Analyse Each Scripture to Determine Its Meaning	140
	Step 3: Deduce Timeless Principles Taught by Groups of Scriptures	141
	Step 4: Construct a Theory to Account for All the Relevant Data	141
	Basic Design for Evangelical Theology	142
	Section 1: Introduction	142
	Section 2: Current Views	143
	Section 3: Biblical Evidence	144
	Section 4: Theory Construction	144
	Section 5: Contemporary Significance	145
	Alternate Design for Evangelical Theology	146
	Section 1: Introduction	147
	Section 2: The Informing Theology	147
	Section 3: The Anchor Text	147
	Section 4: The Developing Theology	147
	Section 5: The Contemporary Significance	147
	Summary	149
15	**Practical Theology**	**151**
	Nature of Practical Theology	151
	Steps in Practical Theology	153
	Basic Design for Practical Theology	154
	1. Introduction	154
	2. Present Situation	154

	3. Preferred Scenario 155
	4. Practical Suggestions 156
	Advanced Designs for Practical Theology 156
	Alternative Design for Practical Theology 157
	Summary 159

16 The Literature Review 161
Why You Must Do a Literature Review 161
How Your Literature Review Will Be Judged 162
How to Obtain Sources for Your Literature Review 163
Summary 166

17 Descriptive Research 167
Understanding Descriptive Research 167
    Its Nature 167
    Its Purpose 168
    Its Characteristics 168
    Its Value 169
    Its Limitation 169
Conducting Descriptive Research 170
    Step 1: Set the Research Objective 170
    Step 2: Review Related Research 171
    Step 3: Design the Approach 171
    Step 4: Develop Instruments 172
    Step 5: Select the Participants (population sample) 174
    Step 6: Describe the Data Collection Procedures 175
    Step 7: Analyse and Interpret the Data 176
    Step 8: Draw Conclusions 177
    Step 9: Write the Report 178
Summary 179

18 Other Types of Theological Research 181
Empirical Research (IMRAD) 181
    Introduction: What Problem Was Studied? 182
    Methods: How Was the Problem Studied? 182
    Results: What Were the Findings? 183
    Discussion: What Do the Findings Mean? 183
Book Reviews 184
    The Values and Types of Reviews 184
    The Components of a Critical Review 184
    The Language and Structure of a Review .186
    Summary 186
Case Studies 187
Congregational Analysis 187

Appendix A
    Common Abbreviations 189
        Books of the Bible 189
        Versions of the Bible 190

Appendix B
    Abbreviations for Journals, Periodicals, Major Reference Works,
    and Series. 193

Select Bibliography 201

Foreword

I do remember well my confusion and bewilderment as I attempted to write my first research paper at the seminary. There were several guides available at the library to help me in this process, but in many cases their lack of clarity added more to my confusion. Dr Kevin Smith has worked hard to provide seminary students with a fresh and helpful guide for their research and writings.

I was glad to receive, a couple of years ago, a copy of the first edition of this book that many students in various countries and regions of the world have found to be a user-friendly guide. Now with this revised edition Dr Smith has added new features to make the book even better.

This guide is characterized by being targeted to seminary students and researchers in theological studies in particular. It is well organized and deals with topics that are hard to find in other guides of this kind, such as plagiarism, software for Bible study, and other types of theological research.

In an age when the global south has much to contribute to global theological education and to various areas of theology, biblical studies and missiology, this book comes at the right time to assist students and researchers. This guide will enable them to present their work in an attractive and intelligible format that complies with international standards of academic writing.

This is a must-have book that ought to be available at each student's desk and at all libraries. Dr Smith, thank you for your much appreciated service to global theological education.

Rev Riad Kassis, PhD
International Director, International Council for Evangelical Theological Education
Director, Langham Scholars Programme, Langham Partnership

Preface

This book emerges from several years' experience working with both undergraduate and postgraduate students at the South African Theological Seminary. It has a single purpose – to help theological students write better assignments and theses. My colleagues and I have witnessed at first hand the struggles and pitfalls facing our students. We felt it was time to put the lessons we have learned on paper in the hope that they will empower future students to learn from their forerunners.

We have divided the work into two parts. Part A addresses academic writing in general. It should be relevant to all students, whether they are writing a first-year assignment or a doctoral dissertation. Part B is written mainly for postgraduate students who are preparing to write a thesis or dissertation. It deals with intermediate and advanced aspects of theological research.

Although I am solely responsible (for better or for worse) for the final writing and editing of every chapter, I am deeply indebted to three colleagues. Dr Mark Pretorius did the research and wrote the first drafts of the chapters on assignment writing and plagiarism. Having assessed countless assignments, he brings years of personal experience to bear on the challenges of writing assignments and avoiding plagiarism. Dr Noel Woodbridge has successfully supervised many theses involving empirical research. He is better qualified than I am to write chapters on practical theology and descriptive research. I am grateful to him for having done it. He also contributed substantially to the chapter presenting a design for exegetical research. Beth Perry assisted greatly in preparing the chapters about referencing, helping to rework the guidelines into a style consistent with SBL requirements.

Because of the valuable input from Beth, Mark, and Noel, and the fact that the content of the work to some extent reflects shared experience, most references to the authors are in the first person plural (we, us, and our). When the references switch to the singular (I, me, and my), they point to my personal comments or experiences.

Our frame of reference comes from the South African higher education system. Although certain aspects, such as the preferred system of referencing and the requirements for length of theses, reflect local norms, we believe most of the book is sufficiently generic to benefit theological students in general.

We use the term *thesis* freely for research reports at bachelor's, master's, or doctoral levels, while reserving *dissertation* for the doctoral level. Thus, we can speak of a PhD thesis or a PhD dissertation, but only of a master's thesis. Some institutions reverse these names, speaking of master's dissertations and doctoral theses. This is simply a matter of institutional preference, so be aware that your institution may use these terms differently to the way we do.

Finally, I would like to express my deep gratitude to those who have helped make this work a reality: to friends and colleagues from SATS who supported the project in various ways, including Reuben van Rensburg, Jenny Mason, Arthur Song, Sam Kunhiyop, Dan Lioy, Frank Jabini, and many more. I am especially grateful for Langham's patience and support during the preparation of the revised edition, most notably Peter Fleck, whose ongoing encouragement helped put this book into your hands.

Kevin Smith
Rivonnia, South Africa, 2015

Part A

Academic Writing

In the first eight chapters, we deal with the fundamentals of good academic writing. How do I write a good assignment? How do I put a scholarly essay together? How do I reference my sources correctly? How do I maintain integrity in my writing? What should a properly formatted paper look like? These are essential questions for all students. The practical advice offered should prove valuable, whether you are fresh out of high school or you are writing a doctoral dissertation.

Chapter 1 deals with how to write a good assignment. We begin with the most common student pitfall – failing to read the question properly. Then we offer guidance on sourcing information to answer the question. Finally, we examine the three component parts – what goes into the introduction, body, and conclusion respectively.

Chapter 2 discusses the dos and don'ts of good academic writing. We examine principles of structuring a coherent argument, look at tips for writing in a strong, clear style, and offer advice about the presentation of the paper.

In chapters 3–5, we turn to referencing sources, a vital aspect of academic writing. In chapter 3, we explain how to use in-text citations when following the author-date system of referencing. Chapter 4 explains how to use footnote citations if you are following footnote-based referencing. Chapter 5 outlines the principles of preparing a bibliography, presenting both referencing methods side by side. Chapter 6 tackles the thorny issue of plagiarism, which has become an epidemic in higher education due to the ease of copying and pasting information off the Internet.

Chapter 7 illustrates how assignments and theses should be formatted, while chapter 8 introduces the use of software for Bible study. This chapter dangles somewhat awkwardly at the end of Part A.

1

Writing Assignments

In most higher education programmes, written essays are a primary form of assessment. The purpose of this chapter is to introduce you to the basics of good assignment writing. Writing an assignment involves two main steps: planning and writing. We shall discuss each stage.

Plan Your Essay

An English proverb says, 'More haste; less speed.' This certainly applies to writing assignments. The most common cause of resubmitted assignments is hasty writing. In their haste to *write* the essay, students fail to plan properly. As one lecturer said, 'Failing to plan is planning to fail!' When you need to write an essay, invest time planning the assignment; you will save more time later.

Understanding the Question

The first and most important part of planning an essay is to understand the question. We know this sounds so obvious that you probably will not pay much attention to it, but we have marked thousands of assignments in which the student simply did not read the question properly. Read the question. Read the question carefully. Read it until you have a crystal clear picture in your mind of what you are being asked to do.

One helpful way of ensuring you understand the question is to take note of key words in the assignment instructions. The action words, in particular, tell what the examiner expects of you. Here are some examples of key words to note:
- *Analyse*: divide the material into sections or elements and discuss these in full.
- *Compare*: identify the similarities and/or differences between ideas, facts, viewpoints, and so on.
- *Contrast*: point out the differences between certain objects or characteristics.
- *Criticise*: point out good and bad characteristics, and give your own opinion after considering all the facts.[1]

---
1. Mark Pretorius, 'How to Write a Good Assignment' (unpublished article, 2008), 4.

If you are not 100 per cent sure what a key word means, look it up in a good dictionary. This is especially important if English is not your first language.

Sourcing Relevant Information

Once you understand the question, you must source relevant information to help you answer it. You may find enough information in the course textbook, reader, or study guide to complete some assignments, but others will require extra research in the library or on the Internet. It is important to know which sources to use and how to use them.

Expectations in terms of the use of sources vary according to the level of your study. In a first-year assignment, you may get away with only two or three mediocre sources. This would not do in a third- or fourth-year term paper, where you would need to use at least twelve quality resources. In a doctoral dissertation, 250–300 scholarly works is about the norm.

When seeking sources for an academic paper, try to find recent, scholarly works. Scholarly works are well researched; they deal more in the realm of facts than opinions. Peer-reviewed journal articles are probably the best sources. Well-researched books are second best. Internet articles are often poor sources. Although there are many well-researched, scholarly articles on the web, there are also thousands of sub-standard ones. Using *only* Internet articles is questionable.

Authorship is a key to assessing its academic value. If the author is a respected scholar or an authority on the topic, the article should be useful. If the author is just a layman expressing personal opinions, be careful of using it. In Wikipedia, for example, *anyone* can edit the articles; there is a real danger that an article is written by someone who does not know a great deal about the topic. By contrast, most of the articles on www.bible.org are written by respected biblical scholars. Rather use Bible.org than Wikipedia.com.

Since you cannot always trust the information picked up from the web, here are a few questions to ask when trying to discern what information is reputable and what is not.
- Is the author identified?
- What makes him or her an expert (or at least a trustworthy source)?
- Is the author with a reputable organisation?
- Is the information biased? Does it push a particular perspective?
- Is the site intended for a specific audience?
- If it discusses an issue, does it present both sides?
- Can you verify factual claims or statements from other sources?

How you use your sources is also important. At the bachelor's level, you may be allowed to cite them uncritically. At the master's and doctoral levels, however, you cannot merely cite and affirm them. You must master your sources, interacting critically with them. At all levels, *interacting* with sources is important. Don't just quote them – discuss, explain, and evaluate them. Don't accept everything you read. Decide whether you agree or disagree with an author, and why.

Don't overuse a single source. This is a common mistake. Students find one good source and quote it as if it were the only and final word on the topic. Even experts hold different opinions about topics. Whenever possible, try to interact with several different sources, especially ones reflecting alternative views. If, for instance, you are charismatic in your doctrinal views, don't use only authors who share your persuasion.

How many sources should you cite? There are no hard-and-fast rules. A fair rule of thumb is one unique work for each page; thus, a five-page paper would have at least five entries in the bibliography, a 200-page dissertation at least two hundred. This guideline works well for long papers, but for short papers, you should aim for more than one per page.

The two most important points to remember about using sources are to (a) use sound, scholarly works and (b) interact with your sources rather than just affirming them. After you have understood the question and gathered relevant information, you are ready to write the assignment.

Write Your Essay

An essay needs three parts – introduction, body, and conclusion. The introduction and conclusion are arguably the most important sections.

> The introduction and conclusion allow a writer to address the overall purpose and significance of an essay. In general terms, the introduction states the intention, while the conclusion defines the achievement of an essay. Together they constitute the frame for your paper, providing the first and last opportunities to convince your reader of its value.[2]

The body is the heart of the essay in which you develop and defend your ideas. To achieve its goals, it needs structure, unity, and argument. Let's look at each section of an essay in turn.

The Introduction

In most assignments, the introduction is a brief 'statement at the beginning of your assignment, which shows how you understand the question and how you plan to answer it.'[3] In length, it should be less than 10 per cent of the essay; this usually means somewhere between one paragraph and one page.

Although there is no standard formula for writing the introduction, it should achieve a few basic purposes. To achieve these, you need to:

---

2. Princeton Writing Program, 'Introductions and Conclusions' (2001; retrieved 10 May 2008, http://web.princeton.edu/sites/writing/Writing_Center), 1.
3. Pretorius, 'How to Write a Good Assignment', 4.

- *State the purpose (problem) of the essay.* The purpose of the essay is to answer a particular question, that is, to solve a problem. Your introduction should clearly state the problem and/or purpose.
- *Introduce the subject and the limits of the essay.* You must introduce the topic of the essay and indicate which aspects of it you will tackle and which ones fall outside the scope of the essay.
- *Present your central thesis about the topic.* A central claim (thesis) provides unity to a well-constructed essay. In one or two sentences, you should state the main point (central claim) you will attempt to support in the essay.
- *Preview the argument (structure) of the essay.* Give readers advance warning of the main thrust of the argument, that is, how the essay is organised, how the flow of thought unfolds.

After reading your introduction, readers should be able to state the topic of the essay (including its limits), the central claim you are making about it, and how your essay goes about making that claim.

The Conclusion

The conclusion should bring your paper to a suitable end. '[T]he goal is to make your reader feel that the argument has fully achieved the goals you have set in the introduction.'[4] You achieve this by two main techniques, namely, *review* and *summary*. You often begin by reviewing the purpose (and problem) as well as the thesis (main claim) that you set out in the introduction. After reviewing the purpose and thesis, you should summarise the argument and state your conclusions.

Like the introduction, the conclusion should be less than 10 per cent of the essay, typically from one paragraph to one page. Pretorius offers three tips for the conclusion:
- Don't introduce new ideas!
- Don't use direct quotations.
- Don't give detailed explanations.[5]

To prevent your conclusion feeling like a dull rehash of the essay, here are a few things you can do to keep it interesting. These tips, however, only apply to advanced essays:
- Indicate how your main point fits into the larger field of study.
- Explain the implications of your research and interpretation.
- Make recommendations for future research on related topics.[6]

The introduction and the conclusion are so crucial to your essay that a reader should be able to offer a good overview of the entire essay just by reading the beginning and the

---

4. Princeton Writing Program, 'Introductions and Conclusions', 3.
5. Pretorius, 'How to Write a Good Assignment', 7.
6. Princeton Writing Program, 'Introductions and Conclusions', 3–4.

end. Therefore, don't be careless in the way you write them. Take time to ensure that they embody all the essential information.

The Body

The body is the main part of your essay. It should take up 80–90 per cent of the paper. Here you should develop your main argument, supporting your main idea with reasons and evidence. In this section, we shall discuss three essential characteristics of an essay's body:

- Structure
- Unity
- Argument

Structure. The body of an essay needs a simple, clear structure. This typically requires one level of headings. In some cases, the *assignment* instructions give you the headings. For example, an *assignment* about what you can learn from David's sins as reported in 1 Samuel 11–12 and Psalms 32 and 51 might ask you to use the causes, character, consequences, and cures as headings. If the instructions do not provide an outline, you must develop a simple set of headings that show the main sections and ideas.

Unity. 'Any scholarly paper is, above all, an exercise in stating, developing and defending an idea . . . (or perhaps a closely related set of ideas).'[7] The main idea (or set of ideas) of your paper, often called *the thesis,* is presented in the *introduction* and developed in the body. The fact that the entire essay *develops* the main idea gives it unity and coherence. You should ruthlessly cut out everything that does not help to develop your thesis.

Argument. The body of the essay not only develops a central idea, it develops the idea *in a logical way.* In academic writing, the logical development of the main idea is called 'the argument'.

> A scholarly essay is an exercise in developing and defending ideas. . . . This analysis and explanation of your claim is called an argument. In effect, the argument of your essay is an answer to the question *Why is the central idea or thesis of this paper valid or plausible?*[8]

An essay written to answer a question typically has two main parts, the *what* and the *why.* The *what* states what you believe to be the answer. The *why* provides your reasons for proposing this answer. Your reasons need to be convincing. 'For each step in the defence of your argument, you will need to provide sufficient *evidence* and an *analysis* of that evidence.'[9]

---

7. Princeton Writing Program, 'Developing a Central Idea' (1999; retrieved 10 May 2008, http://web.princeton.edu/sites/writing/Writing_Center), 1.

8. Princeton Writing Program, 'Developing an Argument' (1999; retrieved 10 May 2008; online: http://web.princeton.edu/sites/writing/Writing_Center), 1.

9. Princeton Writing Program, 'Developing an Argument', 2.

Many assignments do not fit the model of one main idea presented in the introduction followed by a protracted argument (set of reasons) to support the claim. Instead, they weave an idea-argument (what-why) pattern throughout the essay. Each section or subsection starts with an idea (claim); the remainder of that section develops it by way of logical arguments (evidence and analysis). Returning to the example assignment based on David's sins, the section on causes might present four causes. Each cause represents a claim or idea. Each one needs to be argued (that is, the author must present biblical evidence to prove the claimed cause contributed to his sin).

Summary

Throughout your academic career, even if you only do a bachelor's degree, you will write many assignments. These will constitute a large proportion of your course grades. Mastering the basics of essay writing will put you in a good position to score high grades. It may also save you hundreds of hours and lots of money on resubmissions. The first essential is to plan your essay before you start writing. In particular, make sure you understand the question correctly. When you get down to writing the essay, ensure that your introduction clearly states the purpose and thesis of the assignment. In the body, check for unity and sustained, persuasive argument. The conclusion should bring the assignment to a clear, decisive end.

2

Scholarly Writing

The goal of academic writing is scientific precision and clarity. You must say *exactly* what you mean, leaving no room for readers to misinterpret you. This demands that two things characterise your writing style – it must be *simple* and *specific*.

The skill of good academic writing does not come naturally to most. It is learned with practice through the pain of writing and rewriting until the product presents a clear, tightly argued and persuasive treatise. The best way to refine your skill is to write – practice produces progress. The second best is to read skilful writers and learn from them. Our objectives in this chapter are modest – to introduce you to some of the most important secrets and alert you to common pitfalls made by novice writers.

Some Thoughts about Structure

Structure is a key to clarity. A well-organised document that signposts the author's flow of thought at every level is easier to follow than one in which readers need to guess where the author is going and how his ideas relate to each other. This is especially true in academic writing, where the content is often technical and the relationships between key ideas may be complex. To help their readers follow their argument, skilled academic writers employ several techniques:

- triads
- headings
- bridging and summarising
- footnotes

At first, mastering these techniques may seem demanding, but with a little practice, they will eventually become second nature. Let us briefly examine how each one can help you structure your paper for maximum clarity.

Triads

At every level, from an entire dissertation to a single paragraph, you should use *triads* to give your writing clear structure. The idea is simple – every unit of a document should have three parts: introduction, body, and conclusion. Unity and progression should mark the journey from introduction to conclusion.

Triads apply at all levels. At the largest level, a thesis should have an introduction that sets out the research problem and plan, a body that systematically analyses the data pertaining to the problem, and a conclusion that summarises the findings. Each chapter of a thesis needs an introduction stating the topic and purpose of the chapter, a body logically presenting the content, and a conclusion summarising the findings and transitioning to the next chapter. Each section within a chapter should have a clear beginning, logical development, and appropriate conclusion. Triads even apply at paragraph level. Most paragraphs begin with a topic sentence that introduces the subject of the paragraph. The body of the paragraph develops the thesis sentence. The paragraph often ends with a summary or bridging sentence. You can apply the same principles to essays, book reviews, journal articles, and just about every other kind of academic writing.

Triads at the thesis level. A thesis uses a three-part structure. The first chapter is an *introduction* stating the *research problem* and objectives, describing the *research plan*, and previewing the remainder of the study. The body of the thesis consists of a number of chapters presenting and analysing data. The final chapter is the *conclusion*. It summarises the findings of the study and makes suitable recommendations for action and for further research.

Triads at the chapter level. The opening section of a chapter, typically from one to three paragraphs, serves as an *introduction*. It may position the chapter in relation to the previous chapters. It introduces the main topic, states the thesis of the chapter, and previews its flow and structure. The chapter's body, which is typically divided into sections, presents a coherent argument in support of its main thesis. The closing paragraphs summarise the argument and bridge to the next chapter.

Triads at the section level. Each major section of a paper or chapter should have an introductory paragraph and a concluding paragraph. These form a frame around the body, introducing the topic and summarising the main idea(s). The body, of course, presents and defends the main ideas.

Triads at the paragraph level. Most paragraphs have a thesis sentence, which is usually the first sentence. The body of the paragraph develops the thesis by way of explanation, illustration, persuasion, or application. The paragraph ends with a summary, conclusion, or transition sentence, although a formal ending is not always possible.

Triads mark the basic shape of a piece of writing. This is true at all levels, from a single paragraph to an entire book. However, within this basic framework, headings signpost the skeleton of the argument, making its main divisions evident. Let's examine how to use headings properly.

Headings

Headings, if effectively used, provide a structural skeleton that enables readers to see the logic and flow of a document at a glance. Underline the words *if effectively used*. Most students use headings. Only rarely do we encounter a student who has been taught that an essay should be one long string of text unbroken by headings (if you were taught this, now is the time to unlearn it). Many, however, use headings ineffectively. Here are some guidelines for using headings.

Ensure the headings are descriptive of the flow of thought. By surveying the headings, a reader should be able to see at a glance what the logical divisions of your topic are and how the material is organised. The headings summarise the argument. To do this effectively, they must be descriptive of the content they represent. Consider the example below for an essay on Titus. By looking at the headings, you can tell exactly what each section of the essay will cover and how the essay will flow. The headings describe and summarise the content at a glance.

Use numbering or styling to distinguish different levels of headings. Readers should be able to identify the heading level at a glance. There are two ways to help them. First, use different font and paragraph styles for different levels. For example, level one could be bold, centred, font size 14, while level two is italics, left aligned, font size 12. Second, you can number the headings. This example combines styling and numbering:

1. The Background of Titus

1.1. *The Author of the Book*

1.2. *The Context of the Book*

1.3. *The Structure of the Book*

2. The Themes of Titus

2.1. *Appointing Elders*

2.2. *Teaching Sound Doctrine*

2.3. *Silencing False Teachers*

By using both numbers and styles, you can help readers to tell the level of a heading at a glance.

Keep the number of levels manageable. Using too many levels of headings confuses readers. We use headings to provide a clear outline of the argument. When readers see a heading numbered 6.2.4.1.8.3, they feel lost and overwhelmed. One or two levels of clearly marked headings clarify the flow of thought; more than this tends to obscure it.

How many levels are enough? It depends somewhat on the length of your paper. Excluding the title, two levels of headings are enough for most short papers (for example, essays, articles, and so on). Many book publishers limit writers to one or two levels within chapters. In doctoral dissertations, one may stretch to three or, at the most, four levels. Never go beyond four levels.

Ensure that there are no orphan headings.[1] Always pair headings. They divide sections into smaller sections. To have only one heading is like trying to cut a cake into one piece. Your headings divide your text into two or more pieces. Therefore, you cannot have only one heading at a particular level. Do **not** do this:

1. The Background of Titus

1.1. *The Author of the Book*

1.2. *The Context of the Book*

1.3. *The Structure of the Book*

2. The Role of Titus

2.1. *Titus Was an Interim Pastor*

3. The Themes of Titus

3.1. *Appointing Elders*

3.2. *Teaching Sound Doctrine*

3.3. *Silencing False Teachers*

In this outline, section 2.1. is an orphan heading. The author should either delete it or add a corresponding section 2.2.

Bridging and Summarising

Academic writing requires protracted and, in many cases, complex argumentation. The techniques of bridging (also called hinging or transitioning) and summarising help readers to follow the argument. These techniques are so closely related that it is best to treat them as a single aspect of good writing.

Bridging refers to building a connection between two parts of the argument. The connecting sentences or paragraphs function like a bridge, ensuring a smooth transition from one section to the next. The alternative name, hinging, compares the function of these connectors to the way a hinge connects a door to its frame.

You need to build a bridge each time you bring one section of the argument to a close and shift to a new facet. At the very least, this means you need bridging sentences between main sections of an essay. The last paragraph of a chapter and the first paragraph of a new chapter often serve as bridging paragraphs, showing how the two chapters are logically related, how the logical flow of the book or thesis is developed across the two chapters.

Summarising forms a key part of bridging. When you write a bridging paragraph, it typically begins with a brief summary of the preceding argument and then indicates how what is about to follow is the next logical step in the treatment of the topic. The

---

1. Here we are talking about a heading that has no counterpart. There is another kind of orphan heading, namely, leaving a heading dangling at the bottom of a page, separated from the text which follows it. You should avoid both kinds of orphan headings.

opening paragraphs of a book or a thesis often illustrate this principle well. They present a brief review of the argument in the preceding chapter(s) and then state how the flow of thought leads logically to the topic for the new chapter.

Students often forget to make explicit the links between their thoughts. They have been living with and thinking about a research topic for a long time. In their minds, the connections between various elements are self-evident. They forget their readers probably have not thought deeply about the topic, so the relationships between ideas will not be clear to them. Do not leave your readers to infer the links; spell them out.

By regularly pausing to summarise your argument and draw readers' attention to the logical links between what you have said and what you are about to say, you help them follow your train of thought. The more protracted and the more complex the argument is, the more important it is to use the techniques of summarising and bridging to ensure the flow of thought is clear.

Footnotes

What role should footnotes play in academic writing? The answer will vary depending on two things: (a) the system of referencing you use and (b) the attitude of your professor, supervisor, or publisher. Before we explore how these factors influence the role of footnotes, you need to understand that two different kinds of footnotes are used in academic writing, namely, reference notes and educational notes. Reference notes credit the sources used, while educational notes supply additional information the author does not wish to place in the body of the paper.

The author-date referencing system does not use reference notes. In the author-date system of referencing (see ch. 3), you do not use footnotes to cite sources. You cite sources in-text by placing the author's name, date of publication, and page numbers in parentheses. As a result, papers written using the author-date method of referencing use fewer footnotes than papers which cite sources in notes.

The footnote referencing system uses footnotes to credit sources. In this system of referencing, every quotation or allusion to your source material must be credited (cited) in a footnote. In an academic paper, this means there will be *many* reference notes.

Professors and publishers have different attitudes towards the use of educational notes. At one extreme, some prohibit them – if something is worth saying, it is worth working into the body of the text. The opposite attitude holds that the real scholarship is found in the notes. This encourages extensive use of notes to provide technical information. The middle ground seems like a sensible attitude. Try to work as much as you can into the body of your paper, but, if the nature of certain material is either so technical or so peripheral that it would disturb the flow of thought, put it in a footnote. This means the number of footnotes will depend largely on how technical your paper is. A first-year *assignment* seldom needs educational footnotes, but a doctoral dissertation may require many.

Triads, headings, bridging, summarising, and footnoting give your writing clear structure and logical coherence. Use triads – the three-part structure of introduction, body, and conclusion – to structure your writing at all levels. Use two or three levels of descriptive, numbered, styled headings to provide a clear skeleton of each chapter. The more complex your argument, the more you need bridging and summarising paragraphs to help readers follow the argument. Finally, work as much of your material into the main text as possible, reserving educational footnotes for material that would disturb the flow of thought.

In addition to structural guidelines, your academic writing will benefit by applying some stylistic tips. We shall explore a few of the more important ones in the next section.

A Few Tips concerning Style

The style of academic writing differs significantly from everyday writing (for example, letters, emails, stories). In the past, an awkwardly formal style was standard. Today, the trend is towards a less formal style. Here are some dos and don'ts to apply to academic writing. Treat them as good general guidelines, not as hard-and-fast rules.

Keep your writing clear, concise, and concrete. Formal writing used to favour long sentences, piling one prepositional phrase or relative clause upon another. This style is out of favour. Keep your sentences short and simple – the modern way. Favour concrete nouns and active verbs. Do all you can to make your writing reader friendly. Make it your goal to write as clearly and concisely as possible. Expert writers can say the most using the fewest and smallest words.

Write in a modest, understated manner. What you write is not the final word on the matter. Therefore, be cautious in your claims, tentative in your tone. Your writing should reflect a humble, open, teachable attitude. Don't make bold assertions. Avoid broad generalisations. Modest, understated arguments are the most convincing kind.

Restrained use of the first person singular is acceptable. Using 'I' in academic writing used to be forbidden. Writers were taught to use awkward phrases such as 'the author' or 'the researcher' in its place. Nowadays, using 'I' here and there is acceptable as long as you do not abuse it. Do not, however, use 'we' if you are the sole author of the paper.

Avoid generalisations and inexact statements. Avoid words such as 'all', 'always', 'none', 'never', and so forth unless you mean them literally. For example, do not say 'all scholars agree that . . .' unless you know there is not a single dissenting voice. Be specific. Say exactly what you mean. If you say 'most experts . . .', list several of them in a citation. Don't say 'approximately 80 per cent' if you mean '77.3 per cent'; be exact.

Beware of overusing bulleted lists. It is legitimate to use bulleted (or numbered) lists when you want to itemise a number of points. Beware, however, of overusing bulleted lists. Students tend to write bullets as incomplete sentences. As a result, they portray unclear, half-baked thoughts. Bullets become a crutch, a mask for the writer's foggy thinking and lazy writing. Whenever possible, prefer to write your points in a flowing paragraph. When you do use bullets, make sure they express clear, complete thoughts.

Prefer the active voice to the passive. Academic writing must use the passive voice at times, but some fall into the trap of using it most of the time. This results in a dry, lifeless writing style. Whenever possible, write a sentence in the active voice. Try to write at least 80 per cent of your sentences in the active voice.

Avoid clichés or colloquial expressions. The move away from overly formal style in academic writing does *not* mean slang or clichéd language is now acceptable. Vyhmeister lists four levels of English (see Table 1) and suggests academic writing belongs in the category labelled 'standard'.[2]

Formal	Standard	Colloquial	Slang
superlative	excellent	first-rate	cool
exasperating	irritating	aggravating	burns me up
deranged	irrational	crazy	nuts

Table 1: From Formal to Slang Style

For theology students, the great pitfall here is resorting to a preachy style. Do not preach in a research paper. Expressions like 'hallelujah', 'amen brother', or 'come Lord Jesus' belong in church, not in assignments.

Do not use abbreviations in the text of the document. Limit abbreviations to materials in parentheses or footnotes. In the body of your document, write out words like 'per cent' (not '%'), 'that is' (not 'i.e.'), 'for example' (not 'e.g.'). Write out the names of Bible books as well; reserve abbreviations for parenthetical references and footnotes.

Presentation is a third crucial aspect of academic writing. The way you present your essay can make it look professional or amateurish.

General Advice about Presentation

Your reader's first impression of your paper comes from its presentation. Does it look and feel like an academic essay? Does it seem like the writer knows how to write an assignment? In the case of assignments, your reader is your assessor. We suspect the impact of this first impression can be worth as much as 10 per cent in your final grade, because the message it sends up front is, 'Here is a serious, diligent student.' This topic is so important that we shall devote an entire chapter to it later, but a few introductory guidelines are in order here.

---

2. Nancy Vyhmeister, *Quality Research Papers for Students of Religion and Theology* (3rd ed.; Grand Rapids, MI: Zondervan, 2014), 169. Vyhmeister's primer is, in our opinion, the most practical general guide to theological research and writing. We encourage you to use it as a companion volume to this book.

Formatting requirements vary from institution to institution. Most academic institutions have a description of their formatting requirements. All we can offer here are general guidelines for formatting a paper. You should adapt these guidelines to fit the requirements of your institution and your professor.

Paper and margins. In most institutions, the standard paper size is A4 or Letter Size. You will presumably use one of these two paper sizes. For *unbound* research papers, you should leave margins of between 2.5 and 3.0 centimetres on all sides between the edges of the page and the main text (approximately 1.0 to 1.25 inches). For theses and dissertations, which need to be *bound* along the left edge, leave one centimetre extra on the left margin. Headers and footers should be set approximately midway between the edge of the page and the text boundaries.

Fonts, line spacing, and line height. Most academic institutions require essays to be written in 12-point font, and set in either 1.5-line spacing or double-line spacing. In footnotes, reduce the font size to 10 point. Where institutions have preferred fonts, Times New Roman, Arial, and Calibri tend to be favoured. Find out what your institution requires.

Theological papers often use Hebrew and Greek text. Some font sets may not include all the characters needed to type in Hebrew or Greek. The good news is that the standard sets for Arial, Times New Roman, and Calibri now include all the characters necessary to use them as Unicode fonts for biblical languages. Institutions and publications may specify particular Hebrew or Greek fonts.

If you do have to switch to a different font for Greek or Hebrew script, you may encounter a problem – they are 'taller' than most normal fonts. As a result, if you set your line spacing on 1.5, lines containing Hebrew or Greek characters will be higher than those without such characters. To solve the problem, do not use a setting such as '1.5-line spacing'. This varies from font to font. Instead, set your line spacing *exactly*. Go to your paragraph settings and, under line spacing, select 'exactly'. Then enter a value equivalent to 1.5 spacing. For Arial 12 point, this would be 'exactly 21 pt'. This keeps all lines the same height.

Justification. Should you set your paragraphs for *full justification* or *left alignment*? This depends on institutional requirements. Although full justification looks neater and most published books prefer it, many seminaries and universities still abide by an age-old tradition of requiring left alignment. We consider either perfectly acceptable but, once again, it is best to check if your institution specifies.

Spelling and punctuation. English spelling varies from country to country. Set your word processor to fit the regional settings required by your institution and use the same forms consistently. For example, if you use 'English UK' as your default, you should use 'colour' instead of 'color' throughout. Consistency is vital. Do not, however, change direct quotations. If it falls in a quotation, leave 'color'.

In British English, punctuation marks are placed *outside* quotation marks (inverted commas) *unless* the punctuation mark is part of the quotation. In American English, periods and commas are always placed inside the closing quotation mark. US English uses double quotation marks (" ") for direct quotations, whereas UK English tends to use single quotation marks (' ').

Even if English is your fifth language, there is no excuse for having the kinds of spelling and punctuation mistakes in your assignment that the 'spelling and grammar' checker on your word processor will identify. If, referring to a shopping centre, you type 'maul' instead of 'mall', it is forgivable because the spell checker will not flag the error ('maul' is an English word); 'maal', on the other hand, is unacceptable. It shows careless or lazy work because any spell checker will flag it as an error.

We shall return to the subject of formatting in chapter 7. Before we do so, we need to look at a crucial aspect of academic writing, namely, crediting the sources you use. This is so important that we shall devote four chapters to it (chs. 3–6).

Summary

The goal of academic writing is precision and clarity. Structure is one key to achieving this goal. Using triads, headings, bridging and summarising properly adds clarity to your writing and helps your readers follow your argument. Style and presentation are also important; they either help or hinder your article from achieving its purpose. Try to keep your style strong and simple. Make sure you format the document properly, in a way that says, 'This student knows what she is doing' – it may add 10 per cent to your final grade.

We now turn our attention to a critical aspect of academic writing – crediting the sources you use. We shall devote chapters 3–6 to this topic.

3

In-Text Citations

In academic writing, it is imperative that you credit the sources you use. Failure to credit your sources is a form of stealing; we call it plagiarism (see ch. 6). There are two dominant methods of referencing in theological studies. The one is in-text referencing (also known as author-date referencing and as 'the Harvard method'). The other is footnote referencing. Since theological institutions tend to use one or the other, we shall present both methods. This chapter covers in-text referencing; the next chapter explains footnote referencing. You should study this chapter together with its companion chapter about how to compile a bibliography (ch. 5).

The Advantages of In-Text Citations

The in-text method of referencing indicates the source in parentheses in the text of your paper. This explains the name in-text citation. Since the in-text citation typically consists of the name of the author and the date of publication, some call it the author-date method.

In-text citations have two advantages over footnotes. First, in-text citations take less space than footnotes. If you read academic articles which use footnotes, you often find footnotes taking up half the document. A 20-page article may have as many as 100 footnotes. Even if the note only has a few words, it occupies two lines of text. In-text citations occupy less space. Second, in-text citations enable readers to identify the source without breaking their train of thought. Each time you encounter a footnote, you need to break your train of thought and look at the bottom of the page to obtain essential information about the source (endnotes are worse – the information is not even on the same page). In an economical way, in-text citations alert you to the essential information right where you need it.

The Elements of In-Text Citations

In-text citations provide answers to three questions: (a) Who? (b) When? (c) Where? They indicate *who* you are quoting, *when* the source was written, and *where* in the document your quotation can be located. Therefore, a complete in-text citation usually has three parts:

1) *Author*: the first part of an in-text citation gives the surname(s) of the author(s). This immediately credits the people whose ideas you are using. It also helps readers locate the full source in the bibliography, which is arranged alphabetically according to authors' surnames.

2) *Date*: the date of publication follows the author's name. This aids the reader in two ways. First, it distinguishes different sources by the same author. Second, it indicates how recent the cited source is; recent works carry more weight than older ones.

3) *Page*: when you are quoting from or referring to specific parts of a source, insert page numbers to help readers locate the relevant portion. If you are referring to the entire source without special reference to selected parts, you may omit the page numbers.

Putting the three parts together, a standard in-text citation would look like this: (Wilson 2004, 132). A single space separates the author's name and the date of publication. A comma divides the date and page number.[1]

How to Add an In-Text Citation

There are two ways of adding an in-text citation to your paper.

If the name of the author appears in the text, place the date and page number in parentheses either after the name or after the quotation. In general, prefer to put the citation immediately after the author's name. Here are some examples:

> Wilson (2004, 132) explains, 'A series of linking words connect these three psalms.'
>
> Montgomery believes 'Psalm 73 stands at the theological centre of the Book of Psalms' (1999, 149).
>
> Long and White (2006) did not find any conclusive evidence of purposeful redaction in Luke 9:51–19:27.
>
> Njamini (2002, 132–148) explored several potential reasons for the rising divorce rate among Xhosa pastors.

The first two examples contain direct quotations; they illustrate the two positions in which the date and page can be added, either after the author's name or after the quotation. As a rule, the first option is preferred. The third example refers to an entire

---

[1]. There are variations on this style of author-date citations. For example, some add a comma between the author and the date, such as (Wilson, 2004); others prefer to separate the date and page number with a colon, such as (Wilson 2004:132). Still others use the abbreviations p. and pp. to denote page numbers, such as (Wilson 2004, p. 132). These minor variations are not important; the most important thing is to be consistent in your method.

work, so page numbers are unnecessary. Although the last example does not contain a direct quotation, the page numbers indicate the portion of the work where the relevant information can be found.

If the name of the author does not appear in the text, place the author, date, and page number in parentheses at an appropriate place in the sentence. The most common place is at the end of the sentence, before the full stop.

> There 'remains little doubt that Luke 9:51–19:27 depicts a literary journey rather than a literal one' (Bosman 1992, 94).
>
> The majority of commentaries conclude that Paul wrote Ephesians (e.g. Williams 1984; Bond 1991; Long and Brown 1995; Mahlangu 2002; Smith and Ngi 2006).
>
> The allusions to illness in Psalm 6 'may be metaphors for spiritual or national suffering' (Mills 1999, 24; cf. Jabini 2012).

The full citation typically follows a quotation. The period (full stop) comes *after* the citation; other than the closing inverted comma, there is no punctuation mark between the end of the quotation and the citation. The middle example (above) lists a number of sources without any direct quotation. In the last example, the direct quotation comes from Mills; Jabini is a second source supporting the same idea.

When you include a block quotation, the same two approaches can be used. The citation could look like either of these examples:

> Pollock (2007, 198) clarifies the approach as follows:
>
> When faced with an ambiguity in the Greek text that he cannot retain in translation, the translator should place the likelier interpretation in the text and the alternate rendering in a footnote.
>
> It is not always possible to translate word-for-word.
>
> When faced with an ambiguity in the Greek text that he cannot retain in translation, the translator should place the likelier interpretation in the text and the alternate rendering in a footnote (Pollock 2007, 198).

In each of the examples so far, the source had author, date and, where necessary, page numbers. Sometimes your source does not have all three elements. Here are some tips for handling variations.

How to Handle Variations on the Main Elements

Not all in-text citations follow the standard formula of author, date, and page. What if a book has six editors instead of an author? What should you do if no author is named, as often happens with websites? What if there is no date? Electronic books often do not include page numbers; what then? How should you reference a chapter or a section?

We cannot look at every possible problem you might encounter, but we can explain how to handle common problems. If you understand the principles involved, you should be able to solve other problems.

Problems Related to the Author

You will encounter two opposite problems with respect to the author part of an in-text citation: no author and too many authors.

If the work has no author, substitute the title for the author. If the title is long, abbreviate it. The example shows how you could cite an anonymous Internet article called 'The Doctrine of Salvation in the Preaching of George Raymer'.

> 'Jesus died to atone for our sins' ('Salvation in Raymer' 2007, 3).

If the work is an article, the title should be placed in inverted commas. If the work were a book, the title would be italicised.

If the work has 3–5 authors, list all the names in the first citation; thereafter, cite the first author followed by 'and others' (or et al.).

> First citation: (Brown, Smith, Wilkins, and Rebuli 1998, 14)
> Later citations: (Brown and others 1998, 29)
> (Brown et al. 1998, 29)

If the work has six or more authors, cite it using the first author followed by 'and others' (or 'et al.'). In the bibliography, list all the authors.

> 'If we abandon our belief in the doctrine of creation, our belief in the atoning work of Jesus makes no sense' (Flanagan et al. 2004).

Occasionally you will use source documents that have an *organisation as author*. This often happens with government bodies, organisational reports, and institutional documents. In such cases, substitute the name of the organisation for the author. If the name of the organisation is long, write it out in full the first time, but place an abbreviation in square brackets after it; thereafter, use the abbreviation to cite it.

> First citation: (World Council of Churches [WCC] 2014, 12)
> Later citations: (WCC 2014, 19)

Many students err when citing *an article from an edited book* – they cite the editor(s) of the book rather than the author of the article. You should cite by the author of the article. For example, Wood was the senior editor of the third edition of *The New Bible Dictionary* (1996), while Dunn wrote the article 'Baptism'. If you cite from this article:

Incorrect:	(Wood 1996, 120)
Correct:	(Dunn 1996, 120)

The only time you may substitute editor(s) for the author is when the source does not indicate who wrote the article; in such cases, you may substitute either the editor(s) or the title for the author. In general, prefer to use the editors as the 'author'. If a Bible dictionary was edited by Young and Kunhiyop, but gives no indication who wrote the article 'Baptism', you could cite it in either of these ways:

Preferred:	(Young and Kunhiyop 2006, 423)
Accepted:	('Baptism' 2006, 423)

Whichever option you choose, your bibliography entry must match. These would be the corresponding entries.

> Young, Linda P., and Samuel W. Kunhiyop, eds. 2006. 'Baptism'. Pages 420–428 in *The African Bible Dictionary*.
>
> 'Baptism'. 2006. Pages 420–428 in *The African Bible Dictionary*. Edited by Linda P. Young and Samuel W. Kunhiyop.

Problems Related to the Date

Most problems related to the *date* spring from the rise in electronic media. Websites often fail to indicate the date an article was written or published. Electronic books (e-books) may give two dates, namely, the date the printed edition was published and the date of the electronic version; which one should you cite? The content of an online article may change regularly (for example, Wikipedia), so the *exact* date on which you accessed it becomes crucial. Using the examples below as guidelines, you should be able to work out how to handle most situations.

If a source gives no indication of the date it was written or published, you may use the abbreviation 'n.d.' for 'no date'. This is the traditional way of referencing books that give no publication date.

> Example of 'no date': (Tucker n.d., 249)

If an e-book gives publication information for both the printed edition and the electronic edition, use the date of the electronic edition. Cite the version you are using, that is, the electronic edition. For example, the Logos edition of Warren Wiersbe's book *Be Holy* indicates that the printed edition was published in 1994, but the electronic edition in 1996.

Correct:	(Wiersbe 1996, 31) – date of electronic ed.
Incorrect:	(Wiersbe 1994, 31) – date of printed ed.

Some publishers require that you include both dates in your citation, putting the date of the electronic source as the primary date and the date of the print edition as the secondary date. The secondary date is placed between square brackets, like this: (Wiersbe 1996 [1994], 31). This method is rather cumbersome, but has the benefit of giving the reader an accurate sense of how old the original edition of the book is.

If a website does not indicate the date the source was written or uploaded, you may cite it by the date you accessed it. This is not ideal, but it is better than citing it as 'no date'. If you accessed a dateless online resource on 14 January 2014, you would cite it in-text as 2014, and indicate in the bibliography that this was the date of access rather than the date of publication. We recommend that you put the date of access in square brackets to indicate that it was not a publication date.

> Example: (Wilson and Ngi [2014], 24).

Where do you locate the date of publication in a book? Usually on the left-hand page behind the title page. If you look at this page in Johann Mouton's *How to Succeed at Your Master's and Doctoral Studies,* this is what you will see:

> Published by Van Schaik Publishers
>
> 1064 Arcadia Street, Hatfield, Pretoria
>
> All rights reserved
>
> Copyright © 2001
>
> . . . .
>
> First edition 2001
>
> Second impression 2001
>
> Third impression 2002
>
> Fourth impression 2003

Which date should you cite? The publication date is the date of the copyright or the edition, in this case 2001. The other dates are simply reprints. If a book has been through more than one edition, you may see something like this:

> First edition 1984
>
> Second edition 1993
>
> Third edition 2004

In this instance, cite the latest edition, namely, 2004.

Problems Related to the Page

The purpose of including page numbers is to help readers locate the relevant section of the source. Page numbers are not the only way to point readers towards a particular section of a source. Here are some variations on the use of page numbers.

In some circumstances, you may omit any reference to a specific part of the source. In these cases, you simply give author and date (for example, Cook 2004). These are common situations in which this guideline applies:

- You are referring to the whole source rather than to a specific part of it.
- You are citing a work without any page numbers and none of the other guidelines apply.
- You are citing a commentary's discussion of a specific Scripture.

In many sources, section numbers provide an ideal means of referencing. Many documents number sections. We have seen this in web documents, theses, grammars, lexicons, and legal works, to name just a few. If a source contains both page and section numbers, you may choose to cite it by page or by section. Use the symbol § or the abbreviation 'sec.' to point to a section number. The plurals are §§ and 'secs.'

Example from Strong's lexicon:	(Strong 1996, §1499)
Example from a dissertation:	(Long 2013, sec. 2.3.2)

You may cite a chapter number instead of a page number. This happens in two situations: (a) if you are referring to an entire chapter rather than a specific part of a chapter or (b) if an electronic source has chapters, but not pages. You may choose to write out the word 'chapter' or to abbreviate it as 'chap.' or 'ch.' (plurals 'chaps.' and 'chs.' respectively). Here are some examples:

Single chapter:	(Wilson 2002, chap. 3)
Multiple chapters:	(Ndlovu 1997, chaps. 3–7)

When citing dictionaries or lexicons, you can use the Latin abbreviation 's.v.' (meaning 'under the word') followed by the entry. The citation below means you can find the relevant information under the lexicon entry for the word εἰμί, section 2.a.

(Kirsten 1997, s.v. εἰμί 2.a)

The goal is to help readers find the right part of the source as easily as possible. As a rule, page numbers are the most helpful way to achieve this goal. However, if page numbers are not available or there is a better way to achieve the goal, use another way of pointing readers to the right place.

Some Loose Ends

There are four loose ends we need to discuss: (a) how to cite Scripture, (b) how to order groups of citations, (c) how to punctuate in-text citations, and (d) how often to repeat an in-text citation.

How to Cite Scripture

The standard way to cite Scripture is to indicate the book of the Bible followed by the chapter and verse like this: Matthew 18:19. Note that the chapter number and verse number are separated by a colon. Here are some important rules for citing Scripture verses:

- In the text of the document, write out the names of Bible books in full; in parentheses, abbreviate the book names. The preferred abbreviations for books of the Bible can be found in Appendix A. Compare these two examples:

    > Matthew 18:19 promises, 'If two of you on earth agree about anything you ask for, it will be done for you by my Father in heaven' (NIV).

    > The word of God promises, 'If two of you on earth agree about anything you ask for, it will be done for you by my Father in heaven' (Matt 18:19, NIV).

- Whenever you quote directly from a Bible translation, you need to indicate which translation you are using. Use standard abbreviations for this purpose (e.g. NIV for New International Version in the above examples). If you primarily quote from the same translation, after the first quotation add a footnote like this: 'Unless otherwise indicated, all Scripture quotations are from the New International Version.' Then you do not need to add 'NIV' when quoting it.

How to Order Groups of Citations

To emphasise that the consensus of scholarly opinion regards Psalms 9–10 as a single poem, the author of the example below cites twelve scholars who concur with that judgement. This is a common practice in academic writing.

> However, Psalms 9–10 were originally a single psalm, so the heading of Psalm 9 subsumes Psalm 10 (Bratcher and Reyburn 1991; Motyer 1994; Craigie 1998; Broyles 1999; Strugnell and Eshel 2001; Wilcock 2001; Richard 2002; Wilson 2002; Terrien 2003; Miller 2004; Goldingay 2006; Labuschagne 2007).

When you need to cite multiple sources in support of a point, how should you order them? Here are three guidelines:

- You may arrange citations in alphabetical order based on the authors' surnames.

- You may arrange them in chronological order, ascending or descending, based on the dates of publication.
- When citing Scriptures, it is standard to list them in canonical order, that is, in the order of the Bible books.

The next aspect we need to discuss is the punctuation of in-text citations.

How to Punctuate In-Text Citations

In ordinary citations consisting of author, date, and page, use no punctuation between the author and date, and use a comma between the date and page (for example, Williams 2002, 26). When including a *volume number* in the citation, separate the volume and page numbers with a colon; it is optional to use the abbreviations 'vol.' or 'vols.'

Example 1:	Wilmot 2013, 4:428
Example 2:	Wilmot 2013, vol. 4:428

It is technically preferred to use an en-dash to denote a range of pages (e.g. 12–15), although a simple hyphen or minus sign is acceptable (12-15). If the pages or verses are not consecutive, separate them with a comma.

Incorrect:	(White 2011, 19–34 and 94)
Correct:	(White 2011, 19–34, 94)
	(John 14:1–4; 15:1, 7, 10)

Separate citations with a semi-colon. Do not separate them with a comma and do not use 'and' before the last entry in a series.

Incorrect:	(Smit 1996, Thom 2009 and Williams 2004)
Correct:	(Smit 1996; Thom 2009; Williams 2014)
Incorrect:	(Matt 16:18–21, Luke 14:12–14 and John 8:1–11)
Correct:	(Matt 16:18–21; Luke 14:12–14; John 8:1–11)

When you work extensively with certain sources, how often must you provide a full citation? This is the topic for the next section.

How Often to Repeat an In-Text Citation

When working extensively with a source, must you repeat the in-text citation every time? The rule is that you must start fresh in each new paragraph. When you start a new paragraph, you must provide full citation details even if you are still referring to the same source as you were in the previous paragraph. The two paragraphs below show correct practice. Although the citation in the second paragraph is from the same source and the same page as the one in the first, it needs to be repeated in full because it occurs in a new paragraph.

> Van Wyk (2001, 43) explains that there are three ways we might interpret Psalm 6: as a composite of two fragments, namely, verses 1–7 and 8–10; as the prayer of a sick king whose enemies are exploiting his crisis; or as a national prayer in which the allusions to illness are metaphors for national suffering.
>
> 'In my view,' declares Van Wyk (2001, 43), 'the evidence favours the second option.' He offers four reasons for this view. First . . .

Within the same paragraph, these rules apply:

- If a different citation does not intervene, it is not necessary to repeat the citation for subsequent references. If it comes from the same page (or verse or section), the second quotation needs *no* citation; the original citation is assumed to apply. If the second citation refers to a different page, only the new page (or verse or section) number needs to be given. You can use the following abbreviations: p. for one page, pp. for more than one; v. for one verse, vv. for more than one; § for one section, §§ for more than one. For the most part, however, it is not necessary to use 'p.' or 'pp.' You can simply give the page numbers on their own, as long as it is clear from the immediate context that they are page references.

  > p. 14 = page 14
  >
  > pp. 14–19 = pages 14 to 19
  >
  > v. 7 = verse 7
  >
  > vv. 7–11 = verses 7 to 11
  >
  > §14.1 = section 14.1
  >
  > §§14.1–3 = sections 14.1 to 14.3

- If a different citation intervenes, you must provide enough of the citation to make clear what you are citing. The situation occurs when you cite source A, then source B, then source A again. For the second citation from source A, you may give only the name and page number as long as this leaves no doubt about the source's date. If there is any potential for ambiguity, provide a full citation.

  > Mills (2007, 144) announced, 'A literal interpretation of Genesis 1–3 is no longer tenable.' In response to Garrison's (2003, 13–27) 'case for a literal interpretation', Mills (152) claims, 'Dawkins has proved the foolishness of belief in creation'.

Summary

Academic integrity demands that you credit your sources. In-text citations are one way to do so. Each in-text citation should answer three questions: Who? When? Where? In most citations, these correspond to author, date, and page, but there are many variations on the standard citation.

On their own, in-text citations do not provide enough information to enable a reader to find the source. The in-text citation has a companion entry in the bibliography, which provides more complete information about the source.

4

Footnote Citations

Proper referencing is a vital part of academic writing. It is not just a matter of technique, but of integrity. If you do not cite your sources correctly, you are being dishonest. The two main methods of citation used in theological studies are in-text citations, which were explained in the previous chapter, and footnote citations, which we cover in this chapter. You can only use one of these methods at a time. You must find out which method is required, and use it consistently.

Two Types of Footnotes

There are two main types of footnotes: reference notes and educational notes. Reference notes provide information about the sources referenced in the text. Educational notes (they have many other names) provide additional information that the author elects not to place in the body of the text. Whether you are using author-date or footnote-based referencing has no bearing on the use of educational notes. The focus of this chapter is on the use of reference notes.

Advantages of Footnote Citations

Why do some institutions and some publications prefer footnote citations to in-text citations? Footnotes have a few advantages over author-date referencing. First and foremost, footnotes are less intrusive than in-text citations. In-text citations clutter the body of the essay with technical information that may be distracting to readers. Their intrusive power is most pertinent in scholarly essays, which tend to have many citations. Footnotes provide the necessary information about sources without disrupting the flow of the text. If readers want to know about the source, they can read the footnote. If they do not, they need not. Second, footnote citations provide more complete information than in-text citations. Third, footnotes make the inclusion of a bibliography optional. Since the first footnote provides the full bibliographic information, it may be unnecessary to include a bibliography. Because in-text citations only give the author and date, the bibliography is indispensable – it alone provides the information a reader knows to trace the source.

Principles of Footnote Citation

The first note contains the complete publication data, while any subsequent notes for the same source use a shorter version that contains only the surname, (abridged) title, and page number(s). In the examples below, the first entry is for the complete footnote and the second is for the subsequent note.

In the case of a book, the name(s) of the author(s), the title of the book (in italics), and the number(s) of the page(s) cited appear in the body of the note, while the publication information is placed in parentheses. The individual pieces of information in parentheses are separated by semicolons, and ordered as follows:

- editor
- translator
- number of volumes
- edition
- series
- place
- publisher
- date
- electronic edition details

For articles, both the title of the article and the name of the publication in which it was published are placed in the body of the note. The title of the article appears in quotation marks, while the title of the publication is italicised.

Here are some important rules about punctuation:

- In titles, capitalise all words except for articles, coordinating conjunctions, and prepositions. The first word of a title or subtitle is always capitalised.
- The titles of published books and journals are placed in italics, while the titles of articles or unpublished works are placed in quotation marks. You can choose whether to use single or double quotation marks depending on the style requirements for the work.
- Semicolons are used to separate the elements in parentheses in a footnote.
- Colons precede page numbers in journal articles and separate volume and page numbers in multi-volume works.

Abbreviations are used for the titles of many works in footnotes. These include journal titles, commonly used resources such as lexicons or series' of books. A list of some of common and acceptable abbreviations can be found in Appendices A–B.

If a city where the work is published is not well known, include the state or country. You may use any standard system of abbreviations for US states, as long as you are consistent.

Examples of Common Footnote Citations

Although space does not permit us to provide an extensive list of examples, we shall illustrate footnotes for these types of source materials.

Books
1. Books with one author
2. Books with two or three authors
3. Books with more than three authors
4. Books with a translator
5. Books with one editor
6. Books with two or more editors
7. Books with both author and editor
8. Books with author, editor, and translator
9. Revised edition
10. Works with multiple volumes
11. Chapter in a book with an editor
12. Chapter within a titled volume in a series with an editor and volume numbers
13. Commentary in a series with general titles
14. Commentary in a series with general titles and volume numbers

Articles (Journals, Magazines, and Newspapers)
15. Journal article
16. Magazine article
17. Newspaper article
18. Book review
19. Signed article in an encyclopedia or dictionary
20. Article in a lexicon or theological dictionary

Electronic Resources
21. Electronic book (e-book)
22. Webpage

Other Resources
23. Interview
24. Unpublished dissertation or thesis
25. Paper presented at a professional society

Footnotes for Books

1. Books with one author

> 1. James L. Crenshaw, *The Psalms: An Introduction* (Grand Rapids, MI: Eerdmans, 2001), 6–7.
>
> 4. Crenshaw, *The Psalms*, 6.

2. Books with two or three authors

> 2. James L. Crenshaw, Marti Steussy, and Norman Gottwald, *A History of Israel* (Grand Rapids, MI: Eerdmans, 2001), 123–124.
>
> 7. Crenshaw, Steussy, and Gottwald, *A History of Israel,* 142.

3. Books with more than three authors

When a book has more than three authors, only name the first author and add the abbreviation 'et al.' or the words 'and others' in the note.

> 3. Bernard B. Scott et al., *Reading New Testament Greek* (Peabody, MA: Hendrickson, 1993), 16.
>
> 12. Scott et al., *Reading New Testament Greek*, 16.

4. Books with a translator

> 4. J. P. Fokkelman, *Reading Biblical Poetry* (trans. I. Smit; Louisville, KY: Westminster John Knox, 2001), 97–107.
>
> 54. Fokkelman, *Reading Biblical Poetry*, 99.

5. Books with one editor

> 5. Scott Nash, ed., *The Sermon on the Mount: Studies and Sermons* (Greenville, SC: Smyth and Helwys, 1992), 5.
>
> 55. Nash, *The Sermon on the Mount*, 5.

6. Books with two or more editors

If a book has two or three editors, list them all. If it has more than three, only name the first author and add the abbreviation 'et al.' or the words 'and others' in the note. The abbreviation 'eds.' follows the editors' names.

> 6. Steven L. McKenzie and M. Patrick Graham, eds., *The Hebrew Bible Today: An Introduction to Critical Issues* (Louisville, KY: Westminster John Knox, 1998), 39.
>
> 56. McKenzie and Graham, *The Hebrew Bible Today*, 39.

7. Books with both author and editor

When a book has both an author and an editor, you cite the entry by the name of the author and place the editor's name first in the parentheses.

> 7. Edward Schillebeeckx, *The Schillebeeckx Reader* (ed. Robert J. Schreiter; Edinburgh: T&T Clark, 1986), 15.
>
> 25. Schillebeeckx, *The Schillebeeckx Reader*, 15.

8. Books with an author, editor, and translator

> 9. H. Bavinck, *Reformed Dogmatics* (ed. J. Bolt; trans. J. Vriend; Grand Rapids, MI: Baker, 2003), 12.
>
> 22. Bavinck, *Reformed Dogmatics*, 12.

9. Numbered or revised editions

Information about the edition of the book is placed in the parentheses, and uses standard abbreviations, such as 'rev. ed.' or '4th ed.'

> 10. Bernard W. Anderson, *Out of the Depths: The Psalms Speak for Us Today* (3rd ed.; Louisville, KY: Westminster John Knox, 2000), 301–302.
>
> 34. Anderson, *Out of the Depths*, 302.

10. Work with multiple volumes

The first reference notes the work as a whole instead of a particular page in one of the volumes. The second note is a reference to a specific volume and page number.

> 10. Karl Barth, *Church Dogmatics* (ed. G. W. Bromiley and T. F. Torrance; 4 vols.; London: T&T Clark, 2009).
>
> 60. Barth, *Church Dogmatics*, 1:43.

11. Chapter in a book with an editor

The chapter is placed in quotation marks (single or double depending on the rules of punctuation you are following), while the title of the book remains in italics.

> 12. Edith Turner, 'A Visible Spirit Form in Zambia,' in *Readings in Indigenous Religions* (ed. G. Harvey; London: Continuum, 2002), 43–51.
>
> 24. Turner, 'A Visible Spirit Form in Zambia,' 45–46.

12. Chapter within a titled volume in a series with an editor and volume numbers

> 12. Fokkelien van Dijk-Hemmes, 'Mothers and a Mediator in the Song of Deborah,' in *A Feminist Companion to Judges* (ed. Athalya Brenner; vol. 4 of *Feminist Companion to the Bible*, ed. Athalya Brenner; Sheffield, England: Sheffield Academic Press, 1993), 112.

> 62. Dijk-Hemmes, 'Mothers and a Mediator,' in *Feminist Companion*, 4:112.

13. Commentary in a series with general titles

The name of the commentary series should be placed in the parentheses.

> 23. James L. Mays, *Psalms* (Interpretation; Louisville, KY; John Knox, 1994), 57.
>
> 44. Mays, *Psalms*, 57.

14. Commentary in a series with general titles and volume numbers

> 24. Marvin E. Tate, *Psalms 51–100* (WBC 20: Dallas, TX: Word Books, 1990), 29.
>
> 50. Tate, *Psalms 51–100*, 39.

Footnotes for Articles

Whereas the titles of published books are typeset in italics, the titles of articles are placed in quotation marks, but not italicised. The title of the work in which the article is published is italicised.

15. Article in a journal

The standard elements for a journal article are as follows: name of author, title of article (in quotation marks), title of journal (in italics), volume and number of the journal, date, page numbers.

> 13. Mark D. Given, 'Restoring the Inheritance in Romans 11:1,' *Journal of Biblical Literature* 118 (1999): 90–92.
>
> 63. Given, 'Restoring the Inheritance,' 91.

If the journal article is accessed from an electronic database or an online edition of the journal, you may provide the details of the database or website in addition. We consider this optional.

> 43. Gueorgi Kossinets and Duncan J. Watts, 'Origins of Homophily in an Evolving Social Network,' *American Journal of Sociology* 115 (2009): 411, retrieved 28 February 2010, doi:10.1086/599247.
>
> 26. James W. Thompson, 'The Background and Function of the Beatitudes in Matthew and Luke,' *ResQ* 41 (1999): 110, retrieved from the ATLA Religion Database.
>
> 27. David J. Belcastro, 'Thomas Merton: American Monk, Artist and Social Critic,' *Theological Librarianship* 7, no. 2 (2014): 33, retrieved 14 June 2014, https://journal.atla.com/ojs/index.php/theolib/article/view/334/1084.

16. Article in a magazine

15. Alan Millard, 'Biblical Writer Had Early Sources,' *British Archaeological Review* 36 (September/October 2010): 11–12, 17–21.

43. Millard, 'Biblical Writer,' 18–19.

17. Article in a newspaper

16. Noel Woodbridge, 'The Use of Worship Songs in Youth Ministry,' *The Star* (14 November 2007): 4.

24. Woodbridge, 'Use of Worship,' 4.

18. Book reviews in journals

16. J. Andrew Dearman, review of Richard D. Nelson, *Joshua: A Commentary*, *JBL* 118 (1999): 130–31.

116. Dearman, review of Nelson, 130.

19. Signed article in an encyclopedia or dictionary

The articles in an encyclopedia are usually contributed by a variety of authors, and the name of the author is given. It is proper to reference the article under the name of the author. Do not cite it under the name of the editor of the encyclopedia.

18. J. A. Sanders, 'Exile,' *IDB* 2:186–88.

118. Sanders, 'Exile,' 2:187.

20. Article in a lexicon or theological dictionary

If you are dealing with a word or family of words, include the complete title and page range. For example, here we are citing the words lamb and sheep.

19. J. Gess and R. Tuente, 'Lamb, Sheep,' *NIDNTT* 2:410–412.

If you have a subsequent entry, you include only the dictionary reference.

21. Gess and Tuent, *NIDNTT* 2:411.

If you are dealing with a word appearing in an article discussing a group of words, include information only for the word you are using.

22. D. Hill, 'θυρα,' *NIDNTT* 2:30.

Footnotes for Electronic Resources

21. Electronic book (e-book)

An e-book is footnoted in the same way as a print book, with the exception of including the electronic edition or e-reader at the end of the parentheses. If the electronic edition has a different publication date, include it.

> 25. James L. Crenshaw, Marti Steussy, and Norman Gottwald, *A History of Israel* (Grand Rapids, Mich.: Eerdmans, 2001; Kindle ed.), 123–24.

> 55. Crenshaw, Steussy, and Gottwald, *A History of Israel*, 123.

If the e-book was accessed online, provide the URL and the date of access. If the book does not have page numbers, you may substitute a section title, chapter number, or some other marker of location. It is acceptable to place the date of retrieval and the URL inside the parentheses or after them. Either of these would be acceptable:

> 45. Philip Schaff, *The History of the Christian Church* (London: Charles Scribner's Sons, 1910; elec. ed. Dallas, TX: Electronic Bible Society, 1998; retrieved 26 September 2014, http://www.ccel.org/s/schaff/history/About.htm), 57.

> 45. Philip Schaff, *The History of the Christian Church* (London: Charles Scribner's Sons, 1910; elec. ed. Dallas, TX: Electronic Bible Society, 1998), 57, retrieved 26 September 2014, http://www.ccel.org/s/schaff/history/About.htm.

22. Webpage

The most basic entry for a website consists of the author name(s), page title, website title, date of publication, web address, and date retrieved.

> 46. Daniel B. Wallace, 'A Mishnaic Commentary on Matthew 1.19,' *Bible.org* (2013, retrieved 30 October 2014, https://bible.org/article/mishnaic-commentary-matthew-119).

If a website does not provide all the information you need, provide as much as you can. If no author is named, you can use the title of the article/page or the title of the website as a substitute.

> 49. 'Doctrine,' *The Methodist Church of Southern Africa* (retrieved 30 October 2014, http://www.methodist.org.za/theology/doctrine).

Do not hyphenate URL addresses if they need to be continued on the next line. Do not begin the second line of a URL with a dot.

Footnotes for Other Resources

23. Interview

In the case of personal interviews, it is often best to work the details of an interview into the main text. For instance, you can write, 'In a personal interview with Leonard Sweet on 14 July 2014...' When a more formal citation is desired, reference it under the name of the person interviewed, and then mention the name of the interviewer. The three examples below are fictitious, illustrating published, television, and unpublished interviews.

> 27. Christopher L. Peppler, Interview with Jennifer Mason, *Christian News Magazine* (23 July 2007), 7.
>
> 50. Angelina Jolie, Interview with Steve Kroft, *60 Minutes*. CBS, WCBS, 3 February 2009.
>
> 28. John Smith and Jane Doe, Interview with Bongani Njamini, personal interview (Cape Town, South Africa, 11 October 2013).

24. Unpublished dissertation or thesis

Theses and dissertations are not considered to be published works. When referencing a thesis or dissertation, the title is placed in quotation marks, but not italicised. In parentheses indicate the type of work, awarding institution, and date of completion.

> 15. Nancy L. deClaissé-Walford, 'Reading from the Beginning: The Shaping of the Hebrew Psalter' (Ph.D. diss., Baylor University, 1995), 59–64.
>
> 21. deClaissé-Walford, 'Reading from the Beginning,' 63.

25. Paper presented at a professional society

> 22. Susan Ebertz, 'Stories of Our Past as Parables of Our Present: Japanese American Internment Camps in Arizona' (paper presented at the annual meeting of the American Theological Library Association, Scottsdale, AZ, 28 June 2010), 46–48.
>
> 25. Ebertz, 'Stories of Our Past,' 46.

Multiple Citations in One Footnote

In an academic paper, you can reduce the number of footnotes by placing multiple citations in one footnote. 'In a single paragraph containing several quotations, for example, a reference number following the last quotation will permit them all to be cited in one note.'[1]

You can use any logical method of ordering the citations. For instance, if you referred to four sources in a paragraph, and the footnote provides the citation information for

---

1. Kate L. Turabian, *A Manual for Writers of Term Papers, Theses, and Dissertations* (6th ed.; rev. John Grossman and Alice Bennett; Chicago: University of Chicago Press, 1996), §8.16.

all four, it is sensible to list them in the order they are mentioned in the text. If you are listing commentators who share a particular interpretation, you could order them chronologically or alphabetically. The individual sources should be separated by a semicolon. If this is the first time you are citing the work, give the full citation, but if you have cited it previously, use the abridged citation.

5

The Bibliography

Every academic paper ends with a bibliography, a list of resources (books, articles, interviews) used in writing it. In this chapter, we shall discuss how to compile a bibliography.

Types of Bibliographies

There are four main types of bibliography:

1) works cited

2) works consulted

3) selective bibliography

4) annotated bibliography

You should select the one that is most appropriate for your paper. When you have selected it, label it appropriately. If you are using author-date referencing, do not use 'bibliography' as the heading; call it 'works cited' or 'reference list'. If you use an annotated bibliography, the heading should be 'annotated bibliography'. Let us explain how each kind of bibliography works.

1) *Works cited* (or *reference list*). In an author-date system of reference, the bibliography is usually a list of works cited. All and only the works cited in the text of the document are listed in the bibliography, which is headed 'works cited' or 'reference list'. The purpose of the works cited list is to enable readers to locate the sources cited in the paper. Do not list works you consulted, but did not cite.

2) *Works consulted*. This format is more extensive than a list of works cited; it includes all the works you consulted, whether or not you cited them. It indicates all the works that influenced the writing of the paper. Use a list of 'works consulted' to provide your readers with a comprehensive list of works on your topic so that they know all the crucial works you used.

3) *Selective bibliography.* The purpose of a selective bibliography is to list only the most important resources on a topic. It simply points readers to key works.

4) *Annotated bibliography.* In an annotated bibliography, the author adds a few notes after each entry. The annotation provides some information about the resource and/or its significance for the paper. Annotations enrich documents such as research proposals and reading lists.

When writing papers or theses which use an author-date system of referencing, assume that the bibliography should be a list of *works cited* unless you are specifically told to use a different kind of bibliography. The list of works cited should include *all* and *only* the works that you cited in the paper.

If your paper uses footnote-based referencing, it is not imperative to list every work cited in the body, because the initial footnote citation gives the full details of the source. Depending on your purpose, therefore, the works listed in the bibliography do not need to match the sources referenced in the work exactly.

How to Compose a Bibliography Entry

Each entry in a bibliography needs to convey four main pieces of information:

a) who wrote it?	the author
b) when was it published?	the date
c) what is it called?	the title
d) how can it be accessed?	the publication details

There are well-established guidelines for formatting bibliography entries. For the most part, the entry is the same whether you are using in-text or footnote-based referencing. The one consistent difference is the placement of the publication date. In-text referencing systems place the publication date immediately after the author's name, whereas footnote-based methods put the date at or near the end.

Examples of Common Bibliography Entries

Although space does not permit us to provide an extensive list of examples, we shall illustrate bibliography entries for common types of source materials. The examples show the entry for both methods of referencing. The abbreviation FN is used for the footnote method and the abbreviation AD for the author-date method.

Books
1. Books with one author
2. Books with two or three authors
3. Books with more than three authors

4. Books with a translator
5. Books with one editor
6. Books with two or more editors
7. Books with both author and editor
8. Books with author, editor, and translator
9. Revised edition
10. Works with multiple volumes
11. Chapter in a book with an editor
12. Chapter within a titled volume in a series with an editor and volume numbers
13. Commentary in a series with general titles
14. Commentary in a series with general titles and volume numbers

Articles (Journals, Magazines, and Newspapers)
15. Journal article
16. Magazine article
17. Newspaper article
18. Book review
19. Signed article in an encyclopedia or dictionary
20. Article in a lexicon or theological dictionary

Electronic Resources
21. Electronic book (e-book)
22. Journal article in full-text from an online database with a print counterpart
23. Journal article in full-text from an online database without a print counterpart
24. Webpage

Other Resources
25. Interview
26. Unpublished dissertation or thesis
27. Paper presented at a professional society

Bibliography Entries for Books

The first author is listed by surname first, followed by other names. Other authors' names are written in the normal order. The only difference between author-date and footnote systems is the placement of the *date*. In the author-date method, the date immediately follows the author's name, while in the footnote method it comes after the name of the publisher.

1. Books with one author

FN	Crenshaw, James L. *The Psalms: An Introduction*. Grand Rapids, MI: Eerdmans, 2001.
AD	Crenshaw, James L. 2001. *The Psalms: An Introduction*. Grand Rapids, MI: Eerdmans.

2. Books with two or three authors

If a book has two or three authors, list all the authors.

FN	Crenshaw, James L., Marti Steussy, and Norman Gottwald. *A History of Israel*. Grand Rapids, MI: Eerdmans, 2001.
AD	Crenshaw, James L., Marti Steussy, and Norman Gottwald. 2001. *A History of Israel*. Grand Rapids, MI: Eerdmans.

3. Books with more than three authors

When a book has more than three authors, only name the first author and add the abbreviation 'et al.' or the words 'and others' in the note.

FN	Scott, Bernard B. et al., *Reading New Testament Greek*. Peabody, MA: Hendrickson, 1993.
AD	Scott, Bernard B. et al., 1993. *Reading New Testament Greek*. Peabody, MA: Hendrickson.

4. Books with a translator

FN	Fokkelman, J. P. *Reading Biblical Poetry*. Translated by I. Smit. Louisville, KY: Westminster John Knox, 2001.
AD	Fokkelman, J. P. 2001. *Reading Biblical Poetry*. Translated by I. Smit. Louisville, KY: Westminster John Knox.

5. Books with one editor

FN	Nash, Scott, ed. *The Sermon on the Mount: Studies and Sermons*. Greenville, SC: Smyth and Helwys, 1992.
AD	Nash, Scott, ed. 1992. *The Sermon on the Mount: Studies and Sermons*. Greenville, SC: Smyth and Helwys.

6. Books with two or more editors

If the book has two or three editors, name them all and use the abbreviation 'eds.' after the last name.

> FN McKenzie, Steven L., and M. Patrick Graham, eds. *The Hebrew Bible Today: An Introduction to Critical Issues*. Louisville, KY: Westminster John Knox, 1998.
>
> AD McKenzie, Steven L., and M. Patrick Graham, eds. 1998. *The Hebrew Bible Today: An Introduction to Critical Issues*. Louisville, KY: Westminster John Knox.

If the work has more than three editors, you list only the name(s) of the main editor(s), followed by 'et al.' You are free to decide how many of the primary editors to name. The examples below illustrate one and three editors named.

> FN Dennis, Lane T. et al., eds. *ESV Study Bible*. Wheaton, IL: Crossway Books, 2008.
>
> AD Dennis, Lane T., Wayne Grudem, J. I. Packer et al., eds. 2008. *ESV Study Bible*. Wheaton, IL: Crossway Books.

7. Books with both author and editor

When a book has both an author and an editor, list it under the author's name and mention the editor after the title.

> FN Schillebeeckx, Edward. *The Schillebeeckx Reader*. Edited by Robert J. Schreiter. Edinburgh: T&T Clark, 1986.
>
> AD Schillebeeckx, Edward. 1986. *The Schillebeeckx Reader*. Edited by Robert J. Schreiter. Edinburgh: T&T Clark.

8. Books with an author, editor, and translator

> FN Bavinck, H. *Reformed Dogmatics*. Edited by J. Bolt. Translated by J. Vriend. Grand Rapids, MI: Baker, 2003.
>
> AD Bavinck, H. 2003. *Reformed Dogmatics*. Edited by J. Bolt. Translated by J. Vriend. Grand Rapids, MI: Baker, 2003.

9. Numbered or revised editions

You are free to spell out or abbreviate words like 'revised', 'third', and 'edition'.

> FN Anderson, Bernard W. *Out of the Depths: The Psalms Speak for Us Today*. Third edition. Louisville, KY: Westminster John Knox, 2000.
>
> AD Anderson, Bernard W. 2000. *Out of the Depths: The Psalms Speak for Us Today*. Revised edition. Louisville, KY: Westminster John Knox.

10. Work with multiple volumes

When referring to the work as a whole, simply indicate how many volumes. The number of volumes is placed after the names of editors and translators.

> FN Barth, Karl. *Church Dogmatics*. Edited by G. W. Bromiley and T. F. Torrance. 4 vols. London: T&T Clark, 2009.
>
> AD Barth, Karl. 2009. *Church Dogmatics*. Edited by G. W. Bromiley and T. F. Torrance. 4 vols. London: T&T Clark.

11. Chapter in a book with an editor

The chapter title is placed in quotation marks (single or double depending on the rules of punctuation you are following), while the title of the book remains in italics.

> FN Turner, Edith. 'A Visible Spirit Form in Zambia.' Pages 149–172 in *Readings in Indigenous Religions*. Edited by G. Harvey. London: Continuum, 2002.
>
> AD Turner, Edith. 2012. 'A Visible Spirit Form in Zambia.' Pages 149–172 in *Readings in Indigenous Religions*. Edited by G. Harvey. London: Continuum.

In the examples, it might be appropriate at times to substitute the chapter number for the page numbers.

12. Chapter within a titled volume in a series with an editor and volume numbers

> FN Dijk-Hemmes, Fokkelien van. 'Mothers and a Mediator in the Song of Deborah.' Pages 110–114 in *A Feminist Companion to Judges*. Edited by Athalya Brenner. Vol. 4 of *Feminist Companion to the Bible*. Sheffield, England: Sheffield Academic Press, 1993.
>
> AD Dijk-Hemmes, Fokkelien van. 1993. 'Mothers and a Mediator in the Song of Deborah.' Pages 110–114 in *A Feminist Companion to Judges*. Edited by Athalya Brenner. Vol. 4 of *Feminist Companion to the Bible*. Sheffield, England: Sheffield Academic Press.

13. Commentary in a series with general titles

The commentary series has a name, but the volumes are not numbered.

> FN Mays, James L. *Psalms*. Interpretation: A Bible Commentary for Teaching and Preaching. Louisville, KY: John Knox, 1994.
>
> AD Mays, James L. 1994. *Psalms*. Interpretation: A Bible Commentary for Teaching and Preaching. Louisville, KY: John Knox.

14. Commentary in a series with general titles and volume numbers
The commentary series has a name, and the volumes are numbered.

> FN	Tate, Marvin E. *Psalms 51–100*. Word Biblical Commentary 20. Dallas, TX: Word Books, 1990.
>
> AD	Tate, Marvin E. 1990. *Psalms 51–100*. Word Biblical Commentary 20. Dallas, TX: Word Books.

Bibliography Entries for Articles

Whereas the titles of published books are typeset in italics, the titles of articles are placed in quotation marks, but not italicised. The title of the work in which the article is published is italicised.

15. Article in a journal
The standard elements for a journal article are as follows: name of author, title of article (in quotation marks), title of journal (in italics), volume and number of the journal, date, page numbers. The differing placement of the date in the two systems causes some significant differences. Note that in the footnote system the date is placed in parentheses before the page numbers.

> FN	Given, Mark D. 'Restoring the Inheritance in Romans 11:1'. *Journal of Biblical Literature* 118, no. 1 (1999): 89–96.
>
> AD	Farley, Michael A. 2008. 'What Is "Biblical" Worship? Biblical Hermeneutics and Evangelical Theologies of Worship'. *JETS* 52, no. 3: 590–613.

The title of the article is written in regular typescript (not italicised); the name of the journal is italicised. The volume number of the journal follows its name (without any punctuation marks between them), and a colon separates the volume number from the page numbers. Many journals are published two, three or four times each year, and each issue is numbered; the notation above, '52, no. 3: 590–613', refers to volume 52, issue number 3, pages 590–613. Not all journals use issue numbers.

If the journal article is accessed from an electronic database or an online edition of the journal, you may provide the details of the database or website in addition. We consider this optional. Here are three different examples of how to do it.

FN	Kossinets, Gueorgi and Duncan J. Watts. 'Origins of Homophily in an Evolving Social Network.' *American Journal of Sociology* 115 (2009): 411. Retrieved 28 February 2010, doi:10.1086/599247.
AD	Thompson, James W. 1999. 'The Background and Function of the Beatitudes in Matthew and Luke.' *Restoration Quarterly* 41: 109–16. Retrieved from the ATLA Religion Database.
FN	Belcastro, David J. 'Thomas Merton: American Monk, Artist and Social Critic.' *Theological Librarianship* 7 (2014): 31–44. Retrieved 14 June 2014, https://journal.atla.com/ojs/index.php/theolib/article/view/334/1084.

16. Article in a magazine

Magazine articles are cited similarly to journal articles, except that volume and issue numbers do not apply. Instead, the specific edition of the magazine is identified by adding the date of the issue – month if released monthly; exact date if released weekly.

FN	Millard, Alan. 'Biblical Writer Had Early Sources.' *Biblical Archaeology Review* 36, no. 5 (October 2010): 11–12, 17–21.
AD	Hodgson, Taryn. 2014. 'How the Media Is Sexualising Your Children.' *JOY! Magazine*, 17 May, 59–60.

There is an important difference between the footnote and author-date methods. In the footnote method, the date is in parentheses, followed by a colon and then the page numbers. In the author-date entry, the date is separated from the title by a comma, and the page numbers from the date by a comma.

17. Article in a newspaper

Newspaper articles need to indicate the exact date and the page number. The components are similar to those of a magazine article. If the author's name is not known, put the title first. If the newspaper is not well known, you might add the city of publication.

FN	Woodbridge, Noel B. 'The Use of Worship Songs in Youth Ministry.' *The Star* (14 November 2007): 4.
AD	Woodbridge, Noel B. 2007. 'The Use of Worship Songs in Youth Ministry.' *The Star*, 14 November, 4.

Note the difference in the way the date is separated from the title and the page number in the two systems of reference.

18. Book reviews in journals

Book reviews begin with the name of the reviewer. They give the author and title of the work reviewed, followed by the publication details of the work in which the review was published.

> FN   Dearman, A. 'Review of Richard D. Nelson, *Joshua: A Commentary.*' *Journal of Biblical Literature* 118 (1999): 130–31.
>
> AD   Dearman, A. 1999. 'Review of Richard D. Nelson, *Joshua: A Commentary.*' *Journal of Biblical Literature* 118: 130–31.

19. Signed article in an encyclopedia or dictionary

The articles in an encyclopedia are usually contributed by a variety of authors, and the name of the author is given. It is proper to reference the article under the name of the author. Do not cite it under the name of the editor of the encyclopedia.

> FN   Sanders, J. A. 'Exile.' Pages 186–88 in vol. 2 of *The Interpreter's Dictionary of the Bible*. Edited by G. A. Buttrick. 4 vols. New York: Abingdon, 1962.
>
> AD   Sanders, J. A. 1962. 'Exile.' Pages 186–88 in vol. 2 of *The Interpreter's Dictionary of the Bible*. Edited by G. A. Buttrick. 4 vols. New York: Abingdon.

20. Article in a lexicon or theological dictionary

There are variations in the way you reference articles in theological dictionaries. In the footnote method, you typically just reference the work as a whole. The author of the article would be mentioned in the relevant footnote. Here is an example:

> FN   Botterweck, G. Johannes, Helmer Ringgren, and Heinz-Josef Fabry, eds. *Theological Dictionary of the Old Testament*. Translated by Douglas W. Stott. 15 vols. Grand Rapids, MI: Eerdmans, 1974–2006.

When you use the author-date system, your bibliography entry must match your in-text citation. If you cited the author of the article in-text, then you must have a corresponding bibliographic entry for the citation.

> AD   Oepke, Albrecht. 1964–1976. 'γύμνος.' Page 773 in vol. 1 of the *Theological Dictionary of the New Testament*. Edited by Gerhard Kittel and Gerhard Friedrich. Translated by Geoffrey W. Bromiley. Grand Rapids, MI: Eerdmans.

Bibliography Entries for Electronic Resources

21. Electronic book (e-book)

In the footnote method, an e-book is referenced in much the same way as a print book, with the exception of including the electronic edition or e-reader at the end of the entry. If the electronic edition has a different publication date, include it.

> FN   Crenshaw, James L., Marti Steussy, and Norman Gottwald. *A History of Israel*. Grand Rapids, MI: Eerdmans, 2001. Kindle edition, 2013.

When you use the author-date method, the bibliography entry must match the in-text citation. If the print and electronic editions have different publication dates, you must select which one to use in your in-text citation. Although it is acceptable to use the date of the printed work, it is preferable to use the date of the electronic edition. This requires adjustments to the bibliography entry. Here are two acceptable ways of including the two dates.

> AD 1   Crenshaw, James L., Marti Steussy, and Norman Gottwald. 2013 [2001]. *A History of Israel*. Grand Rapids, MI: Eerdman. Kindle edition.
>
> AD 2   Crenshaw, James L., Marti Steussy, and Norman Gottwald. 2013. *A History of Israel*. Grand Rapids, MI: Eerdmans, 2001. Kindle edition.

The primary date is that of the electronic edition that you were using. The date of the original printed edition may be place in square brackets after the date of the electronic edition, or it may be placed after the publication details of the printed book, as it would in footnote-based referencing.

If the e-book was accessed online, provide the URL and the date of access.

> FN   Schaff, Philip. *The History of the Christian Church*. London: Charles Scribner's Sons, 1910. Electronic edition: Dallas, TX: Electronic Bible Society, 1998. Retrieved 26 September 2014, http://www.ccel.org/s/schaff/history/About.htm.
>
> AD   Schaff, Philip. 1998. *The History of the Christian Church*. London: Charles Scribner's Sons, 1910. Electronic edition: Dallas, TX: Electronic Bible Society. Retrieved 26 September 2014, http://www.ccel.org/s/schaff/history/About.htm.

22. Webpage

The most basic entry for a website consists of the author name(s), page title in quotation marks, website title in italics, web address, and date retrieved. If the website indicates a publication date for the article, include it in the usual place.

> FN   Wallace, Daniel B. 'A Mishnaic Commentary on Matthew 1.19.' *Bible.org*. 2013. Retrieved 30 October 2014, https://bible.org/article/mishnaic-commentary-matthew-119.
>
> AD   Wallace, Daniel B. 2013. 'A Mishnaic Commentary on Matthew 1.19.' *Bible.org*. Retrieved 30 October 2014, https://bible.org/article/mishnaic-commentary-matthew-119.

Many websites do not include all the information you wish to reference. If the website does not indicate a publication date, simply omit the date in the footnote method. In the author-date method, substitute the year of retrieval in square brackets. If the website does not name the author, place the title at the start of the bibliography entry. If an organisation is the author, list it as such. The example below has no author and no publication date. The title appears first and the citation date in the author-date entry is the year of retrieval.

> FN   'Doctrine.' *The Methodist Church of Southern Africa.* Retrieved 30 October 2014, http://www.methodist.org.za/theology/doctrine.
>
> AD   'Doctrine.' [2014]. *The Methodist Church of Southern Africa.* Retrieved 30 October 2014, http://www.methodist.org.za/theology/doctrine.

Bibliography Entries for Other Sources

23. Interview

If an interview is listed in the bibliography, the person interviewed is treated as the author. Here are two different examples of interviews.

> FN   Peppler, Christopher L. Interview with Jennifer Mason. *Christian News Magazine* (23 July 2007): 7.
>
> FN   Jolie, Angelina. Interview with Steve Kroft. *60 Minutes*. CBS, WCBS, 3 February 2009.

24. Unpublished dissertation or thesis

Theses and dissertations are not considered to be published works. When referencing a thesis or dissertation, the title is placed in quotation marks, but not italicised. The name of the institution must be provided. If the thesis was accessed online, you should add the URL and date of retrieval.

> FN deClaissé-Walford, Nancy L. 'Reading from the Beginning: The Shaping of the Hebrew Psalter.' Ph.D. dissertation, Baylor University, 1995.
>
> AD deClaissé-Walford, Nancy L. 1995. 'Reading from the Beginning: The Shaping of the Hebrew Psalter.' Ph.D. dissertation, Baylor University.

25. Paper presented at a professional society

> FN Ebertz, Susan. 'Stories of Our Past as Parables of Our Present: Japanese American Internment Camps in Arizona.' Paper presented at the annual meeting of the American Theological Library Association. Scottsdale, AZ, 28 June 2010.
>
> AD Ebertz, Susan. 2010. 'Stories of Our Past as Parables of Our Present: Japanese American Internment Camps in Arizona.' Paper presented at the annual meeting of the American Theological Library Association. Scottsdale, AZ, 28 June.

Punctuation in a Bibliography

The most important thing about punctuating a bibliography is *consistency*. If you read ten different style guides, you will probably encounter ten different sets of rules. As long as you stick to the same system throughout your bibliography, it does not matter too much which set of rules you use.

The most important punctuation details relate to the use of capitals, italics, quotation marks, commas, periods, colons, and brackets. The points below contain our guidelines for punctuating a bibliography. They represent our preferred style. If you choose to use variations on the recommended style, just be consistent.

> a) *Capitals.* In titles, capitalise all words except for articles, coordinating conjunctions, and prepositions. The first word of a title or subtitle is always capitalised.
>
> b) *Italics and underlining.* Italicise the titles of books, journals, and magazines. Do not italicise the titles of articles, theses, dissertations, or papers. Reserve underlining for electronic sources, such as email addresses or URLs.
>
> c) *Periods.* Although there are some differences between UK and US English, as a general rule you should use a period after initials or abbreviations. For instance,

the author Lyndi Pam Tucker would be 'L. P. Tucker.' Also use a period after abbreviations, such as 'eds.' or 'trans.'

d) *Commas.* Study the example entries closely to see where commas are used to separate elements in an entry. There are some variations between the footnote and author-date systems, in that the footnote method sometimes uses colons where the author-date method uses commas.

e) *Brackets.* Whereas some styles place references to editors, editions, and volumes in parentheses, our preference is to keep brackets and parentheses to a minimum. Parentheses are mostly reserved for the publication date of journal or magazine articles in the footnote system, and square brackets for additional publication dates in the author-date system.

How to Order the Works in a Bibliography

The rule for arranging the entries in a bibliography is simple: alphabetise all sources based on the surnames (family names) of the authors or editors. Arrange all the entries in a single alphabetical list; do not divide them into categories (for example, journals, books, interviews). Here are some rules for alphabetising:

- Write the author's name in the first entry; thereafter, use eight underscores. If you have multiple entries for the same author, the order depends on the referencing system. In the footnote method, you order the entries alphabetically by title. In the author-date system, organise the entries in date order; if there are multiple publications from the same year, number them a, b, c, and so on.

    Williams, D. H. 2002.

    _____. 2004a.

    _____. 2004b.

    _____. 2004c.

- When alphabetising author's names, follow the exact order of the letters, ignoring spaces and apostrophes. Alphabetise compound family names by the first part of the compound.

    Brown, Jean-Paul.

    De La Rey, L. W. C.

    De Waard, Anthony J.

    d'Offay, Michael.

    Grudem, Wayne.

    Hall-Lindsay, T. I.

MacMillan, G. Brett.

McArthur, Kenneth R., Jr.

Smith-Jones, L. F.

St Denis, R.

van Rensburg, Reuben D.

- If two authors have the same surname, alphabetise by their initials and/or first names.

    Wilson, D. 2002.

    Wilson, Debra. 2014.

    Wilson, D. L. 1991.

    Wilson, S. J. 2007.

- When a source has no author, alphabetise it by the first word of the title, but ignore the words 'a', 'an', or 'the'.

    New International Version. 1984. Grand Rapids, MI: Zondervan.

    'Serving the Lord with Your Talents.' 2002. Online book. Accessed from www.freebooks.co.za, 2007-11-01.

    Wilson, D. L. 1991. *A Biblical Theology of the Spirit.* Cape Town, South Africa: Acad Books.

    'The Word of God.' 1998. Retrieved 12 October 2007, www.tjl.co.za.

    Zoltan, E. Wilfred. 2007. *The Spirit in the Word.* Johannesburg: SATS Press.

Summary

Every piece of academic writing should end with a bibliography. In an author-date system of referencing, the preferred form of bibliography is a list of *works cited*; other kinds are works consulted, selective or annotated bibliographies.

Bibliography entries are organised alphabetically by the surnames of the authors or editors. Entries need to convey at least four essential pieces of information: Who wrote it? When was it published? What is it called? Where can it be accessed? The exact content and format of entries vary widely depending on the kind of resource it is (for example, book, thesis, journal article, interview, online resource) and the details available for it.

There are many different style and format guides for writing bibliography entries. Rules regarding what components to include, how to order them, how to punctuate and many other details vary. This chapter offered a set of such guidelines. Whether you follow these guidelines or another set of protocols is not terribly important. There is only one non-negotiable rule – be consistent!

6

Plagiarism

Technology – you can love it or hate it, but you cannot ignore it! Whatever your view, it is here to stay. A well-known futurist and theologian was confronting his child about the dangers of technology (computers, the Internet, chat rooms, computer games and the ever-growing popularity of SMS and photos so easily thrown about on cell phones). The child interrupted, saying, 'deal with it dad or go and see a doctor'. Whether we like it or not, we must face the challenges technology presents.

In the technocratic world, people no longer need to go into the office for meetings. Free online conferencing software can facilitate multi-user meetings. You can simply install any number of conference programs available with a camcorder on your computer to enjoy multiple visual interactions without leaving your office or home. Through ever-changing technology, people walk with their fingers, not their feet any more. There are vast amounts of information and modes of transporting this information available at one's fingertips. Anybody with a computer and an Internet connection can enter a cyber world that less than twenty-five years ago was inconceivable to the average person.

Ever-changing technology brings new challenges. The number one challenge academic institutions now face in academic writing is plagiarism. For scholars who worked in academic institutions before the onslaught of technology, the word plagiarism was known, but in a limited way. For example, before computers became part of people's household furniture, the only way they could plagiarise was to go to a library, photocopy a couple of pages from a book and copy the information verbatim. If the person marking the paper was not familiar with the information, the students could easily get away with plagiarising. However, for the budding student, or the experienced scholar in this new age of information, technology creates a great temptation to plagiarise.

Before exploring plagiarism and its dangers, we need to define it.

Defining Plagiarism

According to *The Penguin English Dictionary*, the act of plagiarism is a 'wrongful attempt to pass off another's literary or musical work as one's own; act of copying without permission or acknowledgement'.[1] Joseph Gibaldi addresses the two iniquities of plagiarism. 'Using another person's ideas, information, or expression without acknowledging that person's work constitutes intellectual theft,' Gibaldi said, 'and passing off another person's ideas, information or expression as your own, to get a better grade or gain some other advantage constitutes fraud.'[2]

Plagiarism is a serious offence. Using the work of an author without giving due credit to that author is stealing his or her information or ideas. Besides, it is deceitful because it passes that information on as if it were one's own.[3] In all fairness, though, there are times when a person copies someone else's work unintentionally or out of ignorance of the laws of plagiarism. Plagiarism without the intent to deceive may be a result of carelessness; deliberate plagiarism, however, is a flagrant offence of deception. It is a serious breach of trust.

Because a charge of plagiarism is considered a serious offence, students must avoid even the slightest temptation to use someone else's writings and then claim those writings as their own. This is even more the case if you are a theology student, since we ought to 'reject every kind of evil' (1 Thess 5:22).

Before getting into what constitutes plagiarism and how one can avoid it, it would be wise to discuss how plagiarism has crept into academic circles. Plagiarism has no boundaries. It can affect anyone who has to do research for a paper, whether a student is writing an essay for school or a scholar is researching a doctoral thesis. Technology can tempt anyone to take a shortcut at one time or another, especially as pressure mounts and deadlines loom. Unfortunately, to cut and paste someone else's work and pass it off as your own because of the pressure to succeed in a fast-paced society has been the downfall of many budding academics.

The reality of technology is that one does not need to go and sit in a library for hours poring over books and making copious notes any more. Due to technology, this is fast becoming a practice of the past. Thus, the unfortunate reality is that plagiarism is most prevalent among students who have access to the Internet. The temptation to cut down on one's workload and to free up time for other activities makes plagiarism attractive.

Consider this when it comes to information on the Internet. One of the biggest search engines, Google, has even had its name turned into a verb by its users. We do not say, 'Go to Google if you need information', but, 'Why don't you just Google it?' Google even has plans to make millions of books available online, if it can find a solution to the copyright challenges. The leading universities in the world have begun to offer course content free (for example, MIT and Harvard). They offer MOOCs, sharing lectures and notes. Ready access to such high-quality material makes plagiarism attractive.

---

1. George N. Garmonsway et al., eds., *The Penguin English Dictionary* (Harmondsworth: Penguin Books, 1972), 535.

2. Joseph Gibaldi, ed., *MLA Handbook for Writers of Research Papers* (7th ed.; New York: Modern Language Association, 2009), 52.

3. Ibid.

Research conducted in 2007 by Prega Govender of the *Sunday Times* newspaper revealed that almost every institution of higher learning is being affected by students plagiarising work. We read in the news of high-ranking officials being exposed for plagiarising doctoral degrees, and of professors who have resigned in the face of plagiarism allegations. However, the integrity of institutions remains intact, provided that they take measures to stamp out plagiarism and to deal with offenders.

In a personal communication with Mark Pretorius, Professor Isobel Konyn of the University of KwaZulu-Natal said:

> The impact of the technological highway continues to be felt throughout society. In the sphere of higher education, it has posed new challenges that universities globally are battling to regulate efficiently. Prior to the emergence of the Internet, an academic could know what was available to students in terms of library resources and scholarly writings. Today, the challenge is far greater, and this makes the detection and eradication of plagiarism more difficult.[4]

Many institutions are setting up software packages to reduce this shameful practice. Organisations like Turnitin.com have been created specifically to deal with plagiarism. They enable students and institutions to submit academic papers. The programme checks the submitted documents for plagiarism against its database of sources.

How should we deal with this scourge that is affecting not only the integrity of students but also the integrity of the institutions where they study?

Dealing with Plagiarism

The first step in dealing with plagiarism is to educate students. This should be done the moment they enter an institution of higher learning.

One way is to create a website with questions and answers about plagiarism and require every student to study it before attempting to write an assignment. One could even compel students to sign a declaration that they understand what plagiarism is, and the consequences they face if caught plagiarising. Since many students plagiarise out of ignorance, the quicker we can educate them, the less plagiarism we should find in their assignments. Obviously there will still be students who plagiarise, but at least they will do it knowingly and will have no legal recourse to challenge whatever steps the institution takes against them. Academic institutions must make it clear that they will not tolerate plagiarism and that they are willing to take stern action against students who plagiarise.

The second step is to take disciplinary action against students who plagiarise. Each institution should have its own process in this respect. Depending on the nature and

---

4. Quoted by permission of Professor Konyn of the University of KwaZulul-Natal.

seriousness of the offence, this might involve warning, failure, suspension or expulsion. In most cases, it would involve each of these steps in a progressive procedure.

Avoiding Plagiarism

You avoid plagiarism by properly acknowledging, that is, referencing, all sources. Referencing usually has two elements, attribution and documentation. Attribution is the practice of marking off any ideas and phrases that are not your own, which you do with quotation marks and in-text citations. Documentation refers to providing information about the sources of ideas and phrases that are not your own, and this is done through in-text citations and the bibliography. The case studies below demonstrate why it is important to bear both elements in mind.

Recognising Plagiarism

Students often plagiarise out of ignorance – they think they only need to cite when they use exact quotations, failing to realise that there are many other situations which require giving credit to sources. In this section, we shall answer some questions to help you recognise situations in which you must cite.

Am I plagiarising when I use the author's exact words without quotation marks, but I cite the original source in an in-text citation? Yes, you plagiarise any time you use the author's exact words without using quotation marks, because you are communicating to your assessor that these words are an expression of your personal understanding and thought process resulting from your study.

Am I plagiarising when I merely exchange the author's words with synonyms, as long as I cite a source at the end of the sentence? Yes, you are plagiarising when you use the same sentence structure as the original source because once again the thought and expression of the thought is not original with you. You have not paraphrased the original thought and therefore cannot treat it as though you had done so. You are committing deception, for your marker assumes that all content in your paper without quotation marks is your mental digestion of the facts.

Am I plagiarising when I take the content of the original source and then I put it in my own words, but do not cite the original source? Yes, you have plagiarised, because the content of what you have written did not originate with you. You merely put it into your own words. You must cite the original source after the sentence or paragraph of information that you have paraphrased.

What about using Internet sources that are not copyrighted? Is it plagiarism to use them without citing the source? Yes it is, because, once again, it consists of passing on someone else's research as though it were your own.

What information in my research paper does not need to be cited? You need not cite personal thoughts, opinions, or your evaluation of the thoughts of others. You also do not need to cite a source for information that is considered common knowledge, such as, Table Mountain is in Cape Town or Harare is the capital of Zimbabwe. If you discover that virtually all your sources assume certain information as common knowledge, it is not essential to cite a source for that information. For instance, if you are doing a paper on the Dead Sea Scrolls, you do not need to cite a source to support the fact that they were found in 1947 near the Dead Sea.

Undermining Research

Doing research for written assignments serves a variety of functions in your personal and academic development. For one thing, thinking deeply about the topic as you wrestle with a variety of sources not only enhances your understanding of the subject, it also makes the learning permanent – you will not easily forget what you have personally struggled to grasp. Furthermore, it develops one of the most important life skills you can ever acquire – the ability to think for yourself! You gain the ability to think through diverse opinions on difficult questions, processing and presenting personal convictions. Third, it teaches problem-solving skills. Discovery-based learning empowers you to solve real-life problems. You learn to find the best sources and use them critically. You learn to analyse, compare, summarise and so forth.

When you swap 'cutting-and-pasting' someone else's thoughts for forming your own convictions through personal discovery (research), you cheat yourself of higher education's most valuable lessons. You should be able to say honestly that you have gained understanding and formed convictions through the research you have conducted. When you plagiarise, you violate all the objectives of research and you lose the value of higher education. You are, in fact, wasting time – yours and your teacher's.

Challenging Plagiarisers

If you are prone to taking shortcuts, passing off others' work as your own instead of putting in the work required to think through your sources, we have some questions for you.

1) What learning can take place when you merely 'cut and paste'? There is no evidence that you understand the material until you explain the information you are presenting in your own words.

2) How do you prepare yourself for ministry when you focus on cutting and pasting pieces of information with the intent of deceiving your assessors? Even if you succeed in misleading your assessors, are you not cheating yourself, sacrificing your integrity and betraying your Saviour?

3) What thinking and writing skills do you develop when you substitute someone else's words for your own? Do you not think you are robbing yourself of opportunities to learn critical thinking and communication skills that you will one day need in your ministry?

We understand why students would cheat in a commerce or a law degree, but cheating in a theology degree is like stealing a Bible – how can God possibly bless you for it? What good will a degree in theology do a man without integrity?

Plagiarism is a serious offence. Avoiding it is *your* responsibility. Ignorance is no excuse. You must know what it is and ensure you don't do it. To safeguard yourself remember these words: **you quote it, you note it!**

7

Formatting an Academic Paper

The purpose of this chapter is to offer tips for formatting an academic paper. After describing some principles, we present sample pages to illustrate key aspects of good formatting. We suggest you study them closely and use them as models for formatting your papers.

The Cover Page

The cover page of a thesis or an assignment should contain the following elements:
- The title of the paper
- The name of the author
- The nature of the paper
- The qualification
- The institution
- The date of submission
- The professor or assessor

Figure 1 on page 67 shows the title page of a thesis or dissertation. All the items are centred on the page. The title appears first, followed the author's name. Next comes a description of the nature of the submission; in this example, a dissertation submitted for a degree. If the submission only constituted part of the requirements, the wording would change to 'submitted in partial fulfilment of the requirements for . . .', such as, 'A mini-thesis submitted in partial fulfilment of the requirements for the degree of Master of Theology'. The last three items are the name of the institution, the date of submission, and the names of the supervisors.

Figure 2 on page 68 shows the title page of an assignment for a course. The name of the assignment appears at the top. After the student's name, it states the assignment number, course, programme, and institution. The cover ends with the date of submission and the name of the teacher who will assess it. If the paper were not an assignment, you could substitute labels such as report, portfolio, term paper or book review for 'Assignment 1'. Once again, note that all the items on the title page are centred. Some institutions ask you to write the title of the paper in capitals or in bold or italicised script.

The Declaration and Dedication (only for theses)

Theses and dissertations must include a signed declaration stating that the work is the author's. The declaration appears on a separate page. The author must sign and date it. This is a typical wording:

> I, the undersigned, hereby declare that the work contained in this dissertation is my own original work and has not previously in its entirety or in part been submitted to any institution for a degree.
>
> Signed: _____ Date: _____

A thesis or dissertation may also include a dedication to family, friends or colleagues who have made the study possible. Such a dedication appears on its own page after the declaration.

Abstract

Dissertations, theses and research projects often require an *abstract*. An abstract is a brief summary of the research and its findings. The Princeton Writing Program explains the content and purpose of an abstract like this:

> An abstract is a paragraph, often between 100 and 350 words, that expresses the main claim and argument of a paper. An abstract says everything of central importance in a way that gives the reader a clear overview of what is contained in the essay. It should include the few things you would like your reader to remember long after the details of your paper may be forgotten. Science journals, for instance, usually publish abstracts at the beginning of articles so that readers can make quick decisions about whether the article is relevant or interesting. If the reader decides to read the entire article, the abstract functions as a map of the writer's argument or discussion.[1]

Write the abstract on a separate page before the table of contents. The heading should be 'abstract' or 'summary', written as a main heading. The body of the abstract is written in the same style as the rest of the paper, usually 1.5-line spacing (double spacing in some institutions) and either left aligned or justified. Figure 3 on page 69 contains a typical example of what an abstract should look like. Depending on the requirements of the institution, the page may or may not be numbered (see guidelines below for page numbering).

---

1. 'Abstracts.' *Princeton Writing Program* (1999, retrieved 10 May 2008, http://web.princeton.edu/sites/writing/Writing_Center).

Table of Contents

The table of contents begins on a new page. As a guideline, it should contain main headings and one or two levels of subheadings. In an assignment, the main headings will be the first level of headings in the text. In a thesis, the main headings in the table of contents are usually chapter titles; the first one or two levels of headings within the chapter are also listed in the contents. Each entry in the table of contents contains a page number on the right hand side. If your headings are numbered in your paper, include the numbering in the table of contents.

The diagram (Figure 4 on page 70) shows a fairly typical table of contents for a thesis. Word processors have functions that enable you to automatically generate and update a table of contents. To do this, you need to use the built-in style settings for headings (usually called Heading 1, Heading 2, and so on). The great value of using the built-in function to generate the contents page is that it will always get the page numbers correct and, if you edit the document, it can quickly correct the contents page to match the changed pages.

Normal Pages

Academic institutions set standard guidelines with respect to how the main body of a paper should be formatted. These would be common settings:

Font name: Arial, Times New Roman, or Calibri

Font size: 12 point

Line spacing: 1.5 *or* double

Justification: justified *or* left aligned

Paper size: A4 *or* Letter

Margins: 2.5 to 3.0 cm on all sides (1 to 1.25 inches)

Block quotations: indent ± 1 cm from left and right margins

Headings: legal numbering; stylised

Spelling: English UK *or* US

Page numbers: bottom centre *or* top right

Referencing: author-date system *or* footnote system

These guidelines tell you how to format your submissions. As a student, you should programme your word processor with the default settings (called creating a template). For example, you can set up your processor so that the paper size is A4, the default font is Arial 12, the line spacing 1.5, the spelling English UK, and so on. In particular, you should learn to use *style sheets* in your word processor. Styles typically include defined heading styles; using them properly makes editing your work *much* easier.

A nicely formatted page in an academic paper should look a little like the example in Figure 6 on page 72. The text is typed in 1.5–line spacing with decent margins. There is a block quotation, indented from both margins. The page is clearly numbered and new paragraphs are signposted by leaving a *small* space. It contains a heading that is clearly marked (numbered and bolded). The page looks neat. It does not contain large white spaces between paragraphs.

Now, by way of contrast, look at the sample page in Figure 7 on page 73. The heading does not stand out because it is neither numbered nor styled. There is no header and no page number. The page also illustrates a common error students make – leaving large, ugly gaps between paragraphs. They do this by pressing the 'Enter' key twice each time they begin a new paragraph. *Do not hit 'Enter' twice to start a new paragraph!* There are two acceptable ways to mark a new paragraph. The first is by indenting the first line of each paragraph slightly. If you use this method, you will have *no* extra space between paragraphs. The other is by adjusting your paragraph settings to leave half a line before or after each paragraph. This leaves a *small* space between paragraphs, enough to signpost where a new paragraph begins, but not enough to leave ugly white gaps. You can set your word processor to do this under its 'paragraph' settings (Hint: in MS Word, holding down Ctrl + Shift + 0 will do it). All the examples at the end of the chapter use the second method.

Headers and Footers

The header is the segment of the page above the area where you type the main body of the document. The footer is the corresponding area at the bottom of the page. In the header, write the title of the paper or, for a thesis or dissertation, the chapter title. Insert page numbers in the footer. The first page of a chapter and the title page of an assignment have no header because the title is written at the top of the page. Number the first content page of your thesis or assignment as page 1. You may either leave the front matter (for example, title page, table of contents, and so on) unnumbered or you may number it in a different format (for example, i, ii, iii . . . or a, b, c . . .). You should position your header/footer approximately midway between the text and the margin. Word processors have built-in functions for setting headers and footers. You will need to learn how your processor facilitates a different heading on the first page of a section and how it allows you to use different styles of page numbering for different sections, that is, one style for the front matter and another for the rest of the document.

The First Page

Leave an extra space at the top of the first page of a chapter, article or assignment, as well as at the top of pages such as an abstract, table of contents or bibliography. We suggest you leave approximately five centimetres (2 inches) between the top margin and the title.

Write the title in large, bold, centred text. The first page of the entire document should be numbered page 1. The example in Figure 5 on page 71 shows what the first page of a thesis chapter looks like. There is a gap from the top margin, then the chapter number, followed by the chapter name. Finally, note the gap between the chapter name and the text.

Numbered and Bulleted Lists

If you need to number items in a paragraph, you may do so by placing consecutive numbers or letters in parentheses, such as (1) . . . (2) . . . (3) . . ., or (a) . . . (b) . . . (c) . . . Do not alternate between these two styles; select one and use it consistently. Punctuate these items naturally. If each item is a complete sentence, capitalise the first letter and end the sentence with a period. If the items are parts of a sentence, separate them either with commas or with semicolons. Here is a simple example:

> The Reformers' interpretation of the psalms emphasised (a) the value of the headings, (b) the need to understand the psalms in their historical setting and (c) the prophetic-messianic nature of the psalms, regarding David as a type of the Messiah.

Numbered or bulleted lists should be indented slightly to the right of the left margin and set to use a hanging indent. If each list item is a complete sentence, end it with a period. If all the items form a single sentence, separate them with commas or semicolons and place a period after the last one. If they are just listed fragments, do not use any punctuation marks at the end. A bulleted list containing full sentences looks like this:

- It originated within an eschatological milieu.
- The figures to whom the psalms are attributed were regarded as future-predicative prophets.
- Certain psalms describe a person or event in such glowing terms that the language far exceeds the reality of any historical king or battle.
- The very inclusion of royal psalms in the Psalter suggests that the redactor understood them to refer to a future *mashiah*-king.

Tables and Figures

Tables (see Figure 8 on page 74). Tables are powerful tools for presenting a large amount of data in a compact, visual format that helps readers see it as a whole at a glance. Major style guides (e.g. APA, MLA, SBL, Turabian, Chicago) offer extensive guidelines concerning how to present various data types in tables. If you need to use complex, technical tables to present your data, you need to consult one of them. Each time you use a table, you must label it with three parts: (a) table, (b) number, and (c) descriptive caption, like this: *Table 7: Similarities in the Headings of Psalms 3 and 7*. The label may be positioned either above or below the table (be consistent with your placement). Whenever you allude to such a table in the text of your paper, refer to it by its number (e.g. 'In Table 7, . . .').

Figures (see Figure 10 on page 78). Graphs, charts, maps, diagrams, drawings, and pictures are all classed as 'figures'. Each time you insert one of these in your paper, you must label it for precise identification. The label has three parts: (a) figure, (b) number, and (c) descriptive caption. This is an example: *Figure 6.4: Chart Summarising the Exegetical Process*. All graphs, charts, diagrams, and so forth are labelled 'figure'. The number ensures the figure has a unique identification. The name summarises the content of the diagram. The label may appear either above or below the figure. Be consistent with its placement. Either label them all above or all below; do not chop and change. Having labelled a figure, all references in the text should refer to it by number. If the author wished to refer readers to the example figure above, he would called it 'Figure 6.4'.

Bibliography

The bibliography (see Figure 9 on page 75) might be labelled 'works cited' or 'reference list'. It begins on a new page. Format the title 'works cited' as a level 1 heading. In the case of a paper with chapters, format it as a chapter title, leaving a gap between the top margin and the label. For smaller papers, simply style it like heading level 1. Thereafter, list entries in alphabetical order by the last name of the author(s). The paragraph style for bibliographic entries includes *hanging indent*. Position the first line of the entry against the left margin; indent subsequent lines approximately 1.25 centimetres (½ inch). To create a hanging indent, use the paragraph settings in your word processor. Do not leave a line between entries. Lastly, when there are multiple entries by the same author, do not repeat the name each time. Instead, use a short line for each subsequent entry.

Religious Tolerance and the Exclusive Claims
of the Gospel of Jesus Christ

Roger E. Brown

A Dissertation Submitted for the Degree of
Doctor of Philosophy
at the University of Johannesburg

2015

Supervisor: Prof. J. S. Dlamini

Figure 1: Cover Page of a Thesis

A Critical Evaluation of the Jehovah Witness
View of the Deity of Jesus Christ

Linda W. Steyn

Assignment 1
THE2123 The Doctrine of Salvation
Bachelor of Theology
Baptist Theological Seminary

November 2015

Lecturer: Dr. William R. Domeris

Figure 2: Cover Page of an Assignment

Abstract

At present, research into the editorial shaping of the canonical Psalter holds a central role in psalms studies. In keeping with this trend, this dissertation examines links between Psalms 3-8 in an attempt to discern the critera and objectives the editors used when arranging them.

The study begins with a detailed exegetical synopsis of each of the six psalms in the chosen corpus. This lays a foundation for examining links between the psalms that might have influenced the editors to arrange them in the canonical order. An exhaustive analysis of links first between adjacent psalms and then across the entire corpus follows; the goal is to identify the rationale for the ordering of the psalms.

The analysis suggests that verbal and thematic links provided the main basis of arrangement. The editors' primary objective was to ensure a natural verbal and thematic connection between each pair of adjacent psalms. Although editorial linking is most evident on the level of adjacent psalms, beyond this level the editors do seem to have considered shared terms and similarities in the headings; these considerations were subordinate to shared terms and themes amongst neighbouring psalms.

Figure 3: Abstract

Table of Contents

1. Introduction   **1**
    1.1. Background   1
    1.2. Problem   3
    1.3. Objectives   4
    1.4. Delimitations   5
    1.5. Design   6
    1.6. Definitions   7
    1.7. Hypothesis   8
    1.8. Overview   10

2. History of Psalms Studies   **11**
    2.1. Introduction   11
    2.2. Ancient Approaches   12
    2.3. Historical Criticism   14
    2.4. Form Criticism   17
    2.5. Redaction Criticism   20
    2.6. Recent Literary Studies   26
        2.6.1. Studies on the Entire Psalter   27
        2.6.2. Studies on Collections of Psalms   40

Figure 4: Table of Contents

Chapter 1
Introduction

1.1. Background

Throughout most of the twentieth century, psalms research was dominated by the form-critical approaches of Hermann Gunkel (Gunkel 1926; Gunkel and Begrich 1998) and his student and successor Sigmund Mowinckel. Gundel's method was to "define psalms according to categories of literary genres (*Gattungen*) and to discover the original life-setting (*Sitz im Leben*)" (Mitchell 1997, 50). Mowinckel laid great stress on the importance of the cult as the setting for which the psalms were written and in which they were used. He attempted to reconstruct Jewish festivals and position specific psalms within certain festivals. Common to both form-critical schools was a tendency to view psalms individually, to see little or not literary relationship between adjacent psalms or collections of psalms.

Gerald Wilson's (1985) dissertation, *The Editing of the Hebrew Psalter*, was a landmark event in psalms research. Unlike the form criticals, Wilson argued that the psalms were carefully org-

1

Figure 5: First Page

Figure 6: Properly Formatted Page

Chapter 2: Literature Review

The leading conservative voice of the middle nineteenth century was Hengstenberg (1845-1848), who defended the ascriptions of authorship in the headings, the purposeful arrangement of the Psalter and the presence of messianic prophecy in the psalms. He heavily influenced Delitzsch (1887), whose work on the Psalms represents the high-water mark of nineteenth century studies. Mitchell (1997:46) summarises Delitzsch's contributions perfectly.

> Delitzsch ... achieves the best balance between criticism and tradition of all nineteenth century commentators. He generally supports the validity of the headings....

> He notes that the order of the lyrics cannot be explained purely on the basis of chronological evolution, and indicates evidence of editorial activity in the Psalter, noting concatenation in particular. In the light of this, he detects 'the impress of one ordering spirit'.... Delitzsch also maintains that a central theme is discernable in the collection, that is, concern with the Davidic covenant and its ultimate fulfilment in a future Messiah. He perceives the eschatological hope not only in the redactor's mind, but also in the mind of the individual psalmists.

In spite of the influence of Hengstenberg and Delitzsch, by the end of the nineteenth century the current of psalms studies was flowing away from the traditional view of the Psalter as a largely Davidic collection that was purposefully arranged to a critical view that it was a piecemeal collection of anonymous, post-exilic lyrics compiled for use as the hymnbook of the second temple. The great commentaries of the early twentieth century (e.g., Cheyne 1904; Briggs & Briggs 1906 & 1907; Kirkpatrick 1906) reflect the scepticism of the period.

16

Figure 7: Poorly Formatted Page

Chapter 6: Composition of Psalms 3-8

	Psalm 3	Psalm 7
genre	מִזְמוֹר	שִׁגָּיוֹן
author	לְדָוִד	לְדָוִד
occasion	בְּבָרְחוֹ מִפְּנֵי אַבְשָׁלוֹם בְּנוֹ	אֲשֶׁר־שָׁר לַיהוָה עַל־דִּבְרֵי־כוּשׁ בֶּן־יְמִינִי

Table 6.3: Similarities between the Headings of Psalms 3 and 7 (Hebrew)

	Psalm 3	Psalm 7
genre	a psalm	a shiggaion
author	of David	of David
occasion	when he fled from the presence of Absalom, his son	which he sang to the Lord concerning the words of Cush, a Benjamite

Table 6.4: Similarities between the Headings of Psalms 3 and 7 (English)

Might the compilers have used Psalms 3 and 7 as some sort of literary frame around the previously existing group of Psalms 4-6? Tate (2001, 347) has suggested that the presence of historical notes in the headings of Psalms 3 and 7 identifies them as "the framing ...

Figure 8: Page with Tables

Works Cited

Alden, Robert L. 1974. 'Chiastic Psalms: A Study in the Mechanics of Semitic Poetry in Psalms 1–50.' *Journal of the Evangelical Theological Society* 17: 11–28.

Allen, Leslie C. 1996. '§2376. זמר.' Pages 1116–1117 in the *New International Dictionary of Old Testament Theology and Exegesis*. Edited by Willem A. VanGemeren. Volume 2. Carlisle, UK: Paternoster.

_____. 1998. *Psalms 101–150*. Word Biblical Commentary 21. Dallas, TX: Word Books. Logos Edition. Oak Harbour, WA: Logos Research Systems.

Althan, Robert. 1999. 'Atonement and Reconciliation in Psalms 3, 6 and 83.' *Journal of Northwest Semitic Languages* 25: 75–82.

Anderson, A. A. 1972. *Psalms*. 4 vols. The New Century Bible. London: Oliphants.

Andersen, Francis I., and Dean A. Forbes. 2005. *The Hebrew Bible: Andersen-Forbes Phrase Marker Analysis*. Oak Harbour, WA: Logos Research Systems.

Anderson, George W. 1965. 'Enemies and Evildoers in the Book of Psalms.' *Bulletin of John Rylands Library* 48, no. 1: 18–29.

Anderson, R. D., Jr. 1994. 'The Division and Order of the Psalms.' *Westminster Theological Journal* 56: 219–241.

248

Figure 9: Bibliography

8

Software for Bible Study

The advances in software for Bible study have changed the landscape of biblical and theological research. Where biblical scholars used to spend hours meticulously combing over the text in search of parallels, sifting through a Strong's concordance trying in vain to locate all the occurrences of a particular Greek word, paging through an analytical lexicon to double check their parsing of a rare verb, all the while being surrounded by piles of reference works, they can now generate a report that gives them all the same information in less than a minute. Such is the power of Bible study software.

In this chapter, we aim to summarise the benefits and limitations of software packages, and then illustrate some of the features of existing software. We realise that this is a continually changing landscape, so what is groundbreaking technology today might be commonplace tomorrow. If you are an experienced user of Bible software, you may pick up a tip or two here, but our primary objective is to whet the appetite of those who have not yet ventured into this world.

The Benefits of Software

Electronic resources offer many benefits compared to their print-based companions. The benefits can be summed up in terms of saving time and improving accuracy. For instance, if you wanted to find all the occurrences of the word *agapaō* in the New Testament, it would have taken hours of searching using the old print-based tools, and then you might well have missed a few. Using software, you can find all the occurrences in a few seconds and be confident that you have them all. If you have the right resources in your collection, you can also extend your search to include the Septuagint and the Greek Fathers; admittedly this may increase the search time to as much as a minute!

The ease of access is wonderful. Instead of piles of books open on your desk, you have a carefully ordered electronic interface with the resources you need neatly stacked. You can open the exact book you need to exactly the right place with one or two clicks of your mouse. If you reduce the clutter around you, you reduce the clutter within you too. When you use printed reference books, you have to page through them to find the relevant information. Electronic editions can be searched and they are tagged, so that you open directly to the right place.

If you have some knowledge of Greek (or Hebrew), but not enough to read the original languages fluently – not too many can, even among those who teach them – morphologically coded electronic editions can break the text and the language open. For instance, when you point at a Greek verb, its parsing information is displayed. If you are not sure what a Hebrew word means, you can click on it and open five lexicons directly to entry for that word. If you want to know how the word *pisteuō* is used in the New Testament, you can search for all occurrences; the report will indicate how many times it is used in each book of the Bible (Figure 10).

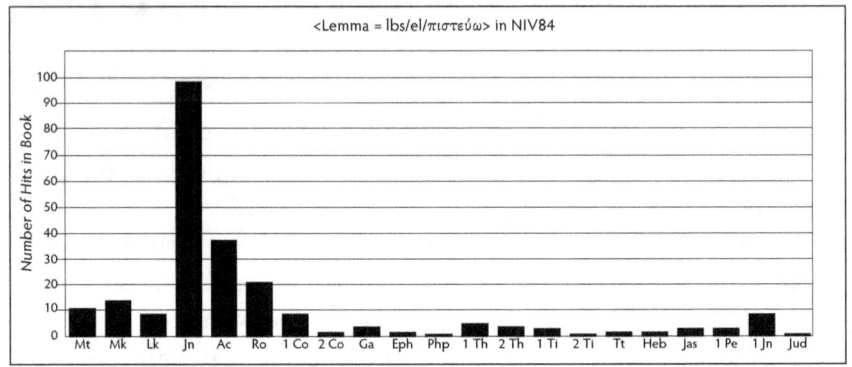

Figure 10: Pisteuō in the New Testament by Hits per Book

If you have no knowledge of Greek or Hebrew, the tools can still open up a measure of access to the original language texts. You can easily identify the underlying Greek or Hebrew words and search for other occurrences of the same words. You can open lexicons to the correct entries, which is difficult to do in a printed resource if you do not know the alphabet.

We love the portability that electronic resources provide. You cannot carry your Greek and Hebrew texts together with essential dictionaries and analytical lexicons to church, can you? Actually, you can – on your phone! You can take a whole library of resources everywhere you go, and consult them instantly.

The Limitations of Software

The value of software relates largely to its power to analyse and search Greek and Hebrew texts. This also gives rise to its greatest limitation. To give a man a search engine and a few dictionaries and lead him to believe that he is now ready to study 'the Greek' courts disaster, much like arming a soldier with a cap gun and sending him into battle in the sincere but misguided belief that it is a bazooka. Nothing compensates for real proficiency with the language, and a little learning can be dangerous. How irksome to hear a pastor who has a morphologically coded Hebrew text and a Strong's dictionary wax lyrical about why the NIV translation of his preaching portion is flawed. The ease of access to parsing information can contribute to lazy study of the languages; students never learn to parse correctly because the software does it for them.

Software packages are at the most powerful when managing reference works, the kind that you consult for particular information. We prefer our lexicons and commentaries as e-books. After all, who reads a lexicon cover to cover? But ordinary books are not as useful as e-books. If you intend to read a book from start to finish, you would probably prefer not to do it on your computer screen. Admittedly, the growing number of e-readers, tablet computers, and large-screen smartphones does make e-books more reader friendly, so this limitation might become obsolete in time.

The Categories of Software

The software programmes fall into three main categories (Figure 11), although we suspect the second group is gradually being replaced by the third.

Commercial Products	Free Downloads	Online Applications
Logos Bible Software	e-Sword	lumina.bible.org
Bible Works	The Word	biblearc.com
	The Sword Project	biblewebapp.com
		scholarsgateway.com

Figure 11: Three Categories of Software

The commercial products are the gold standard. Programmes like Logos Bible Software and Bible Works make large collections of premium publications available, with powerful search engines and reporting tools. Their power amazes, but their price alarms. The second group are free programmes that you can download and install on your computer. These normally contain a number of free Bibles and books, with the option to purchase additional works that are not available for free. They are powerful study tools, though not in the same league as the commercial trendsetters because they are mostly limited to works in the public domain. They cannot, therefore, incorporate the best lexicons, commentaries, and morphological tools. The third category consists of online applications. These resemble the free downloads, but operate online. Instead of downloading them onto your computer, you use them over the Internet. They have similar powers and limitations as the free downloads.

Free Online Applications

The number of promising free online Bible study applications is growing. The better ones all offer similar features, and share most of their strengths and weaknesses. Each typically has one or two features that you wish could be combined in one application.

For illustrative purposes, we are going to demonstrate two of them. We shall use Lumina. Bible.org (Lumina) to illustrate some tools for New Testament studies and BibleWebApp (WBA) to do likewise for the Old Testament. Our purpose is not to endorse these two in particular; it is merely to illustrate the kinds of features these applications offer.

New Testament and Greek

The most likely way to use Lumina for Bible study is to have an English text open on the left and a Greek text on the right.

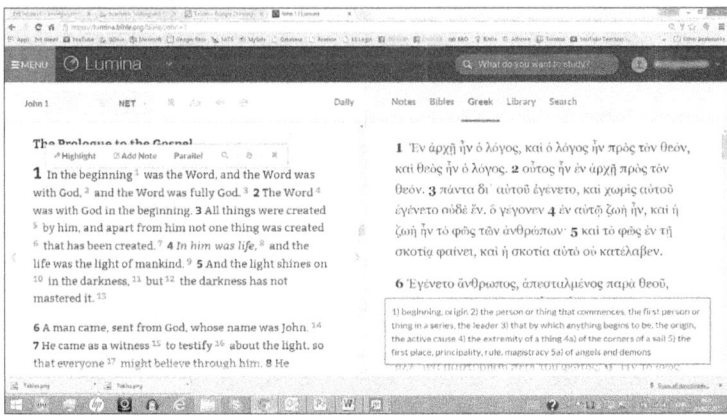

Figure 12: Parallel English-Greek Bibles in Lumina

Figure 12 shows English and Greek texts open in parallel windows. The Greek and English texts are linked, such that when you click on a word in either text, it highlights the corresponding word in the other. When the word 'beginning' is chosen on the left, the corresponding Greek word ἀρχῇ is highlighted on the right.

When you click on the word 'beginning', a pop-up opens above the word with options to highlight, add a note, view the verse in parallel translations, search, share, or bookmark. If you click on the *search* icon, these options appear:

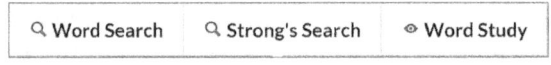

Figure 13: Search Options in Bible.org

The 'Word Search' lists all occurrences of the word 'beginning' (with the option to include other forms like 'begins', 'began', and 'begun') in the English Bible. You can filter the results to show the whole Bible, OT, NT, or any single book of the Bible. Figure 14 shows results for *beginning* in the gospel of John. You can get different results by changing the English translation you are searching. This is a powerful tool for Bible study.

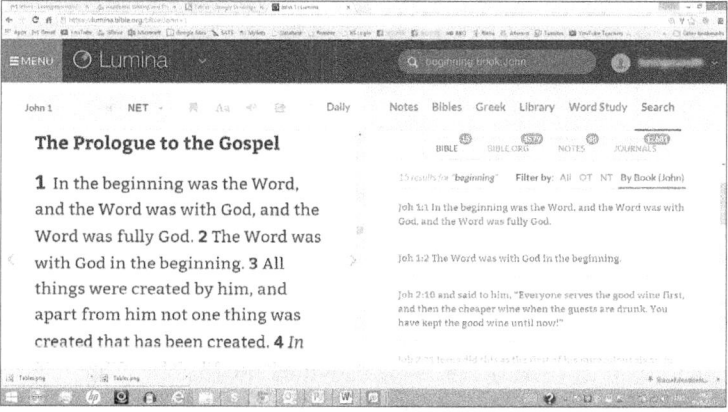

Figure 14: Word Search in Bible.org

The 'Strong's Search' (Figure 13) works similarly to the 'Word Search', except that it searches for the underlying Greek word. Each Greek word in the NT text is assigned a number. The word *archē* ('begin') is number 746. When you search by Strong's number, the search returns all occurrences of the Greek word *archē* (#746) in the NT. The results will be different to searching for the English word 'begin', because in some contexts *archē* does not mean 'begin', so the English search will not include those verses. Figure 15 shows part of the search result for Strong's #746 in the NT.

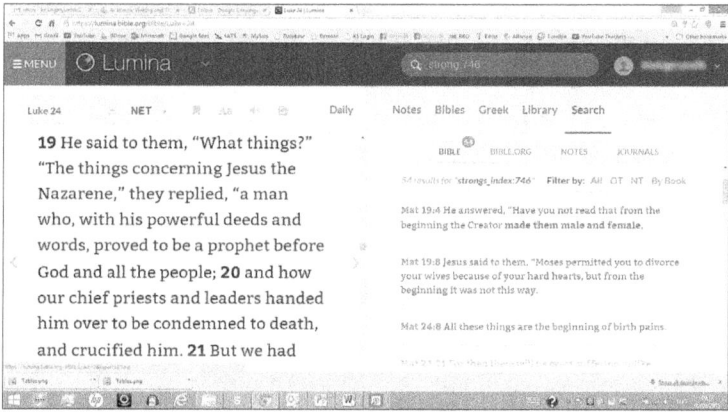

Figure 15: Strong's Search in Lumina

The 'Word Search' opens the entry for the underlying Greek word in the Strong's dictionary. Unfortunately, Strong's not a dictionary suitable for serious research, so this feature has limited value.

When you click on a word in a Bible window (see Figure 12), a pop-up window appears at the bottom of the Greek text with some information about the Greek word (Figure 16).

> **Morphology:** N-DF-S **Strong's:** 746 **Transliterated:** archē
> **Root:** ἀρχή
>
> 1) beginning, origin 2) the person or thing that commences, the first person or thing in a series, the leader 3) that by which anything begins to be, the origin, the active cause 4) the extremity of a thing 4a) of the corners of a sail 5) the first place, principality, rule, magistracy 5a) of angels and demons

Figure 16: Information about a Greek Word

The most helpful part of this is that it provides morphological information. In this instance, it tells you that *archē* in John 1:1 is a noun, dative feminine singular (N-DF-S). If the word in focus were a verb, the dialogue box would provide parsing information. The remaining information in the pop-up appears to come from Strong's dictionary.

Since it is not our purpose to promote Lumina (Bible.org), we shall revert to the BibleWebApp to illustrate similar functionality for the Old Testament and Hebrew. Before we do so, we should mention that the Lumina application also links to the large number of articles and resources on the Bible.org site, and allows you to incorporate them into your research.

Old Testament and Hebrew

In all of the free applications, the functionality for studying the Old Testament (that is, Hebrew texts) is less advanced than the corresponding functionality for the New Testament. Nevertheless, the free apps are improving all the time, and do offer some valuable and powerful Bible study tools. The examples below are all drawn from the BibleWebApp programme.

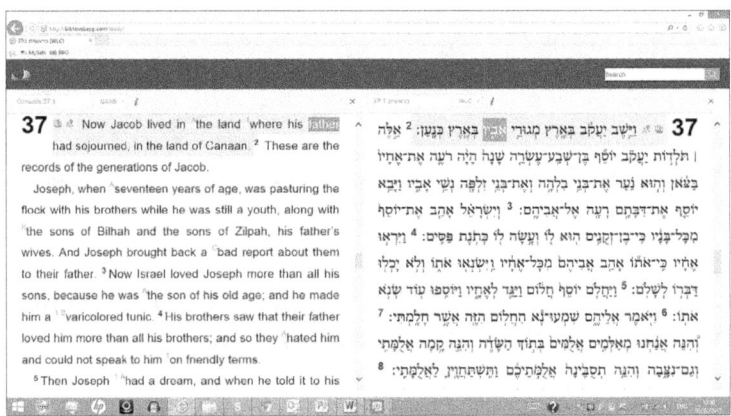

Figure 17: Parallel English-Hebrew in BWA

Figure 17 shows the screen with English and Hebrew texts open in parallel. If you point at a word in either text, the corresponding word is highlighted in the parallel text. The software provides similar functionality to what we observed earlier in the Greek examples. For example, if you click on a word, a little pop-up opens with the Hebrew word (Figure 18), the Strong's number, and a dictionary entry for the word.

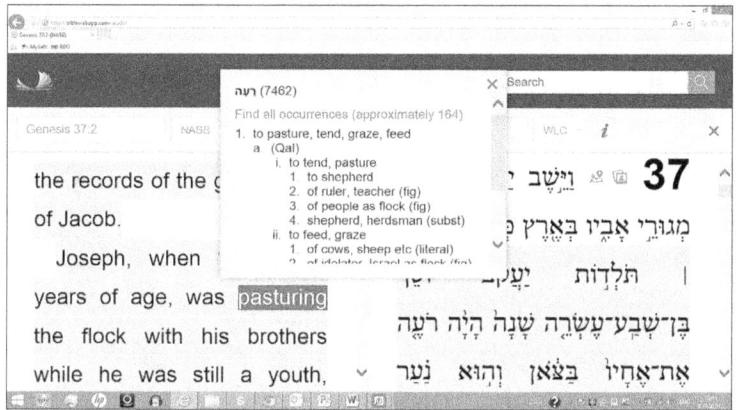

Figure 18: Information Pop-up in BWA

The pop-up in Figure 18 has a link to find all occurrences of the Hebrew word. If you click on it for the word 'pasturing' (Heb. רָעָה), the search returns all occurrences of Strong's number H7462. Figure 19 shows the result for a word search of 'generation' (H8435).

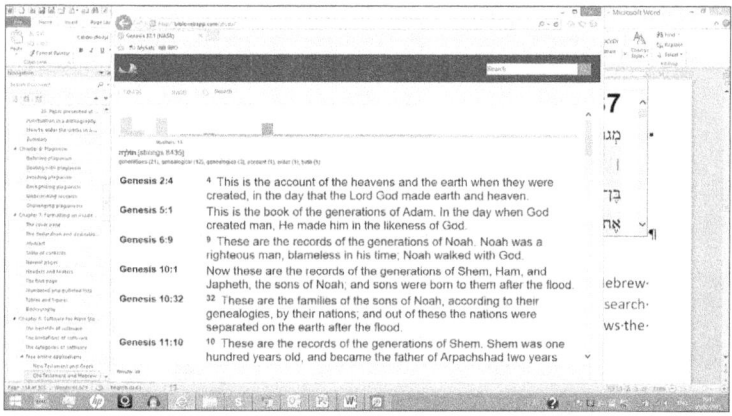

Figure 19: Strong's Word Search in BWA

This is an informative report. The bar chart at the top of Figure 19 indicates the frequency of the word by book of the Bible. If you point your mouse at one of the bars, the name of the OT book and the number of times the word occurs in that book is displayed. The graphic shows 'Numbers: 13', indicating that the word occurs thirteen times in

Numbers. You can see at a glance that Genesis, Numbers, and 1 Chronicles are the books where most of the occurrences appear.

If you point at a word in the Hebrew text, parsing information is displayed at the bottom of the screen. If you click on the word, a pop-up appears with parsing information and a dictionary entry (Figure 20). At present, not all Hebrew words have morphological data tagged, but the coding is improving all the time.

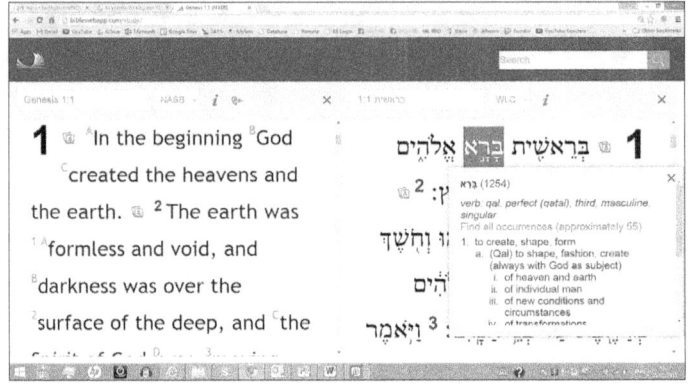

Figure 20: Information Pop-up for Hebrew Words in BWA

One final feature of BibleWebApp that is useful is the ability to create visual filters. For example, two visual filters have been added in the screenshot below (Figure 21). Qal perfect-tense verbs are marked in light blue, while feminine construct nouns are shown in yellow. This is useful for students learning the language, and wanting to highlight all words with particular grammatical qualities in the text.

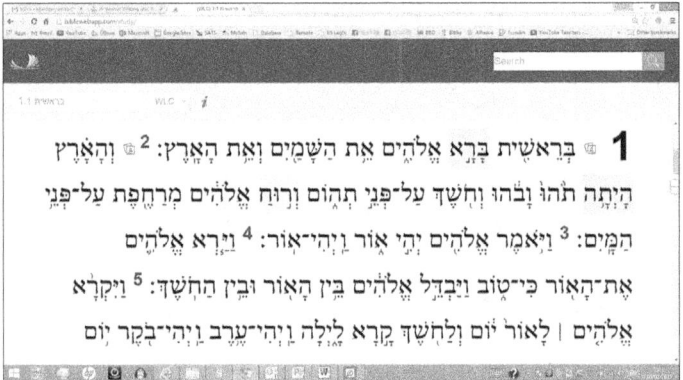

Figure 21: Visual Filters in BWA

This quick tour is sufficient to illustrate the potential in free Bible study applications. They place in your hands a convenient way to study the Greek and Hebrew texts without being an expert in the biblical languages. They furnish help parsing, reading parallel texts, finding occurrence of words in the Bible or its individual books, and much more. Their greatest limitation is that they cannot provide quick links to the best lexicons.

Commercial Software Programmes

The premier commercial programmes can do everything the free online applications do – and much, much more. You can purchase the best available lexicons, grammars, commentaries, dictionaries, and atlases, not to mention countless Greek and Hebrew editions, interlinears, reverse interlinears, and so on, as books in your collection.

Logos 5 comes with a number of pre-configured reports for studying biblical texts. The reports draw on the resources in your collection to provide data about the passage. For example, if you choose the 'Passage Guide' and type 'Rich Young Ruler', the search returns Matthew 19:16–22 with content organised under various headings. Under the heading cross-references, you can find verses directly or indirectly related to this text (Figure 22).

Ex 20:13 | "You shall not murder.	Dt 5:17 | " 'You shall not murder.	25:46; Mk 10:17, 18, 19, 20, 21, 22, 23, 24, 25, 26, 27, 28, 29, 30, 31, 12:31; Lk 10:25, 26, 27, 28, 12:33, 16:9, 18:18, 19, 20, 21, 22, 23, 24, 25, 26, 27, 28, 29, 30, 19:8; Jn 12:25; Ac 2:45, 4:34, 35, 13:48; Ro 2:4, 10:5, 13:9; Ga 3:10, 12, 5:14; Php 3:6,	7; 1 Ti 6:17, 18, 19; Jas 2:8, 11
Ex 20:14 | "You shall not commit adultery.	Ex 20:12, 13, 14, 15, 16; Le 18:5, 19:18; Dt 4:40, 5:16, 17, 18, 19, 20, 6:17, 7:11, 11:22, 28:9; Ne 9:29; Ps 25:8, 34:8; Eze 20:11, 13, 21, 33:31; Na 1:7; Mt 5:21, 27, 43, 48, 6:19, 20, 15:4, 18:8, 19:23, 24, 25, 26, 27, 28, 29, 30, 22:39,		
Ex 20:15 | "You shall not steal.			
Ex 20:16 | "You shall not bear false witness against your neighbor.			

Figure 22: Cross-References in Passage Guide

Next there is a category for *parallel passages*. This shows other passages of Scripture that record similar events or sayings.

Mark 10:17–31	Matthew 19:16–20:16	Luke 18:18–30
¹⁷And as he was setting out on his journey, a man ran up and knelt before him and asked him, "Good Teacher, what must I do to inherit eternal life?" ¹⁸And Jesus said to him, "Why do you call me good? No one is good except God alone. ¹⁹You know the commandments: 'Do not murder, Do not commit adultery, Do not steal, Do not bear false witness, Do not defraud, Honor your father and mother.' " ²⁰And	¹⁶And behold, a man came up to him, saying, "Teacher, what good deed must I do to have eternal life?" ¹⁷And he said to him, "Why do you ask me about what is good? There is only one who is good. If you would enter life, keep the commandments." ¹⁸He said to him, "Which ones?" And Jesus said, "You shall not murder, You shall not commit adultery, You shall not steal, You shall not bear false witness, ¹⁹Honor your	¹⁸And a ruler asked him, "Good Teacher, what must I do to inherit eternal life?" ¹⁹And Jesus said to him, "Why do you call me good? No one is good except God alone. ²⁰You know the commandments: 'Do not commit adultery, Do not murder, Do not steal, Do not bear false witness, Honor your father and mother.' " ²¹And he said, "All these I have kept from my youth." ²²When Jesus heard this, he said to

Figure 23: Parallel Passages in the Passage Guide

The 'Passage Guide' provides two graphic displays, one for *topics* related to the passage (Figure 24) and another for *words* in the text (Figure 25). In both reports, the size of the font is intended to represent the prominence of the topic or word in the passage. By clicking on any word, you can initiate a detailed study of that word or topic.

adultery beggars character Evidence Giving God Immortality indecision invitations luxury Mother murder Neighbor parents religion Riches stewardship storing Treasure youth...

Figure 24: Topics in the Passage Guide

Figure 25: Words in the Passage Guide

The 'Exegetical Guide' generates an analysis of a passage based on the Hebrew or Greek text. The report shows quick links to text-critical apparatuses, grammars, visualisations, and ends with a word-by-word presentation of the text. For the Matthew account of the story of the Rich Young Ruler, the text-critical apparatus for the SBL edition of the Greek New Testament looks like this (Figure 26).

16 αὐτῷ εἶπεν WH Treg NA28] εἶπεν αὐτῷ RP
- Διδάσκαλε WH Treg NA28] + ἀγαθέ RP
- σχῶ WH Treg NA28] ἔχω RP

Figure 26: Textual Variants in the SBL Apparatus in the Exegetical Guide

The word-by-word analysis shows the Greek and English texts in parallel at the top, then presents each Greek word on the left with a drop down-menu that links to any grammars or lexicons in your collection that have an applicable entry (Figure 27). You can control how many links you want to see, to increase or decrease the complexity of the report.

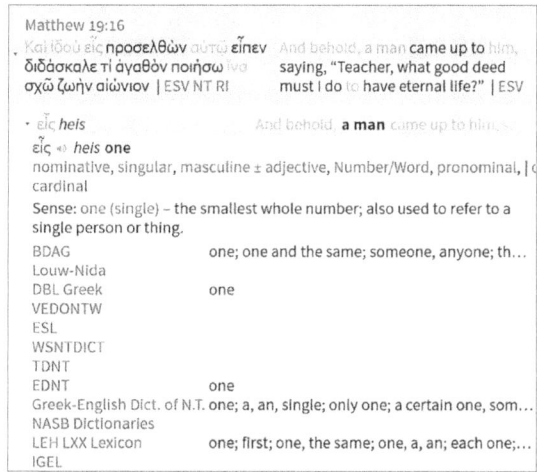

Figure 27: Word-by-Word Analysis in the Exegetical Guide

Logos 5 also offers a 'Sermon Starter Guide'. You can input a topic or a text, and hit 'go'. For instance, you can type 'give' or 'giving' to begin researching a message about giving. The report returns information under headings such as 'theme', 'passages', 'illustrations', and 'outlines'. Under 'theme', for instance, you will have links to related topics like almsgiving, generosity, and tithing. Under 'passages', you find a few important biblical texts highlighted, a list of pericopes that relate to giving, and an option to find more (Figure 28).

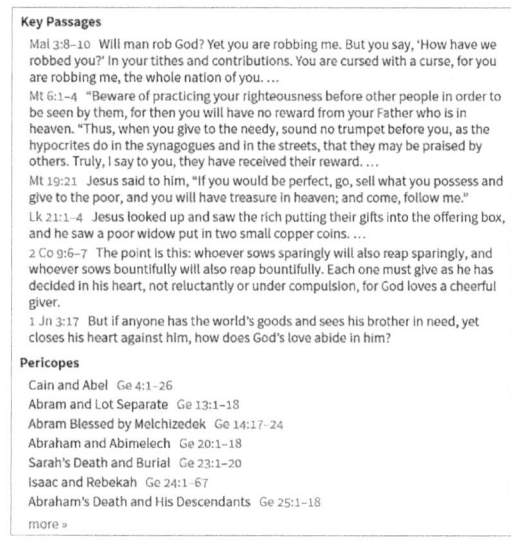

Figure 28: Passages in the Sermon Starter Guide

Logos offers a feature to compare Bible translations. You select whichever ones you want to compare. You specify your base translation (far left in Figure 29), and the display shows how much the other translations differ from it and where those differences lie.

NKJV	ESV	NET	LEB	NIV84
Mt 19:16 Now behold, one came and said to Him, "Good Teacher, what good thing shall I do that I may have eternal life?"	Mt 19:16 NowAnd behold, onea man came and saidup to Himhim, saying, "GoodTeacher, what good thing shalldeed must I do that I mayto have eternal life?"	Mt 19:16 behold, onesomeone came up to him and saidto Him, "GoodTeacher, what good thing shallmust I do that I mayto gain eternal life?"	Mt 19:16 NowAnd behold, onesomeone came up to him and saidto Him, "GoodTeacher, what good thing shallmust I do so that I maywill have eternal life?"	Mt 19:16 Now behold, onea man came up to Jesus and said to Himasked, "GoodTeacher, what good thing shallmust I do that I mayhaveto get eternal life?"

Figure 29: Comparison of Bible Translations

If you have difficulty placing events in their proper epochs and keeping track of where people and events fit in relation to one another, the 'Timeline' function is amazing. You choose a period of history, and the report gives you bird's-eye view of who, what, and when (Figure 30).

Figure 30: Timeline for the Inter-Testamental Period

We have not tried to spell out the values and applications of these functions. They should be fairly self-explanatory. How much you 'get out' of a product like Logos depends on how much you 'put in'. In other words, the more books you have in your collection, the more information the reports provide.

∙ ∙ ∙

Computer technologies have changed the whole world beyond recognition. This is equally true of the world of Bible study and biblical research. Free software places in the hands of every student of Scripture a set of tools that Paul the apostle and Calvin the reformer could only have dreamed about. The commercial products take the power of the tools to an altogether different dimension. Finding information has become the easy part. Dealing with the massive amount of information available and interpreting it sensibly is the challenge now.

Part B

Theological Research

We now turn our attention to more advanced topics related to theological research. The focus here is on postgraduate research, particularly on helping master's and doctoral candidates prepare for and write theses and dissertations. This does not mean these chapters are only for postgraduate students. The models and methods of research in chapters 11–16 should be valuable to all theology students.

After a brief orientation to thesis requirements in higher education (ch. 9), we devote three chapters to preparing research proposals. Chapter 10 speaks about the research proposal as a whole, while chapters 11 and 12 tackle the two main sections of the proposal – the problem and the plan respectively.

The last six chapters, 13–18, deal with models and methods for theological research. First, we present models for doing biblical exegesis (ch. 13), systematic theology (ch. 14), and practical theology (ch. 15). These can work as models for papers from large assignments to full theses. Lastly, we analyse specialised methods of research that typically make up a component of a theological study. Most theses contain literature reviews; chapter 16 offers pointers for doing a literature review. Practical theology often requires descriptive survey research. In chapter 17, we introduce this specialised kind of research. We close, in chapter 18, with an overview of how to do a few other kinds of research, such as book reviews, case studies, empirical studies, and more.

9

Thesis Requirements

Our focus throughout the second half of this book will be on [post]graduate[1] research, particularly on writing theses and dissertations. Since thesis requirements differ substantially from country to country, from institution to institution, and even from programme to programme, the norms and standards suggested here are only guidelines. In theology, theses are written at three levels: bachelor's, master's, and doctoral. Table 2 illustrates the expectations at each level.

Bachelor's Thesis	Master's Thesis	Doctoral Thesis
10,000–15,000 words	40,000–50,000 words	80,000–100,000 words
Students must systematically analyse the selected topic in the field of study.	Students must master the selected topic in the field study.	Students must add new knowledge to the field of study.

Table 2: Thesis Requirements at Each Level of Study

You can see from the table that the length and level of the thesis increases dramatically each time you move from the bachelor's towards the doctoral level. At the master's level, you must *master* the literature and issues pertaining to the topic of your thesis. At the doctoral level, you must do all that is required at master's level and more – you must advance the existing state of knowledge in the field of your study. At the bachelor's level, the requirements are more modest. You do not have to contribute new knowledge. You do not even have to master all the existing knowledge on your topic. You only have to demonstrate the ability to research a topic systematically and critically and present your conclusions in a well-organised, well-argued report. Let's briefly explore these requirements in a little more detail.

---

1. In some countries, studies at the level above a bachelor's degree are called *graduate studies*, while in others they are known as *postgraduate studies*. For the remainder of this book, we shall use the term *postgraduate*.

Bachelor's Level

Many bachelor's degrees do not require a thesis. Where a thesis is required at the bachelor's level, it typically functions as a moderate-sized capstone project in which students can show their ability to apply the research skills they have acquired throughout the degree programme. The bachelor's thesis would typically be between 10,000 and 15,000 words (30–50 typed pages). This *excludes* the preliminary pages (title page, table of contents, list of figures, and so on), bibliography, and appendices. Depending on the nature of the research, the bibliography should contain approximately 30–50 entries. These should be academic works, not popular literature.

All the bachelor's thesis must demonstrate is the ability to carry out a protracted research project in a chosen field of study. It does not need to present original research. It must demonstrate these skills:
- Identify a research problem.
- Select appropriate research methods.
- Gather and analyse data.
- Interact critically with existing literature.
- Present a sustained, logical argument in writing.
- Cite and reference sources correctly.
- State conclusions and recommendations.

A topic such as 'What Romans teaches about justification' would be permissible as a bachelor's thesis, since the student does not need to contribute new knowledge or master the entire, vast body of literature on the topic.

Master's Level

Thesis requirements at the master's level vary greatly. At one end of the spectrum, in some masters' programmes the thesis constitutes the entire degree. The thesis itself is expected to be about 50,000 words, and must embody a high level of independent research and writing. Although this model of master's degree is foreign to many, it is a demanding process since the research standards required are lofty. At the other end of the spectrum, in some masters' programmes the final thesis is essentially a capstone paper at the end of a large body of coursework. It functions much like a bachelor's thesis at the end of a bachelor's degree, and might be as short as 15,000 words. However, in most masters' degrees the thesis expectations are in-between these two extremes. The master's thesis is a sizeable research project, culminating in a document of approximately 20,000–25,000 words.

Major Thesis	Standard Thesis	Capstone Paper
50,000 words	25,000 words	15,000 words
150–200 works cited	75–100 works cited	50–75 works cited

Table 3: Thesis Requirements in MTh Degrees

In writing their theses, master's candidates must demonstrate the ability to design and conduct a research project. They must demonstrate mastery of their subject, including the research methods that relate to it and the existing literature on it. All the requirements for the bachelor's thesis apply to a master's thesis, but with the added expectation of *mastery*. A master's thesis need not contribute new knowledge, but it is desirable that it demonstrate a fresh approach to the topic; it should not be a dull rehash of familiar territory.

'What does Romans teach about justification?' would not be a suitable topic for a master's thesis. There are two reasons for this. First, it would be difficult to demonstrate mastery of the vast body of literature on this topic. Second, so much has already been written that this thesis would likely be a dull review of the familiar. 'How to communicate the doctrine of justification by faith to the Hottentot people in the Kalahari' would give a thesis a fresh perspective *if* the Hottentots, for cultural reasons, found the doctrine confusing or offensive.

Doctoral Level

The standards and expectations for a research doctorate are quite well established worldwide. A PhD dissertation should be recognisable regardless of where it is written. The same cannot be said for the thesis component of a professional doctorate, such as a Doctor of Ministry dissertation. The guidelines that follow relate primarily to the PhD dissertation.

The length of a doctoral dissertation is much less important than the quality of the research. A reasonable guideline in terms of length would be about 80,000–100,000 words, but in practice PhD dissertations can be as short as 50,000 words or as long as 150,000 words. They are judged on two main criteria:
- Does it make a substantial original contribution to existing knowledge?
- Is it publishable (either the entire dissertation or key parts of it)?

Ironically, therefore, 'What does Romans teach about justification?' might be perfectly feasible as a doctoral thesis. The onus would be on researchers to bring a fresh perspective to the current understanding of the topic. They would need to make a substantial addition to current theory. If their dissertation did not do this, being a dull rehash of current knowledge, they would fail at examination.

Summary

This, then, is a broad general framework for thesis writing. The thesis is a project at the bachelor's level. At master's level, it ranges from a moderate-sized capstone paper to a substantial research undertaking. Doctoral dissertations must contribute innovate, original research.

You are likely reading the chapters that follow in preparation for writing a thesis. As you work through them, you should keep this framework in mind. The chapters are general in nature. You will need to contextualise your planning to the appropriate level. In particular, you should find out what specific requirements your institution and programme lay down for the thesis component, and prioritise those specific guidelines over the general ones laid out in this primer.

Now, without further delay, let's move on to the most important part of writing any thesis – the research proposal.

10

The Research Proposal

Every theological research project should begin with a research proposal. Before you may write the thesis, a panel of experts needs to approve your proposal. A professor may require you to submit a brief proposal for a term paper. Even if a project does not require a formal proposal, you will benefit from preparing one for yourself; it will focus your thoughts and give your research direction. The ability to conceptualise and write a quality proposal is the mark of a person ready to do independent research.

In this chapter, we are going to look at the research proposal as a whole – its value, components, and preparation. The two chapters that follow will each tackle one of the two main parts of the proposal, the research problem and the research plan, in greater detail.

The Value of a Research Proposal

A research proposal 'is a document that outlines how you *propose* to undertake your research studies.'[1] Essentially, it outlines *what* you will research and *how* you will research it. The 'what' part is called the *problem*; the 'how' part we call the *plan*. A proposal describes a problem and sets out a logical, systematic plan to solve it.

Whether it is a 1-page outline for your own use or a detailed doctoral proposal, writing the research proposal is the most difficult and the most important part of the entire research project. If you rush through this step, you will have a poorly conceived research problem and plan. This makes the rest of the study difficult. But if you invest time and effort to produce a first-class proposal, the rest of the study should fall into place.

The greatest value of a proposal is that it keeps the research project on course. It gives direction and focus to the project. It prevents you taking rabbit trails – time-consuming, energy-sapping digressions. If you invest the time and energy at the start of your project to think through *what* you will research and *how* you will go about it, formulating a clear picture in your mind of your destination and the route you will take to get there, your journey should progress without delay or detour.

---

1. Johan Mouton, *How to Succeed in Your Master's and Doctoral Studies* (Pretoria, South Africa: VanSchuik, 2001), 44.

For example, if you carefully and precisely formulate your research problem, keeping it narrow and focused and identifying which aspects to include and exclude, you dramatically reduce the amount of reading you need to do. This saves time. If your problem is vague and fuzzy, you will read five times as much because you have no clear yardstick to distinguish what you must read from what you need not read. Similarly, if you think through the essential steps you must take to solve the problem, you reduce the likelihood of wasting time gathering data you do not need.

In short, prepare a good proposal and your research will flow; prepare a poor one and it will flop. An old adage – 'failing to prepare is preparing to fail' – certainly applies to research. Yet students often do a poor job of preparing their proposals. Why? Partly due to ignorance – not understanding the nature of research well enough to plan the project. We suspect over-eagerness is an even bigger cause. In their haste to get on with 'the real work', they slap together a poorly conceived proposal. Preparing a quality proposal is hard work. It requires much reading and reflection. It is time-consuming. However, in the long run, it saves time. Therefore, we urge you – invest quality time in the proposal. Prepare it well. What you sow into the proposal, you will reap in the thesis.

If you are convinced of the value of preparing the proposal properly, you will be wondering what elements should go into a research proposal. Views differ from one researcher to another. In the next section, we shall present our preferred breakdown of the elements that belong in a proposal.

The Elements of a Research Proposal

A research proposal consists of two main parts: the research problem and the research plan. The first part, the research problem, addresses 'the what' of the study; it describes the problem the researcher will attempt to solve. Part two, the research *plan*, focuses on 'the how' of the study; it explains how the researcher will go about solving the research problem. Let us examine each part.

Part 1: The Research Problem

The first part of the proposal should *state the research problem* with the utmost focus and clarity. The problem the researcher will attempt to solve needs to be defined and delimited with such precision as to leave no confusion or ambiguity as to what the research is about and what it aims to accomplish. The more clearly and precisely the research problem is laid out, the more focus the research will have.

> Your problem should be so clearly stated that anyone anywhere in the world (who reads English) may read it, understand it, and react to it without help. If the problem is *not* stated with such clarity and precision, then you are merely

deceiving yourself that you know what the problem is. Such self-deception will merely cause you trouble later on.[2]

What components should you include in your description of the research problem? We suggest you include these elements in this order:

1. The Statement of the Problem
    1.1. The Main Problem
    1.2. The Key Questions
    1.3. The Hypotheses [if relevant]

2. The Elucidation of the Problem
    2.1. Delimitations of the Study
    2.2. Definitions of Key Terms [if relevant]
    2.3. Presuppositions of the Researcher [if necessary]
    2.4. Preliminary Literature Review

3. The Value of the Study
    3.1. Theological Value
    3.2. Practical Value

The notable omission from the list is a section on the background to the problem. The first time I wrote about research methodology, I followed Mouton who suggests that a section on the background of the problem precede the statement of the problem.[3] Since writing that course, I have evaluated about one hundred research proposals by students working from the model I presented. I am convinced that including a background section tends to hinder students more than it helps them. The heading 'background' lures all except the most gifted students into writing a long-winded social narrative that seldom sheds much light on the research problem. For many students, it serves as a decoy. After writing several pages about social ills in their communities, they are unable to shift focus from the practical to the academic, from real-life problems to a research problem. Under the heading 'the problem', they describe a broad, undefined social problem that is unsuitable for theological research. For this reason, I consider it best to exclude a background section from the research proposal. Essential background information can be presented in the section about the value of the study. However, many professors expect or even require a background section. If you are preparing a thesis proposal, you should check with your professor whether he wants you to include a section on the background to the study.

The statement of the problem. Begin your research proposal with a direct statement of the research problem. State the problem as a single sentence (at most a short paragraph). You may formulate it as a statement, a question, or an objective. In large research projects,

---

2. Paul D. Leedy, *Practical Research: Planning and Design* (6th ed.; New York: MacMillan, 1993), 63.
3. Mouton, *Master's and Doctoral Studies*, 48.

the main problem is usually too large to solve without dividing it into smaller units. In such cases, break the main problem down into 2–6 sub-problems; we are calling these 'key questions', but many call them 'sub-problems' or 'objectives'. A hypothesis is a calculated guess as to what the answer to a research question will be. A hypothesis must be directly related to a research problem or question. Thus, you may have a hypothesis for the main problem and, if you wish, one per sub-problem.

The elucidation of the problem. If you begin with a direct statement of the research problem, there will be loose ends to tie up. This section clarifies the nature of the research by explaining the delimitations, definitions, and presuppositions of the study and by presenting a preliminary literature review. Under delimitations, you narrow the focus of your study by indicating what you will *not* research, that is, what you will exclude. The sections on definitions and presuppositions help your readers to understand the things you treat as 'givens' (what you assume to be true) and how you use important terms. The literature review places your planned research in the context of related scholarship, helping readers to appreciate how your study relates to what others have done.

The value of the study. The first part of the proposal ends with a motivation for doing the study. You may motivate the study at a practical and/or theoretical level. This section provides an opportunity to introduce some essential background information by indicating how the proposed research will help to address social needs in a community. You may explain who should benefit from the research and how they might benefit.

We shall discuss each of these elements in more detail in the chapter on the research problem. Now let us examine the elements that constitute the second part of the proposal, the research plan.

Part 2: The Research Plan

Research follows a problem-solution format; so does the research proposal. The first part sets out the research problem; the second part presents a plan to solve it. The research plan contains three sections: design, methodology and bibliography.

    4. The Research Design
        4.1. The Structure
        4.2. The Timeframe
    5. The Research Methodology
        5.1. The Data
        5.2. The Tools
        5.3. The Steps
    6. The Bibliography

In certain cases, it may be necessary to add a section indicating the qualifications of the researcher to do the research. For example, if the proposed study requires advanced analysis of the Greek text of the New Testament, the researcher needs to be competent to perform such analysis. If an empirical study depends on specialised psychometric testing, the researcher needs the skills and licence to perform the testing. In general, the qualifications of the researcher to carry out the research can be worked into the discussion of methodology at appropriate points.

The research design. Your first decision is what kind of study is best suited to solve the *research problem*. For example, can you use a purely literary approach or do you need an empirical component? Later in the book, we shall present a variety of standard designs for theological research – exegetical studies, systematic theology, empirical research, case studies, and so on. The chosen design largely dictates the logic and structure of the study. In large projects, such as theses or dissertations, the proposal needs to include proposed timeframes; these serve as a progress agreement between student and supervisor.

Research methodology. To assess the validity of a research project, one must know *exactly* how the researcher will conduct the study. You should explain step by step how you intend to do the research. The best way of doing this is to work through your proposed study one section (or one sub-problem) at a time, describing the research tools (methods) you will deploy and indicating what data you will collect, how you will collect it, and how it will be analysed.

Bibliography. End your proposal with a list of *Works Consulted*, indicating the scope of your reading up to the point of submission. The majority of the entries should be relevant scholarly works. Avoid sources that are out of date (older than 25 years) and those classified as 'popular' instead of 'academic'; do not clutter your bibliography with irrelevant books (those not directly related to your topic) or with online articles. You must show that you know what the major works on the topic are.

We shall discuss each of these elements in more detail in the chapter on the research plan. The final matter we need to address in this chapter is the preparation of the research proposal.

The Preparation of a Research Proposal

Students are notorious for being careless in the way they prepare research proposals. As members of a committee that evaluates proposals for masters' theses and doctoral dissertations, we are appalled by the sloppiness with which many proposals are prepared. Students write the name of the degree programme incorrectly; their work is littered with spelling errors and grammatical errors; it abounds with imprecise language, fuzzy logic, unsubstantiated claims, and unjustified generalisations or assumptions.

Take care with the preparation of your research proposal. Based on the proposal, your professor(s) will make a decision as to whether you are capable of conducting serious research. Your proposal needs to make a positive impression. Sloppiness in the presentation of your proposal sends the wrong message. No professor looks forward to working with a lazy, careless student.

What are the important errors to avoid when preparing a research proposal? Here is a checklist of questions to consider:

- *Did you carefully check the spelling and grammar?* Even if you have to write the proposal in a second or third language, there is no excuse for the kinds of spelling, typing, and grammatical errors that can be corrected by using the spelling and grammar checking functions on your word processor. Proofread your proposal several times before you submit it.
- *Does your proposal conform to the requirements of the institution?* Find out if the institution has set requirements for the following: (a) line spacing, font type and size, margins, and so on; (b) the components of the proposal; and (c) referencing and bibliography. Make sure your proposal conforms to all the institution's requirements.
- *Did you write the name of the qualification correctly?* If the degree is a Master of Theology programme, do not carelessly call it a Master of Arts or an MA.
- *Is your language precise and modest?* Be modest in your claims. Do not promise more than you can deliver. Support all claims with evidence. Say exactly what you mean. It is your responsibility to be so precise that you leave no room for readers to misunderstand your proposal.

Pay attention to detail when you prepare a research proposal. Do not be careless or sloppy. The research proposal is the most important part of writing a thesis. It needs to convince a panel of professors that you are capable of doing independent research.

Summary

A research proposal governs and directs a research project. This is the most difficult and most important part of many research endeavours. In the long run, the time and energy invested in conceptualising the project pays dividends.

Research proposals have two main parts – the research problem and the research plan – the *what* and the *how*. First it describes a problem; then it presents a plan to solve it. See Table 4 for a list of the components included in each section of a proposal. These two parts are so crucial that we shall devote the next two chapters to exploring them in detail. In the following chapter, we shall explore how to construct each element of the research problem.

The Components of a Research Proposal
Part 1: The Research Problem
1. The Statement of the Problem
1.1. The Main Problem
1.2. The Key Questions
1.3. The Hypotheses
2. The Elucidation of the Problem
2.1. Delimitations of the Study
2.2. Definitions of Key Terms
2.3. Presuppositions of the Researcher
2.4. Preliminary Literature Review
3. The Value of the Study
3.1. Theological Value
3.2. Practical Value
Part 2: The Research Plan
4. The Research Design
4.1. The Structure
4.2. The Timeframe
5. The Research Methodology
5.1. The Data
5.2. The Tools
5.3. The Steps
6. The Bibliography

Table 4: The Components of a Research Proposal

11

The Research Problem

The goal of all research is to solve a problem. If you do not have a problem needing a solution, a question crying out for an answer, you do not have anything to research. Therefore, formulating a research problem is the most important and, for many students, the most challenging part of the entire thesis-writing process. Every thesis is a systematic attempt to answer a single research question, to solve one overarching research problem. In this chapter, we are going to examine the steps involved in formulating a research problem.

The Process at a Glance

The quest for a research problem begins with a *provisional research idea* (see Figure 31). This might be a topic that interests you, such as divorce, judgement, or prophecy. It might be a particular book of the Bible or a passage of Scripture, perhaps the book of Psalms or Matthew 24–25. Often the research idea originates with a real-life problem in your community or your church, problems such as the neglect of children's ministry in your denomination, the devastating impact of poverty or HIV/AIDS in your community, or ministering in a culture that practices polygamy. The crucial thing to realise is that the *provisional research idea* needs to be refined into a suitable research problem.

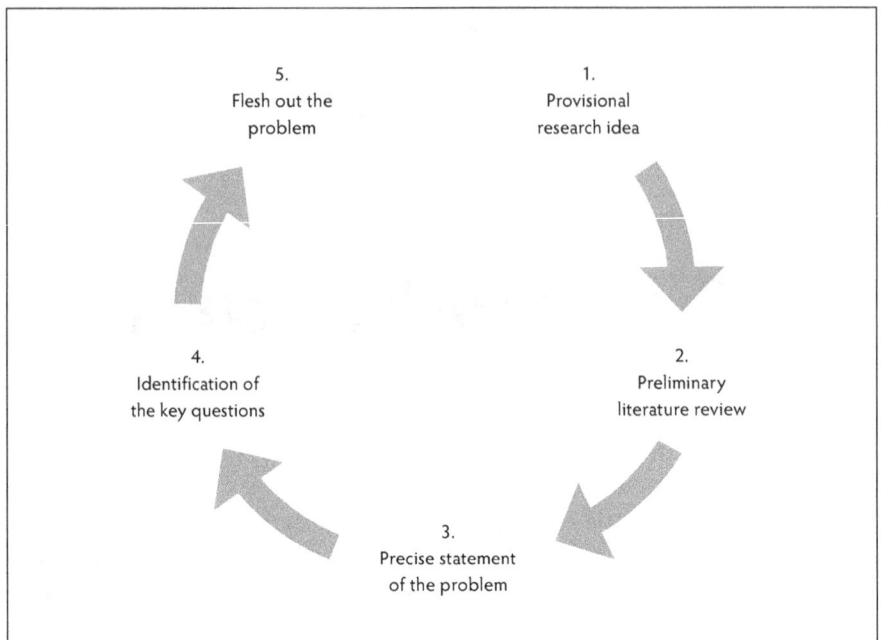

Figure 31: Formulating the Research Problem

When you have a provisional research idea, the next step is to conduct a preliminary study of the topic. You can do this by skimming the literature available on the topic, conducting a *preliminary* literature review. This is a vital step. By surveying literature related to your topic, you will get a good idea of what the issues and debates are, what others have done, what needs to be done, and so forth. It helps you to clarify your thinking on the issue and identify some key research questions.

When you have read broadly on the topic, you need to narrow your research idea down to *a single* research problem and formulate it precisely in one sentence, as a statement, a question, or an objective. This is a crucial moment in the research project. Whatever question or objective you commit to here will control the entire thesis. The research problem statement is not just an appealing question or a desirable objective; it is a narrow, focused, precisely formulated statement of a research problem that is informed by familiarity with existing research (literature) on the topic.

The fourth step is optional, but usually desirable. Although the research problem states the overarching question or objective of the thesis, it is helpful to break this problem statement down into a set of key questions that must be answered in order to solve the main problem. These *key questions* are logically related to the main problem. They break the main problem down into smaller, more manageable units. By answering the key questions, you should solve the main problem. We recommend that you try to identify between three and five key questions.

The final step is to *flesh out the problem* by thinking through the elements that form the elucidation of the problem (delimitations, definitions, presuppositions) and the value of the study. This process helps you to clarify and focus the research problem further.

In summary, then, the process of formulating the research problem has five steps (see Figure 31):

1) Identify a provisional research idea

2) Conduct a preliminary literature review

3) Formulate the main research problem

4) List 3–5 key research questions

5) Flesh out the research problem

Since this is such a crucial part of research, we need to examine each step in greater detail.

The Research Idea

Your research begins with something that interests you, such as a field of study, a practical problem, or a biblical question. This is not yet a research problem, but it is the starting point. Ideas for theological research usually come from one of two worlds: the real world or the research world.

- *Real life.* Research in the field of practical theology often begins with a real-life problem. Real-life problems are practical problems in the church and/or community. For example, the HIV/AIDS epidemic has caused a host of practical problems in communities and churches in Africa. These include large numbers of orphaned children, aging grandparents raising infants, superstitions about causes and cures of HIV/AIDS, church-based prejudice towards HIV-positive people, a great need for family-based health care, and many more. Any of these could serve as the point of departure for a research project.
- *Research.* The point of departure for research in the fields of biblical studies and systematic theology (and some topics in practical theology) lies in existing research. As you study the Scriptures and read scholarly books and articles, you will begin to note which questions have been answered and which ones remain to be answered. The 'gaps' in current research provide opportunities for further research. For example, while studying the gospel of Matthew a student discovered that judgement is a major theme; he noticed that Matthew uses the phrase 'weeping and gnashing of teeth' six times (out of seven in the Bible), yet found that nobody has done an in-depth study of this phrase and its

contribution to Matthew's theology. This gap in existing scholarship paved the way for his thesis.

We repeat: research begins with something that *interests you*. This is vital. Research is a long, lonely, demanding task. You need to find your topic fascinating. You need to love your chosen field. Do not allow yourself to be persuaded to research a topic that does not capture your attention.

The Preliminary Literature Review

When you have a research idea in mind, you need to begin the process of refining it into a focused research problem. The process of refining the research idea into a research problem is challenging. Mouton observes that students seldom have difficulty identifying potential research ideas. 'The real challenge, however, is to take that idea and transform it into a research problem or research question. In my experience, most students find this a very difficult and time-consuming process.'[1]

The first step in refining your research idea into a research question is to do a preliminary literature review. The idea is to scan academic writings related to your topic to see what has been done and what questions remain unanswered (or unasked). As you scan the literature, new questions and creative angles for examining your topic will emerge. Here are three examples of how the literature survey helps you to develop a research idea.

1) A preliminary literature review will alert you to current trends in your field of interest. Being aware of these trends helps you to channel your study into a research gap. I began my first doctoral thesis with a general interest in Bible translation. My promoters, aware of a recent development, alerted me to a few recent publications. The articles proposed a new philosophical framework for translation. I immediately recognised a gap for further research – nobody had yet examined the theoretical or practical implications of using the new framework to develop an approach to translation.

2) A preliminary literature review will help you to delimit your study to ensure that it is doable. Your initial research idea will be too broad to serve as a research problem; you need to narrow it. A new master's candidate began with an interest in what the Old Testament teaches about the Holy Spirit. Realising that he needed to narrow his focus, his supervisor advised him to review existing literature on the subject; she gave him some tips to help him get started. As he read widely on his research idea, he reduced the scope first to the prophetic books, then to Zechariah alone. Another candidate began with an interest in researching what heaven will be like for believers. She began with the feeling

---

1. Mouton, *Master's and Doctoral Studies*, 149.

that not much research had been done on the topic, but soon discovered there was a vast body of writing on it. She settled on researching what a single text in Revelation teaches about heaven.

3) A preliminary literature review may alert you to the fact that your research idea is not doable. A colleague assisted a master's candidate who was determined to write her thesis about justification in Romans. He cautioned her that the topic has been so thoroughly covered that there is no point in another study retracing familiar territory, but his words fell on deaf ears. They agreed that she would read broadly about justification in Romans; if she could identify a gap in the existing literature or come up with a fresh perspective, she could proceed. She could not, so she had to return to the drawing board.

These are some of the values of doing a literature survey as step two. It may lead you to abandon a poor research idea early. If the preliminary survey confirms that the idea has potential, it helps you to identify gaps in the existing research and to narrow the scope of the planned research.

The Main Problem

Step three is to state the main research problem in a single sentence. A well-formulated main problem, which is clear and focused, is crucial for effective and efficient research. The research problem can be formulated as a statement, a question, or an objective. It does not matter which form you use. The following examples illustrate how the main problem can be formulated as a question, statement, or objective without altering its basic meaning.

Statement	Question	Objective
The research will examine how churches in Swaziland should minister to polygamous families which join the church.	How should churches in Swaziland minister to polygamous families which join the church?	The main objective of the study is to determine how churches in Swaziland should minister to polygamous families which join the church.

Statement	Question	Objective
The research will attempt to discover the criteria and objectives the editors of the Psalter used to arrange Psalms 42–49.	What criteria and objectives did the editors of the Psalter used to arrange Psalms 42–49?	The objective of the research is to determine the criteria and objectives the editors of the Psalter used to arrange Psalms 42–49.

The Golden Rule: The golden rule for formulating a research problem is that you must state it in a single sentence!

Whether you choose to formulate the problem as a statement, a question, or an objective, you must write it in a *single sentence*. If you cannot state it in one clear sentence, the problem is not yet clear in your mind. The more simply and precisely you state the research problem, the easier your task will be later. As stated in the previous chapter:

> Your problem should be so clearly stated that anyone anywhere in the world (who reads English) may read it, understand it, and react to it without help. If the problem is *not* stated with such clarity and precision, then you are merely deceiving yourself that you know what the problem is. Such self-deception will merely cause you trouble later on.[2]

How does one transform a research idea into a problem statement? (We shall assume the problem will be stated as a question, but the same principles apply if you prefer to formulate it as a statement or an objective.) Every question has two components:

1) Subject: what you intend to study

2) Complement: what you intend to find out about it

A few simple examples should help you to understand the two elements:

Subject	Complement	Question
leaders	why they leave churches	'Why do good leaders leave churches?'
heaven	what it will be like	'What will life in heaven be like?'
Psalms 3–8	what message they convey	'What are the main teachings of Psalms 3–8?'

By way of review, the process of formulating a question is as follows:
- Subject: decide what subject you want to study
- Complement: decide what you want to discover about it
- Question: put the two parts together as a question

Each of the examples above was a simple question. A good *research question* is usually more complex. The same principles apply to more complex questions. The difference usually lies in the subject, which tends to be more specific in a research question.

---

2. Leedy, *Practical Research*, 63.

Subject	Complement	Question
leaders in Baptist churches in KwaZulu-Natal	why many are leaving	'What factors are causing pastors to leave Baptist churches in KwaZulu-Natal?'
heaven in Revelation 21:1–8	what heaven will be like	'What does Revelation 21:1–8 teach about life in heaven?'
the arrangement of Psalms 3–8	the reason the editors put them in this order	'What does the arrangement of Psalms 3–8 reveal about the editors' objectives?'

In each of these examples, the subject is much narrower (more precise) than in the simple questions in the previous example. We have narrowed the subject from 'leaders' to 'Baptist leaders in KwaZulu-Natal'. You could not research all leaders everywhere, but you could research a particular group of leaders (Baptist) in a limited area (KwaZulu-Natal). An in-depth study of all the passages of Scripture that speak about heaven would be impractical, but a study of what one key passage (Rev 21:1–8) teaches is realistic. We have narrowed the subject to make the study doable. Similarly, an exegetical study of Psalms 3–8 is not practical. By narrowing our focus to *the arrangement of* Psalms 3–8, the scope of the study becomes manageable.

What often happens is that you begin with a broad subject in mind (research idea), but, as you read widely on that topic (preliminary literature review), you begin to narrow the scope of the study by choosing to focus on one particular aspect of the broad subject – from leaders to Baptist leaders in KwaZulu-Natal, from heaven to heaven in Revelation 21:1–8, from Psalms 3–8 to the arrangement of Psalms 3–8. What you have done is *delimit* the scope of the subject.

Finally, here are two practical tips to help you avoid common traps that catch novice researchers. First, do not formulate your main problem in a way that permits a *yes* or *no* answer. A good theological research question should seldom permit 'yes' or 'no' as an answer. Rather ask 'what are the causes of church splits?' than 'is Satan the cause of church splits?' 'What does Matthew 19:1–12 teach about divorce and remarriage?' is a better question than, 'Does Matthew 19:1–12 permit a divorced person to remarry?' Second, do not ask a question to which you know the answer. Thesis candidates often begin with a hidden agenda. They are convinced of something and intend to use a thesis to announce their conviction to the world. They fail to realise that a thesis is research, not propaganda. Research must seek solutions to unsolved problems, answers to unanswered questions. If you are convinced you know the answer to your question before you begin the study, your bias will prevent you from doing justice to the study. Either write a book expressing your convictions or select a different topic for a thesis.

In summary, then, formulate your main problem in a single sentence. It may take the form of a statement, question, or objective. It needs to indicate both what you will study (the subject) and what you wish to discover about it (the complement). In a research problem, the subject area should be narrowly delimited. Avoid questions permitting a yes or no answer; do not ask loaded questions on which your mind is made up.

The Key Questions

Although a research project seeks to solve a single research problem, the main problem is usually too large to treat as a whole. Therefore, it often helps to break it down into a few key questions. Answering the key questions leads naturally to solving the main problem. In a thesis, there is often one key question for each chapter (except the introduction and conclusion).

You need to be aware that various authors (and supervisors) use different terms for the same things. For example, the main research problem may be referred to as the problem, question, aim, objective or purpose of the study. What we are calling the key questions are often referred to as either subordinate problems or research objectives. Regardless of the preferred terminology, there is always a main problem (or question or objective) that is broken down into a series of smaller problems (or questions or objectives).

To identify the key questions, ask yourself what specific questions you need to answer in order to answer the main question. If you ask the right questions in the right order, your study will fall into place naturally. Here is an example:

Main problem	How should churches in Swaziland minister to polygamous families which join the church?
Key questions	1. What cultural practices related to polygamy pose pastoral challenges to the churches?
	2. How do the churches currently handle these pastoral challenges?
	3. What biblical principles should pastors bear in mind as they minister to polygamous families?
	4. What practical steps do churches need to take to enhance their ministry to polygamous families?

We could now easily convert this list of questions into a thesis title and outline:

Title	How churches should minister to polygamous families in Swaziland
Chapter	1. Polygamy in Swaziland: a problem practice
	2. How churches currently handle the problem
	3. Biblical principles for handling polygamy
	4. Towards an effective ministry approach

Here is another example:

Main problem	How does the Old Testament practice of tithing taught in Malachi 3:8–12 relate to New Testament believers?
Key questions	1. What did the Old Testament teach with regard to tithing?
	2. What did Malachi 3:8–12 mean to its original readers?
	3. What does the New Testament teach with respect to tithing?
	4. How does the message of Malachi 3:8–12 relate to New Testament believers?

Note that if the researcher successfully answers all the key questions, she will have answered the main question. Can you see how each key question could easily represent one chapter of a thesis (or section of an article)? A thesis outline for this study might look like this:

Title	How tithing in Malachi 3:8–12 relates to Christians
Chapter	1. Tithing in the Old Testament
	2. Exegesis of Malachi 3:8–12
	3. Tithing in the New Testament
	4. Tithing and the Christian

Once you have identified the main problem and the key questions, your research project starts to take shape. You have, in embryo form, the title of your study, the main problem you need to solve, the logical sequence of steps to solve it and the key to a working outline. The final step in formulating the research problem is to flesh out the details.

Fleshing Out the Problem

The final step is to flesh out the research problem. This involves completing these parts:

- The hypotheses
- The delimitations
- The definitions
- The presuppositions
- The value

We shall discuss each of these components.

The Hypotheses

What is a hypothesis? According to Leedy, 'Hypotheses are tentative, intelligent guesses posited for the purpose of directing one's thinking toward the solution of the problem.'[3]

---

3. Leedy, *Practical Research*, 75.

When you have formulated a research problem, you make an educated guess as to what its solution will be. This educated guess guides your thinking. You set out to determine whether the data supports your hypothesis (initial theory). This helps you to focus your analysis of the data.

Theologians do not agree about whether a hypothesis is an essential element of a *theological* research proposal. In many other disciplines, testing a hypothesis is by far the best approach. Medical research is a good example; the researcher suspects particular treatment may help those suffering with a disease, so he designs a series of experiments to test his hypothesis. In theological research, hypotheses are not always essential. This is another matter on which to consult your supervisor for his preferences.

If you do decide to base your study around a hypothesis, then your entire analysis should be designed to determine whether the evidence supports it as the solution to the research problem. At the end of the study, you must accept, reject or modify your hypothesis. We use 'accept' or 'reject' instead of 'prove' or 'disprove' because research findings do not constitute absolute proof. Furthermore, *proving* your hypothesis is *not* the goal of research; *testing* it is. Whether you accept, reject or modify it has no bearing on the success of your study. If the evidence points towards a different conclusion to what you envisaged when you began, so be it. If you feel pressure to prove your hypothesis, you may distort the data so as to succeed. Settle in your heart early that there is no pressure to accept it; this will help you remain objective. In fact, it reflects well on your rigour and objectivity if your findings do not support your hypothesis.

Hypotheses are directly related to research questions. Therefore, you may have one and only one hypothesis per research question. This means you may have one main hypothesis related to the main problem and one subordinate hypothesis per key question. We say 'may' because many researchers prefer to work with only a main hypothesis. Once again, if you are preparing for a thesis, check what your supervisor expects.

The Delimitations

Delimitations are self-imposed limitations, that is, the ways you choose to limit the scope of your research. They state what you will *exclude* from the research, what you will *not* study. They refine the problem by demarcating its boundaries. They help to make the study doable by reducing its scope. They help you to focus on what is relevant to your problem and avoid following rabbit trails. Leedy's remark is true:

> Only a researcher who thinks carefully about the problem and its focal center will distinguish between what is relevant and what is not relevant *to the problem*. All irrelevancies to the problem must be firmly ruled out in the statement of delimitation.[4]

---

4. Ibid., 74.

The delimitations directly affect the scope of the findings. If you delimit your study to 'the Zulu speaking believers in the Assemblies of God in the Gauteng Province', you cannot draw conclusions that apply to the Assemblies of God throughout South Africa.

What kinds of delimitations tend to form part of theological research? These are some common types of delimitations (do not treat it as an exhaustive list):

- *Canonical: limiting your study to a selected corpus of Scriptures.* A term paper may not be able to address 'what the Old Testament teaches about life after death', but it may be able to do justice to 'afterlife in the book of Psalms'.
- *Geographical: limiting your study to a particular region (or regions).* To research the training needs of pastors' wives in Kenya, you would need to interview wives from all across the country; this may not be possible. By limiting the research to Nairobi, it becomes doable.
- *Cultural: limiting your study by cultural or language divisions.* Could you research the question, 'How does traditional African culture view the spirit world?' We doubt it. Although they share much common ground, African cultures are not uniform in their worldview. It would be more feasible to ask, 'How does traditional Agikuyu culture view the spirit world?'
- *Historical: limiting your study to a specific period.* If it aims to be comprehensive in depth, historical research usually needs to limit the period it covers. The shorter the period, the greater the depth in which you can examine it.
- *Ecclesiastical: limiting your study to certain churches or denominations.* You could not do an empirical study of the causes of church splits in Argentina; there have been thousands. You might be able to research the causes of splits in Assemblies of God churches in Argentina (perhaps with added historical and geographic delimitations).
- *Conceptual: limiting the conceptual elements to be covered.* A thesis evaluating 'the translation of texts relating to the deity of Christ in the New World Translation' need not engage christological literature as a whole. Under delimitations, the researcher can motivate not delving deeply into doctrinal debates.

The title may include some of the major delimitations. For example, a title such as 'identifying causes of church splits in the Baptist Union of South Africa between 1980 and 2005' contains three delimitations – ecclesiastical (Baptist Union), geographic (South Africa), and historical (1980–2005). Under delimitations, you might motivate your choice of these delimitations and, if necessary, add other delimitations that do not appear in the title.

The Definitions

The purpose of the definition of terms section in a research proposal is to help your readers follow your argument. It should define terms as *you* will use them in your research. It does not matter whether or not your readers agree with your definition. By alerting readers to what *you* mean when you use a particular term, you help them to follow your argument and reduce the likelihood of misinterpretations.

Which terms should be defined? First, you should only define terms that are pivotal to understanding your research proposal. In other words, stick to terms crucial to the study. Less pivotal terms can be defined when they first occur in the study. Second, you should define any term an informed reader may either not understand or may misunderstand. Three categories occur regularly:

- *Uncommon technical terms.* You can assume your readers will be fairly well informed with respect to theological jargon. Define key terms they may not know. If your topic is Bible translation, you do not need to define *dynamic equivalence*, but you should define *indirect translation* (a new approach based on a communication model called relevance theory). A doctoral dissertation on the ethics of genetic engineering need not define *utilitarianism*, but ethicists may not know exactly what *somatic engineering* is.
- *Terms with more than one attested meaning.* If a key term in your proposal has more than one attested meaning in scholarly literature, you need to state what you mean by it. Some use the term *missio Dei* to refer to God's mission to reconcile all human beings to himself, while others use it with more socio-humanitarian overtones. Attested uses of *biblical theology* include a twentieth-century movement, an approach to OT and NT theology, and simply theology that is biblical in approach. The meaning ascribed to *baptism in the Holy Spirit* varies from one church movement to another. When using these kinds of terms, you must state what you mean by them.
- *Terms you are using with particular nuances.* If you intend to use a term with slightly different connotations to its standard use in scholarly literature, explain the difference. In Ethiopia, *evangelist* has a special meaning. Many churches have two full-time workers, a pastor and an evangelist. When Ethiopians speak of *the evangelist*, they mean something slightly different to what most Christians would.

You should *not* define terms informed readers will understand. One of our MTh students wrote two paragraphs in his thesis defining *the Old Testament*; this insults informed readers. Even terms such as justification, situation ethics, deism, or source criticism do not require definitions unless you are using them in with different nuances to their standard usage.

How many terms should be defined? There is no standard answer. As a rule, define as many as necessary, but as few as possible. Some studies need no definitions; others are rich in technical jargon and require many definitions. Readers of theological research tend to be well informed regarding theology. Therefore, an exegetical study using standard terminology might not require any definitions. However, if a theology student writes a doctoral dissertation on the ethics of genetic engineering in which he delves into medical procedures, he may need to define many terms since his readers may not be as familiar with medical terms.

This discussion of definitions of terms relates to the process of formulating a research problem in a research proposal. In a research report, such as a thesis, you may elect to include a more comprehensive glossary. Alternatively, many terms can be defined when they first occur in the body of the report.

The Presuppositions

Presuppositions (also called assumptions) are 'the givens' that undergird your thinking and approach. They are the things you take for granted, what you consider self-evident, the foundational truths on which you build your study.

Your presuppositions may or may not be true. You might, for example, base your study on the philosophical foundation laid by an earlier piece of research. If that research is later disproved, yours may be too. In the 1960s, Eugene Nida was the leading Bible translation theorist in the world. He developed his ideas based on the best linguistic theories available at the time. Today, linguistic models have changed, calling some of Nida's views into question.

Your readers may or may not share your presuppositions. By stating your presuppositions, you alert your readers to your personal bias and help them to follow your argument. If your exegesis of a gospel text assumes Matthean priority, a reader who believes in Markan priority may have trouble following your train of thought. Although she may disagree with your view, by alerting her to the fact that your study presupposes Matthean priority, you empower her to understand your analysis.

Which presuppositions do you need to state? Any that materially influence your study. 'An important task in research thinking is to ask the question: "Which of my presuppositions affect the way I think and write?"'[5] How might your personal bias (for example, church affiliation, theological persuasion) prejudice your interpretation of the data? Which beliefs or theories are foundational to the research? Asking these kinds of questions will help you to pinpoint presuppositions you need to state.

Since scholarly literature does not agree regarding whether Isaiah 40–66 was written by Isaiah in the eighth century BC, if you take this for granted *and* doing so materially affects your argument or conclusions, you need to state it as a presupposition. If you set out to analyse whether 1 Corinthians 13:10 supports the cessation of spiritual gifts, your church and theological background (for example, Pentecostal or Reformed) will significantly affect your objectivity; therefore, mention your background. Perhaps your convictions regarding the inspiration of Scripture or your preferred hermeneutic methods are so crucial to your study that you should declare them up front.

---

5. Vyhmeister, *Quality Research Papers*, 101.

The Value

The final section of the problem should motivate the study by explaining its value. Depending on the nature of the study, the value may be theoretical and/or practical. You should describe how the study promises to contribute to current knowledge (theoretical value) and/or to present realities (practical value).

When you discuss the practical value of the study, you should address *who* should benefit, *why* they should benefit and *how* they should benefit. Since the model we are recommending does not begin with an introduction section, this is the place to provide a little background information. Briefly describe the present realities and how the proposed research may help to address them. But please keep this section short and sharp, a few paragraphs at most. Do not wander off on a five-page lament about the social ills of society.

This is an example of a well-written 'value' section for a thesis entitled: 'Practical proposals for raising the profile of children's ministry in Assemblies of God churches in Zimbabwe':

> Speaking as a leader in the Assemblies of God in Zimbabwe, casual observation suggests that children's ministry is widely neglected in the denomination's churches. Few churches appear to devote a significant percentage of their budget to children's ministry. The children's ministries that exist seem to focus on entertaining the children so they do not disturb the adults' worship service rather than on evangelising, discipling and equipping children for ministry.
>
> This study will help to raise the profile of children's ministry in the Assemblies of God in three ways. First, by means of a descriptive survey it will provide accurate data regarding the present state of children's ministry. Second, its analysis of the biblical and scholarly materials will underline the importance and value of prioritising children's ministry. Last, and most important, it will develop a feasible strategy for raising the profile of children's ministry among churches and church leaders in the denomination.

In just 150 words, this proposal indicates who will benefit (the Assemblies of God in Zimbabwe), why they will benefit (children's ministry is undervalued) and how they will benefit (raising the profile of children's ministry). It provides enough background information to understand the context of the study and enough motivation to persuade readers of the study's value.

Summary

A research proposal consists of two sections: the research problem and the research plan. The process of developing a research idea into a full research problem involves five steps:

1) Identify a provisional research idea

2) Conduct a preliminary literature review

3) Formulate the main research problem

4) List 3–5 key research questions

5) Flesh out the research problem

    The initial research idea is just something that interests you; it may or may not prove to be a feasible research area. To help decide if it is a good research idea, you need to preview the literature in the field. Your reading will help you to isolate and formulate a specific research problem. Since this main problem is often too large to tackle as a whole, divide it into a few key questions that represent the logical steps from problem to solution. Lastly, flesh out the problem section of your proposal by addressing the hypotheses, delimitations, definitions, presuppositions and value of the study.

12

The Research Plan

The research plan constitutes the second half of the research proposal. The first half presents the research problem. The second half sets out a plan to solve it. The plan needs to be thorough, describing every step the researcher intends to take in solving the problem. Many research proposals fail dismally here. They set out the plan in such vague, general terms that one really has no idea *exactly* how the candidate intends to solve the problem. The research plan should be presented in such detail and with such clarity, that a different researcher, simply by studying the proposal, could duplicate the study.

We suggest the research proposal should include three sections under the research plan:
- The research design
- The research methodology
- The annotated bibliography

We shall devote one section of this chapter to each of these three parts.

The Design

The research design is the general approach you will use to solve your research problem. The most important part of the design is *the structure* of the study. The other standard element is the *timeframe*.

The structure. By structure, we mean identifying logical, sequential divisions of the study. What major steps will be needed? How should these steps be ordered? These steps will form the major parts, chapters or sections of the research report (paper, thesis or dissertation). When you know the steps and their sequence, it is usually easy to work through them one by one determining the exact methodology needed for each.

In the simplest terms, theological research tends to be one of two types: literary or empirical. Since all theological research involves some literary research, we tend to define a study as *literary research* if it has no empirical component, but as empirical research if it contains fieldwork. Research under the banner of biblical studies and systematic theology is usually literary, while many studies under practical theology are empirical.

As a broad, general rule, research in practical theology often begins by examining a present situation, then formulates a biblical model of what should be, and culminates with developing a practical response. Analysing the present situation often requires empirical research. In systematic theology, one typically begins with a thorough analysis of current views, then analyses the biblical evidence (the bulk of the study), and concludes with a short section on the significance of the findings. The biblical analysis needs four steps: identify all the Scriptures, analyse each one in context, deduce timeless principles and construct a theory to explain all the data. Exegetical studies often move from a discussion of the context of a passage to a detailed examination of the text itself and conclude with a look at its significance. We shall discuss each of these models in detail in chapters 13–15.

You should *not* simply adopt one of these designs uncritically. Your research problem must control the design of your study; it dictates what steps are needed and the best order in which to follow them. Therefore, it controls which model is most appropriate and how, if at all, you should customise or modify it to suit your objectives.

As you study these research designs, you will notice that every model has substantial biblical *and* practical components. This reflects our convictions that theology should be both biblical and practical. This might seem obvious to you, but not all scholars share these values. Many institutions make little room for the Bible in their approach to either systematic or practical theology. When an institution does not view the Bible as God's inerrant and authoritative word, it tends to approach systematic theology as an exercise in analysing theological views and theories rather than a disciplined study of the Bible's teachings. Similarly, it tends to approach practical theology as a pragmatic exercise, permitting theses that closely resemble the social sciences in that they are exclusively empirical in design.

We favour a Bible-based approach to all theology. While we value both the writings of scholars and the findings of empirical research, we consider these subordinate to the revealed truth of the word of God. For us, therefore, systematic theology is first and foremost a study of what God has revealed about a particular topic. Similarly, practical theology is first and foremost an investigation of how the truth of God's word applies to the real-life circumstances and problems we encounter in the world.

We also embrace an approach to theology that emphasises its practical application for the church and the believer. Therefore, all three models move from theory to practice, from doctrine to application, from belief to behaviour, from ideas to implications. This is not the norm for postgraduate theological research. Rarely do theses in the domains of systematic theology and biblical studies make a serious attempt to apply their exegetical or doctrinal findings to churches or believers. Because we believe that God, his kingdom and his word are applicable to every area of life and that his teachings are given to meet human needs, we strongly encourage every thesis to deal with 'significance and suggestions'.

The timeframe. If you are writing a thesis or conducting funded research, your proposal must include a proposed timeframe for completing each phase of the study. This serves as a kind of contract between student and supervisor or between researcher and funder.

In the vast majority of cases, master's and doctoral students grossly underestimate the time it will take to complete their research. When you draft a research proposal, allow more time than you think you will need for each step. Full-time students should be able to complete full master's thesis in 1–2 years,[1] and a doctoral dissertation in 2–3 years. The averages for part-time students are 3–4 years for the master's and 4–6 years for the doctorate. We suggest you assume it will take you towards the upper end of these averages and spread out your proposed dates accordingly. If you finish faster than proposed, nobody will complain.

The presentation. In your research proposal, the research design section should begin with a brief description of the type of study, followed by a chapter outline with dates and notes attached. These elements should be included:

- The type of research being undertaken
- The steps and their sequence
- The nature of the data involved (literary or empirical)
- The chapter outline with brief notes
- The proposed dates of completion

Here is a possible design section for a thesis addressing the question, 'How should churches in Swaziland minister to polygamous families which join the church?'

Research Design

The proposed study falls within the field of practical theology. Solving the main problem will require four major steps. First, the study will describe the challenges that cultural practices related to polygamy pose to churches in Swaziland. Then, it will examine how churches currently handle these challenges. Next, it will present biblical principles Swazi pastors should bear in mind when ministering to polygamous families. Finally, it will conclude with some practical guidelines for pastors to implement.

The study will contain both literary and empirical components. There is little written material available on steps 1 and 2, so the researcher will gather these data through empirical means. Step 3 requires a literary approach, analysing selected texts that have relevance to ministry in polygamous settings.

The thesis will require six chapters. Here is a proposed outline with intended dates of completion:

1) *Introduction* (Mar. 2009). The introduction will present the research problem and the research plan.

2) *The challenges of ministering in polygamous settings* (Dec. 2009). The study must begin with an understanding of the challenges of ministering in the Swazi culture.

3) *The current approaches of Swazi pastors* (Feb. 2010). The next logical step is to document and evaluate current approaches to the challenges.

---

1. This applies to situations in which the entire master's degree is based on a thesis of approximately 50,000 words. Reduce the time by half if your thesis is more in the order of 20,000–25,000 words.

4) *Biblical principles for ministering in polygamous settings* (Aug. 2010). Thereafter, a detailed analysis of the biblical principles relating to polygamy and ministry to those who practise it is needed.

5) *Biblical, ministerial model for Swazi pastors* (Nov. 2010). In the light of the data presented in chapters 2–4, the researcher will attempt to develop a model for ministering to polygamous families in Swaziland.

6) *Conclusion* (Dec. 2010). The final chapter will summarise the research and make suggestions for pastors in Swaziland.

The design section, as this example illustrates, gives a comprehensive outline of the process the researcher will follow, without going into detail about *exactly how* he will do each step. The methodology section answers the question, how exactly will you do each step?

The Methodology

In the design section, you presented a broad overview of the steps necessary to solve the research problem. Now, in the methodology section, you take each step in turn and describe *exactly how* you plan to do it. You need to describe each step in sufficient detail so that, by the end of the study, others can confirm that you did what you promised to do and did it properly.

The results of your research will be judged on one criterion above all others – how well you choose and implement your methodology. Did you choose appropriate methods to solve your research problem? Did you implement your chosen methods consistently and competently? If you commit yourself to a diachronic approach, examiners will ask whether you really did a diachronic study. If you promise to exegete key texts, they will check that you did proper exegesis. If you undertake a descriptive survey, did you use proper data collection and analysis techniques?

The best way to do the methodology section of a research proposal is to take each step in the research design and explain exactly how you plan to do it. For each step, you should discuss *the data* you need and *the tools* you will use.

The Tools

What we are calling tools, others called methodologies (plural). It is important to distinguish between research methodologies (tools) and your methodology.

Research methodologies are proven ways of solving certain problems. They are like tools in a toolbox. If you are building a cabinet, at different stages you will use different tools (saw, screwdriver, hammer, pliers). Each tool was designed for a particular task. In the same way, a researcher has a toolbox with a variety of methodologies – tried and tested methods of solving particular problems. An expert researcher has mastered the art of knowing when and how to employ each tool to solve problems.

Your methodology is a description of the steps you will take to solve your particular problem. Drawing from your toolkit of methodologies, you will select and use appropriate tools for each step. In your methodology, you must describe which tools you will use, as well as when, how and why you will use them. You may use many different methodologies in your methodology or you may use only one or two. You must select and use the appropriate tools for each task.

You can only use tools you own. Similarly, you can only employ methodologies if you are aware of them. Therefore, we shall quickly present a whirlwind survey of some of the methodologies (tools) commonly used in theological research. This survey is not intended to be complete. We just want to give you an idea of the kinds of hammers, chisels, spanners, saws and screwdrivers in a research toolbox.

Methodologies used primarily in conceptual argumentation. The methodologies here are different ways of engaging conceptual literature in a philosophical debate. Regardless of the field of study, your research could draw on a variety of these at different stages. These include:

- *Dialogical:* simply engaging in dialogue with different authors' viewpoints.
- *Comparative:* comparing different views, analysing their similarities and differences.
- *Complementary:* harmonising different theories or views by moulding them into a single, logically coherent whole.
- *Epistemological:* critiquing the philosophical foundation on which a theory or an argument is based.
- *Polemical:* arguing for or against a particular viewpoint.
- *Analytical:* breaking down a theory or a concept into its logical components or constituents.
- *Synthetic:* putting together previously unrelated concepts or components to form a new entity (theory, model).

Methodologies used primarily in biblical exegesis. The methodologies here are examples of interpretive tools used in the exegesis of Bible passages. You may need to use several of these tools when engaging the biblical text.

- *Textual criticism:* reconstructing the original text by weighting variant readings.
- *Historical criticism:* reconstructing the history of the text or the history in the text.
- *Lexical analysis:* conducting word studies on key words.
- *Syntax analysis:* analysing the grammar of the text.
- *Discourse analysis:* analysing the discourse features showing the flow and coherence of a pericope.
- *Structural analysis:* examining the literary and semantic structure of a text.
- *Source criticism:* analysing and/or reconstructing the sources an author used.
- *Form criticism:* examining the literary forms and the life-settings in which they were used.

- *Redaction criticism:* exploring the theological message of a text.
- *Rhetorical criticism:* studying the literary artistry or rational argument of a text.

Many of these tools are defined and deployed differently by varying schools of theology. The presuppositions of the user can dramatically affect how the tool is used. Therefore, it may be necessary to indicate how you define and apply some of these tools.

Methodologies used primarily in field research. The methodologies listed here are ways of gathering primary data. Each method is susceptible to misuse, so you should be sure you understand how to use a method correctly when you elect to employ it in your study.

- *Questionnaire*: a series of written questions a researcher supplies to subjects, requesting their response. Different kinds of questions solicit different types of data (for example, open or closed questions, quantitative or qualitative questions).
- *Interview*: a series of questions a researcher addresses personally to respondents. The interview can be structured or unstructured. As with questionnaires, different questions solicit different kinds of data.
- *Survey*: a statistical tool designed to provide a broad overview of a representative sample of a large population.
- *Case study*: the collection and presentation of detailed information about a particular participant, looking intensely at an individual or small participant pool, drawing conclusions only about that participant or group and only in that specific context.
- *Observation*: in fieldwork, observation occurs when the researcher observes the subjects; in *participant observation*, a researcher systematically observes people while joining in their activities; in *action research*, a researcher observes without participating.
- *Focus group*: a group discussion to solicit views about a focus area.

We shall discuss some of these empirical methods in more detail in later chapters. However, using them properly in complex studies may require more specialised training than we can provide here. If necessary, we urge you to read works offering specialised guidance on these methods.

We must emphasise that all these methodologies are simply *the tools of the trade.* Just as a handyman uses a variety of tools to complete a job, so too the researcher uses various methodologies at different stages of a study.

The Data

You must address all critical questions relating to the data you will use. Here are some examples:

- What data do you need?
- If they already exist, how will you access them?
- If they do not exist, how will you collect them?
- How do you intend to analyse and interpret them?

For the literary components of your study, you should list the primary and major secondary sources you plan to use and how you intend to use them. For empirical components, you should address matters such as the nature and scope of the population, the selection of sampling techniques, data collection instruments and techniques, data analysis and interpretation and any other aspects of significance (see ch. 17 for a detailed description of survey research).

We turn now to how you should present your methodology in the research proposal.

The Presentation

When you write up the methodology section of your proposal, describe your methodology for each stage of the study. In an orderly, step-by-step fashion, explain what you will do to solve the problem. Discuss the data and the tools. Defend your choice of methods for each step by explaining your rationale. The crucial thing is to use the right tool for each job, to employ appropriate methodologies for each aspect of the research project.

By way of example, let's consider the example study on how to minister to polygamous families in Swaziland. How exactly would we do the first phase of the study, describing the challenges Swazi pastors face ministering in a polygamous culture? Unless someone has previously conducted a similar study, the data probably do not exist, so the researcher will need to collect them herself. How will she do it? Should she use questionnaires, interviews or focus groups? Whichever tool (or tools) she chooses, whose views should she survey (for example, pastors, elders, missionaries, members, polygamists)? How many (per group) will comprise the sample? Will the sample be representative of the population? What data will be solicited? How will the integrity of the data be insured? How will the data be analysed? These are the kinds of questions the methodology section should address.

Turning to the chapter on the biblical principles, what sources will be used? Will she conduct a diachronic (across time) survey of biblical passages that touch on the study topic? Will she do detailed exegesis of selected texts? If so, which texts and what exegetical steps will be used? Are there existing studies that can serve as the point of departure for this section? If so, what are they and how will the researcher engage them (for example, dialogue, synthesis, comparison)?

What we are trying to illustrate is that for each major division of the study, the researcher should describe the steps she intends to follow in as much detail as possible. The last section of the research plan is an annotated bibliography. Let's discuss it briefly.

The Bibliography

Research requires mastering existing literature on your chosen topic. Your research proposal needs to show that you have done a significant amount of preliminary reading – you have scanned the field and read some key works. You can show your preliminary reading by including an annotated bibliography with at least twenty entries.

What is an annotated bibliography? Whereas a simple bibliography lists the works cited or consulted, an annotated bibliography adds a one- or two-sentence explanation of why the work is relevant to the research topic. From the annotation, it should be clear why the work cited will be a valuable resource for the study. Here is a sample annotated bibliography for an exegetical thesis on Psalm 3:

> Kselman, John S. 'Psalm 3: A Structural and Literary Study.' *Catholic Biblical Quarterly* 49 (1987): 572–580. This article analyses the structural markers in the Hebrew text of Psalm 3, critiques various views of the psalm's structure and proposes a new structural interpretation.
>
> Sarna, N. M. 'Legal Terminology in Psalm 3:8.' Pages 171–181 in *Shaarei Talmon,* edited by M. Fishbane and E. Tov. Winona Lake: Eisenbrauns, 1992. Sarna examines the terminology in Psalm 3:8, noting its legal connotations. His article is helpful for evaluating the main theme(s) of the psalm.
>
> Terrien, Samuel L. *The Psalms: Strophic Structure and Theological Commentary.* Grand Rapids: Eerdmans, 2003. This is a major commentary on the Book of Psalms. Terrien's greatest contribution lies in his analysis of each psalm's structure and flow of thought.

What common mistakes do students make when compiling the bibliography in a thesis proposal? In dealing with our students, we often encounter these mistakes regularly:

- *Outdated works.* The majority of entries should be from the last 10–15 years. The dates are among the first things we look at when we skim the bibliography in a research proposal. We do not want to see the majority of entries from the 1960s. Entries older than twenty-five years should be seminal works in the field.
- *Popular works.* A thesis is a piece of theological *research*. It needs to engage with academic literature, which is the product of research. Popular and devotional books (as opposed to academic sources) express the opinions and experiences of the author, but those views may not be well researched. The majority of works should be academic resources.
- *Irrelevant works.* Students often fill up their bibliography by listing resources unrelated to the proposed research topic. If your thesis topic is 'the work of the Holy Spirit in Luke's gospel', do not list Steven Covey's *Seven Habits of Highly Effective People* in the bibliography. When we see this, we immediately suspect you have been too lazy to do a proper job and are listing works for the sake of reaching twenty entries.
- *General works.* Try to include as many specialised books and articles as possible. Although one-volume commentaries, Bible dictionaries or systematic theology textbooks may prove helpful during the study, specialised works are more valuable. For a thesis proposal on Psalm 3, Kselman's article on the structure of Psalm 3 is more helpful than *The New Bible Commentary.*

If your topic touches on several major areas, your bibliography should include entries relevant to each major part. If you are researching leadership in the Salvation Army in

South Africa, your bibliography should not be limited to titles on leadership. There should be some dealing with the Salvation Army, especially the Army in South Africa.

Our seminary requires that all research proposals include an annotated bibliography with at least twenty entries. This is a minimum. For certain topics, the supervisor may require additional preliminary reading, especially at the doctoral level. For the works included, he wants to see recent, relevant, specialised, academic works. Resist the temptation to pad your bibliography with outdated, irrelevant, general, popular titles.

A word of advice – *start compiling your thesis bibliography from day one!* Each time you consult a book or an article, add it to your bibliography. Writing the bibliography is frustrating at the best of times, but if you leave it to the end of the process, it can be almost impossible. We recommend that you open a file on your computer called 'Bibliography' and update it every time you find a new source.

13

Biblical Exegesis

Biblical exegesis is an in-depth, inductive examination of Scripture in which the exegete systematically applies established hermeneutic tools (exegetical methods) to discover the meaning and implications of a text of biblical text. Serious exegesis meets all the criteria of research. The object of enquiry is the biblical text. Exegetical methods are research methods. The objective is to resolve an interpretive problem in the text to determine its meaning and significance.

Although this chapter offers some guidelines for an exegetical procedure, its goal is to provide a framework for doing exegesis as theological research. For detailed treatment of exegetical procedures, students should consult some of the many excellent exegetical guides.

Presuppositions of Evangelical Exegesis

As interpreters, we all approach the biblical text with a set of presuppositions that govern our exegesis. Since these presuppositions influence our exegesis, we should state them openly. My hermeneutic presuppositions influence the method presented in this chapter. If your views differ significantly from mine, you should still find the chapter helpful, but you may need to adapt it. These are my convictions:

1) The Scriptures are the inspired word of God and are inerrant in the autographs.

2) The primary goal of biblical interpretation is to discover the author-intended meaning, that is, the message the Holy Spirit led the human author to convey to the original readers. Furthermore, the Holy Spirit guided the writing process to ensure the intended message is faithfully communicated in writing.[1]

3) Each text has one primary author-intended meaning; therefore, each passage can have only one correct interpretation. I reject all forms of *sensus plenior*

---

1. In ordinary communication, this is often not true. What we say may not accurately represent what we intend to communicate. Because the Holy Spirit superintended the writing of the scriptures, he ensured that the human authors wrote exactly what he intended.

(multiple meanings), especially the idea that the text can mean something to us that it could never have meant to its original readers.

4) The Bible should be interpreted literally, that is, at face value according to the normal rules of communication. For this reason, I favour grammatical-historical exegesis.

5) Although a text has only one meaning, it may have many valid applications. The applications derive from the one meaning; they are concrete applications of the same timeless truth.

6) Exegesis must be relevant and valuable to today's believers. To complete his work, an exegete must move from interpretation to application, from the past to the present, from the there-and-then to the here-and-now.

These convictions underlie my approach to exegetical studies. If your presuppositions differ significantly, you may need to adjust the model I am about to present.

Design for an Exegetical Study

Whether it is a 10-page term paper, a 100-page thesis, or a 300-page dissertation, an exegetical study has five main parts: (1) introduction, (2) context, (3) meaning, (4) significance, and (5) conclusion. In a term paper, these would be sections of the paper. In a thesis, each might be one chapter. In a dissertation, each part could require several chapters.

Section 1: The Introduction

The opening section provides framework for the study. It covers such elements as the boundaries of the passage, the reason for selecting it, problems in the text, scholarly views (short literature review) on the passage and its problems, a brief description of the research approach and an overview of the remainder of the study.

- *The passage*. Explain your reasons for choosing the text and how you delimited its boundaries.
- *The objectives*. The general objective of exegesis is to expose the meaning and significance of the biblical text. If your exegesis will focus on particular exegetical problems in the text, describe them; your objective will be to solve these problems.
- *The perspectives*. Summarise the major scholarly perspectives on the text, especially different approaches and alternate solutions to exegetical problems.
- *The plan*. Preview the remainder of the study, describing the approach, methodology and structure.

Section 2: The Context

This part deals with all aspects relevant to the historical and the literary contexts of the book in which the selected passage is located. Most exegetical studies require a section devoted to the book in which the passage is located. This section should cover whichever of these elements are relevant to the research:

- *The general background of the book.* The general background encompasses issues related to the *authorship, date* and *audience* (recipients) of the book. Unless these matters are crucial to the argument, they can be addressed briefly in the thesis.
- *The historical context of the book.* The historical context relates primarily to the quest for the *occasion* and *purpose* of the book. A secondary aspect of this section is to explain any aspects of the historical setting (milieu) of the book that are crucial to understanding its message.
- *The literary context of the book.* At this level, the literary context has to do with the book's *structure* and *argument* (that is, flow of thought). How an interpreter understands the overall structure and argument of the book has an influence on how he understands the meaning of the passage.
- *The theological themes of the book.* For some studies, a survey of the major *themes* and *motifs* of the book is necessary. In particular, this section should analyse what the whole book teaches about themes relevant to the focal point of the selected passage.

Section 3: The Meaning

This section is the heart of the exegetical study, consisting of an in-depth analysis of the text.

1) *Preliminary analysis.* The preliminary exegetical work entails two main tasks: analyse textual variants and translate the passage.
    - *Textual criticism.* Examine textual variants and discuss any meaningful ones.
    - *Translation.* If you are familiar with the original language, it is valuable to produce your own translation of the passage. Where difficult translation decisions have to be made, the translation should include notes explaining the problem, listing translation options and motivating the choice. If you are unable to produce your own translation, you may substitute by comparing various good translations. Write out the text of the translation you will be

using as your main text together with notes discussing significant alternate renderings.[2]

2) *Contextual analysis.* Study the immediate historical and literary context of your pericope. You should give due attention to whichever of these aspects of the pericope context are relevant:
   - *Historical setting.* Determine the underlying historical occasion the author was addressing and analyse any historical or cultural allusions in the text.
   - *Literary context.* Examine attention to the literary context of the passage, which includes the immediate context, the book context and the canonical context.

3) *Verbal analysis.* Investigate the actual words in the passage, their meaning (lexical analysis) and relationships (grammatical analysis).
   - *Lexical.* Analyse the meaning of key words and phrases to discover their significance in the text.
   - *Grammatical.* Examine any significant grammatical features in the passage (for example, verb tenses, genitive phrases, conditional clauses, and so on).

4) *Literary analysis.* Examine the literary features of the passage to determine their influence on the meaning of the passage. Under the banner of literary features, we include:
   - *Genre.* Identify the general and specific genre of the passage and how it influences the interpretation of the text; for example, if the text is Matthew 8:18–22, the general genre is 'gospel', while the specific genre is 'pronouncement story'.
   - *Structure.* Analyse the relationship between parts of the passage; techniques such as sentence diagrams or semantic structure analyses are helpful.
   - *Composition.* For some texts and some studies, matters relating to traditions, sources, redaction and life-settings require investigation.
   - *Rhetoric.* Examine the stylistic features of the text that may influence its meaning; these include compositional techniques such as figures of speech, repeated words, catch phrases and markers of emphasis.

5) *Exegetical synthesis.* In this section, you should begin to pull together your exegetical findings. The primary question you want to answer here is this: What was the author trying to communicate to his readers through the text? To answer this question, you might need to answer such questions as these:
   - What are the major concerns or issues the passage addresses?
   - What is the impact of the combination of genre, literary devices and structure on the meaning of the passage?

---

2. The translation is usually done in two phases. At the start of your study, produce a provisional translation. Then, after you have conducted an in-depth study, go back and refine the translation in the light of your observations.

- What is the relationship between the motifs and the concerns of the passage?
- What is the relation of these motifs and concerns to the historical setting of the book?

Section 4: The Significance

No exegetical thesis is complete until it addresses the contemporary significance of the passage, answering the question: What difference does it make? This section may explore two kinds of significance: (1) theology and (2) application.

1) *Theology: the doctrinal significance of the passage.* Here the thesis should expound what the passage teaches us (a) about God, (b) about creation (especially ourselves), and (c) the relationship between God and creation.
    - What universal truths (principles) does the passage teach?
    - How does it harmonise with the whole teaching of Scripture?
    - What contribution does it make to Christian doctrines?

2) *Application: the practical significance of the passage.* The study should make *at least one application* of the passage to contemporary Christianity. The application should focus on the central idea in the exposition of the passage.
    - Identify the target group at which you will aim your application. Then give attention to how you can (a) explain the original meaning of the text to them and (b) help them connect with the truths in the text.
    - Identify how the text applies to today's situation. The focus may be upon (a) the life of the individual Christian and/or (b) the life and ministry of the church.

In many institutions, exegetical studies do not include a major section on the significance of the text. Students may leave the research in the there-and-then without building bridges to the here-and-now. In our opinion, exegesis is not complete until it links the biblical text with the real work, the past with the present, allowing the ancient message to speak to our modern context. Since not all professors require (or even desire) this component, we recommend you ask your professor what he expects.

Section 5: The Conclusion

The conclusion may or may not be a separate section of the study. In some exegetical studies, the section about 'significance' *is* the conclusion. It briefly summarises the exegetical findings, then closes with a discussion of the significance (doctrinal and/or practical) of those findings. In other studies, the conclusion is a separate, short section summarising the problem, process and findings of the study and possibly proposing further research.

Writing Up an Exegetical Study

How should you write up an exegetical study? The answer depends somewhat on the length of the study. The exegetical design presented above outlines the logic of the study and the elements that typically fall under each main section, but it does not dictate the outline of the study. The most common way to organise the report on an exegetical study is what we call the commentary structure.

The Commentary Structure

This approach moves through the passage verse by verse, presenting relevant exegetical insights as they occur in the pericope. It needs an introduction section and a section discussing the overarching background issues, but it presents most of the exegetical details in the verse-by-verse discussion. The commentary integrates the historical, cultural, redactional, grammatical, lexical and other types of observations. It may discuss the significance (doctrinal and practical) within the commentary or in a separate section.

An exegetical study can be organised under the following categories:

1. Introduction
    1.1. The Passage
    1.2. The Problems
    1.3. The Perspectives
2. Context of the Book
    2.1. General Background: Author, Date and Audience
    2.2. Historical Context: Occasion, Purpose and Milieu
    2.3. Literary Structure: Structure and Argument
    2.4. Theological: Themes and Motifs
3. Exegesis of the Passage
    3.1. Text and Translation
        Present the working translation of the text (your own or an existing one) followed by notes discussing relevant textual variants and translation alternatives.
    3.2. Meaning for the Original Readers
        Move through the text verse by verse discussing all the points relevant to its meaning, such as key words, grammar, customs, geography, rhetoric, redaction, and so on.
    3.3. Significance for Today's Readers
4. Conclusion
5. Bibliography

An alternative to a commentary arrangement is a topical arrangement. This is less popular, but well suited to certain studies.

The Topical Structure

An alternative structure, a topical outline, uses each step in the exegetical process as a heading (or, in longer studies, a chapter). So, for example, under *grammatical analysis* you discuss all-important grammatical features; composition might be discussed under a heading such as *redaction criticism*. The name 'topical outline' derives from the fact that the analysis of the text is discussed under topics or in categories.

These could serve as the headings for a topical study:

1. Introduction
2. Text and Translation
3. Exegetical Analysis
4. Contemporary Significance
5. Conclusion
6. Bibliography

The body of the study falls under the heading 'exegetical analysis' on the outline. This section presents exegetical data arranged under headings that represent steps in the exegetical process. The nature of the study dictates which headings are included. Any exegetical process might be used as a heading (for example, lexical analysis, grammatical analysis, form criticism, literary context, discourse features, historical context, and so on).

In general, the commentary method is a better way to present an exegetical study. The student should default to the commentary approach unless there is a good reason for preferring a topic arrangement.

Summary

Exegesis is a form of research. Its general objective is to uncover the text's author-intended meaning for the original readers and its significance for today's church. On occasion, its specific objective is to solve a particular interpretive problem in the passage. To achieve these objectives, it deploys a variety of exegetical methods as its research methods.

A detailed exegetical analysis of the chosen pericope lies at the heart of exegetical research. Preliminary study of the book in which the passage is located lays a foundation for the exegesis, while exploring its doctrinal and/or practical significance links the exegesis to the present.

There are two acceptable ways of writing up an exegetical study, namely, the commentary style and the topic approach. The commentary method proceeds verse by verse, presenting exegetical observations as they relate to the text. The topical approach arranges the main body of the study under topical headings.

Section 1: Introduction

Section 2: Context

Book of the Bible
General Background
Historical Context
Literary Context
Theological Themes

Section 3: Biblical Evidence

Preliminary Analysis	Literary Analysis	Verbal Analysis
Textual Criticism	Genre	Lexical
Translation	Structure	Grammatical
	Rhetoric	

Exegetical Synthesis
What the author was trying to say

Section 4: Contemporary Significance

Theology:	Application:
Doctrinal Significance	Practical Significance

Section 5: Conclusion

Figure 32: Design for an Exegetical Study

14

Systematic Theology

For evangelicals,[1] systematic theology is *a systematic study of what the Bible teaches about a topic*. Can we justly call doing systematic theology *research*? The answer depends on *how* we do it, the method we use. If we begin with the presupposition that the task of theology is to systematise the teachings of Scripture, the manner in which we proceed should meet all the criteria of research. In this chapter, we shall discuss the presuppositions and steps of evangelical systematic theology. Based on these presuppositions and steps, we shall present two models for doing evangelical theology.

Presuppositions of Evangelical Theology

The point of departure for evangelical theology is the conviction that the Bible is God's full and final revelation. Three vital presuppositions of evangelical theology derive from this conviction. First, God has spoken in his word. Since we have an inspired, inerrant, authoritative, sufficient word from God, our task is to identify and summarise what it teaches. Second, as a corollary to this, because the word of God comes from the mind of God, it forms a harmonious whole, without inner contradictions (provided we interpret it correctly). Third, although the Bible's teaching is a coherent whole, it does evidence progressive development over time. Progressive revelation implies that each new revelation builds on the foundation of earlier revelation on the same topic.

The evangelical approach to systematic theology differs vastly from the liberal approach. Because liberal theologians do not begin with the assumption that God has spoken authoritatively in Scripture, they have to resort to speculation. Lacking a solid, objective point of departure, their theological method amounts to little more than creative speculation as to what God might be like. Theology thus degenerates into a subjective, conceptual comparison of what others, whether ancient writers or recent theologians, have written.

---

1. Evangelical (conservative) scholars approach systematic theology differently to their liberal counterparts. Our approach reflects conservative presuppositions. We use the term 'evangelical theology' with the meaning 'systematic theology practised in a conservative, evangelical manner'.

By taking as its starting assumption the fact that God has spoken in his word, evangelical systematic theology can proceed in a truly scientific manner. Ware explains that a two-fold process lies at the heart of the scientific method, namely, (a) data collection by observation and (b) theory construction.[2] As a physicist gathers data by observing experiments and proceeds to formulate a theory to explain all the data in a harmonious way, so a systematic theologian gathers data by careful exegesis of the biblical text (observation) and develops a theory to account for all the data. Like every other science, systematic theology 'moves beyond inductive itemisation to the synthesis of theory construction'.[3]

Steps in Evangelical Theology

The task of the systematic theologian is to construct a model that accounts for what all the relevant Scriptures teach about a topic. This task requires four steps.

Step 1: Identify All the Scriptures That Address the Topic

This is a crucial preliminary step. If your research is to be credible, it needs to account for *all* the relevant data. If you omit certain texts, their implications may alter or discredit your theory. A pitfall to avoid is selecting Scriptures that support your preferred outcome and overlooking those that challenge it.

The scope of many research projects does not permit an exhaustive inductive study of all the Scriptures addressing a topic. If there is a large body of biblical materials to cover or if you are writing a short paper, you should delimit your study. There are several ways to do this. For example, instead of covering all Scriptures on the deity of Christ, you could limit your study to those that call him 'God' (Greek, *theos*) or you could limit your study to cover only the pastoral epistles.

Step 2: Analyse Each Scripture to Determine Its Meaning

The objective of this stage is to permit each Scripture to speak for itself, that is, to mean whatever the original author intended. To achieve this goal, you need to conduct an inductive, exegetical study of each selected text. This corresponds to the observation stage of the scientific method, gathering the raw data from which you will construct your theory.

Exegesis is the bedrock of theology. Your theology will never be better than your exegesis. If your analysis of the individual texts is flawed, your interpretation of all the

---

2. Bruce Ware, 'Method of Evangelical Theology,' *BiblicalTraining.org* (2001; retrieved 25 March 2008, http://www.biblicaltraining.org/class.php?class=TH503).

3. Ibid.

data, your final theological model, will also be flawed. For this reason, if you want to do theology, you must develop your exegetical skills. In particular, learn Hebrew and Greek. We marvel at the number of aspiring systematic theologians who consider learning the biblical languages unimportant. If theology must be built on exegesis – as it surely must – learning the languages is not optional.

When you have completed your exegetical study of a text, state its teaching about the topic in propositional form, either as a single proposition or a series of them. Reducing each text's contribution to propositions lays a good platform for the next step.

Step 3: Deduce Timeless Principles Taught by Groups of Scriptures

After you have completed your exegetical study of each text and stated its contribution to the topic in propositional form, the next step is to reduce the mass of data to a limited number of timeless truths (propositions). The objective of this step is to deduce the major truths; that is, to group the many data into categories and summarise them as generalisations. Based on the individual observations (inductively observed facts), we deduce necessary generalisations. This process is called deduction.

Ware illustrates the process with the doctrine of the Trinity. When all the exegesis is complete, four main truths emerge from the data:

1) There is one God.

2) The Father is God.

3) The Son is God.

4) The Spirit is God.[4]

These four truths are deduced from the mass of biblical evidence. However, they do not yet represent a full-fledged doctrine, because they do not indicate how the four truths relate to each other. Therefore, the theologian's task cannot end here. He must develop a model that explains how they relate.

Step 4: Construct a Theory to Account for All the Relevant Data

Step 3 leaves you with a minimum number of major truths derived from exegesis of the key texts. The last step is to construct a theory or a model that accounts for all the data in a unified way. Ware calls this process *retroduction*, which he describes as looking at the data and asking how we can best make sense of it.[5] He quotes John Warwick Montgomery's definition of retroduction:

---

4. Ware, 'Method of Evangelical Theology', lecture.
5. Retroduction is also called abduction.

> Retroduction is the creative ordering of relevant data into a conceptual fabric that exposes the relationships among those data in a way that enhances their native meanings.

The goal is to formulate a conceptual model that accounts for all the data and clarifies the relationships between them. Such a model enhances the native meanings of the data making the links between them clear. The Christian doctrine of the Trinity is a theological construct that goes far beyond the four main propositions (see above). Understanding how the statements are simultaneously true and appreciating the relationships between the persons of the Trinity greatly enhances our grasp of the data.

Constructing a viable theological model is an iterative process. First examine the data and formulate a tentative theory to account for it all. Then return to the data and ask if the proposed understanding does justice to it. Does it account for all the data? Does it elucidate the relationships between the data? Is it logically consistent? If the answer to any of these questions is 'no', you must re-examine the data. As you re-examine it, you either modify your original theory or construct a different model.

Data do not dictate their own interpretation. Different theological systems emerge because alternate models are proposed to account for the data. The Calvinist and Arminian views on election represent two completely different models for explaining the same data. Postmillennialism, amillennialism and premillennialism present three synopses of the biblical data regarding the millennium. The task of a systematic theologian is to analyse the data as objectively as possible and develop a model that best accounts for all the data, elucidating how they fit together.

How do we put all these pieces together into a working design for a research project in systematic theology? We are going to offer two models. In the next section, we shall propose a basic model for systematic theology. The basic model attempts to cover all the texts in the selected corpus, whether it is the entire canon or a part of it. In the following section, we shall offer an alternate model that anchors the study in a single, major text of Scripture.

Basic Design for Evangelical Theology

In essence, the basic model has five logical divisions, each of which form a main section of the study (see Figure 33).

Section 1: Introduction

The introduction states the 'what', the 'why' and the 'how' of the study. Under the banner of the what, it states the problem, key questions, delimitations and hypothesis. The why section indicates the value of the study. The how part describes the methodology and concludes with a preview of the flow of the study.

Section 2: Current Views

The study needs to be conducted with a thorough understanding of existing research on the topic. This section offers a clear, objective description of each of the major current views on the issue under investigation.

Typically, the treatment of each view should cover such elements as:

- *Key scholars and their works.* Base the presentation of each view on the writings of its most significant contributors. Wherever possible, demonstrate first-hand familiarity with the writings of the most important advocates of the view. Your description should not be based on second-hand reports of their beliefs (translations of foreign-language works are acceptable). Furthermore, while it is appropriate to include seminal works by older theologians, the focus should be on *current views* as expressed in recently published books and articles.
- *Definitions, descriptions and debates.* You should clearly define and describe each major view. You should also expose the main points of debate surrounding it, including the presuppositions on which it is based.
- *Arguments and counter-arguments.* You should state the main arguments used in support of each view and how the view counters objections. As used here, 'counter-arguments' refers to arguing in favour of the view by answering objections and criticisms to it. (The arguments *against* each view are usually presented as part of the argument for the alternate views.)
- *Scriptural interpretation.* Where relevant, the description of each view should indicate how its advocates interpret the Scriptures, both their general approach to the Scriptures and their specific handling of important passages.
- *Strengths and weaknesses.* A critique of the obvious strengths and weaknesses of each view needs to be built into this section in an appropriate manner. We say *obvious* strengths and weaknesses because you have not yet done the study, so you are not yet qualified to comment beyond the level of what is self-evident.

We do not intend these bullets as headings. They indicate the ingredients that form part of the recipe for a good description of a current view. You must mix the ingredients properly.

Naturally, you are free to delimit the perspectives you cover in this section. For example, if covering an ethical issue such as abortion, you may need to include all views (both Christian and non-Christian perspectives). Alternatively, when analysing certain issues, you may wish to delimit the study to focus on the perspectives within a particular faith community (for example, Pentecostal or Reformed).

In the field of systematic theology, the description of current views will *usually* be based on literary sources; however, this is not necessarily the case. There is no reason why this section cannot incorporate empirical research (fieldwork) to discover the current views of a particular community. For example, if you were researching the beliefs of Baptist pastors in Cameroon regarding the inspiration of the Scriptures, you might draw your data from published works, denominational archives and surveys or interviews with Baptist pastors.

The summary of existing views on the topic sets the stage for your own in-depth analysis of the issues, which necessarily begins with an exegetical study of the biblical texts addressing the topic.

Section 3: Biblical Evidence

The next major section of the research consists of a thorough inductive analysis of the relevant biblical texts. This phase of the study constitutes the bulk of the study. In a thesis or dissertation, it may require several chapters. The process itself divides logically into two distinct phases: induction and deduction. The *induction* phase consists of an exegetical study of each text touching on the topic. When it is complete, you will have a mass of isolated data. The *deduction* phase reduces this mass of isolated data into a few generalisations, that is, into the smallest possible number of propositions.

Induction: Exegesis of Passages

As a Christian committed to developing a biblical worldview, you must strive to build your theology exegetically. This step calls for you to identify and analyse all the relevant biblical texts. The number of texts and the level of the study will determine how deep the exegesis needs to be. However, unlike when doing an exegetical study, it is not necessary to document every stage of your exegesis. You may report only the results of your exegetical study, commenting on the relevant aspects of the text as they relate to the topic of the research.

Deduction: Extraction of Propositions

The exegesis will leave you with a host of data, all tied to the truth implications of specific texts. To work with this data in a way that enables you to construct a theory to explain it, you need to reduce it to a manageable number of propositions. Divide the ideas that emerge from the exegetical phase into categories, leaving nothing out. Then formulate propositional statements that encompass all the data in each category. When this process is complete, you will have the key ideas for which you will need to account in your theory construction section.

Section 4: Theory Construction

Once you have analysed the relevant texts (induction) and isolated the key ideas they teach (deduction), you need to put all the data together to form a holistic picture of what the Bible teaches about the issue (retroduction). This is theory construction. Your goal is to construct a model that accounts for all the biblical evidence in a unified manner, making the relationships between the individual data clear. When you have devised a tentative model, go back to all the exegetical data and check that your model adequately accounts for each datum without distorting it. Keep revising your model until it does so.

Every major evangelical systematic theology contains numerous examples of how expert theologians go about this process. What are dichotomy and trichotomy? They are models designed to explain all the biblical evidence regarding the constitution of man. What is the doctrine of the substitutionary atonement? It is a theory attempting to explain all the biblical data on the reason for and significance of Jesus' death. The scholars who write these textbooks have followed the above processes; when you read their books, you are seeing the result of their analysis, their proposed model with a sample of the evidence added as proof texts.

Section 5: Contemporary Significance

The task of theology is not complete, in our opinion, until its significance for today's church and its believers is considered. The final section of the study should explore the contemporary significance of the study. You can do this at two levels, namely, doctrinal and practical.

The entire discussion in this concluding section needs to be overtly and intentionally tied to the main issue driving the research agenda. Do not allow your discussion of the significance of your study to focus on peripheral details. Major on the majors.

For many studies, the volume of biblical data available on the topic combined with the length of the study make the basic model unsuitable. In such cases, the researcher has three options: (a) narrow the topic; (b) reduce the corpus; or (c) use a different design. The alternative design presents a way of handling a large number of texts in a more focused manner than the basic design.

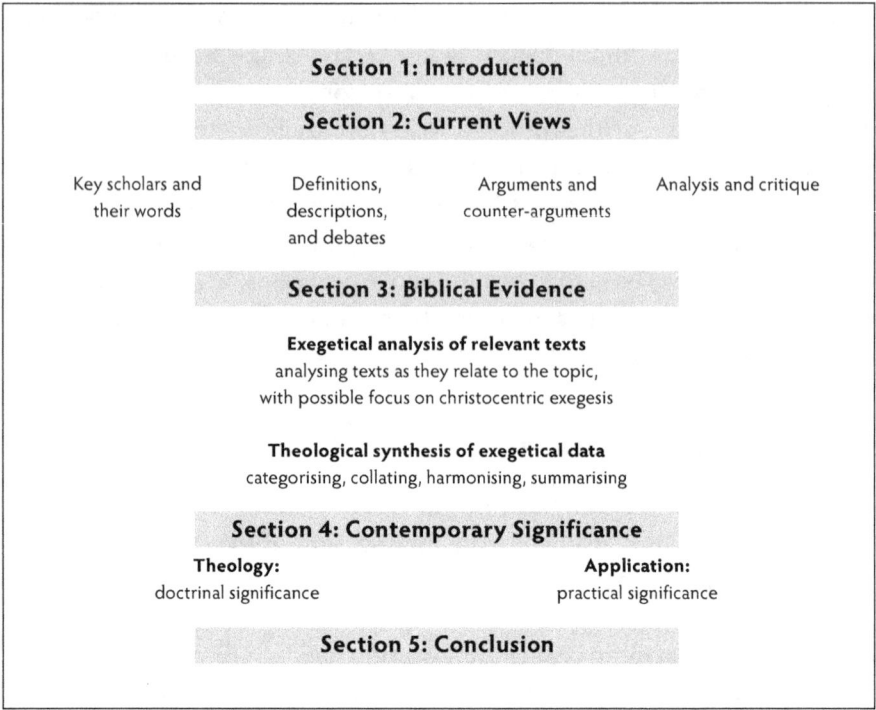

Figure 33: Design for Systematic Theology

Alternate Design for Evangelical Theology

You cannot always conduct a full exegetical study of what the entire Bible teaches about a chosen topic in a single research project because this often requires in-depth exegesis of a large number of texts, a task that is not doable in one study. However, it is possible to conduct an in-depth exegetical study of one or two key texts *and* allow your exegesis to be informed by a thorough survey of other relevant texts. In such cases, the study is anchored in a key passage. Earlier biblical passages are analysed in relation to the *anchor text*; these provide the *informing theology*. Subsequent texts may be analysed for how they elucidate or develop the theme of the anchor text.

Figure 34 on page 148 shows the basic approach. The main biblical text on the topic serves the anchor text. A detailed exegetical analysis of this text lies at the heart of the study. To place the anchor text in its theological context, the study begins with a synopsis of the informing theology, that is, what earlier passages of Scripture have taught to lay a conceptual foundation for the key text. The teaching of the key text is further elucidated by how later texts of Scripture have added to its teaching or applied it. The study closes with a discussion of the contemporary significance of the teaching. Aside from an introduction, these four parts typically constitute the structure of the study. In some cases, you may need to include a chapter on 'current views', identical to the one in the basic design.

Section 1: Introduction

See the corresponding section under 'basic design for evangelical theology'.

Section 2: The Informing Theology[6]

Conduct an exegetical survey of the antecedent biblical texts that form part of the informing theology of the anchor text, leading to a synthesis which systematically summarises the combined teaching of the relevant texts on the issue. Two steps are involved:

Step 1: identify and analyse relevant texts. This step calls for you to identify and analyse all the relevant biblical texts. The number of texts and the level of the study will determine how deep the exegesis needs to be. It is not necessary to document every stage of your exegesis. You may report only the results of your exegetical study, commenting on the relevant aspects of the texts as they relate to the topic of the thesis.

Step 2: synthesise and summarise the overall teaching. Once you have analysed the relevant texts, you need to put all the data together to form a holistic picture. This involves categorising, collating, harmonising and summarising the exegetical data. In short, it is systematising the teachings of texts you analysed. Do all this with an eye on how they impact upon the main research question and the anchor text.

Section 3: The Anchor Text

The heart of the study is a detailed exegetical study of the anchor text, which ought to be a major biblical passage dealing with the topic under investigation. For a detailed description of how to conduct an exegetical study, see the chapter on 'how to do an exegetical study'.

Section 4: The Developing Theology

This section is similar to the one on the informing theology, except that it examines how the key theme is further developed and applied in subsequent biblical passages.

Section 5: The Contemporary Significance

See the corresponding section under the 'basic design for evangelical theology'.

---

6. If a literature review addressing contemporary views is deemed necessary, it will be section 2 and the informing theology will become section 3.

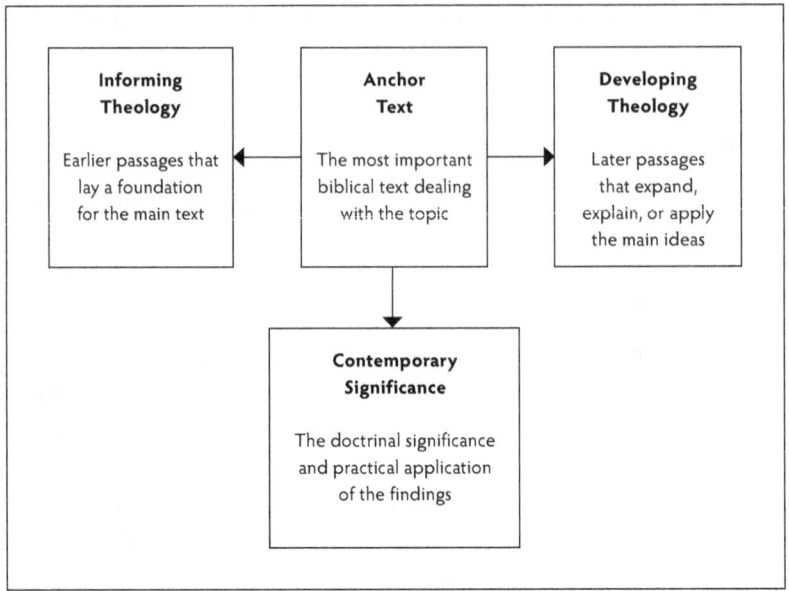

Figure 34: An Alternate Design for a Theological Study

Christopher Peppler uses a variation of this model for what he calls 'christocentric exegesis'. The words and works of Jesus (namely, the gospels) lie at the centre of this model. They are informed by the Old Testament and explained and applied in the remainder of the New Testament (see Figure 35).

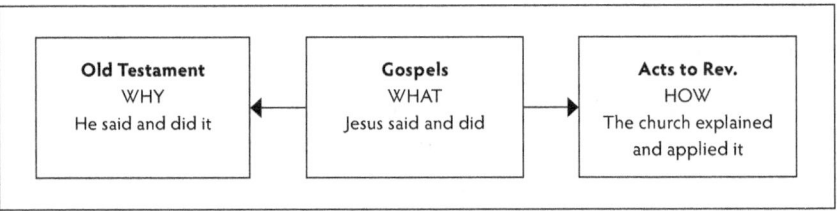

Figure 35: Christocentric Exegesis

This model of christocentric exegesis is a favoured approach at the South African Theological Seminary. Wherever possible, we strive to ground our exegesis in the words and works of Jesus. We recognise that sometimes this exegetical model may not be applicable because all the key biblical texts lie outside of the gospels, but wherever possible we encourage you to give 'what Jesus said and did' a prominent place in your exegesis and theology.

Summary

The purpose of this chapter is to provide an orientation to doing research in the field of systematic theology. An evangelical approach to systematic theology begins with an essential presupposition – God has spoken in his word. The task of evangelical theology, therefore, is to identify all that he has said in the Scriptures, analyse each relevant text, extract the key principles as propositions and construct a theological model to account for all the data.

We offered two designs for research projects. The first is the basic design for evangelical theology. It begins with a survey of current views on the topic, then proceeds to analyse the scriptural evidence by following three main steps – induction, deduction and retroduction – and concludes by exploring the significance of the research findings. The alternative design anchors the study around a key text, analysing how earlier texts serve as its informing theology and later texts develop and apply its ideas.

15

Practical Theology

Although practical theology is often the most beleaguered of the theological disciplines, we have come to hold it in the same high esteem that Schleiermacher did when he referred to it as the queen of the theological disciplines. Far from being the soft option for those who cannot do 'real' theology, research in practical theology requires expertise in each of the other branches of theology (biblical studies, systematic theology, church history, and missiology), but it also requires an extra set of skills – studying Christian actions and practices using empirical research tools. Moreover, practical theology is the branch of theology that most directly relates theology to everyday life and ministry, for which reason it should be held in esteem by any theologian or leader who loves the church.

Nature of Practical Theology

What is practical theology? In the early days, practical theology was viewed as the branch of theological study that applied theology to life and ministry; it was *applied* theology. While the other disciplines advanced the frontiers of understanding, practical theology had the mundane task of adapting their insights for pastoral ministry (the 'clerical paradigm'). This reductionistic view of practical theology as the application of 'real' theology to pastoral practice has rightly been eclipsed.

Today we view practical theology as a branch of theological research. It is the branch of theology that studies Christian praxis, that is, Christian action in service of Christ, the church, and the kingdom of God. It studies the complex relationship between Christians' beliefs and actions – how their beliefs inform their practices, and how their practices reflect their beliefs. It does this with both informative and transformative goals. The practical theologian is a man (or woman) of faith seeking to understand Christian praxis and ministry, and a servant of God seeking to transform ministry praxis so that it is maximally faithful to God and optimally effective in the world.

Practical theology brings contemporary faith and praxis into critical dialogue with Scripture, theology, and history, so that it might ensure that ministry is faithful to God and effective in its context. This includes pastoral ministry, but is not limited to it. It includes application to life, but is not limited to it. Practical theology rightly covers preaching, teaching, children's ministry, youth ministry, missions, counselling, pastoring, and leadership, because it strives to inform best practice in these domains of Christian ministry.

As a field of research, practical theology combines sociological research and theological reflection to solve real-life problems. Its point of departure is a problem in the real world, that is, a real-life situation or practice that is not as it should be. By means of a rigorous analysis of the problem, its causes and possible solutions, the researcher seeks to transform the situation. He seeks an in-depth understanding of the 'the world as it is', critically reviews Scripture and other influential sources to understand 'the world as it should be', then to correlate the two sets of data to develop a strategy 'to contribute to the world's becoming what God intends that it should be'.[1]

Cowan distinguishes between *contemplative* and *transformative* approaches to theology. Contemplative theologies are content to reflect on the world as it really is, but transformative theologies are determined to change the world into what it should be. Although biblical studies and systematic theology can be practised in a transformative way, practical theology is the most directly transformative branch of theology. Research in the field of practical theology begins with a real-life problem and hopes to end with a workable solution that will change the situation.

Cowan stresses that practical theology research has four crucial characteristics: (a) correlational, (b) hermeneutical, (c) critical and (d) transformative.

- *Correlational.* It evaluates the relationship between 'the world as it is' and 'the world as it should be'. It seeks an accurate understanding of the present situation and the preferred scenario.
- *Hermeneutical.* It requires the ability to interpret accurately both 'our world and our traditions'. Practical theologians use two tool sets, one to interpret the present situation and another to exegete the Scriptures.
- *Critical.* It 'requires that we explicitly evaluate the inherited understandings that guide our interpretations and actions'.
- *Transformative.* Its underlying drive is to bring the world into greater harmony with the word.[2]

Thus the goals of practical theology research are to examine the world to understand the real-life problem, examine the word to see what God's ideal is, and then develop an action plan to transform what is into what should be. These three goals provide the backbone of a working model for doing practical theology.

---

1. Michael A. Cowan, 'Introduction to Practical Theology', *Loyola Institute of Ministry* (2000; retrieved 2 June 2006, http://www.loyno.edu/~mcowan/PracticalTheology.html).
2. Cowan, 'Introduction to Practical Theology', online.

Steps in Practical Theology

Whereas systematic theology usually moves from theory to practice, practical theology embraces a practice-theory-practice movement. This means that it begins by trying to understand a contemporary situation or practice, then seeks to understand biblical, theological, and historical sources related to that situation or practice, and concludes by seeking ways to improve the present situation or practice. This rhythm of practice-theory-practice characterises all major approaches to research in practical theology.

By adding an initial step of identifying a problem or practice to research, Michael Cowan produced an attractive four-step sequence for doing research in practical theology. We can refer to it as the LIM model.[3]

Step 1: Identify a real-life problem. The point of departure is a problem in the real world, one that we have noticed and which concerns us. This is usually something of concern in the church or community. Based on our initial, unscientific observations and reflections, we state a problem and the underlying forces at work that are causing it.

Step 2: Interpret the world as it is. The research itself begins with a systematic investigation of the situation. By doing descriptive research, using both empirical and literary methods, you set about interpreting the what, the how, and the why of the problem. *What* is the real situation (your first impressions might be mistaken). *How* did the present situation develop? *Why* is the situation the way it is? The objective is to produce an accurate description and a reliable interpretation of the present reality, based on solid research.

Step 3: Interpret the world as it should be. For Christian scholars, this means trying to understand the will of God in relation to the situation or practice. We do this by re-examining the normative sources of our faith tradition. For evangelical theologians, the Scriptures hold centre stage, but sources from church history or influential theologians are included. We critically re-examine (exegete) our normative sources in the quest to understand how they speak afresh to the situation or practice we are studying.

Step 4: Interpret our contemporary obligations. The final step is to develop a feasible action plan that faithfully represents the will of God as interpreted in our faith tradition and provides a doable remedy to the problem. Cowan describes the ideal: 'We plan an adequately detailed intervention based on the possibility that we have chosen, implement it carefully, and rigorously evaluate both what practical difference it made . . .'[4] Not every study can end with implementation; often the researcher must be content with offering recommendations.

These four steps contain the seeds of a simple, logical model for research projects in the field of practical theology.

---

3. Ibid.
4. Ibid.

Basic Design for Practical Theology

The dominant approach to research in practical theology follows a practice-theory-practice design. This means that the research begins by studying present practice, then turns to theological theory, and returns to propose preferred practice. This flow of thought dominates practical theology today. Although the details differ, all variants of the practice-theory-practice design have the same essential movement. They begin with an *in-depth* study of a situation or practice. Next they turn to normative sources to formulate a theological response to the situation or practice; the normative sources might include Scripture, tradition, church history, models of good practice, scientific theories, and so on. They end by returning to practice, attempting to plan an intervention to improve praxis.

In a practice-theory-practice design, researchers are not allowed to assume that they know the present situation accurately. They must research it thoroughly to ensure that their presuppositions and premises are true. Since the real nature of the present situation is assumed to be unknown, the direction that the study of Bible and theology will take cannot be predicted with certainty until the empirical analysis of the situation has been completed. The questions that researchers take to their normative sources come from the study of the situation, so they can only be tentatively formulated before the first phase of the research has been completed.

A thesis based on Cowan's LIM model would probably follow these phases.

1. Introduction

Articulate concerns directly related to the selected topic, state a particular problem, present the aims of the study, formulate a feasible hypothesis and indicate your research methodology.

2. Present Situation

In this stage,[5] you interpret the world as it is. This involves describing the situation as follows:
- Present a *historical survey* to develop a picture of the history of the situation. Depending on the nature of the situation, you can do this by using published works, relevant archives and records, or interviews with witnesses and participants.
- Describe the present situation, both in terms of *what* is happening (the facts and realities) and *why* it is happening (the forces at work shaping the realities). Do this by conducting empirical research (fieldwork, questionnaires and

---

5. The logical flow of some studies dictates that the present situation be presented after the preferred scenario.

interviews) and/or by doing a *situation analysis* (a literature survey in the social sciences).

This portrayal of the present situation describes in detail a real-life situation or practice in need of improvement. The accuracy and objectiveness of the analysis are crucial for the remainder of the study. If the situation is well analysed, it lays a solid foundation for planning a biblical and practical response. This part of a practical theology study is so crucial and complex that we have devoted an entire chapter to descriptive research. You should study it in conjunction with this chapter on practical theology.

3. Preferred Scenario

The goal of this stage is to formulate a theological vision of the preferred scenario, interpreting the world as it should be. You need to develop this vision by critically re-examining the normative sources of your faith tradition.

What is a *faith tradition*? Cowan, who is Roman Catholic, includes scriptural texts, theological classics, and church teachings as elements of a faith tradition.[6] For evangelicals, the Scriptures alone are normative, but church traditions, church history, theological texts, and denominational positions constitute a history of interpretation within a faith community. These traditions significantly influence the way we understand the teachings of Scripture. We cannot engage Scripture afresh unless we are aware of how these historical forces at work in our faith community and tradition have shaped our reading of Scripture. Although the goal of this phase of the study is to present a theological vision of a preferred scenario that is based on a biblical perspective, to do so we must critically re-examine both the Scriptures and the other aspects of our faith tradition that shape our interpretations of the Scriptures.

If you are writing a thesis in the field of practical theology, what is expected with reference to the biblical analysis? Usually, this takes the form of a survey or overview analysis of scriptural teachings related to your topic. You should work through the Scriptures in an organised manner, explaining how they address your topic. For the most part, you do not need to conduct an in-depth exegetical analysis of every passage, but you do need to ensure that your interpretations are sound and that any inferences you draw, or applications you propose, derive from the text. You may need to conduct detailed exegesis of a few pivotal texts. Even in your overview, you need to engage authorities on the texts you treat, especially major scholarly commentaries. If you are writing a master's thesis or a doctoral dissertation, you must demonstrate proficiency at working with the biblical texts. Do not be fooled – adding the label 'practical' in front of 'theology' does not relieve you of the need for handling the biblical and theological aspects of the thesis competently.

---

6. Cowan, 'Introduction to Practical Theology', online.

4. Practical Suggestions

Conduct *action planning* to provide a *practical framework* for transforming the present situation into the preferred scenario. Recommend feasible responses to the present situation (a list of possible interventions or action steps) in the light of:

- your historical and empirical analysis of the present situation (the world as it is);
- your synopsis of relevant biblical and theological resources to suggest a preferred scenario.

In certain instances, a research project extends to the implementation and evaluation of the action plan. In most student research, however, the study ends with practical suggestions to move from the present situation (the world as it is) towards the preferred scenario (the world as it should be).

Advanced Designs for Practical Theology

The attractiveness of Cowan's LIM model lies in its user-friendliness. It can be used for a wide range of studies. Don Browning and Richard Osmer have each popularised more advanced designs that follow the practice-theory-practice movement.[7]

Browning champions a practice-theory-practice design. His approach has four movements:

1) The first movement endeavours to provide a thick description of theory-laden practices. The objective is to understand the practice fully and accurately.

2) The second movement explores what normative Christian texts really imply for our praxis. This involves critically re-examining relevant Scriptures and other theological sources.

3) The third movement seeks to fuse the 'horizons between the vision implicit in contemporary practices and the vision implied in the practices of the normative Christian texts'. It re-examines the practice and the texts in the light of one another, being open to modify practices and reinterpret texts.

4) The final movement endeavours to answer the key questions, 'How shall we live?' and 'What shall we do?' This is the *strategic* response. Browning proposes that it must answer four questions:

   a) How do we understand the concrete situation in which we must act?

---

7. Don S. Browning, *A Fundamental Practical Theology: Descriptive and Strategic Proposals* (Minneapolis, MN: Fortress, 1991); Richard R. Osmer, *Practical Theology: An Introduction* (Grand Rapids, MI: Eerdmans, 2008).

b) What should our praxis be in this context?

c) How do we defend our proposed praxis?

d) What rhetoric and strategies should we use to communicate and implement our proposed praxis?

Osmer also sees the practice-theory-practice design as requiring four tasks, but his are slightly different to Browning's. When compared with Browning, Osmer expands the first practice step into two tasks, but does not have a specific task dedicated to a correlation and 'fusion' of horizons. Here are Osmer's four tasks:

1) The *descriptive* task asks, 'What happened?' We begin with an empirical study of a situation or practice.

2) The *interpretive* task asks, 'Why did it happen?' We draw on theories from the natural, social, and human sciences to explain the situation or practice.

3) The *normative* task asks, 'What should happen?' We explore Scripture, theology, and models of good practice.

4) The *strategic* task asks, 'What shall we do?' We devise a strategy to improve the situation or practice.

Alternative Design for Practical Theology

Although research in practical theology usually follows a theory-practice-theory design, that is not the only way to undertake research in practical theology. You can undertake the task of improving praxis by moving from theory to practice. This is a well-established approach in Doctor of Ministry dissertations, which often divide logically into two main parts: first a theoretical foundation and then a practical application to a specific context. The theoretical foundation covers the biblical and theological bases, as well as relevant theory from the human and social sciences (for example, history, psychology, sociology, leadership, education). The practical section often includes an empirical study of the context or situation (case study; descriptive survey), before moving towards the application of theory to practice.

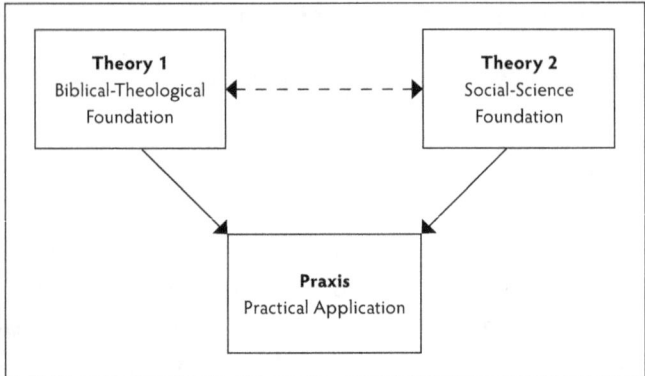

The point of departure is a question about practice that emanates from observation or experience. Unlike research using the practice-theory-practice approach, the researcher does not proceed to undertake a detailed study of the situation that gives rise to the question. Praxis gives birth to a question, which is assumed to be valid. A detailed description of the situation is not deemed to be necessary before the researcher can study the theoretical foundations for a response. Rather, after deriving a research problem from praxis, the researcher turns to the Scriptures and the sciences to formulate a theoretical foundation for application.

The natural outline for this type of study would be along these lines:

1) Introduction

2) Theory 1: Biblical-Theological Foundation

3) Theory 2: Social-Science Foundation

4) Praxis: Practical Application

5) Conclusion

The introduction would provide a brief description of the real-life context that gives rise to the research question; it would state the research problem and outline the research plan. The praxis section might require two chapters if one is needed for an empirical study of a ministry context, and another to provide a ministry strategy. In many cases, the praxis section can be covered in a single chapter.

As an example, consider a pastor who has observed a growing number of his congregants developing addictions to Internet pornography. He hopes to find an effective ministry strategy to help men break free of their addiction. The question is born out of observation and experience (Christian men struggling with pornography) and the objective is to develop a strategy for effective ministry (to help them overcome their addiction). The researcher begins by seeking to understand *addiction to Internet pornography* from a scriptural and scientific perspective. He undertakes a topical study of the Bible's teachings, before turning his attention to scientific research. He discovers a growing body of neurological and psychological research that shows how pornography affects brain and behaviour. Armed with considerable insight into the Internet pornography as a phenomenon, the researcher turns his attention to his ministry context. He uses the understanding that he developed of Internet pornography to design a small-scale empirical study of the phenomenon in his context, and then develops an informed and holistic ministry plan to address the problem in his own church.

This theory-practice design for research in practical theology has similarities and differences when compared with the practice-theory-practice designs. The two approaches both seek to improve ministry praxis. They begin with a concern about praxis and they end with a strategy to improve praxis. However, in the theory-practice design, the situation or practice merely raises the question for research. The research does not initially attempt an in-depth study of the present praxis. Although the context raises the question, it is not focal to the initial part of the inquiry. Rather, the researchers examine scriptural and scientific sources to formulate a theoretical (theological) perspective on the topic as a whole. The theological study is not governed by the context. This contrasts with the practice-theory-practice models, in which researchers take the questions raised by an in-depth study of the present practice to their normative sources, so that the theological reflection is in direct response to questions that surface during the empirical study.

Summary

Practical theology covers a vast, diverse array of subjects. As the queen of the theological disciplines, it has the noble and beautiful task of studying Christian ministry and praxis with the goal of helping it to become as faithful as possible to God's will. Research in practical theology usually begins with a detailed analysis of the present practice, then re-examines normative sources for insight, and returns to reform or enhance practice. The elegant simplicity of this practice-theory-practice approach might conceal the fact that to do practical theology well requires a high level of ability to interpret the world and the word.

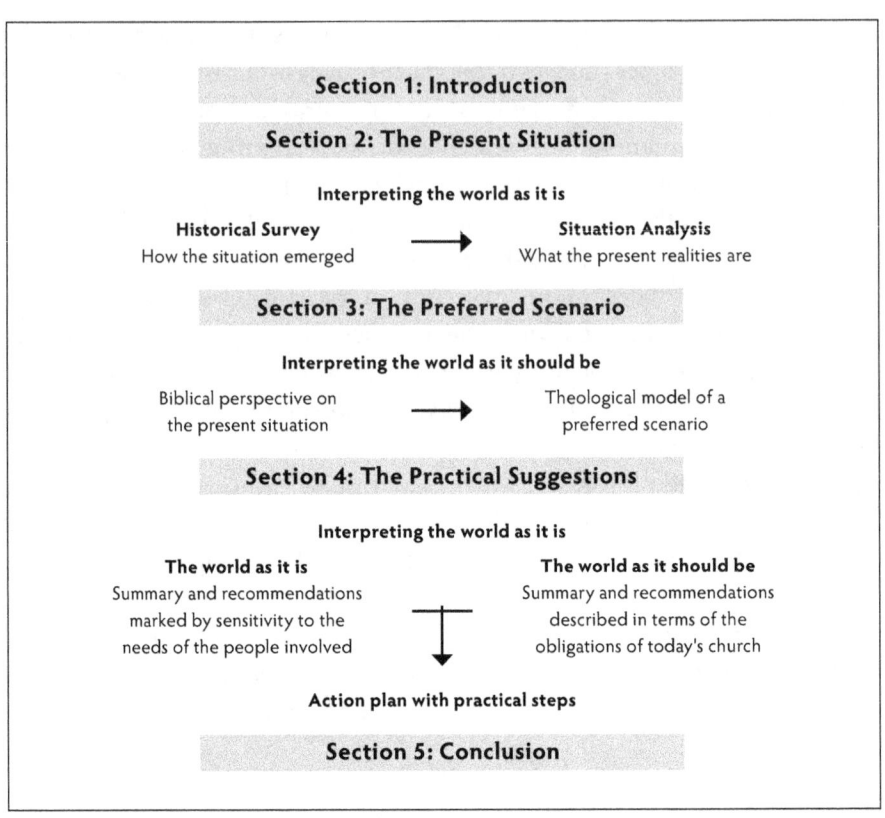

Figure 36: Design for Practical Theology

16

The Literature Review

'It is essential that every research project begins with a review of the existing literature.'[1] In many theses, chapter 2 is a literature review. Even if a thesis does not contain a separate chapter for its literature review, it must demonstrate awareness of the history of research and interact with the major contributors in the field.

Some prefer to call it a review of scholarship, since as a researcher your interest does not lie in just any kind of literature; it lies in scholarly writings. 'In short, you are interested in the most recent, credible and relevant scholarship in your area of interest.'[2] Others refer to it as a history of research, because it provides a bird's-eye view of previous research leading to the point at which your study enters the debate.

Why You Must Do a Literature Review

Why is a review of research such a crucial part of writing a thesis? What are the most important reasons for conducting a literature review at the start of every research project? There are many reasons. For example, a literature review will help you to:
- avoid duplicating research that has already been done;
- identify gaps in the existing research that call for further study;
- interact with the most recent theories and empirical findings; and
- narrow your research idea in the light of greater insight into the field.

You cannot just dive into a topic that interests you. You must position your inquiry within the context of questions that have already been asked and answered. You want to research questions that either have not been answered yet or have, in your judgement, been answered inadequately. Doing a thorough literature review helps you to channel your energy, focusing on real gaps and needs. It also helps you to approach your research from an informed perspective, aware of how others have handled similar studies and what their findings have been. In the long run, it saves time!

---

1. Mouton, *Master's and Doctoral Studies*, 86.
2. Ibid., 87.

How Your Literature Review Will Be Judged

In all things, if you know what is expected, it is easier to meet the expectations. So what is expected in a literature review? Mouton lists four criteria by which a literature review is judged.[3]

1) *It should be exhaustive in its coverage of the main aspects of the study.* If your study touches on four interrelated aspects, your literature review must cover all four aspects. Furthermore, it must show that you are familiar with *all* the major studies on each aspect.[4] If your topic touched on the doctrine of the Holy Spirit in the book of Acts and you did not mention the extensive debate between Gordon Fee and Roger Stronstad in the 1990s, your examiners would conclude that you had not done a thorough job. You must cover all the major contributions.

2) *A good review is fair in its treatment of authors.* Theological students are notorious for allowing bias to creep into their research. When reading first-draft master's proposals, we often get the feeling the student already knows the answers to his questions. He has made up his mind, and intends to use the thesis to prove it. This attitude is incompatible with research, which requires objective, open-minded inquiry. When the researcher is biased, his treatment of sources in the literature review is often unfair. If he disagrees with a source, he does not present a fair summary of its views and arguments. Sometimes, the problem is not so much bias as sloppiness – the researcher has not personally read the source, so he is unable to do it justice. To write a good literature review, you must conscientiously read the works you review and present an unbiased, accurate evaluation of them.

3) *A literature review should be topical and not dated.* By 'topical', we mean up-to-date and of current interest. While it often needs to begin with a brief historical overview, the bulk of the review should be devoted to the current state of the debate. What are the current hot-potato issues in the field? Who are the major spokespersons for different views? What recent publications have contributed to the discussion? Your review should answer these kinds of questions.

4) *A good literature review should be well organised and interpretive.* A literature review should *not* read like an annotated bibliography, merely a list of works with a few words about each. Instead, it should reveal your interaction and interpretation of the history of research. That is, you must interact with key works in a way that shows how you interpret the history of scholarship. This implies organisation. There are various ways to organise the review. The best

---

3. Ibid., 90–91.
4. This is true at the master's and doctoral levels, but less is required at the bachelor's level.

for your study might be chronological, by schools of thought, or by divisions of your study. The system you choose must allow it to show your interpretive interaction with scholarship.

These, then, are the essential criteria. Your review should be exhaustive, objective, current and interpretive. We have looked at *why* a literature review is important and *what* it should look like. Now let's turn to *how* to obtain the sources you need.

How to Obtain Sources for Your Literature Review

Conducting a literature review is daunting chiefly because it is difficult to identify and access all the relevant literature. In other words, you must face two challenges:
- You must identify all the relevant literature on your topic.
- You must access most of the literature you have identified.

If you have ready access to a major theological library, you should have little difficulty accessing information. If, however, you are a distance education student and do not have access to a top library, identifying and accessing relevant literature is one of the greatest research challenges you will face. But, do not be discouraged – you can succeed! How? Let's answer that in a 'question-and-answer' style.

What tools do I need to identify and access relevant literature? You need two tools: a library and the Internet. During your study, you will need access to a good theological library. This may mean you have to travel to the nearest one and spend a couple of weeks there. During my doctoral studies, I made three two-week trips to the University of Stellenbosch to use the library. While there, I photocopied as much as I could so that I could use the resources at home.

You must have access to Internet-based resources! In the early stages of your research, this is even more helpful than a library. There are two reasons for this: (a) there are many good e-books and e-journals available full-text online and (b) even if a particular resource is not available full-text, you can become aware of its existence when it appears in your search results. Also, you may be able to find abstracts or book reviews of these works.

What kinds of literature am I seeking? The general answer is *high-quality academic sources,* particularly recent ones (the last 10 years). To be more specific, you should focus on three major kinds of sources:
- *Journals.* Journal articles are *the best source* of academic literature. They are shorter and more up-to-date than books.
- *Books.* You must access major books in your field, especially seminal works and major scholarly treatments.
- *Theses.* Theses are academic research; if someone else has done related research, you need to be aware of it and engage it.

By the way, the bibliography is one of the first things assessors look at when assessing a thesis! What do they look for? First, recent publications – books and articles from the last ten years. Second, quality resources – the major titles and the best journals on the topic. Third, key authors – the leading scholars, specialists in the field.

How do I find the key books on my topic? Here are some simple ways of finding key resources quickly:

1) Read literature reviews. Academic publications – monographs and theses – typically begin with a literature review (just as you will do). In their reviews, they will identify the key authors and works, briefly summarising their content and contribution. The works that receive the most attention are the most important in the field! They are must-read resources for you.

2) Study bibliographies. When you locate a key resource (book, article or thesis), study its bibliography for other relevant titles. You will be amazed how quickly you will locate all the critical works in your field. Everyone will quote them, so they are easy to find – just look for the names that come up time and time again.

3) Search online bookstores. The largest bookstore in the world is www.amazon.com. Amazon lists almost every published book. Go there and search on the key words or topics of your study; you will find every significant book on the topic (even some that are not yet published). You will also find book reviews and some links to related books. The value of this kind of search is that you will find the latest releases, sources that were not included in literature reviews and bibliographies.

4) Use Google scholar and Google books. Normal Google searches and alerts will probably be of limited value because you will find too many popular (as opposed to scholarly) resources. However, there are two Google initiatives that can be goldmines for sourcing information: Google scholar and Google books.

Google scholar (http://scholar.google.co.za) is a search facility that locates scholarly (as opposed to popular) sources on the web. You can find journal articles, theses and dissertations, research papers, and so on. Many of the results can be viewed full-text on the Internet; others can be previewed. As contrasted with a normal Google search, the results from a Google scholar search will have much greater academic value.

Google books (http://books.google.co.za) is an initiative to make published books available online. A vast number of books have already been uploaded; more are being added daily. Books in the public domain (no copyright restrictions) are full-text. Copyrighted works are also uploaded full-text, but you cannot read the entire text. You can, however, search the full-text of the book, view the contents pages and read excerpts (sometimes quite substantial extracts). The site often provides links to reviews of the book.

How do I find journal articles on my topic? The old way was to go to a library and search its catalogues for articles. If you have access to a major theological library with a sizeable collection of journals, this is still helpful. However, many journals are now available on the Internet. Online journals occur in two forms: (1) full-text: you can download the actual article; (2) citation: you find the bibliographic entry and, sometimes, the abstract. Obviously, full-text articles are more helpful because you can access them immediately. The problem is finding them. There are a few ways:

Databases. There are massive collections of articles on searchable databases. These databases are specifically designed for research purposes and are used mainly by university libraries.

- *EBSCOhost* is the world's largest collection of journals; find out if your institution subscribes to it. You can access many articles and book reviews full-text.
- *JSTOR* (www.jstor.org) is a project designed to make journal resources available online. The platform already includes a vast collection. You can conduct a full search of all resources on the site and you can access all the articles full-text.
- *ATLA and ATLAS* is the largest listing of academic works for theology. Many of the entries only contain bibliographic information, but a significant minority can be accessed full-text. Searching ATLA will give you a good idea of what has been written on a theological topic. ATLAS contains many of the articles listed on ATLA in full-text.
- *OT and NT Abstracts* (available on EBSCOhost) provide brief abstracts of almost every important book or article published in the fields of Old or New Testament studies. The abstracts cover works published in all major theological languages, but all the abstracts are in English. Skimming the abstracts related to your topic is a great way to begin a literature review. Within a couple of hours, you can form an idea of what is happening in a field of study by reading dozens of abstracts. (I always begin my biblical research here!)
- *Religion and Philosophy Collection* contains more than 300 full-text journals! All the articles are available full-text. It provides extensive coverage on a wide range of topics in theology, religion and philosophy.
- *The Theological Journal Library* is a collection with approximately 500 volumes of journals from Bible-based publications on CD-ROM. You can search and view extracts of articles online at www.galaxie.com/journal.php. The collection is reasonably affordable, so you may even consider buying your own copy.
- *SA e-Publications* (www.sabinet.co.za) is an online platform that publishes electronic versions of South African journals, including a sizeable *religion collection*. The platform is fully searchable and all the articles are full-text.
- *Directory of Open Access Journals* (www.doaj.org) is a large collection of online journals that can be searched, including a good number of religious and philosophical journals; the articles are available full-text.

- *Ingenta* (www.ingentaconnect.com) allows you to search a religion database with sixty-three journals (all religions). All articles are searchable, but not all are free; most are pay-per-view.

In addition to these collections, there are literally hundreds of scholarly journals available on the Internet. Google scholar will help you to find the ones that relate to your topic.

How do I find theses and dissertations on my topic? In addition to looking on institutions' websites, you should try www.tren.com. The Theological Research Exchange Network is a library of over 10,000 theological thesis/dissertation titles representing research from many different institutions. TREN also makes available conference papers presented at annual meetings of several academic societies. The level of access to documents varies. For some, you can only view the bibliographic information and need to purchase the thesis or paper. Others have previews/abstracts that you can peruse. A few are available free.

Summary

A review of existing scholarship is an essential first step in most research projects. It helps you avoid duplicating what others have done, identify gaps, interact with recent findings and narrow your research idea. Your review must focus on scholarly sources, and should be exhaustive, objective, current and interpretive. Journals, books and theses are valuable scholarly sources. Internet sites may be helpful, but should be used with care. If you do not have easy access to a good theological library, you can access many of the best sources online.

17

Descriptive Research

Descriptive research, also referred to as survey research or descriptive survey research, is a key research tool for studies in the field of practical theology. Many studies in practical theology involve fieldwork (empirical) research in which the researcher uses interviews, surveys, and/or questionnaires to gather original data about a church, community, organisation, event, custom, or something else. The purpose of this chapter is to offer practical guidelines for doing descriptive research in theological studies.

Understanding Descriptive Research

Its Nature

> Descriptive research does exactly what its name says: it describes, usually one or more characteristics of a group of people, technically called a population. Sometimes the information gathered is strictly quantitative – numbers and percentages; other times it is qualitative, including the 'why' along with the 'how many'.[1]

Like all research, descriptive research seeks to examine a problem. It typically uses data derived from interviews, questionnaires, surveys and case studies to form the conclusions and recommendations of a study or report. Descriptive research provides data about the subject of the study, describing the who, what, when, where and how of a situation. It provides a systematic description that is as accurate and factual as possible. This approach lends itself well to statistical (quantitative) research. However, it can also be qualitative in nature, seeking to describe a phenomenon.

Technically speaking, questions relating to the causes and cures for a situation fall outside the scope of pure descriptive research. In a qualitative study, the researcher may probe the population's views as to what caused a situation and/or how to cure problems, but in doing so he is reporting someone else's subjective perceptions rather than factually and objectively describing causes. Good descriptive research usually lays a solid platform

---

1. Vyhmeister, *Quality Research Papers*, 30.

from which the researcher may diagnose causes and propose cures, but these steps are inferences drawn from the description, not part of the description itself.

Its Purpose

The main goal of descriptive research is to describe the data and characteristics about the problem or issue being studied. In other words, the purpose is to make reality known. You may draw conclusions and take decisions based on the description.[2]

In technical language, according to Isaac and Michael,[3] descriptive research serves four main purposes:

1) collecting detailed information that describes existing phenomena;

2) identifying problems or justify conditions and practices;

3) making comparisons and evaluations; and

4) determining what others are doing with similar problems or situations and benefit from their experience in making future plans and decisions.

In the context of ministry in the local church, descriptive research is designed to report current ministry conditions or strategies. Based on the description, the researcher may critically evaluate the research findings and suggest ways to improve the ministry situation.[4]

Its Characteristics

Leedy indicates that the descriptive survey has the following salient characteristics.[5]

1) The descriptive survey method deals with a situation that demands the technique of observation as the principal means of collecting the data.

2) The population for the study must be carefully chosen, clearly defined and specifically delimited in order to set precise parameters for ensuring discreteness to the population.

3) Data in descriptive survey research is particularly susceptible to distortion through the introduction of bias into the research design. Particular attention should be given to safeguarding the data from the influence of bias.

---

2. Ibid., ch. 4.

3. Stephen Isaac and William B. Michael, *Handbook in Research Evaluation* (San Diego: EDITS, 1971), 18.

4. 'Applied Research Project' (2005, retrieved 19 March 2008, www.dts.edu), online.

5. Leedy, *Practical Research*, 187.

4) Although the descriptive survey method relies upon observation for the acquisition of the data, that data must then be organised and presented systematically so that valid and accurate conclusions can be drawn from them.

Its Value

The following points highlight the significance of descriptive research.[6]

1) Descriptive research describes the current and present phenomena, problems, and/or opinions.

2) This method is very easy and direct to use and, hence, is a popular and widely used research method.

3) Descriptive research not only describes the current problem, but also many times suggests valuable solutions to the problems.

4) Descriptive research is helpful in developing the data collection tools like questionnaires, schedules, checklists, and so on.

5) By dealing with the relationships between or among the variables, descriptive research is useful in developing new generalisations, principles or theories, which possess universal validity and utility.

Its Limitation

Descriptive research can accurately describe a situation and report common perceptions as to possible causes and cures, but it cannot objectively diagnose causes or prescribe cures. It can lay a sound, factual platform from which the researcher can infer likely causes and propose practical solutions, but the researcher must recognise these as extrapolations from the results of the survey study.

In other words, it cannot establish a *causal* relationship between variables.[7] Patwardhan cautions that descriptive research,
- does not focus on the 'why' in trying to understanding phenomena;
- cannot be used for prediction and control purposes.[8]

Failure to recognise these limitations of the method will cause researchers to overstate their conclusions. If you are aware of them, it will safeguard you against this tendency.

---

6. 'Types of Research in Education' (2008, retrieved 19 March 2008, bhojvirtualuniversity.com), online.

7. 'Educational Research' (2005, retrieved 18 March 2008, http://www83.homepage.villanova.edu), online.

8. H. Patwardhan, 'Research Design and Implementation' (2007, retrieved 18 March 2008, http://bb.cutn.sk/discus/messages/31352), online presentation.

Conducting Descriptive Research

The descriptive research process may be divided into nine steps:

1) State the objective

2) Review related research

3) Design the approach

4) Develop the instruments

5) Select the participants

6) Describe the data collection procedures

7) Analyse and interpret the data

8) Draw conclusions

9) Write the report

For the rest of this chapter, we shall look at each of these steps in a little more detail.

Step 1: Set the Research Objective

All research is directed by a research problem or objective. In a theological thesis, the main research problem will govern the objective of the descriptive component of the study (see ch. 10). When the main research problem is divided into sub-problems or key questions, one of these will set the objective for the empirical study. In rare cases, the descriptive research project will be the entire project. Whether it forms the entire study or part of a larger study, the descriptive survey must be guided by a specific problem and a clear objective. You must state the objective of the descriptive research in a single sentence.

All we have said previously about stating research problems applies here too. The value of the study is particularly important in this kind of research, since it must be of sufficient significance to motivate potential respondents. The objective governs every other aspect of the study. It determines the selection of research design, the kind of information needed, the selection of participants, the sample size, the questions to be asked, and much more.

Typically, the objective (or question or problem) will use wording that points to the research method to be employed, at least to its *quantitative* or *qualitative* nature. For example, 'What influence does growing up in the home of an evangelical minister have on one's adult church involvement?' suggests a qualitative study. On the other hand, 'What is the correlation between a church's teaching about giving and the percentage of their income that its members give to ministry?' suggests a quantitative approach.

Step 2: Review Related Research

Before you rush off and conduct your own descriptive study of a population, you should demonstrate familiarity with related research projects. You should discuss *previous research* in the same field (or relevant, related fields). Your review should seek to accomplish the following:

- Summarise the findings of other research projects along the same line of enquiry as your study.
- Summarise the findings of other studies that have some degree of relevance to the proposed study.
- Evaluate the appropriateness of the methods used for other similar studies. In this point, you should indicate the conclusions drawn by researchers who have previously reviewed the related research.
- Indicate any applications of previous research findings to professional practice.

This review of related research is typically presented in a section called 'literature review'. The literature review often requires an entire chapter. If it is rather short, include it in the introductory chapter of a thesis. For research in theology, you must also provide a biblical-theological and theoretical basis for the project, explaining the rationale for your research design. This description must be informed by previous research on this and related topics.[9]

Step 3: Design the Approach

When you know what you need to know (a clear objective) and how other studies have achieved similar goals (review of research), the next step is to decide on the best way to obtain the information you need. Personal interviews may be appropriate to gather some data (qualitative research). Using a *questionnaire* is the best way to glean other information. You can obtain certain kinds of information from *records*. Personal *observation* is also valid. For each of these different approaches, you need to develop a strategy. You must be able to provide a clear rationale for each kind of data collection tool you plan to use. Your rationale should indicate *why* this is the most suitable method to achieve the objective. Your strategy should also describe in detail *how* you intend to use each approach. If you plan to conduct interviews (or questionnaires), describe how many interviews, who will be interviewed, why those people, how long the interviews will take, how you will access the interviewees, what data will be gathered, and so on. If you plan to use records or archives, indicate what is available and how you will access it.

For example, will you interview all the deacons? If not, how will you select those you choose to interview? When and where will you do the interviews? Will the survey of the church members' impressions of the deacons' work be anonymous? How can you get the

---

9. 'Applied Research Project', online.

greatest number of church members to reply to your survey? The research design needs to address these and other practical questions.[10]

Step 4: Develop Instruments

You can use a variety of data collection methods, including questionnaires, interviews and observations.

Questionnaires (mainly for quantitative research)

The questionnaire as an instrument used in surveys. Data sometimes lies buried deep within the minds or within the attitudes, feelings or reactions of men and women. As with oil beneath the sea, the first problem is to devise a tool to probe below the surface. A commonplace instrument for observing data beyond the physical reach of the observer is the *questionnaire*.[11]

> Surveys have become increasingly popular in recent years. People are asked what kind of toothpaste they use, for which political candidate they will vote, or how they feel about interracial marriage. Some surveys are done orally. Some use questionnaires to which a person must respond in writing. While information obtained from a questionnaire is extensive, it tends to be shallow. This type of research is called *quantitative* and depends to a great extent on numbers.[12]

Preparing questionnaires. Preparing questionnaires takes much time and expertise. Questionnaires should be attractive, brief and easy to complete. A well-prepared questionnaire can obtain data that describes reality and elicits the information that is required.

Do's and don'ts when preparing questionnaires. Here are some practical guidelines to help you in constructing questionnaires. The list is by no means an exhaustive one, but it provides some of the key components of a well-written questionnaire. First, the dos:
- Do start your questionnaire with a title and introduction or welcome message.
- Do provide confidentiality and anonymity.
- Do follow the KISS (keep it simple, stupid) principle.
- Do write questions and responses with clear objectives, concise language, complete sentences, simple words and correct spelling and grammar.
- Do be specific in asking each question.
- Do place personal and confidential questions at the end of the questionnaire.

---

10. Vyhmeister, *Your Indispensable Guide to Writing Quality Research Papers: For Students of Religion and Theology* (Grand Rapids, MI: Zondervan, 2001).
11. Leedy, *Practical Research*, 187.
12. Vyhmeister, *Quality Research Papers*, 37.

- Do require respondents to read each question carefully by varying the way you ask the questions.
- Do design mutually exclusive responses.
- Do allow 'don't know' and 'not applicable' responses where appropriate.
- Do test your questionnaire by means of a pilot study.

Now for some don'ts:
- Don't be vague.
- Don't ask double-negative questions.
- Don't use many abbreviations, acronyms or clichés.
- Don't ask objectionable or value-laden questions.
- Don't ask leading questions.
- Don't ask open-ended questions unless necessary.
- Don't ask 'double-barrelled' questions.
- Don't ask hypothetical questions.
- Don't ask respondents to make unnecessary calculations.
- Don't ask non-essential questions.

Types of questions. 'Many different kinds of questions appear in questionnaires. However, they can all be classified as either *open* or *closed*.'[13]

- *Open questions.* An open question allows respondents to answer however they wish, without prompting. Because answers vary so greatly, tabulating open questions is involved and time-consuming.
- *Closed questions.* In closed questions, respondents choose from a list of given answers. These questions are easy to answer, but the answers may not be very accurate.

Pre-testing the questionnaire (pilot study). Conduct a pilot study to gather information about deficiencies in the questionnaire and ideas for improving it. Test the questionnaire with 5–10 respondents who do not form part of the main study. This provides the questionnaire, as a research instrument, with greater validity.

Interviews (mainly for qualitative research)

Interviews permit a deeper and fuller understanding of the attitudes of the respondents. Whereas the survey (using questionnaires) may have room only for 'agree' and 'disagree' answers, an interview can tell the researcher why the person disagrees or agrees. Interviewing takes time but provides information not available through a survey. In order for an interview to afford the best information possible, the interviewer should record the conversation. However, an audio recording can only be made with the express permission of the person interviewed. Go to the interview with a written outline of the

---

13. Ibid., 38–39.

questions to be asked. The conversation may depart from this outline, but at least you will have a framework for your interview.[14]

Summary of the steps of handling an interview. Leedy recommends the following steps for successfully handling the interview as a technique for gathering data for research. They are simple, but very important:

1) Set up the interview well in advance.

2) Send the agenda of questions you will ask the interviewee.

3) Ask for permission to record the interview.

4) Confirm the date immediately in writing.

5) Send a reminder together with another agenda of questions ten days before the interview.

6) Be prompt, follow the agenda, and have a copy of your questions for your interviewee in case he has mislaid his copy.

7) Following the interview, submit a typescript of the interview and get either a written acknowledgement of its accuracy or a corrected copy from the interviewee.

8) After you have incorporated the material into your research report, send that section of the report to the interviewee for final approval and written permission to use the data in your report.[15]

Step 5: Select the Participants (population sample)

Sampling. Choose the sample so carefully that you can see all the characteristics of the total population.[16]

> When Gallup polls want to know which candidate the citizens are going to elect, they do not ask each registered voter. They sample the population. That is, they poll a representative group. Regardless of the kind of instrument used to get information – survey, interview, checklist – sampling is a way to get a lot of information from not so many people. For a sample to represent the total population, it must have all the characteristics of that population. A sample should be large enough to represent the population and it must

---

14. Ibid., 41.
15. Leedy, *Practical Research*, 195.
16. Ibid., 200.

contain the same types of people in the same proportion in which they appear in the total population.[17]

Sampling techniques. When selecting participants, use an appropriate sampling technique. Ensure that participants are both able and willing to provide the desired information. Vyhmeister describes three main sampling techniques:

- *Representative sampling.* To represent the population, the sample should include in proportion all the different kinds of people in the group. Thus, a representative sample (often called a stratified sample) will include men and women, old and young, rich and poor, black and white, and whatever other kinds of people are in the larger group.
- *Random sampling.* Random sampling is a technique used to ensure – as far as possible – an unbiased representation of the population. Here 'random' does not mean 'chance'. The researcher designs ways to achieve this by polling every tenth name on the list or interviewing every fourth candidate. Random sampling can be applied to the total population. For example, every sixth member of the church – regardless of age, sex or other factors – receives a questionnaire.
- *Cluster sampling.* Cluster sampling selects sample clusters. For example, Brian wants to study Baptist churches in the Western Cape. He finds twenty-nine churches affiliated to the Baptist Union of South Africa. Analysing them by race, he finds sixteen are predominantly black, nine white, and four coloured. He divides them by size, noting that three have over 300 members, fourteen have 100–300 and ten less than 100. After he divides the churches into categories, he can randomly choose one church from each category.[18]

Step 6: Describe the Data Collection Procedures

Collecting the data is an exciting part of the research. After all the hard work of preparing, it is fun to send out the questionnaires and get them back. The ideal would be to have a 100 per cent return, that is, to have every one of the questionnaires completed and returned in time for the tabulation. This rarely happens. Either a letter gets lost, or a respondent fails to return the questionnaire or a questionnaire is not filled in correctly – and the survey results give information on a limited part of the population.

Procedures for collecting the information needed in the research deal with questions such as: How will the data be collected? Who will collect the data? What procedures will be used? Data collection procedures can be divided into two phases: the preparation phase and the collection phase.

---

17. Vyhmeister, *Quality Research Papers*, 35.
18. Ibid., 35–36.

Preparation phase: prepare the cover letter. When sending out questionnaires, include a cover letter with each one. The cover letter should do the following:
- Briefly explain the significance of the study. (Please note, the significance does not lie in the fact that you are doing a thesis; it lies in the value of your research to the community or the church. Helping you finish a thesis will not be important to most people.)
- Briefly describe what is being asked of the respondent and why.
- Address the potential respondent personally and individually.
- Provide an endorsement by the research supervisor to add credibility to the letter.
- Guarantee the respondent complete anonymity and confidentiality.
- State a specific date (deadline) by which the questionnaire should be returned.
- Sign the letter personally.
- Provide a self-addressed, stamped return envelope.

Collection phase: follow-up strategies. The response rate of returning completed questionnaires tends to be low (30–50 per cent). For this reason, researchers need to use certain follow-up strategies to increase the response rate.

Initial follow-up strategies can increase the response rate up to 20 per cent. We recommend two early strategies. First, send a reminder by SMS, email or postcard. A little later, send a second packet with a new, positively worded cover letter, and another self-addressed, stamped, return envelope.

Secondary follow-up strategies can increase the response rate up to 10 per cent. The most effective of these techniques is to telephone the slow responders to encourage them to return the completed questionnaire.

You must record and systematise the data gleaned through the survey. When you have retrieved enough questionnaires, record every piece of data in an organised fashion.[19]

Step 7: Analyse and Interpret the Data

Raw data do not convey meaning on their own. You need to analyse, organise and interpret the data. You need to collect the data and then treat them with appropriate analytical techniques. In the case of quantitative data, these techniques will include tools of statistical analysis. For qualitative data, you need a system of coding, organising and analysing non-numerical data.

When analysing numerical data (in other words, when doing quantitative research), you may use one or more of these data analysis tools:
- *Discriminant item analysis*: Provide the response rate for each item as well as the total sample size and the overall percentage of returns, since not all

---

19. Leedy, *Practical Research*, 216; Vyhmeister, *Quality Research Papers*, ch. 4.

respondents will answer questions (that is, a numeric profile/tally of your results, percentages, and so on).
- *Cluster analysis*: Group items into clusters that address the same issue and develop total scores across an item cluster in order to avoid 'information overload'.
- *Inferential (analytic) statistics*: Use the statistics to test your hypothesis.

Qualitative data, on the other hand, are not numerical in nature. They include observations, journal entries and existing documents (for example, archives, minutes). Most often, however, they take the form of open-ended responses to surveys or interviews. To present such data in a succinct, accurate and honest manner, you need to code, organise and discuss/analyse them.

- *Coding*. To protect the anonymity of your respondents, use a coding system. For example, the code MGBC could conceal these properties: M for male, G for Gauteng province, B for Baptist denomination and C for aged 40–49.
- *Organising*. To help your readers to follow your discussion, you need to find a sensible way to organise and present your data.
- *Discussing*. Finally, you need to comment on the trends you observe and the likely reasons for them. This constitutes analysing or interpreting it.

There are many specific techniques for doing the analysis. Most of them revolve around identifying similarities and differences between responses, dividing them into groups or categories, and then discussing the trends and the possible causes for them.

While analysing your data, you should relate your findings to existing theories and interpret your results in their light. You should also see if your findings build a new theory or confirm existing ones.

Step 8: Draw Conclusions

The research process must result in conclusions. These conclusions will be valid to the extent that the underlying data collection and analysis is properly done. The process of drawing conclusions has three main steps: (a) state the findings; (b) verify their credibility; and (c) consider their implications. We shall discuss each step in a little more detail.

State the findings. You should present the findings of your research as clearly and concisely as possible, relating the results to the research problem. If you asked a question, what answer did you discover? If you tested a hypothesis, do your findings lead you to accept or reject it?

The strength of your findings may range from conclusive to inconclusive; between these two poles are tentative *conclusions*. Your *conclusions* are *conclusive* if you believe they represent the definitive answer to the problem. They are *inconclusive* when the data conflict, failing to suggest a clear answer. Most *conclusions* fall into the *tentative* category. This occurs when the data suggest a solution, but you are not yet able to claim it as the final word on the matter. As a rule, it is best to understate rather than overstate your *conclusions*.

If your study revolves around testing a hypothesis, both 'accept' and 'reject' are acceptable research results. You should not feel pressured to 'prove' your hypothesis. If you do, it will cause you to distort the data analysis to ensure a positive outcome. This compromises the research.

Validate their credibility. You should check, double check and check again to ensure that the data do indeed support the *conclusion*s you draw from them. Did you analyse and interpret the data correctly? Might there be influential factors or causes you overlooked? Are there other plausible ways to interpret the data? Are your *conclusion*s based on facts rather than opinions? Are the data sufficient to justify the claims you base on them? These are the kinds of questions you need to ask to ensure your findings are credible.

Consider their implications. The final step is to consider the implications and applications of the findings. What practical or ministerial implications do you see? Who might benefit? What principles can be drawn from the study? This issue of drawing principles is both necessary and dangerous. On the one hand, your study is likely based on a small, specific population, so it is dangerous to generalise broadly as if what is true of that population is true in general. On the other hand, there likely are common elements your population shares with other communities, who may also benefit from the research. To strike the balance between these two, it is appropriate to discuss broader applications of your findings (to other populations), but it is wise to do so in tentative, understated language, recognising that your *conclusion*s apply directly to the actual population you studied and only indirectly to others.

In most research projects, the study does not speak the final word on the topic. The researcher recognises the need for further, related research to clarify or corroborate the findings. He can see how his study has gone one step beyond previous research, but also realises there are many more steps to be taken. If this describes how you feel at the end of your study, you should end it with some recommendations for further research.

Step 9: Write the Report

The last and most important step of a study is to write an appropriate and clear report of what you have done and found, so that others may also take advantage of this new knowledge. The report typically has five sections.

Introduction (covers step 1). As in all other research, there must be an introduction. This gives the background, the definition of the problem, the purpose, the limitations and delimitations, and the definition of terms.

Literature review (covers step 2). Following the introduction, a descriptive research thesis needs to have what is termed as a 'review of literature'. This section reports on the preparatory reading, both on the topic or population investigated (youth, deacons, women administrators, and so on), the methodology used (surveys, scales, rankings, and so on), and the theoretical framework, if appropriate.

Research method (covers steps 3–6). This section deals with the research method employed. You should describe step by step everything you did – the approach (qualitative or quantitative), the instruments, the sample size and sampling techniques, the data collection procedures and any other steps or details that someone would need to know if she wanted to duplicate your study. Two matters are of particular importance here. The first is to describe how you developed, tested and applied the questionnaire, or, in the case of interviews, to describe in detail how you planned and conducted them. The second is to explain the procedures you used to organise and analyse the data.

Results (covers step 7). What did you discover? The topics are organised in some logical way and described in turn. Often the questions of the survey are taken one after the other, or, if the questionnaire is long, by related groups of questions.

Consider including all your hypotheses, questions, objectives, or purposes as well as the data needed to address each one and the measures needed to collect the data. Finally, describe the method you will use to analyse the data.

Records of data resulting from observations may be presented in the form of tables, charts, graphs, and other summary and trend-indicating techniques.

Summary (covers step 8). Finally, summarise the whole process. On the basis of the summary, draw conclusions and make recommendations for further study.

If you are writing a theological thesis, the descriptive study probably only constitutes one major section of the study. We recommend you conduct and report the descriptive study section as we have described the process here. For example, a thesis in practical theology using the LIM model could have three main parts. The part containing the descriptive study, the 'present situation' part, could be written up in the form of a descriptive research report.

Summary

Descriptive research is a valuable ministry tool for developing an accurate portrait of a present reality to lay a platform for diagnosing causes and prescribing cures. There are two main forms, namely, quantitative and qualitative. Quantitative studies employ surveys and questionnaires to gather data that lend themselves to statistical analysis, while qualitative approaches rely on interviews, focus groups or personal observations; the data collected do not lend themselves to statistical analysis.

18

Other Types of Theological Research

We want to close our treatment of research models by discussing some methods that do not warrant their own chapter, but are valuable tools for ministry and research. First, we present the IMRAD model for reporting empirical research. IMRAD is *the standard* way or reporting empirical research in the natural and social sciences. Second, we offer guidelines for doing a critical book review. Third, we discuss how to do a case study as research. Fourth, we provide some suggestions for doing congregational analysis.

Empirical Research (IMRAD)

In most sciences, there is a standard structure that is followed by the vast majority of theses. It is known as IMRAD, which stands for **I**ntroduction, **M**ethods, **R**esults **A**nd **D**iscussion. If a Conclusion is added, this leads naturally to this outline for a study:

1) Introduction

2) Methods (and Materials)

3) Results

4) Discussion

5) Conclusion

The empirical component of a theological study can often be presented using the IMRAD model. In some cases, the entire empirical study can be presented in a single chapter, which covers all the components of IMRAD. In a large-scale empirical study, an entire part of the dissertation is devoted to the empirical study, with a chapter for each phase.

Introduction: What Problem Was Studied?

'The introduction should supply sufficient background information to allow the reader to understand and evaluate the results . . . without needing to refer to previous publications on the topic.'[1] According to Day and Gastel, the Introduction should cover the following:

1) Present clearly and concise the nature and scope of the research problem.

2) Review briefly pertinent literature to orient the reader to the topic.

3) State and briefly motivate the method of investigation.

4) Summarise the principle results of the research.

5) State the principle conclusions suggested by the results.

As you can see, the Introduction section presents a summary of the entire study: problem, literature, methods, results, and conclusions. You are not writing a novel, in which building suspense is part of a literary strategy. In academic writing, your aim is to communicate information as efficiently as possible. The Introduction section of your IMRAD study should enable your readers to understand the entire study without needing to read the remaining sections. If readers want to understand the research in greater detail, they can continue reading.

Methods: How Was the Problem Studied?

Reliable results depend upon valid methods – the selection and implementation must be sound. In the hard sciences, researchers aim to describe their experiments in sufficient detail to allow other researchers to reproduce the experiment, to evaluate the validity of the results, and to judge the extent to which the conclusions can be generalised.[2] In the social science, which is where most empirical studies in theological research is positioned, similar concerns should be addressed. If readers wish to undertake a similar study in their context, they should have enough insight to do so. You should describe and defend your research methods in a manner that demonstrates the validity of the findings.

The first choice you need to motivate is whether to undertake a *quantitative* or a *qualitative* study. Be sure that you have read enough about these two approaches to make a sensible choice. We often see theological students attempt to describe and defend their choice without reading enough to understand either. Their ignorance of methods shines through, and calls into question the competence of the research to undertake the research.

---

1. Robert A. Day and Barbara Gastel, *How to Write and Publish a Scientific Paper* (6th ed.; Cambridge: Cambridge University Press, 2006), 57.
2. Day and Gastel, *How to Write and Publish a Scientific Paper*, 60.

If you choose a quantitative study, you need to discuss the sampling methods, the research instrument (the questionnaire), and the data analysis methods. You motivate the delivery method for the questionnaire; if you choose an electronic survey, consider the influence on your sample. If you choose a qualitative study, you must choose which [combination] of the qualitative approach, such as interviews, focus groups, case studies, participant observation, or appreciative enquiry.

Results: What Were the Findings?

The results section must *present the data*. However, it is normally necessary to select the data that you present so as to faithfully represent the findings without trying to present everything. 'The fool collects facts; the wise man selects them.'[3]

If your data are quantitative, meaning that they can be represented numerically, then they are often best presented in the form of graphs, charts, or tables, accompanied by an explanatory narrative that makes the graphic representation easy to understand. If your data are qualitative – words instead of numbers – you should present them in narrative form. For the most part, you can summarise points of agreement (for example, 'seven of the ten pastors interviewed believed that . . .'). You should always note dissenting voices. Direct quotations should be reserved comments or statements so significant that it is imperative to use the exact words of the respondent.

The results can often be presented by following the order of the questions in a questionnaire or an interview. You state the question, present the data, then summarise observable patterns in the data. Ensure that you present the results in a short-and-sweet manner, avoiding unnecessary words, especially non-essential repetition (redundancy).

Discussion: What Do the Findings Mean?

The discussion section interprets the data, exploring and explaining their meaning and significance. Day and Gastel argue that many research projects are sound up to this point, but are ruined by verbose discussions that fail to capture the significance of the data accurately. They recommend that this section of the study should do the following:

1) Present the principles, relationships, and generalisations implicit in the data.

2) Acknowledge exceptions, lack of correlation, or unsettled points.

3) Show how your results compare or contrast with previous research.

4) Discuss the theoretical implications and practical applications of the results.

5) State the conclusions clearly, summarising the evidence for each conclusion.[4]

---
3. John Wesley Powell, quoted in Day and Gastel, *How to Write and Publish a Scientific Paper*, 67.
4. Day and Gastel, *How to Write and Publish a Scientific Paper*, 70.

Book Reviews

The Values and Types of Reviews

A book review is a special kind of theological writing. Students may be required to write book reviews on prescribed readings. Scholars write reviews of new publications in their field of expertise. Reading reviews is a valuable means of keeping abreast of the vast body of literature being published. So many works are published each year that it is impossible to read every work in a field; by reading good reviews, you can keep track of the latest research.

Book reviews fall into two types: descriptive and critical. Descriptive reviews simply summarise a book. Our interest lies in the critical review. Critical reviews describe and evaluate books. The reviewer critiques it against accepted standards and supports his evaluations with evidence.

The Components of a Critical Review

The first step in doing a book review is to read the book carefully and take notes. You should read it at least twice, preferably with a gap between readings. In your first reading, familiarise yourself with the book and form initial impressions. In the second reading, test your impressions and gather evidence to support your conclusions.[5]

There are many ways to write a critical review. As a rule, the review should have one central thesis (main point) and should be organised logically to support that thesis.[6] The review must have four components, which may or may not be used as headings to organise the review:

1. Details of the book
Provide a full bibliographic entry for the book. Include the total number of pages in the book. Some reviews also list the price and ISBN number.

2. Background of the author
Do some research about the author – her qualifications, background, church affiliation, ministry position or experience, previous publications, and so on. *Briefly* note anything about the author that sheds light on the book.[7]

---

5. Grenville Draper, 'Writing Book Reviews' (2007, retrieved 8 December 2007, http://library.uwaterloo.ca), online.

6. Ian Colford, 'How to Write a Book Review' (2000, retrieved 8 December 2007, www.library.dal.ca), online.

7. Los Angeles Valley College, 'How to Write a Book Review' (2005, retrieved 8 December 2007, www.lavc.edu), online.

3. Description of the purpose

The description should *not* be a summary of the book. Rather, it should extract and state the author's main purpose and thesis (authors often state their purpose in the preface or introduction), then describe how he sets about achieving the purpose and developing the thesis. Those who read your description should have a clear understanding of the book's main purpose and how the author went about achieving it.

4. Evaluation of the book

The longest and most important part of the review is to evaluate the book: (a) How effectively did the author develop his thesis? (b) How well did she achieve her purpose? It is crucial to evaluate the book against the author's stated purpose. If the author set out to write a devotional commentary for teenagers, criticising her for failing to evaluate textual variants is unfair. Similarly, you would not blame someone writing 'a layman's guide to Bible doctrines' for leaving out technical data. However, a critical commentary that neglects important variants or an academic monograph that fails to engage critical sources should be exposed.

State how well you believe the author has achieved his purpose, then back up your conclusion with evidence from the book. Here are some criteria you might use to evaluate a theological book:

- *Bible*. Does the author engage Scripture adequately? Is her exegesis consistent, thorough and sound?
- *Scholarship*. Does the author demonstrate familiarity with relevant recent scholarship? Does he engage that scholarship appropriately and sufficiently?
- *Presuppositions*. Does the author state his assumptions honestly? Are they appropriate? Does personal bias undermine his objectivity or cloud his judgement?
- *Organisation*. Is the book clearly and logically structured? Does it use suitable structural devices to support its purpose (for example, tables, indexes, transitions, headings).
- *Methodology*. If it is a research work, is the author's methodology sound and suitable? Did she describe it transparently?
- *Accuracy*. Has the author done thorough research? Did you notice any factual errors? Does she represent others' views fairly and truly?
- *Suitability*. How suitable is the book for its target audience? Is it readable? Is it interesting? Is it useful?
- *Comparisons*. How does the book compare with other works in the field? What contribution does it make? Does it meet accepted norms?
- *Impact*. How did the book affect you? What was your personal response to it?

The Language and Structure of a Review

The tone of your review should reflect a courteous and gracious attitude. Even if you disagree with the author, write in a collegial manner. Many academic debates are conducted in a manner unbecoming of the gospel of Jesus Christ. Scholars use combative language to humiliate those who hold opposite views. We urge you, in all your writings, to treat others as brothers in Christ.

You might structure your review by using the four components as headings (see above), but you need not do so. Many reviewers prefer to weave components 2–4 into a flowing essay. If you write the review in an essay format, arrange it around the central thesis of your evaluation and use the normal three-part structure: introduction, body and conclusion.

- *Introduction.* The opening statement should set the tone for the review. Colford suggests a statement about either (a) the review's thesis, (b) the author's purpose, or (c) the book's significance as good options for the opening sentence.[8]
- *Body.* The body should develop your review in a clear, organised manner. It should weave together description and evaluation, providing evidence in support of its judgements.
- *Conclusion.* 'The concluding paragraph may sum up or restate your thesis or may make the final judgement regarding the book. No new information or ideas should be introduced in the conclusion.'[9]

Even if you use the four components as headings, you could still apply this three-part structure to the material under the two main headings, namely, the description and the evaluation.

Summary

Book reviews rank among the most valuable types of theological writing. They enable readers to keep abreast of recent trends without needing to read every new work. Although descriptive reviews have some value, critical reviews are much more valuable.

The objective of a book review is to evaluate how well the author has achieved her purpose. The review should describe her purpose and explain how she tried to achieve it. The reviewer should state how well he believes the author has achieved her purpose, supporting his conclusions with evidence from the book.

---

8. Colford, 'How to Write a Book Review,' online.
9. Ibid.

Case Studies

Vyhmeister describes a case study in pastoral research this way:

> It studies one situation, the activities of one group, or one incident. Naturally, a pastor's case study looks at an event or person or situation related to ministry. It must analyze the background of the incident, all of the factors that contribute to the interplay and interaction, and what actually happens.[10]

A case study of a pastoral ministry issue requires four steps.[11]

1) *Observation.* The case itself is written out based on careful observations. You may use any of the tools of descriptive research (including personal observations) to compile the case. All essential details must be included in a written description of the case.

2) *Analysis.* 'Once the case has been written out, the next step is to carefully analyze the events, interactions and reactions of the person or persons involved in the case. . . . The task of analysis is to understand, not to make judgements regarding the rightness or wrongness of anyone's actions.'

3) *Interpretation.* Now the case is critiqued theologically. 'The key question is: What do the Bible, theology, and the church's tradition and doctrine say about the case?'

4) *Action.* The study ends with action planning, where 'one evaluates any action already taken and outlines appropriate future pastoral strategies for responding to the case'.

A case study can range in size from a short paper to a full thesis. It is, in essence, a specific form of practical theology research. A specific kind of case study that can be valuable in ministry is congregational analysis.

Congregational Analysis

An excellent work on how to do congregational analysis is *Studying Congregations in Africa* by Jurgens Hendriks.[12] We highly recommend his book, both as a valuable primer for doing practical theology and, especially, as a comprehensive blueprint for studying a church. Hendriks' thinking is too detailed to summarise briefly here. What we can offer is

---

10. Vyhmeister, *Quality Research Papers*, 54.
11. Ibid., 55–59, *passim*.
12. H. Jurgens Hendriks, *Studying Congregations in Africa* (Wellington, South Africa: Lux Verbi, 2004).

a much-simplified guide for analysing congregations, which might help leaders to make informed decisions.

The simplified method has four steps. It requires that one conduct a detailed study of a church's history, culture, theology, and experiences. Here are nine questions you should try to answer:

- What is the history of your church?
- What is the culture of the area in which you live?
- What is the culture represented in your church and how does the culture of the area reflect there?
- What is the primary theology/message represented at your church?
- What are some of the major experiences your church has been through?
- What was your experience the first time you entered the doors of your church?
- What kept you coming back?
- In the course of this study, what did you learn about your church that you did not know before?
- How might a contextual analysis help your church in making major decisions?[13]

Tom Steffen suggests that *narrative research* offers another way to research a congregation.[14] The goal is to *tell the story of the church*. He suggests five steps in the process:

1. Conduct a 'church story timeline'.

2. Conduct ethnographic research.

3. Conduct focus groups.

4. Exegete the stories.

5. Announce findings and discuss chapters.[15]

We should also mention the qualitative method of measuring congregational health that Christian Schwarz developed.[16]

---

13. 'Contextual Analysis of a Congregation' (retrieved 3 June 2008, www.mccchurch.org/resources/smallgroup/contextualanalysis.htm).

14. Tom A. Steffen, *Reconnecting God's Story to Ministry* (Waynesboro, GA: Authentic Media, 2005), ch. 8.

15. By chapters Steffen means the chapters in the story of the church, not chapters in a research report.

16. Christian Schwarz, *Natural Church Development: A Guide to Eight Essential Qualities of Healthy Churches* (Carol Stream, IL: Churchsmart Resources, 1996).

Appendix A

Common Abbreviations

The abbreviations listed in this appendix are all derived from the *SBL Handbook of Style*. For extensive lists of acceptable abbreviations, you should consult the *SBL Handbook*.

Books of the Bible

Old Testament Books			
Gen	Genesis	Song	Song of Songs
Exod	Exodus	Isa	Isaiah
Lev	Leviticus	Jer	Jeremiah
Num	Numbers	Lam	Lamentations
Deut	Deuteronomy	Ezek	Ezekiel
Josh	Joshua	Dan	Daniel
Judg	Judges	Hos	Hosea
Ruth	Ruth	Joel	Joel
1–2 Sam	1–2 Samuel	Amos	Amos
1–2 Kgs	1–2 Kings	Obad	Obadiah
1–2 Chr	1–2 Chronicles	Jon	Jonah
Ezra	Ezra	Mic	Micah
Neh	Nehemiah	Nah	Nahum
Esth	Esther	Hab	Habakkuk
Job	Job	Zeph	Zephaniah
Ps/Pss	Psalm/s	Hag	Haggai
Prov	Proverbs	Zech	Zechariah
Eccl	Ecclesiastes	Mal	Malachi

New Testament Books			
Matt	Mathew	Col	Colossians
Mark	Mark	1–2 Thess	1–2 Thessalonians
Luke	Luke	1–2 Tim	1–2 Timothy
John	John	Titus	Titus
Acts	Acts	Phlm	Philemon
Rom	Romans	Heb	Hebrews
1–2 Cor	1–2 Corinthians	1–2 Pet	1–2 Peter
Gal	Galatians	1–3 John	1–3 John
Eph	Ephesians	Jude	Jude
Phil	Philippians	Rev	Revelation

Apocrypha and Septuagint			
Bar	Baruch	Ep Jer	Epistle of Jeremiah
Add Dan	Additions to Daniel	Jdt	Judith
Pr Azar	Prayer of Azariah	1–4 Macc	1–4 Maccabees
Bel	Bel and the Dragon	Pr Man	Prayer of Manasseh
Sg Three	Song of the Three Young Men	Sir	Sirach/Ecclesiasticus
Sus	Susanna	Tob	Tobit
1–2 Esd	1–2 Esdras	Wis	Wisdom of Solomon
Add Esth	Additions to Esther		

Versions of the Bible

These are standard abbreviations for major Greek, Hebrew, and English editions of the Bible.

ASV	American Standard Version
BHQ	*Biblia Hebraica Quinta*
BHS	*Biblia Hebraica Stuttgartensia*
CEV	Contemporary English Version
ESV	English Standard Version
GNB	Good News Bible (a.k.a. TEV)
GW	God's Word
HCSB	Holman Christian Standard Bible
KJV	King James Version
LEB	Lexham English Bible

LHB	Lexham Hebrew Bible
MKJV	Modern King James Version
MT	Masoretic Text
NA28	*Greek New Testament: Nestle-Aland, 28th Edition*
NASB	New American Standard Bible
NET	New English Translation (NET Bible)
NIRV	New International Reader's Version
NIV	New International Version
NKJV	New King James Version
NRSV	New Revised Standard Version
RP	*Greek New Testament: Majority Text* (Robinson and Pierpont)
RSV	Revised Standard Version
SBLGNT	*Greek New Testament: SBL Edition*
TEV	Today's English Version (a.k.a. GNB)
UBS5	*Greek New Testament: United Bible Societies, 5th Edition*

Appendix B

Abbreviations for Journals, Periodicals, Major Reference Works, and Series

Below is a selected list of standard works and accepted abbreviations for them.

ANTC	Abingdon New Testament Commentaries
AcOr	*Acta Orientalia*
AJBS	*African Journal of Biblical Studies*
AARDS	American Academy of Religion Dissertation Series
ABQ	*American Baptist Quarterly*
ATLA	American Theological Library Association
AB	Anchor Bible
ABD	*Anchor Bible Dictionary*
ABRL	Anchor Bible Reference Library
ACCS	Ancient Christian Commentary on Scripture
ACW	Ancient Christian Writers.
ANQ	*Andover Newton Quarterly*
AUSS	*Andrews University Seminary Studies*
AThR	*Anglican Theological Review*
AASOR	Annual of the American Schools of Oriental Research
ANF	*Ante-Nicene Fathers*
ArBib	Aramaic Bible
Arch	*Archaeology*
AsTJ	*Asbury Theological Journal*
ATJ	*Ashland Theological Journal*
AJT	*Asia Journal of Theology*
AJSR	*Association for Jewish Studies Review*

AugStud	*Augustinian Studies*
Aug	*Augustinianum*
ATR	*Australasian Theological Review*
ABR	*Australian Biblical Review*
BBMS	Baker Biblical Monograph Series
BEB	*Baker Encyclopedia of the Bible*
BAG	Bauer, W., W. F. Arndt, and F. W. Gingrich. *Greek-English Lexicon of the New Testament and Other Early Christian Literature.* Chicago, 1957
BAGD	Bauer, W., W. F. Arndt, F. W. Gingrich, and F. W. Danker. *Greek-English Lexicon of the New Testament and Other Early Christian Literature.* 2d ed. Chicago, 1979
BDAG	Bauer, W., F. W. Danker, W. F. Arndt, and F. W. Gingrich. *Greek-English Lexicon of the New Testament and Other Early Christian Literature.* 3d ed. Chicago, 1999
BK	*Bibel und Kirche*
BiBh	*Bible Bhashyam*
BRev	*Bible Review*
TBT	*The Bible Today*
BT	*The Bible Translator*
BHK	*Biblia Hebraica.* Edited by R. Kittel. Stuttgart, 1905–1906, 1925², 1937³, 1951⁴, 1973¹⁶
BHQ	Biblia Hebraica Quinta
BHS	*Biblia Hebraica Stuttgartensia.* Edited by K. Elliger and W. Rudolph. Stuttgart, 1983
Bib	*Biblica*
BA	*Biblical Archaeologist*
BARead	*Biblical Archaeologist Reader*
BAR	*Biblical Archaeology Review*
BI	*Biblical Illustrator*
BibInt	*Biblical Interpretation*
BR	*Biblical Research*
BTB	*Biblical Theology Bulletin*
BSac	*Bibliotheca sacra*
BJS	Brown Judaic Studies
BDB	Brown, F., S. R. Driver, and C. A. Briggs. *A Hebrew and English Lexicon of the Old Testament.* Oxford, 1907.
BBR	*Bulletin for Biblical Research*
BBS	*Bulletin of Biblical Studies*

BASOR	*Bulletin of the American Schools of Oriental Research*
BASORSup	Bulletin of the American Schools of Oriental Research: Supplement Series
CTJ	*Calvin Theological Journal*
CBC	Cambridge Bible Commentary
CGTC	Cambridge Greek Testament Commentary
CML	*Canaanite Myths and Legends.* Edited by G. R. Driver
CJT	*Canadian Journal of Theology*
CBQMS	Catholic Biblical Quarterly Monograph Series
CBQ	*Catholic Biblical Quarterly*
CHR	*Catholic Historical Review*
ChrCent	*Christian Century*
ChrLit	*Christianity and Literature*
CH	*Church History*
CQ	*Church Quarterly*
CQR	*Church Quarterly Review*
Chm	*Churchman*
CW	*Classical World*
Colloq	*Colloquium*
CUL	*A Concordance of the Ugaritic Literature.* R. E. Whitaker. Cambridge, Mass., 1972
CTM	*Concordia Theological Monthly*
CTQ	*Concordia Theological Quarterly*
Cont	*Continuum*
CTR	*Criswell Theological Review*
CRBR	*Critical Review of Books in Religion*
Crux	*Crux*
CurBS	*Currents in Research: Biblical Studies*
CurTM	*Currents in Theology and Mission*
DSD	*Dead Sea Discoveries*
Di	*Dialog*
DCH	*Dictionary of Classical Hebrew.* Edited by D. J. A. Clines. Sheffield, 1993–2015
DissAb	Dissertation Abstracts
DRev	*Downside Review*
DOP	*Dumbarton Oaks Papers*
EncJud	*Encyclopaedia Judaica.* 16 vols. Jerusalem, 1972.
ER	*The Encyclopedia of Religion.* Edited by M. Eliade. 16 vols. New York, 1987
ERE	*Encyclopedia of Religion and Ethics.* Edited by J. Hastings. 13 vols. New York, 1908–1927. Reprint 7 vols., 1951.

EECH	*Encyclopedia of the Early Church.* Edited by A. di Berardino. Translated by A. Walford. New York, 1992.
ETR	*Etudes théologiques et religieuses*
EuroJTh	*European Journal of Theology*
EvJ	*Evangelical Journal*
EvQ	*Evangelical Quarterly*
EvT	*Evangelische Theologie*
EDNT	*Exegetical Dictionary of the New Testament*
ExpTim	*Expository Times*
FCB	Feminist Companion to the Bible
FoiVie	*Foi et vie*
GOTR	*Greek Orthodox Theological Review*
GRBS	*Greek, Roman, and Byzantine Studies*
L&N	*Greek-English Lexicon of the New Testament: Based on Semantic Domains* (Louw and Nida)
Greg	*Gregorianum*
HBD	*HarperCollins Bible Dictionary*
HTR	Harvard Theological Review
HTS	Harvard Theological Studies
HAR	Hebrew Annual Review
HS	Hebrew Studies
HUCA	Hebrew Union College Annual
HvTSt	*Hervormde teologiese studies*
HeyJ	*Heythrop Journal*
HR	History of Religions
HolBD	*Holman Bible Dictionary*
HBT	*Horizons in Biblical Theology*
IJT	*Indian Journal of Theology*
ICC	International Critical Commentary
ITC	International Theological Commentary
Int	*Interpretation*
IBC	*Interpretation: A Bible Commentary for Teaching and Preaching*
IB	*Interpreter's Bible* (e.d. G. A. Buttrick, 12 vols.)
IDB	*The Interpreter's Dictionary of the Bible*
IBS	Irish Biblical Studies
ITQ	Irish Theological Quarterly
IEJ	Israel Exploration Journal
IOS	Israel Oriental Society

JB	Jerusalem Bible
JBQ	*Jewish Bible Quarterly*
JE	*The Jewish Encyclopedia*
JQR	*Jewish Quarterly Review*
JSQ	*Jewish Studies Quarterly*
JSSR	*Journal for the Scientific Study of Religion*
JSNT	*Journal for the Study of the New Testament*
JSNTSup	Journal for the Study of the New Testament: Supplement Series
JTC	*Journal for Theology and the Church*
JBR	*Journal of Bible and Religion*
JBL	*Journal of Biblical Literature*
JCS	*Journal of Cuneiform Studies*
JECS	*Journal of Early Christian Studies*
JEH	*Journal of Ecclesiastical History*
JFSR	*Journal of Feminist Studies in Religion*
JJS	*Journal of Jewish Studies*
JNES	*Journal of Near Eastern Studies*
JNSL	*Journal of Northwest Semitic Languages*
JR	*Journal of Religion*
JRE	*Journal of Religious Ethics*
JRelS	*Journal of Religious Studies*
JSS	*Journal of Semitic Studies*
JSem	*Journal of Semitics*
JAAR	*Journal of the American Academy of Religion*
JAOS	*Journal of the American Oriental Society*
JETS	*Journal of the Evangelical Theological Society*
JTS	*Journal of Theological Studies*
JTSA	*Journal of Theology for Southern Africa*
Jud	Judaica
KD	*Kerygma und Dogma*
KBL	*Lexicon in Veteris Testamenti Libros* (Koehler and Baumgartner)
HALOT	*The Hebrew and Aramaic Lexicon of the Old Testament* (Koehler, Baumgartner, and Stamm)
LD	Lectio divina
LTQ	*Lexington Theological Quarterly*
LCC	Library of Christian Classics
LSJ	Liddell, H. G., R. Scott, H. S. Jones, *A Greek-English Lexicon*. 9th ed. with revised supplement. Oxford, 1996

LB	*Linguista Biblica*
LCL	Loeb Classical Library
LQ	*Lutheran Quarterly*
MSJ	*The Master's Seminary Journal*
MDB	Mercer Dictionary of the Bible
Mid-Stream	*Mid-Stream*
MM	Moulton, J. H., and G. Milligan. *The Vocabulary of the Greek Testament.* London, 1930. Reprint, Peabody, Mass., 1997
Neot	*Neotestamentica*
NAC	New American Commentary
NCE	*New Catholic Encyclopedia*
NCB	New Century Bible
NIBCNT	New International Biblical Commentary on the New Testament
NIBCOT	New International Biblical Commentary on the Old Testament
NICNT	New International Commentary on the New Testament
NICOT	New International Commentary on the Old Testament
NIB	*The New Interpreter's Bible*
NPNF[1]	Nicene and Post-Nicene Fathers, Series 1
NPNF[2]	Nicene and Post-Nicene Fathers, Series 2
NovT	*Novum Testamentum*
Numen	*Numen: International Review for the History of Religions*
OTE	*Old Testament Essays*
OTL	Old Testament Library
OTS	Old Testament Studies
Or	*Orientalia* (NS)
ODCC	*The Oxford Dictionary of the Christian Church*
PEQ	*Palestinian Exploration Quarterly*
PSTJ	*Perkins (School of Theology) Journal*
PRSt	*Perspectives in Religious Studies*
Per	*Perspectives*
Pneuma	*Pneuma: Journal for the Society of Pentecostal Studies*
Presb	*Presbyterion*
PSB	*Princeton Seminary Bulletin*
PIBA	Proceedings of the Irish Biblical Association
QR	*Quarterly Review*
QC	*Qumran Chronicle*
RechBib	Recherches bibliques

RTR	*Reformed Theological Review*
RelSoc	*Religion and Society*
RelEd	*Religious Education*
RelS	*Religious Studies*
RelSRev	*Religious Studies Review*
ResQ	*Restoration Quarterly*
RevExp	*Review and Expositor*
RevistB	*Revista biblica*
RB	*Revue biblique*
SP	*Sacra pagina*
SJOT	*Scandinavian Journal of the Old Testament*
SJT	*Scottish Journal of Theology*
ScrB	*Scripture Bulletin*
SecCent	*Second Century*
Semeia	*Semeia*
SemeiaSt	Semeia Studies
STRev	*Sewanne Theological Review*
SOTSMS	Society for Old Testament Monograph Series
SNTSMS	Society for New Testament Monograph Series
SBL	Society of Biblical Literature
SwJT	*Southwestern Journal of Theology*
SLJT	*St. Luke's Journal of Theology*
SBTQ	*St. Vladimir's Theological Quarterly*
StudBib	Studia Biblica
SJ	Studia judaica
NovTSup	Supplements to Novum Testamentum
VTSup	Supplements to Vetus Testamentum
Tarbiz	*Tarbiz*
Text	*Textus*
Them	*Themelios*
Theol	*Theologica*
TDNT	*Theological Dictionary of the New Testament*
TDOT	*Theological Dictionary of the Old Testament*
TTE	*The Theological Educator*
TNLT	*Theological Lexicon of the New Testament*
TLOT	*Theological Lexicon of the Old Testament*
TS	*Theological Studies*

TWOT	*Theological Wordbook of the Old Testament*
TD	*Theology Digest*
ThTo	*Theology Today*
TimesLitSupp	*Times Literary Supplement*
TJT	*Toronto Journal of Theology*
TJ	*Trinity Journal*
TTJ	*Trinity Theological Journal*
TynBul	*Tyndale Bulletin*
TNTC	Tyndale New Testament Commentary
TOTC	Tyndale Old Testament Commentary
USQR	*Union Seminary Quarterly Review*
VT	*Vetus Testamentum*
VTSup	Vetus Testamentum Supplements
VC	*Vigiliae christianae*
WDB	*Westminster Dictionary of the Bible*
WTJ	*Westminster Theological Journal*
WW	*Word and World*
WBC	Word Biblical Commentary
ZAW	*Zeitschrift für die alttestamentliche Wissenschaft*
ZNW	*Zeitschrift für die neutestamentliche Wissenschaft und die Kunde der älteren Kirche*

Select Bibliography

Alexander, Patrick H., John F. Kutsko, James D. Ernest, Shirley Decker-Lucke, and David L. Petersen, eds. *The SBL Handbook of Style: For Ancient Near Eastern, Biblical, and Early Christian Studies*. Peabody, MA: Hendrickson, 1999.

American Psychological Association. *Publication Manual of the American Psychological Association*. Sixth edition. Washington: American Psychological Association, 2001.

Banz, Clint. *Research Methods*. Landsdale: Calvary Baptist Theological Seminary, 2003.

Barber, Cyril J., and Robert M. Krauss. *An Introduction to Theological Research: A Guide for College and Seminary Students*. Second edition, revised and expanded. University of America Press, 2000.

Browning, Don. S. *A Fundamental Practical Theology: Descriptive and Strategic Proposals*. Minneapolis, MN: Fortress, 1991.

Cowan, Michael A. 'Introduction to Practical Theology.' *Loyola Institute for Ministry*. 2000. Retrieved 2 June 2006, http://loyno.edu.

Danker, Frederick W. 'Multipurpose Tools for Bible Study.' Minneapolis: Augsburg Fortress, 2003.

Day, Robert A., and Barbara Gastel. *How to Write and Publish a Scientific Paper*. Sixth edition. Cambridge: Cambridge University Press, 2006.

Garmonsway, George N., et al., eds. *The Penguin English Dictionary*. Harmondsworth: Penguin Books, 1972.

Gibaldi, Joseph, ed. *MLA Handbook for Writers of Research Papers*. 7th ed. New York: Modern Language Association, 2009.

Hendriks, H. Jurgens. *Studying Congregations in Africa*. Wellington, South Africa: Lux Verbi, 2004.

Isaac, Stephen, and William B. Michael. *Handbook in Research Evaluation*. San Diego: EDITS, 1971.

Lategan, Laetus O. K., ed. *An Introduction to Postgraduate Supervision*. Stellenbosch, South Africa: Stellenbosch University Press, 2008.

Leedy, Paul D. *Practical Research: Planning and Design*. New York: MacMillan, 1993.

Lester, James D. *Writing Research Papers: A Complete Guide*. Fourth edition. Glenview, IL: Scott and Foresman, 1984.

Mouton, Johan. *How to Succeed in your Master's and Doctoral Studies*. Pretoria: VanSchuik, 2001.

Myers, William R. *Research in Ministry: A Primer for the Doctor of Ministry Program*. Chicago: Chicago Theological Seminary, 2000.

Osmer, Richard R. *Practical Theology: An Introduction*. Grand Rapids, MI: Eerdmans, 2008.

Patton, Michael Q. *Qualitative Research and Evaluation Methods.* London: Sage Publications, 2002.
Ritter, Robert M. *The Oxford Guide to Style.* Oxford: Oxford University Press, 2002.
Silva, Paul J. *How to Write a Lot: A Practical Guide to Productive Academic Writing.* Washington: American Psychological Association, 2007.
Swales, J. M., and C. A. B. Feak. 2004. *Commentary for Academic Writing for Graduate Students: A Course for Nonnative Speakers of English.* Second edition. Michigan: University of Michigan Press.
Taylor, Stan, and Nigel Beasley. *A Handbook for Doctoral Supervisors.* London: Routledge, 2005.
Turabian, Kate L. *A Manual for Writers of Research Papers, Theses and Dissertations.* Seventh edition. Edited by W. C. Booth, G. G. Colomb and J. M. Williams. Chicago: Chicago University Press, 2007.
Vyhmeister, Nancy Jean. *Your Indispensable Guide to Writing Quality Research Papers: For Students of Religion and Theology.* Grand Rapids, MI: Zondervan, 2001.
Vyhmeister, Nancy Jean. *Quality Research Papers: For Students of Religion and Theology.* Third edition. Grand Rapids, MI: Zondervan, 2014.
Ware, Bruce. "Method of Evangelical Theology." www.biblicaltraining.org. 2001. Accessed 25 March 2008.

Langham Literature and its imprints are a ministry of Langham Partnership.

Langham Partnership is a global fellowship working in pursuit of the vision God entrusted to its founder John Stott –

to facilitate the growth of the church in maturity and Christ-likeness through raising the standards of biblical preaching and teaching.

Our vision is to see churches in the majority world equipped for mission and growing to maturity in Christ through the ministry of pastors and leaders who believe, teach and live by the Word of God.

Our mission is to strengthen the ministry of the Word of God through:
- nurturing national movements for biblical preaching
- fostering the creation and distribution of evangelical literature
- enhancing evangelical theological education

especially in countries where churches are under-resourced.

Our ministry

Langham Preaching partners with national leaders to nurture indigenous biblical preaching movements for pastors and lay preachers all around the world. With the support of a team of trainers from many countries, a multi-level programme of seminars provides practical training, and is followed by a programme for training local facilitators. Local preachers' groups and national and regional networks ensure continuity and ongoing development, seeking to build vigorous movements committed to Bible exposition.

Langham Literature provides majority world preachers, scholars and seminary libraries with evangelical books and electronic resources through publishing and distribution, grants and discounts. The programme also fosters the creation of indigenous evangelical books in many languages, through writer's grants, strengthening local evangelical publishing houses, and investment in major regional literature projects, such as one volume Bible commentaries like *The Africa Bible Commentary* and *The South Asia Bible Commentary*.

Langham Scholars provides financial support for evangelical doctoral students from the majority world so that, when they return home, they may train pastors and other Christian leaders with sound, biblical and theological teaching. This programme equips those who equip others. Langham Scholars also works in partnership with majority world seminaries in strengthening evangelical theological education. A growing number of Langham Scholars study in high quality doctoral programmes in the majority world itself. As well as teaching the next generation of pastors, graduated Langham Scholars exercise significant influence through their writing and leadership.

To learn more about Langham Partnership and the work we do visit **langham.org**

www.ingramcontent.com/pod-product-compliance
Lightning Source LLC
Chambersburg PA
CBHW080431230426
43662CB00015B/2244